THE
FLYING GREEK

TO BILL HUSSAR
WITH BEST WISHES.

[signature]

WWII FIGHTER ACE
10 AERIAL VICTORIES

Related Titles from Potomac Books

Jungle Ace: The Story of One of the USAAF's Great Fighter Leaders, Col. Gerald R. Johnson by John R. Bruning

Red Partisan: Memoirs of a Soviet Resistance Fighter on the Eastern Front by Nikolai I. Obryn'ba

Spitfires, Thunderbolts, and Warm Beer: An American Fighter Pilot Over Europe by Philip D. Caine

THE
FLYING GREEK

AN IMMIGRANT FIGHTER ACE'S WWII ODYSSEY
WITH THE RAF, USAAF, AND FRENCH RESISTANCE

Col. Steve N. Pisanos, USAF (Ret.)

Potomac Books, Inc.
Washington, D.C.

Library of Congress Cataloging-in-Publication Data

Pisanos, Steve N., 1919-
The flying Greek : an immigrant fighter ace's World War II odyssey with the RAF, USAAF, and the French resistance / Steve N. Pisanos.
p. cm.
Includes bibliographical references and index.
ISBN-13: 978-1-59797-078-5 (hbk. : alk. paper)
1. Pisanos, Steve N., 1919- 2. World War, 1939-1945—Aerial operations, American. 3. World War, 1939-1945—Aerial operations, British. 4. World War, 1939-1945—Campaigns—Western Front. 5. World War, 1939-1945—Underground movements—France. 6. World War, 1939-1945—Personal narratives, American. 7. Fighter pilots—United States—Biography. 8. Greek Americans—Biography. I. Title.
D790.2.P57 2008
940.54'4973092—dc22

2007050087

ISBN-13: 978-1-59797-078-5

(alk. paper)

Printed in the United States of America on acid-free paper that meets the American National Standards Institute Z39-48 Standard.

Potomac Books, Inc.
22841 Quicksilver Drive
Dulles, Virginia 20166

First Edition

10 9 8 7 6 5 4 3

This book is dedicated
to all of the aviators who fought America's enemies during World
War II and the wars in Korea and Vietnam;
my parents; my wife, Sophie; my children,
Jeffrey and Diane; and my boyhood friends.

CONTENTS

FOREWORD

This is a remarkable book. Steve Pisanos has an incredible memory for seemingly every detail of his adventurous life. I would not have believed he had such a talent for autobiography—or, for that matter, for history itself. Although, as I review our first meeting, I know I should have been wise even then.

My assignment as a United Press correspondent during World War II was covering the air war. One of my favorite airdromes to visit was Debden, just outside the English Midland town of Saffron Walden. Debden was occupied by undoubtedly the most colorful collection of fighter pilots in the U.S. Army Air Force. These pilots were so eager to enter the war they had joined the British Royal Air Force (RAF) long before Pearl Harbor brought their native homeland into the conflict. They were shipped to England via Canada and formed three RAF Eagle Squadrons, the 71, 121, and 133. Their RAF training and their gung-ho spirit immediately took a toll on the German Luftwaffe. Their enthusiasm for tangling with the Nazi foe gave a special character to their base, which was a great place for a correspondent to uncover the stories of the aerial conflict that would play a major part in the Allied victory to come.

Fairly early on in their English sojourn, the United States joined the war and the three Eagle Squadrons were absorbed into the U.S. Army Air Force. The groups would always be considered the Eagle Squadrons, but their official designation became the 4th Fighter Group of the 8th Fighter Command.

On one of my visits to Debden, one of my (now) good friends, a great pilot named Deacon Hively, asked if I'd met one of the pilots—a man who was not American but actually Greek.

"He's a great little guy and a helluva pilot," I recall Deacon saying, "but his English isn't so hot. He's got a great story but I don't know about the English. Anyway, you've got to meet him."

I did meet him, and of all the people I've interviewed in a lifetime of journalism, Steve Pisanos ranks right among the most interesting. He was a good-looking chap, neatly groomed in his flight suit, and had a winning smile that covered his chagrin at not finding in the English language the exact word he was seeking. He spun the almost unbelievable story you'll find in extraordinary detail in this volume. I knew I had a great article in my notebook: a dramatic story of a poor boy from Greece who was so determined to fly that he defied his parents and the laws of several nations to come to what he was certain was the land of opportunity—America. His is a Horatio Alger story, set in the exciting world of flight and deadly duels above the clouds, capped with success and recognition beyond even his seemingly impossible dreams.

With that story in my notebook, I reluctantly took my leave of 4th Group that day at Debden and caught the train for London. As they so often were in wartime England, the train was jammed with people and I had only standing room in one of the coaches. We had been under way for twenty minutes or so when the train was shaken with such a roar that passengers, I among them, cried out in fear and ducked away from the windows. We were being buzzed at extremely low altitude by a P-47, the newest of the American fighter planes, given the name Thunderbolt, probably because of their powerful engines and deafening noise.

The plane that had buzzed us made another pass, and this time the daring pilot wagged his wings as he sped over us. I guessed—and established later that I was right—that it was my Greek lieutenant wishing me good-bye.

I was warmed by his gesture and overheated by my fellow passengers' comments. One of the more complimentary statements was along the lines of "Look at that damned fool American! He'll kill us all!"

He didn't kill any of us—but before the war was over, he had a record number of kills of German bombers and their fighter escorts in aerial duels, he escorted our B-17s over continental Europe, and he helped protect England from the Luftwaffe's desperate last stand.

My interview with this amazing young pilot was printed in *Stars and Stripes* and the British press, and I like to think my article played a part in Steve's selection as the first foreigner to be awarded American citizenship for volunteering to fight with our military forces. His story is one of a young boy who dreamed of flying and, with remarkable determination, ambition, and courage, made his dreams come true and helped win World War II.

Walter Cronkite
New York, New York
February 2005

——————————————Acknowledgments

Writing the story of my life was like taking a journey to an unknown destination. I have spent countless hours, days, and nights during the past eight years putting down on paper the episodes and adventures I have experienced since I came into this world. I used my memory, which is still good considering the bygone years, and notes that I have kept since childhood.

Even though my writing experience was somewhat limited in 1995, I started recording my odyssey in longhand from the beginning. I chose not to reveal my story to a ghostwriter or to dictate it into a tape recorder, as some of my friends had suggested. The task of writing my story myself was not as simple as I first thought it would be. I struggled throughout the process, changing and rewriting each chapter, to ensure that the events of my life were presented exactly as they had occurred.

At times I felt that I had embarked on an endless undertaking and seriously considered quitting the game, but I was inspired, almost continuously, by the support of many friends who insisted and encouraged me to keep on writing. Truthfully, if it had not been for this inspiration, I wou never have completed the manuscript.

First and foremost, I wish to express my deepest gratitude to two friends from World War II, the late Col. Francis "Gabby" Gabreski, America's top European ace, and Maj. Don S. Gentile, another high-scoring European ace and a longtime friend. These men were the first to encourage me to put my life's story in a book when we were serving as test pilots at Wright Field, Ohio, in 1945 and 1946.

Another wartime comrade I am indebted to is Jim Goodson, who, after publishing his own book, *Tumult in the Clouds*, about the Royal

Air Force Eagle Squadrons and 4th Fighter Group pilots in World War II, told me, "once I'd begun to push the pencil, I never wanted to stop." Thank you, Jim, for the wise advice.

A special thanks also goes to my friends Richard Braley, Arthur Elder, and Wally Gray, my classmates at Polaris Flight Academy, where we were trained by the RAF to fight the Luftwaffe. Also, thanks to Ward Boyce, the longtime executive director of the American Fighter Aces Association; Arthur Cocagne, my bridge partner; Jack Bray and Norris Hanford, my golf partners; and many other friends, for their profound inspiration and earnest encouragements to keep writing.

I wish also to extend my sincere thanks and appreciation for their devotion and untiring efforts to three wonderful ladies who spent many hours in the tedious task of typing the hundreds of handwritten pages that made up the manuscript and who also made useful suggestions, which I appreciate: Beverly Eastland, Bambi Brown, and Kristine Litewski.

A special thanks also goes to Tim Latta and Corinne Brown of the Sir Speedy Printing Shop for their help and generosity in copying my countless handwritten pages, which I had prepared for typing.

My sincere gratitude also goes to an astute and sympathetic friend, Jason Josephlynch, who, with skillful attention, scrutinized and condensed the draft copy of the story I had put together and made invaluable grammatical corrections that I had overlooked.

I also had the good fortune to be introduced to James O'Shea Wade, a profound and true intellectual and a master in the literary editing business, who spent many hours editing and fine-tuning the text, putting everything in perspective in a most professional manner that made the manuscript shine and ready for the publisher. My sincere thanks, James.

I'd be remiss if I failed to thank my wonderful wife and life partner, Sophie, the woman I am lucky to have been married to for more than six decades—not only because she was patient with me during the writing process but also because she helped me spell words I could not find in the dictionary. My heartfelt gratitude also goes to my two adult children, Jeffrey and Diane, for their love and support throughout the writing process and for the interest Jeffrey showed in monitoring the progress of my work to the end. Without a doubt a good part of what appears in this book was a surprise to my wife, my children, and all of my friends, as they learned about experiences I had had during a different and long-ago era.

I am grateful also to an extraordinary lady, Mrs. Betty Olesen, who spent considerable time retyping many pages of the edited manuscript.

And, lastly, I wish to express my sincere thanks to the team of professionals at Potomac Books, who not only believed that *The Flying Greek* story deserved to be published in book form but also devoted invaluable time in preparing the manuscript and getting the book off the press and into the public's hands.

CHAPTER 1

EARLY DAYS

I was born on November 10, 1919, in our house at 87 Petras Street in Kolonos, a suburb of Athens, Greece. My birth certificate, as registered with the mayor's office in Athens, bears the legend "Spyridon, son of Nicholas and Athena Pisanos." During my childhood, I was known as "Spiro." I was the third child in a family of five boys and a girl.

My father was born in 1890, in the village of Vatica, in Sparta. He was one of six brothers, all of whom became fishermen at an early age, like their father before them. When the brothers lost their two fishing boats in stormy seas between Peloponnese and Crete, they moved to Athens to look for other opportunities. My father found work as a Pezonaftis (a Marine) aboard the cruiser *George Averof*, and he served during the 1912–13 Balkan War and World War I. After the wars, my father worked in Athens in the Office of the Secretary of the Hellenic Navy, Periklis Rediadis.

My father met my mother at the secretary's residence, where she was working in the kitchen as one of the cooks. My mother was born in 1894 on the island of Cephalonia in the Ionian Sea. She had lost her parents when she was young and had been raised by her older brothers, Dionysios and Menelaos. They were farmers who produced wine, melons, and olive oil. At an early age, mother decided that she could not build a life in her village, so she made her way to Athens.

My father and mother were married in 1916. When father was released from the navy, they settled in Kolonos, where they established a home. With help from Mr. Rediadis, my father found work as a conductor with Athens' streetcar company. Eventually, he became a motorman for the electric train operating between Omonia Square in Athens and the port of Piraeus.

Life was not easy for my parents. As their family grew, feeding everyone became more and more difficult. Although my father had a good job, his pay was only just enough to buy food and pay the rent. Our clothes were cheap and didn't last long; our shoes often went without repair.

The house at 87 Petras Street, where my five siblings and I were born, had only two small rooms, certainly inadequate for a family of eight by today's standards. The adobe-built house had a tiled roof that kept us dry and a large courtyard where my father kept a chicken coop with several residents who regularly provided our family with fresh eggs. We shared an outdoor privy in the courtyard with another family, and our only source of running water was a faucet in the courtyard.

LIFE IN KOLONOS

Kolonos was about two kilometers from the Athens Central Railway Station and about six kilometers from the center of Athens. The neighborhood was named after the nearby Kolonos Hill. At the top of the hill was the monument to Oedipus, a tragic Greek figure made famous in Sophocles' Oedipus Trilogy. Surrounding the monument was a beautiful park full of pine, cypress, and pepper trees. Many people from the neighborhood, particularly the young, spent the evening hours in the park, sitting on the flat boulders by the monument or strolling up and down the paths.

Adjacent to the Oedipus monument was an outdoor coffee shop owned and operated by the Kapralos brothers. Every summer evening until midnight, Christos Kapralos played music over the coffee shop's loudspeakers, entertaining his customers and anyone who might be walking by or sitting near the boulders. My friends and I often gathered by the boulders near the monument to listen to the music blaring from the loudspeakers. We watched the groups of people, particularly the girls from our school, strolling by, and on occasion, we fought the boys from other schools who also congregated in the area, until the adults sitting at Kapralos Coffee Shop broke up the melée.

In addition to our fights with boys from other areas of Kolonos, my friends and I made other sorts of trouble. We tampered with the city trams and lit firecrackers on the tram tracks. We caused power outages by crossing wires in electrical junction boxes and engaged in a raid on succulent figs in an Albanian farmer's orchard. The farmer caught us in the act once and managed to put some buckshot from his shotgun into my friend's rear end as we frantically scaled the orchard's wall.

When we reached our late teens, however, life grew serious. On an unusually hot October weekend, six of us decided to bike over to Agios Andreas (Saint Andrews), a beach area east of Athens. After going swimming, we rode our bikes to the small fishing and resort village Rafina, which was a few kilometers away. We were eating *barbunia* (mullet) for lunch at a taverna by the sea when a dark faced gypsy woman and her little girl approached our table. The woman told us, in broken Greek, that she could read our palms and tell us our fortunes for two drachmas each. At first we hesitated, but then we said, "What the heck? Let's try. We have nothing but the money to lose."

Mitsos Jamgis, the oldest member of our gang, was the first one to offer his hand to the gypsy woman. After she looked at his right palm, she said, "Your fortune will be a disturbing and difficult one. You will encounter many problems in your life, but you will overcome them and you will marry a nice and beautiful woman, who will guide you and make you happy." She told my friend Artemis that he too would marry a rich woman and have many children. She then moved on to Mimis Vimakis. "You should prosper in life and you will be married to a nice woman, but you will not have many children."

Then, she came to me. She took my right hand and looked into my eyes. After she examined my palm, she said, "And you, young man, your life will take you to a far away place. You will cross a big ocean to a place where you will find your destiny."

I think the gypsy's predictions led all of us to start seriously considering who we would be and what we would do when we grew up. Mimis and I were approaching our seventeenth birthdays, and others in our group were well into their eighteenth years. Well all decided that it was

3

time to abandon the shenanigans that we had been involved in as youngsters and to conform to society's rules. We gave up fist fighting and
pranks and began to meet at the Kapralos Coffee Shop, as the other
adults did, instead of at the boulders in the park.

On our way to the coffee shop one evening, we encountered a group
of boys from another neighborhood, trespassing on our turf. Closer scru-
tiny revealed that their leader, Panayotis Chronopoulos, was among them.
Panayotis was a smart, stubborn, and tough boy who didn't give up easily in a fight. His gang and ours had fought before.

As we approached our longtime rivals, intending to walk through
their path, I whispered to my friends quietly, "Keep cool, you guys, and
don't say anything. Just keep on walking."

Unfortunately, we exchanged a few words and then blows with
Panayotis and his group. The brawl quickly escalated and soon we heard
police whistles. It was time to lick our wounds and run away. I took a
quick inventory of my injuries. I had a bloody nose and cuts all over my
face. My clean white shirt was torn and bloodied, and I was a little shaken
up. My right fist was numb.

When I arrived home that evening, it was dark and my father was
still at work. He was not due to come home until late that night. My
poor mother started to cry when she saw my face.

"Mom," I said, "we got into a fight that someone else started. We
couldn't help it. These guys provoked us to fight, and when they attacked us, we had no choice but to defend ourselves."

At breakfast the next morning, my father took one astonished look
at my face and exclaimed, "What kind of face is that? I thought you had
given up fist fighting and here you are, all banged up. Who did this to you?"

I explained to my dad that the other boys had started the fight, and I
was amazed when he said he believed me.

"But I want to emphasize again, as I have before," he said, "fighting
will get you nowhere, only to jail. And, remember, those who go to jail
have no future; their lives are shattered forever."

My wounds healed after only about ten days, but, the next time I
met with my friends, I solemnly assured them that my fighting days
were over.

4

CHAPTER 2

IN LOVE WITH AIRPLANES

I was twelve years old and walking to school on a summer morning in 1932 when a humming sound caught my attention and made me look up in the quiet blue sky. The humming became louder and louder until I saw a biplane, painted in the olive livery of the Hellenic Air Force, dive toward Kolonos Hill. The airplane flew so low that I was able to see the aviator's head, covered with a leather helmet and goggles, poking out of the open-air cockpit. As the plane recovered from its dive, it rolled into a left turn, came around again, and flew directly at the high point of the hill, almost to the spot where I was standing. As it came around the second time, the aviator waved at me. Then he zoomed up and flew away toward Mount Parnis, where Tatoi Aerodrome was located.

From that day on, school and books meant nothing to me and each day, while walking to school, I kept a lookout for another aerial demonstration. I was rewarded when, days later, the same biplane flew over Kolonos Hill, almost at the same time in the morning. Once again, the aviator performed spellbinding acrobatic maneuvers.

This time, I was able to collect my thoughts enough to ask myself about the aviator. Who was he? Was he from Kolonos? Why was he showing off here? Was he showing off for a girlfriend? Or to impress his parents? I was puzzled and, of course, fascinated by the aviator's frequent demonstrations. I became obsessed with airplanes, drawing them at school and thinking about them as I fell asleep. Day and night my thoughts drifted away with the olive-colored biplane.

One day, I woke up in the morning to get ready for school. I went outside and looked up in the cloudless Athenian sky, and suddenly I was struck with a deep burning desire to become a military aviator. I began to dream that I was in the cockpit of that Greek air force biplane; I dreamed I was flying over Athens, the

Acropolis, and Kolonos Hill, soaring over the Greek countryside and the sea with its hundreds of islands. On that day I promised myself that I would become an aviator and fly such an airplane no matter what.

Flush with my new dream, I decided to visit Tatoi Aerodrome, the home of the Hellenic Air Force Academy, to watch the airplanes up close. I knew that Tatoi was located at the foothills of Mount Parnis, but I didn't know how to get there and I didn't want to ask anyone for directions because I thought they might tell my father. I revealed my ambition only to Mimis Vimakis, my best friend. On the way to school the day I decided to become a military aviator, I saw Mimis as he was walking up Petras Street. I joined him and told him that I planned to skip school and walk to Tatoi by following the railroad tracks.

"The train that goes to Larissa passes through the Tatoi Aerodrome and I am certain that by following the tracks I will find my way there. If the teacher wants to know why I am not in school, tell him that I am not feeling well," I said.

At first Mimis hesitated to lie for me, but eventually he gave in. Mimis and I parted, and I began to walk briskly toward the railway tracks a few blocks away. From the tracks I began my long trek to Tatoi. By about 11:00 a.m., I had reached the narrow, paved road that led to the aerodrome's entrance. My heart was thumping fast as I walked down the road watching the airplanes take off, fly around the base, and land. At the end of the road, I found a gate with an armed guard. I approached the guard and asked him if I could go into the aerodrome to watch the airplanes.

"No," he said. "You are not allowed to go into the base or to stand out here. This is a military post, and you are on a military road. No civilians are allowed here without permission. You must go back to the train station and watch from there."

Having walked so far from Kolonos, I was disappointed that I couldn't enter the base, but I did as the guard ordered and settled close to the barbed wire fence that protected the base on the side near the railway station. From my makeshift observation post, I watched the airplanes. There were biplanes and single-winged craft, some painted silver and others painted olive green, like the one I had seen over Kolonos Hill. I watched until 1:00 p.m., when the flying stopped. I assumed the aviators had gone to lunch and considered staying to see more in the afternoon. But, because I had a twenty kilometer hike back to Kolonos, I decided that it was best to head for home.

When I arrived home, exhausted from the day's events, my mother asked why I was late from school. I told her that I had stopped at Mimis's house to eat lunch. In fact I was starving, but because of my lie, I had to wait until suppertime to eat. The night passed without anyone from the family realizing that I had missed school that day. I continued to visit Tatoi Aerodrome whenever I could.

One afternoon Mimis came by my house to tell me that a new movie was playing in uptown Athens. It was the story of the air war during World War I.

"I don't know the name of the film," Mimis said, "but I know you will want to see it."

After my mother gave me permission to go, I joined Mimis and we hurried to the Hellas Movie House on Athinas Street off Omonia Square. The film's title in Greek, as advertised in the papers, was *Air Fighting in the Western Front*, but later on, I learned that the movie's actual title was *The Dawn Patrol*. It featured Richard Barthelmes and Douglas Fairbanks Jr.

As we entered the darkness of the almost full theater, we realized we had missed the movie's beginning of the picture, and when it ended, we decided to stay until the next screening to catch the part we had missed. We loved the movie so much that we stayed until the end of the second screening. When we walked out of the theater, I was elated. I returned to the movie house to watch *The Dawn Patrol* again and again during the month that followed. The aerial combat between the British and the Germans was thrilling. Every time I watched the movie, I became more convinced that my dream to become an aviator was not a mistake.

On our way to see *The Dawn Patrol* the third time, Mimis and I arrived at Omonia Square and found that the theater hadn't opened yet. We decided to walk up Stadium Street toward Sintagma Square to kill time until the theater opened. As we were passing by a bookstore, Mimis called my attention to a book titled *The Red Baron: The Exploits of the Greatest Aviator of World War I*, by Manfred Von Richthofen. We immediately went inside the store, and Mimis agreed to loan me the ten drachmas I needed to buy the book.

I clutched the book with both hands as we watch *The Dawn Patrol* for fear of losing it. Before I went to sleep that night, I read some fifteen pages of the Red

Baron's adventures. I read the entire book within two days, and then I started to review page after page at my leisure in hopes of memorizing everything about the man who dominated the sky over the Western Front during World War I.

After reading Richthofen's book, my zeal to visit Tatoi Aerodrome increased. I was never too tired to walk the distance to Tatoi to watch the airplanes fly. On the days that I had classes in math or other subjects that I didn't like, I skipped school to visit the aerodrome. After one of my visits, I returned home dreadfully late.

My mother, who always tried to defend me in front of my father when I did something wrong, could not help me this time. When I arrived home, she told me that my father had gone to school to see why I was late coming home. When my father returned, he wanted to know where I had been. I explained that after school I had gone with some of my friends to play soccer. What a lie! My father did not accept the story and asked again where exactly I had been. After another round of lies, I was forced to confess that I had gone to Tatoi to watch the airplanes.

Father was furious at me for going to Tatoi, but he was even angrier because I had lied to him. He took out his belt and began to whip me. He continued beating me until he became so frustrated that he dropped his belt and left the house, heading for the coffee house on Lenorman Street. But my punishment continued the following day. My father locked all my street clothes away so I would not be able to leave the house.

Even after my punishment, I continued to visit Tatoi. Because walking the twenty kilometers took too long, I decided to start taking the bus or train. On the next school holiday, I walked to the bus stop at Omonia Square early in the morning. Since my father had cut my small weekly allowance to punish me for lying, I had no money to buy a ticket for the ride—but I didn't intend to buy a ticket. I planned to get a free ride by hanging onto the ladder at the rear of the bus and jumping off when the bus reached Tatoi. My plan was foiled, however, when I discovered that the bus company had recently upgraded to modern German-type buses with a ladder on the side near the front door. I realized if I wanted to continue visiting the aerodrome I would have to find a way to make money.

I started doing various odd jobs for people in my neighborhood, and through my diligence, I rapidly accumulated enough spending money to buy several bus tickets to Tatoi. I even had cash left over for the movies.

One of my part-time jobs was taking care of the garden at the residence of Mr. George Papazoglou. Mr. Papazoglou's son-in-law, Mr. Eric

Hans, was involved in the old man's tobacco business, and when he was around, he would give me a tip. One day, as he dug for change in his pocket, he asked me what I wanted to be when I grew up. When I told him that I was determined to be an aviator, he looked me in the eye and said, "You know, Spiro, I was an aviator in the war. I was in the German Air Service, first in the Number 2 Squad-ron. Then I was transferred to Number 11 Squadron, which was commanded by Manfred Von Richthofen."

"You, Mr. Hans, met Baron Richthofen?" I was astounded.

"Oh, yes," he said. "I flew in many flights with Manfred and his brother, Lothar, against the French and British."

The day after I spoke with Mr. Hans was a holiday and the first day of my father's two-week vacation. It was a cloudless day, and at about midmorning, my father asked me to take a walk with him up to Kolonos Hill to the Kapralos Coffee Shop. We walked in silence most of the way, but once we had settled at a table in the coffee shop, my father confronted me.

"Spiro," he said, "I am very disappointed with you. You have been lying to me constantly. You have been missing school to the point that your teacher is concerned about your standing and disturbed by your lack of interest in school. Being your father, I am also worried about your future. You are carefree and reckless, always looking for a fight with others.

"Tell me," he continued, "why are you going to Tatoi to see the airplanes? My boy, airplanes crash; they kill people. There is no future with the airplane."

Although my father could not shake my love of airplanes, his remarks about my lying, manners, and behavior touched a nerve. I apologized to him for lying and promised I would never lie to him or anyone else again. But I begged him not to try to talk me out of flying because I wished with all my heart to become a military aviator.

"Some day, Dad, I will succeed and you'll be proud of me," I said.

TATOI AERODROME

When the school year came to an end, freeing me from books and assignments, I couldn't wait to visit Tatoi. On the first day of summer vacation, I woke up early in the morning and caught the train to the aerodrome.

When I arrived at the Tatoi station, I decided I no longer wanted to watch the planes from the perimeter. I had to find a way into the aerodrome. After some reconnaissance, I started to trek through some two-hundred yards of a vineyard in hopes of reaching the canyon-like dry riverbed that led to the base's western boundary. By the time I made it to the riverbed, my clothes and knees were filthy from my crawl through the vineyard. After a lengthy walk through bushes, weeds, and small trees, I reached the northern part of the aerodrome, but I still had to climb up the steep riverbed. When I reached the top, I was surprised to find myself not only near the base but inside. The barbed wire fence through which I had watched the airplanes before apparently did not surround the entire property, and I had actually penetrated the aerodrome's defenses.

10

I walked leisurely through the base so as not to arouse any suspicion. After crossing the road from the main gate on the base's south side, I found myself behind the last in a row of hangars. As I walked to the front of the hangar, I noticed soldiers opening the huge sliding doors, no doubt in preparation to pull out some biplanes.

I stayed off to the side as the mechanics began to pull the airplanes out. To my great surprise, the five that emerged were identical to the first biplane I saw over Kolonos Hill. Once the mechanics had readied the planes, a van carrying five aviators dressed in flying suits with parachutes on their shoulders drove up. The aviators walked around their flying machines, then climbed and settled in their cockpits. Seconds later, they started their engines, almost simultaneously.

One biplane, which appeared to be maneuvered by the leader of the group, moved ahead and the other four followed. I watched the five biplanes as they taxied on the immense expanse of grass that made up the airfield. The airplanes stopped at the south end of the field, and the aviators in each machine revved up their engines in preparation for takeoff. The leader pulled forward and faced north, while the other four biplanes positioned themselves in formation, two to their leader's left and two to his right. Suddenly all five airplanes started to move forward with a tremendous roar, and in seconds, they were off the ground and up in the air.

Later, I learned these biplanes were British-made Gloster Mars, high-performance single-seat fighters with 325-horsepower Armstrong Siddeley Jaguar engines. The Gloster Mars was a conversion of the British Nieuport Nighthawk fighter. The Hellenic Army Air Force had purchased twenty-five Gloster Mars from England and with them had formed two pursuit squadrons. One was stationed at Tatoi Aerodrome and the other one was based at Sedes Air Base in the north.

I was amazed at the spectacular sight of the five biplanes taking off in formation. Until this point, I had been worried about being caught, but suddenly, I didn't care if the military police or anyone else spotted me and demanded to know what was I doing there. Watching the takeoff was worth my train trip to Tatoi, my struggle to enter the base, and any trouble I might find myself in.

I stayed where I was for almost an hour, watching other airplanes taking off and landing. Then, just after noon, I decided to retrace my steps and make for the railroad station. Although I passed some military vehicles and soldiers walking up and down the road, no one seemed to notice me, and I left the base without difficulty.

ADOLESCENCE IN ATHENS

I continued to enter and exit Tatoi through the riverbed throughout that summer of 1936. In retrospect, I am amazed that no one ever detected or challenged me while I was inside the base. I can only suppose those who saw me assumed I was the son of someone who worked there.

As I continued to visit Tatoi, I became bolder and started to talk to some of the mechanics, including, of all people, my brother's friend, Warrant Officer Gerasimos Gavrilis, who turned out to be a pleasant and friendly man in his mid-twenties. Gerasimos was the chief of maintenance in Hangar One, where the Hellenic Air Force Academy's training airplanes were kept. Thanks to Gerasimos, I was allowed inside the training hangar. I took on various chores, such as sweeping the hangar floor and cleaning the workbenches in the engine and fabric shops. Sometimes I helped push the airplanes out of the hangar into the flight line. There weren't enough mechanics to do all the jobs in the hangar, and so my presence was welcomed. I spent much of my time in the morning on the flight line, watching the arrival of instructor aviators and their cadets who were preparing to go aloft in their Avro-504 and Morane-Saulnier training airplanes.

One day, as I was sweeping the floor in Hangar One, a uniformed officer entered and asked to see the chief of maintenance—Gerasimos—who was called immediately from the engine shop. The officer, I later learned, was Squadron Leader George Fragistas, the head of instructor pilots at Tatoi. He wanted to know the status of an Avro-504 airplane that had been damaged in a ground loop by one of his students. Gerasimos gave the officer a report as they both stood by the damaged airplane near the fabric shop. After their conversation, Gerasimos returned to the engine shop while the squadron leader started to walk toward the small hangar door.

On his way out of the hangar, the officer noticed me, as I stood between two hangar mechanics named Kostas and Aris, holding a broom in my hands. "What is this boy doing here?" he demanded.

Kostas, the talkative one, answered, "This is Spiro, Sir. He is our helper."

The officer regarded me with a conspicuous lack of enthusiasm. "He can't be allowed in the hangar. He is a civilian and only a boy. He should stay out of here."

On saying this, Fragistas stalked out of the hangar. I stood rigid, my heart beating fast. I feared the officer would return with the military police. But when Kostas told Gerasimos what the squadron leader had said, my friend approached me and said, "Spiro, don't worry. I will talk to Wing Commander Haralambos Potamianos, the training school commander, whom I know well."

Gerasimos' words calmed me enough that I was able to finish my chores that day.

During my visits to Tatoi, I learned a great deal about aircraft. With Gerasimos's assistance, I sat in the cockpit of almost every one of the airplanes the Greek air force used at Tatoi: the British Avro504, the French Morane-Saulnier, the Potez, the Breguet, the Atlas, and, of course my favorite, the Gloster Mars. In 1936 and 1937, I spent considerable time in the maintenance facilities, mostly the engine and repair shops, watching the mechanics work. As I watched, I asked all sorts of questions about the airplanes, the engines, the power behind the propeller, the airframes, and the theory of flight. I had enough sense then to write down some of the basics. This effort turned out to be most beneficial to me later in my life.

Airplanes and engines weren't the only things I learned about during my visits to Tatoi. I also learned about the Hellenic Air Force and its rules, regulations, and traditions. In addition I inquired about the Air Force Academy to ascertain the prerequisites for entering the elite school. I knew that simply graduating high school wasn't enough. I had to be at the top of my class.

Further, all applicants were tutored extensively prior to applying to the academy in order to pass the difficult entrance exam. The tutoring wasn't free; the applicant and his family had to pay the cost. I was worried because my father didn't have that kind of money to spend on my education. And even if he had such funds, I doubted he would be willing to spend his money on a venture involving airplanes.

I was also concerned about an unwritten government policy that stipulated that preference for entrance into any military academy in Greece be given to those applicants from military families or with some military background. The technicians and other workers at Tatoi had differing ideas on whether this requirement was rigidly enforced. Some believed that the policy was in place to allow certain officials in the military academies and the government, at that time under the dictator Gen. John Metaxas, to select the men they wanted to become military officers.

If I could find someone in authority who knew about the entrance rules to ask for some advice, I could resolve my uncertainties about the application process. Luckily, I ran into Squadron Leader Fragistas outside the hangar one day.

"I see," he said when he saw me, "you managed to stay here. That's fine. But, with the propellers from the airplanes running continuously, this is a dangerous area. This is no place for a boy of your age."

"Sir, I understand and appreciate your concern. I am being careful every moment," I said. "I love the airplanes and like helping out. Some day I would like to become an aviator like you. I beg you, Sir, please don't send me away."

As I spoke, I realized Fragistas was the man I should ask for help with admission into the Air Force Academy. "Sir," I blurted out, "what advice would you give me as one with a burning desire to become a military aviator? I would do anything possible to achieve my goal. I want to learn to fly airplanes. I want to be up in the sky. My great wish is to attend the Air Force Academy when I finish high school."

The squadron leader advised me first to finish my schooling. He said finishing high school was the easy part. Even some of the top students, who had considerable tutoring, had failed to pass the academy's entrance examination. He told me the secrets to success were to be a top level student in every high school subject, including sports and to, above all, be in excellent health.

"Sir, does it matter if my father is not an active duty military man?" I asked.

"Aye, things would be much simpler if your father was serving in the military. But don't let that stop you. You go on with your studies and prepare yourself."

I thanked the squadron leader for his advice and shook his hand.

Determined after my talk with Squadron Leader Fragistas, I started to study harder and continued to work after school to earn spending money. I still visited Tatoi occasionally to see and be with the airplanes I loved.

One day I found the opportunity to tell my father about the conversation I had with the squadron leader. I told him the major obstacle to my acceptance into the Air Force Academy would be coming up with money for the tutoring I would need to prepare me for the entrance examination. My father's face darkened.

"Well, didn't I warn you that it was going to be difficult for you to pursue this business with the airplanes?" he said. "As for the money you need for tutoring, I can only say I just don't have it, son, so don't count on me being able to help you. Spiro, you need to rethink the academy and reevaluate your plans for the future. You must look for another line of work."

HOW (NOT) TO BUILD AN AIRPLANE

After some time away, I returned to the aerodrome again. I had noticed that on numerous occasions previously that the pilots sometimes offered rides in the training airplanes to the mechanics. One day, Gerasimos said that he would try to coax one of the instructors to take me up for a ride. He almost succeeded in arranging for my first flight, but as the pilot, Flight Officer Dimitrios Spinoulas, who had seemed initially agreeable, watched me approach his aircraft, he balked.

"I am sorry, Mr. Gavrilis, but I can't do it. He is a civilian, and it is against the regulations to take a civilian up for a flight."

I was initially discouraged by this news, but then I had an idea: since the Tatoi pilots wouldn't take me up in one of their airplanes, I would build my own. I didn't know anything about airplane construction. My brother Yannis, however, was a year away from graduating as a mechanical engineer from an engineering institute and had considerable knowledge of mechanical plans and drawings. One Sunday morning, I cornered Yannis while he was sitting in our yard, studying one of his many technical books.

"Yannis, what do you know about the construction of airplanes?" I asked.

"Oh, a little," he replied.

"I mean building an airplane from scratch."

"Not a lot," he said. I proceeded to pepper him with questions about the structure and mechanics of airplanes

He looked at me and asked, "Why all these questions? Are you contemplating in building an airplane?"

"Oh," I said, casually, "not exactly. I just wanted to learn something about the process of airplane construction. That's all."

A few days later, while we were playing soccer after school, I spotted the Opel sedan that had been abandoned long ago by the creek, opposite the soccer field. When the game was over, I approached Mimis Vimakis and asked him to go with me to the sedan to check out its engine. Mimis agreed.

The car had no wheels, and all the windows were smashed. After several tries, we managed to open the hood. As we looked inside and stared at the small engine, I noticed the fan at the front of the engine housing. Immediately, I saw how the fan could be replaced with a propeller when we built my airplane.

"What is it with you, Spiro?" Mimis asked. "Why are you looking at this corroded engine?"

I explained to my friend that Yannis had told me that a lightweight engine could be adapted to function in an aircraft. Then, I revealed my plan: We would use a wheelbarrow to move the engine to the yard at my house. Then, we would ask Yannis and maybe Gerasimos for help. Mimis thought my plan was a good one and agreed to meet me at the car the next afternoon to help me carry the engine to the yard. Excited as we parted for the night, we agreed to say nothing to anyone.

The following day, Mimis and I met at the abandoned sedan. With the tools we'd brought with us, we started to work loosening the bolts that secured the | engine to the Opel's chassis. By late afternoon, and after some scraped knuckles and bruised fingers, we had the engine ready to move, but it was too heavy for the two of us to lift. We recruited Mitsos Jamgis, the strongest guy in our group, to help us. The next afternoon the three of us met at the abandoned sedan and, with a great deal of effort, heaved the engine out of the car and into the wheelbarrow. My two friends helped me push the wheelbarrow home and unload the engine behind the chicken coop at my house. Stage one of my plan was finished. Stage two would be a bit more difficult.

Days later, my father found the engine as he was going to the chicken coop to retrieve some eggs. He wanted to know what the engine was doing there and where it had come from. I told him that my friends and I had taken it from the abandoned sedan by the field where we play soccer and that we could use the engine to drive the propeller of a small airplane, which I planned to build myself.

My father looked me in the eyes and said, "You are dreaming, son." Without another word, he turned away from me and walked into the house. That was the last I heard from my father on the subject of the Opel engine.

When Yannis found out about the engine, he immediately raised objections.

"You can't build an airplane just like that. Think for a moment. You will need a large closed space, material, special tools, and money. Do you have any money?"

"No," I said, "but I will work and make some."

"No way," he said. " You will need thousands and thousands of drachmas. Where do you think you'll get such money? Listen, Spiro," he said, "it isn't as easy as you think. Engines for airplanes are designed and built to be operated in the air. Automobile engines are built strictly for ground operation. You can't mix the two."

I realized he was right.

CHAPTER 3

VOYAGE OF DISCOVERY

Mimis, Mitsos Jamgis, Takis, Artemis, and I decided to celebrate New Year's Eve 1937 in downtown Athens. We were strolling along Stadium Street, between Omonia and Sintagma Squares, when the pealing of church bells all over Athens greeted the new year. As was tradition, my friends and I wished each other happiness and good fortune in what was left of our last year of high school. When I shook hands with Mimis, I said to him quietly, "I have a hunch, Mimis, that 1938 will be a decisive year for me."

That January, we returned to classes and to our familiar routine, which included playing soccer with our classmates after school. During one of these after-school soccer matches, my classmate Elias told me that his cousin Dimitris, one of the top students in his class, had failed the written entrance examinations for the Hellenic Air Force Academy, even after having been tutored for the entire summer. I asked Elias for specifics on what had happened, and he said that in general the examinations were extremely difficult. This was sobering news, and I began to abandon the idea of attending the Air Force Academy and to think about leaving Greece to fulfill my dream.

Leaving Greece for America was my most obvious option. I had learned a great deal, or so I believed, about America from the many movies I had seen during my childhood, including aviation films such as *The Dawn Patrol*, *Wings*, *Lilac Time*, and *Hell's Angels*. I had also read books and magazine articles describing the unlimited opportunities in America. Greece did not offer boundless opportunities, at least not for me, and my chances of becoming an aviator in my homeland, no matter how hard I worked, were slim to none.

I began to find and speak with people who had traveled to Europe, America, and other countries around the world. I even visited the American consulate in

Athens to get information. From my inquiries, I learned, in the late 1930s, traveling to America for business required a passport and a visa and emigration and, permanent residence required a U.S. citizen's sponsorship. In addition, I needed a significant sum of money to pay my way. Even if I had been able to secure the necessary documents and money, I doubted Greece's military government would have allowed me to leave my home country. In a few years, I would be twenty-one, the age at which I would, by law, have to serve for two years in the Greek armed forces.

I concluded that I could not leave Greece legitimately as a passenger on a vessel bound for America. So, I began to seriously consider stowing away on a U.S.-bound ship. This idea popped into my mind after I read an account of a Greek orphan boy, about my age, who had stowed away successfully on a Greek passenger liner headed to Egypt, where he joined his uncle who lived there. I had also read about others from Greece, England, and Germany who managed the same feat in order to get to the New World during the early part of the twentieth century. To stow away on a ship successfully, I concluded, I would need to have guts, courage, determination, and some common sense. Above all, I would have to be in good shape to endure hunger and frigid weather at sea, and I would have to have patience to cope with the miserable claustrophobia onboard a ship. With this in mind, I started a strenuous daily exercise routine.

I also took every opportunity to visit Piraeus, the harbor that served Athens, to carry out a thorough reconnaissance, noting which areas would be impossible to enter and finding others that afforded access to cargo vessels of all sizes, both of Greek and foreign registry. The tough part, I realized, would be smuggling myself aboard a freighter. I concluded that the odds would be more in my favor if I attempted to stow away on a passenger ship. My target was the gigantic Italian liner *Rex*.

When the ship next called at Piraeus, I was ready. I left a note for my family explaining that I was going to America and made my way to the dock. But when I arrived there, I could not figure out how to board the ship undetected, at least not in the daylight. I decided to return home. Still, I was determined not to give up. I made my way back to Piraeus the next morning, the day the liner was due to depart for New York. I saw my opportunity as I watched the crowd of passengers boarding the ship—and the porters in their blue coats carrying luggage up the gangway. I picked up two small suitcases, put one on my right shoulder and carried the other one with my left hand, just as the porters in blue coats did. I started to climb the gangway, tucking my head, which was covered by my fisherman's cap, into my sweater's high collar. My heart pounded from the fear that someone would discover my ruse, but I reached the ship's deck without incident, passed the uniformed guard, and made a right turn into a passageway. I was aboard the *Rex*!

The porters' supervisor spotted me almost immediately and turned me in to one of the ship's guards. I was, of course, escorted off the ship; I had no hope of getting aboard now. My tail between my legs, I returned home and fell back into my regular routine.

Fortunately, a chance meeting with a visiting Greek-American boy about my age named Harry Apostol put me on the right path. Harry spent hours teaching me a bit of English, telling me about life in America, and outlining the process of becoming a U.S. citizen. When I revealed to him my plans to stow away, Harry convinced me that it would not only be dangerous but also futile. I would almost certainly be discovered and returned to Greece. He told me I was better off finding a job as a crew member on a Greek merchant ship and working my way to America. The Greek merchant marine had one of the largest fleets in the world at the time, and many jobs were available for Greeks who wanted to go to sea.

"With luck," Harry said, "the ship you sail on will one day be bound for an American port, and when your ship arrives in the United States, you can just walk away and stay there. That is how my father came to America."

JOINING THE MERCHANT MARINE

I abandoned my plans to stow away and focused on finding work on an ocean-going freighter. One day I went to Piraeus and saw a sailor smoking a cigarette while leaning over the rail of a small but beautiful coastal freighter. I asked him a few questions about his ship, and then I inquired about getting into the merchant marine. He told me to approach someone who owned a ship and simply ask for a job. In fact, he had landed his job as a sailor from his uncle, who owned the coastal freighter. Unfortunately, I didn't know any ship owners, and I did not have any relatives who might know one.

"Then you will have to go through the Seamen's Union," said the sailor. "First, of course, you have to get your Seaman's Certificate in order to join the union. Then the union will try to find you a job. Do you know anyone who belongs to the Seamen's Union? Such a person could help you get started."

When I told the sailor I did not know anyone who belonged to the union, he then directed me to the union's offices in Piraeus. I thanked him for the information

19

he had provided me and said good-bye. I had already spent considerable time at the harbor that day, so I decided to head home and visit the union another day.

While sitting on the train that afternoon, I thought about who in Kolonos might be a sailor in the merchant marine. I closed my eyes for a moment and suddenly remembered Fotis, the son of a shoemaker I had once worked for. Fotis had served in the Royal Hellenic Navy, and when he completed his tenure in the military, he joined the merchant marine.

The next day, after school, I went to the shoemaker's shop and found Fotis looking after the business while his father was away. While we shined shoes, I told him about my interest in the merchant marine, and he was, as I had hoped, a font of information. First, he told me about the Merchant Marine Academy, where sailors went if they wanted to become a ship's officer. Other schools trained individuals to be merchant marine engineers, who took care of the boilers, engines, and other machinery on a ship. If I wanted to be a crew member, a deck sailor, or a fireman on a ship, I didn't need to go to school. I only had to obtain a Seaman's Certificate and membership in the Seamen's Union.

When shipping companies needed nonofficer crew members, they normally went to the union to fill a certain number of the open positions. Alternatively, I could register with a maritime shipping employment agency that recruited and assigned crews for shipping companies. If I joined an employment agency, Fotis told me I would have to pay a fee based on the salary I received as a crewmember aboard a ship.

Fotis went on to tell me that I could obtain a Seaman's Certificate from the Ministry of Merchant Marine, which was located in Piraeus. Several maritime employment agencies and the Seamen's Union office were in Piraeus also. To get my Seaman's Certificate, I needed a copy of my birth certificate, two passport-size photos, and one hundred drachmas—the fee for certification.

The following week I traveled to Piraeus again to visit the Ministry of the Merchant Marine. When I arrived at the huge building, a doorman directed me to an office on the ground floor where applications are submitted for the Seaman's Certificate. I found the right office and asked the young woman inside how to apply for a Seaman's Certificate. While I was waiting for her to find the application forms, I noticed a large photograph of a man with the notation "Defkalion Rediadis, Minister of the Merchant Marine" hanging on the wall.

"Hey," I thought, "Periklis Rediadis was the minister of the navy when my father served as a Marine. Is this man a relative of my father's former boss?"

When the lady brought me the application papers, I asked her if I could speak to Mr. Rediadis directly. She sent me to his office on the second floor, where I encountered his secretary, a woman named Maria. Maria told me Mr. Rediadis was in London and wouldn't return to the office until the following week. I asked her whether Mr. Rediadis was related to the Mr. Periklis Rediadis who was once the minister of the navy.

"Oh, yes," she said, "Mr. Periklis and Mr. Defkalion Rediadis are brothers. Mr. Periklis is now the minister of economy in Athens."

I told Maria that my father and mother had met when they both worked for Mr. Periklis. After explaining that I was returning the following week to submit my application papers for a Seaman's Certificate, I asked her if I could make an appointment to see her boss. She told me an appointment would probably not be a problem and she would mention me to the minister when he returned from London.

A week later, I woke up early, and instead of going to school, I dashed to Omonia Square to catch the electric train for Piraeus. I arrived at the ministry building around 10:00 a.m., and Maria greeted me as I entered the minister's office.

"Ah, Mr. Pisanos," she said, "Mr. Rediadis is on his way to the office. He should be here any moment. I spoke to him on the phone this morning, and I mentioned your name."

I tried to concentrate on what I was planning to say to Mr. Rediadis, but I was unable to form my thoughts for our meeting. While I was racking my brain for a way to open my conversation with Mr. Rediadis, a well-dressed middle-aged man walked into the office and said, "Good morning, Maria."

The secretary replied, "Mr. Rediadis, this is Spiro Pisanos. I spoke to you about him on the phone this morning."

"Oh, yes," Mr. Rediadis said. "So you are Spiro, Athena's son."

"One of them," I said. "Do you remember my mother, Sir?"

"You bet," he said. "I remember both your father and mother. Even after they were married. I ate your mother's cooking when I lived with my brother Periklis in his house, where your mother worked. Your mother, my boy, is an excellent cook, the best we ever had in our kitchen."

We went into the minister's office to discuss my situation, and Mr. Rediadis agreed to help me find a position on a ship owned by one of his acquaintances. He also asked his secretary to handle my Seaman's Certificate application. I thanked him for being so kind and helpful. I shook his hand, and as I was leaving his office, he asked me to mention him to my parents.

"I will," I told him. I said good-bye to Maria, who told me that I should have my certificate soon.

Early in March 1938, I visited Maria's office to pick up my Seaman's Certificate. A week later, Mr. Rediadis informed me that he had secured a position for me as an assistant fireman on the freighter *P. Margaronis*, which had just returned from a voyage to South America and was in port until the end of March. Unfortunately, Mr. Rediadis did not know the *P. Margaronis*'s new destination. He told me only that I would have to visit the ship's operations manager to be briefed on my new job and receive a thorough physical.

On the night after my briefing and physical, during dinner, I informed my family that I was going to sea and intended to settle someday in America. My siblings reacted in shock; my mother began to cry. My father, to my surprise, was happy with my decision.

"Maybe by being at sea," he said, "you will become more disciplined and grow up. This decision will keep you off the streets and out of trouble."

I was leaving at a time when school was still in session, and I did not expect the school to honor my graduation because I would miss so many classes before the year's end. I told my father that I planned to finish school in America. He said he would look into securing my Greek high school diploma.

"By the way, Dad," I said as dinner was ending, "Mr. Defkalion Rediadis asked me to give you his regards."

"Where did you see him?" my father asked, surprised.

"I visited his office at the merchant marine in Piraeus. In fact, he is the one who helped me get the job on the *P. Margaronis*. He's the minister of the merchant marine."

The next day after school, I asked all of my friends to meet me at the Kapralos Coffee Shop. I told them about my plans to go to America by ship and about my desire to settle there and learn to fly.

"But as I go away, I am taking with me the memories of our friendship," I said, ending my short farewell speech. "That will remain always with me wherever I may be. And if all goes well, someday I will return to Kolonos and tell you stories of where I have been and what I have accomplished."

My friends sat in silence when I finished speaking. I had to fight the tremors within me, to keep myself from crying. The silence was soon broken by Mitsos Jamgis, who said, "I don't believe it. I will when I see you climb the ship's gangway."

"That, my friend, you'll see and soon," I assured him.

OFF TO SEA

On March 18, 1938, the shipping company informed me that the *P. Margaronis* was to depart on March 25, Greek Independence Day. I was to report on the ship not later than 6:00 p.m. on the twenty-fifth. My last few days in Kolonos were busy, as I packed my bags and spent time visiting relatives in the neighborhood. After saying good-bye to my friends, I paid a last visit to the Tatoi Aerodrome, where I, although I did not know it then, saw Gerasimos Gavrilis for the last time. I also said farewell to Mr. Hans, whose tales of Baron von Richthofen had in part inspired my passion for airplanes.

On March 20, I visited the *P. Margaronis* while it was coming out of repairs in dry dock, to see what my new home at sea would be like. The ship was a general cargo vessel of approximately ten thousand tons. It was of Greek registry, its homeport was Piraeus, and it had been named after a Greek ship owner, as was common among Greek ships. The ship's exterior was black down to the waterline, and below that line, its huge hull was covered with a dark brownish red paint that, I was later told, was specially made to resist corrosion. The superstructure above the upper deck, as well as its four lifeboats, had been recently painted creamy white.

Early in the morning on March 25, Mimis, Takis, the two Mitsos, my three younger brothers, and I visited the new grade school on Distomou Street. The school was the center of the Greek Independence Day celebration in our town. We stayed at the celebration until about noon, when we returned to our home on Kathemias Street, where family friends and relatives had gathered to see me off and wish me well with my new life at sea. As expected, my mother and my sister, Chrisoula, started to cry when I walked into the house.

After many kisses, hugs, and blessings, I broke away from the people who had come to see me leave. I picked up the two small bundles that held all of my belongings. All of the visitors, as well as my parents and Chrisoula, followed me through the courtyard out to the street door. Since my friends and brothers wished to accompany me to the harbor, Mitsos Jamgis had commissioned a large taxi to take us to Omonia Square, where we caught the electric train for Piraeus. At about 3:00 p.m. the harbor taxi pulled up at the pier. I unloaded my belongings from the trunk of the taxi and placed them by the gangway, as my friends and brothers admired the enormous ship that would be my new home.

My young brother, George, who loved the sea, kidded, "Spiro, why don't you take me with you so I can be your helper?"

"Next trip," I told him, smiling.

I shook hands with and hugged everyone, and they wished me good luck and reminded me to write. As I started to climb the gangway, my heart began to thump.

Suddenly Mitsos Jamgis hollered from below, "I believe you now, Spiro, but you son of a gun, I am going to miss you."

When I reached the top deck I dropped my belongings, turned around, and waved to the guys below as they prepared to pile back into the waiting taxi. After checking with an attendant, I was directed toward the ship's stern and my sleeping quarters, where I ran into a group of crew members who had also just arrived onboard. I introduced myself to the men. A sailor who appeared to be an old hand helped me move my things into a small cabin with a cozy bunk.

"This is your place, Spiro," he said.

Without wasting time, I changed clothes and headed topside. There, I met the other crew members, including the deck hands Kostas, Takis, Argiros, and George, and a merchant marine cadet named Diamantis.

George told me I had been assigned to the third shift below and then introduced me to my shift mates, the firemen Kostas and Stelios. The firemen were brothers, and Kostas was the younger of the two. I immediately liked them; they were polite and clean-cut.

I was standing by the rail that evening when Kostas came up from below to tell me that it was time to go to the galley in the ship's midsection to pick up our evening meal. Kostas explained that as the assistant fireman, I would pick up all the meals for our shift and carry them on a big tray to the small dining room astern. At times when two trays of food are to be picked up at the galley, he would come along to help, especially if the sea was rough and the ship was pitching and rolling.

Because it was my first night onboard, Kostas accompanied me to the galley. As we walked there, Kostas said, "It appears that all the crew is aboard, except some of the officers and the captain. The captain's name is Patroklos. I've never met him, but I've heard that he is an old timer and a master of the sea."

We picked up our dinner and headed astern. That evening I learned that the ship's crew consisted of thirty-five men, including the captain; the first, second, and third officers; an additional cadet officer; the wireless operator, who spoke several languages; the cook, Mr. Moriatis; and a pantryman who assisted the cook. A steward looked after the captain and the officers and was also in charge of the ship's provisions. The crew was divided into two main groups: those who manned the engine room and the boiler area below and those who handled all activities on the top deck and the bridge.

The chief engineer, assistant chief, and second and third engineers manned the engine room. In the boiler section, there were four six-hour shifts, each manned by two firemen and their assistant fireman or coal handler. I was an assistant fireman.

The deck crew consisted of several sailors who worked in various parts of the ship during the day and steered the ship from a station on the bridge. In charge of the deck sailors was the *Lostromos* (boatswain), who allocated and supervised daily tasks. The list of these tasks was never-ending; at any time, somewhere on the ship, somebody was painting, chipping, and priming corrosion spots or repairing the mechanical equipment on the deck. By the time the crew had repainted or repaired everything on the ship, the place where the work had been started would need to be painted again.

After dinner, Kostas and I went topside for some fresh air, and I had the chance to ask him about my job.

"It's pretty simple," he said. "You work below in the coal storage area, and you move coal with a wheelbarrow and dump it into the open pit. But you have to work fast so that the firemen below will always have ample coal to feed the firepits. The pits power the boilers that, in turn, generate the steam that powers the engines. I'll show you exactly what to do when we go below for our first shift."

Later that night, the ship's captain and pilot came aboard and made their way to the bridge to steer the ship out of the harbor. Thirty minutes after they arrived, the *P. Margaronis* started to pull away from its berth. The deck sailors retrieved the mooring lines that held the ship to the pier and pulled them aboard at the bow and stern. A harbor tug assisted the ship in pulling away from the pier. When the turn was completed, the tug had pulled the ship into the channel that would take us into the open sea.

As the *P. Margaronis* reached the channel, the tug released the towing line and pulled away. I stayed astern by the rail and looked at the lights of Piraeus and, in the far distance, Athens, as the ship began to move inside the channel on its own power. As we passed the lighted harbor entrance, I could see the splendid panorama of the two cities and the Bay of Faliron. I was excited to be aboard the ship on my way to a new and challenging life at sea, but at the same time, I was sobered by the thought that I might never have a chance to see this magnificent view of my birthplace again.

When I went down to my cabin that night, I noticed Stelios's cabin door was wide open, and I stopped by to ask him if he had heard anything about our destination. He had heard that the ship was going to Oran in Algeria to pick up a load of iron ore. From there, we would go to either Cardiff or Baltimore to unload the cargo. I had never heard of these two cities and did not know then that Baltimore was in the United States.

The next morning Stelios knocked on my door at 5:00 a.m. We had to eat and be ready to relieve the shift below by 6:00 a.m., so I lost no time getting up, washing, and putting on my work clothes. I left my cabin and walked to the galley in the dawn light to pick up our breakfast. It was chilly on deck, but the sky was clear and the sea was extremely calm. I took the food to our dining room, where Kostas and Stelios were waiting for me. Once we had finished eating, we headed for the ship's midsection and waited until the bell sounded 6:00. The midnight shift surfaced from below, covered in black soot from working with the coal.

Yannis, my counterpart on the midnight shift, gave me a few tips as I prepared to start my work below. I thanked Yannis for the help and then descended with the others to the boiler room. As he had promised the night before, Kostas accompanied me to the coal storage area, one deck above the boiler room, to show me where to pick up the coal and where to dump it. He was very helpful to me at the outset; he wanted to be sure that I did the right thing.

After a brief demonstration, Kostas left the storage area to join Stelios below. I started to move the coal, following the tips Yannis and Kostas had given me. I shoveled coal from the dimly lit storage area into a huge wheelbarrow, pushed it some fifty feet away, and dumped it into an open pit twenty feet deep. Halfway down, the pit opened into two passages that routed the coal to the two firemen's stations in the boiler room. I was to keep the pit full at all times, so that gravity would provide a steady supply of coal for the firemen, who shoveled the coal almost continuously into the four furnaces. Since the furnaces used coal continuously, the distance from the storage area to the pit continuously increased, and each day, I found myself traveling farther than I had the previous day.

Even though I had kept fit at home by running and exercising, I wasn't prepared for shoveling mountains of coal. After that first six-hour shift, I had difficulty climbing the stairways. I was completely exhausted. Every joint in my body ached. Even though I had had the foresight to wear gloves and heavy socks during my shift, blisters appeared on my hands and feet. I began to worry about my aching back because I knew that I would not get any breaks in the next few weeks. But I knew that I would simply have to do the best I could to endure whatever lay ahead.

When I reached my cabin astern after the first shift, I had no desire to wash my sooty, sweaty face and hands. I wanted only to throw myself into my bunk and go to sleep for a week. Kostas and Stelios assured me that the job would become easier for me in a week or so, after my body had become accustomed to the strain. In fact they were right. After several days, I could work a full shift and not ache all over.

ORAN AND INTO THE STORMY ATLANTIC

On the evening of our third day at sea, we arrived outside the Harbor of Oran. The following day, the ship's chief engineer released most of the engine crew to go ashore. Kostas, Stelios, a sailor named Nikos, and I left the ship together to explore the city. As we walked into the center of Oran, I noticed that the people were dressed in white, dress-like garments, similar to those worn by the Arabs in the Middle East. However, many of the buildings in the city did not look Arabic, but Spanish. Nikos, who had been in Oran before with another ship and had spent almost a month there, explained that, though Oran was currently an Arab, Muslim city, it had, at different times in the past, been controlled by the Spanish, the Turks, and the French.

That afternoon, after walking through town and having lunch and coffee at a French café, we returned to the ship. Word came from the officers' quarters that night that we were not going to Cardiff because another company ship was going to pick up the load for England. The *P. Margaronis* was bound for Baltimore. When I heard from Stelios that Baltimore was in America, my spirits soared. I was careful though, not to show my excitement, even to my new friends. I was worried that they might tell others and ruin my plan.

It took three full days to load the ship with iron ore. My thoughts drifted back to that gypsy woman in Rafina when she read my palm and told me that I was destined to cross a big ocean. How right she was. In the early evening of the third day, we left Oran and began the long voyage across the Atlantic. As I carried out my shipboard duties, I thought about how I would leave the ship and how I would travel from Baltimore to New York. I badly needed a map of America, which I could not find aboard the freighter. Ships carried only charts of the ocean, not of landmass.

One day I asked Kostas where I might find a map of America, explaining I wanted to know where Baltimore was located. He referred me to Stelios, who had a U.S. guidebook with maps in it. Stelios pulled out the map from the book and showed me Baltimore. It was on America's east coast between the U.S. capital of Washington, and Philadelphia, Pennsylvania.

"It's about three hours by train from New York City," he said.

That night we steamed through the Straits of Gibraltar and entered the Atlantic. The next afternoon, just before I took my usual post-lunch nap, I noticed that the sun, which had been shining all morning, was hidden behind clouds and the wind had picked up somewhat. Small waves were striking against the side of the ship. The change in the weather concerned me, but Stelios eased my worries, saying, "It is normal for the temperature to drop and the wind to rise when you are sailing into an ocean. In this case, though, the wind and waves could indicate bad weather ahead."

After I crawled into my bunk that night, I tried to work out how quickly the ship, at its present speed, would cover the 3,200 miles Stelios said lay between Gibraltar and Baltimore. I calculated that we would reach our destination in about ten more days, provided we didn't run into bad weather en route.

Late in the evening of our fourth day in the Atlantic, the sea became choppier, with some waves high enough to splash the ship's lower decks. I noticed on my way to the galley that evening that the *P. Margaronis* had begun to roll and pitch slightly. During the night the wind started to whistle louder and the ship's rolling and pitching became even more noticeable. The following morning, as we were on our way to our shift, Stelios told us he had heard from a sailor who had come from duty on the bridge the previous night that an unusual weather system was developing in the western Atlantic. We'd probably have to cope with high winds and rough seas in the next few days.

"The western Atlantic Ocean is known to be the ugliest storm-swept area of water in the world," Kostas said, adding "We should be running into the rain any moment."

It started to rain that afternoon, at lunchtime. Word came down from the bridge that all hands were needed to secure portholes, doors, and hatches, and that we should take precautions when moving about topside. The light rain and the *P. Margaronis*'s tossing continued all day and into the night.

That night, the wind blew furiously, and I could hear the splashing and banging from the waves crashing against the side of our ship. When I woke up the following morning, I struggled to get dressed and had to fight my way through the corridors of the rolling ship to pick up breakfast from the galley. That evening, when I was on my way to the galley, I found Kostas there and he offered me help carrying the food.

"Given the way the ship is rolling," he said, "we must have encountered a cross sea. Such seas can be a menace to the ship."

To ease my evident alarm, he tried to reassure me that the *P. Margaronis* would come out all right.

The next day, when I reached the coal storage area below, I found that because seasickness had kept me from eating the day before I didn't have the strength to push the wheelbarrow or shovel the coal. Kostas had sensed my predicament and came to my rescue. He told me to sit down, rest for a while, and eat some crackers that he had brought along. He warned me not to drink any water, which would upset my stomach further. In my place, he shoveled coal and pushed several loaded wheelbarrows. I was most grateful. If it weren't for his help, I would have been unable to finish my shift.

When the bell sounded at noon, I dropped everything and immediately headed topside to get fresh air. Kostas and Stelios followed close behind. I looked at the swirling waves crashing against our ship and fear came over me. The bow and stern of the *P. Margaronis* were now dropping deeper into the sea, and huge waves continued to crash over the deck. Stelios suggested that we have our lunch in the midsection instead of carrying the food trays astern. A storage space below the galley had been converted into a temporary resting area, to be used by the ship's crew whenever the ship encountered inclement weather at sea and it was difficult to walk safely astern to the crew quarters.

George, one of the sailors responsible for steering the ship, had also taken refuge in this space that afternoon. As we ate, Stelios asked George about the weather and conditions ahead. George told us we were heading for the center of an ungodly storm and the sea was only going to get nastier as we approached it. He added that, when the radio operator had briefed the captain that morning he had said that some of the reports from eastbound ships destined for Europe were garbled, indicating that the storm was strong enough to interfere with communications.

"The sea appears rough now," George said, "but we haven't seen anything yet."

George's words proved prophetic. The next several days saw the ship tossed by huge swells that dwarfed even our large freighter. The ship's bow soared steeply upward, then crashed down onto and through the next wave, raising the stern up in the air. The furious and savaged sea had no mercy for our ship.

Whenever we surfaced on deck, the ugly dark clouds were much lower than they had been before, and they were always accompanied by heavy rain. We could hear nearby thunder, although the heavy downpour obscured any lightning.

The sailors could not work topside anywhere aboard the ship. The firemen, though, without rest, continued to shovel coal into the furnaces while the ship fought the menacing waves one after the other. My diet of crackers, bread, and as little water as I could stand left me lightheaded and dehydrated. Even with a strenuous effort that left me exhausted, I was barely able to complete my shifts. After work, I stared at the waves through the porthole in our resting place in the ship's midsection. We could not walk astern at all and were forced to spend the nights on the floor in the storage space with the rest of the crew.

Two days into the storm, I forced myself to eat a small portion of my lunch and drink a little water. After lunch, my shipmates and I were resting when we were suddenly roused by a loud bang. A large wave had scooped up the ship causing the bow to slam into the sea. I heard the engine stop and immediately assumed we were in trouble. The ship creaked, groaned, and shuddered as it thundered down into the valley created by the next wave. For a moment I thought the ship would succumb to the storm in the furious Atlantic, but then, the ship's engine started to run again.

Fearful, I asked Kostas, "What's going on?"

"When the bow section of a ship dips deeper than normal into the sea, its stern rises up in the air, exposing the ship's propeller well above the waterline," he explained. "The duty crew on the bridge signals the engine room below to cut the power to the engines to prevent the propeller from running at high speed and breaking loose from its shaft. A ship without a propeller in a stormy sea is doomed to go down."

I awoke just before dawn on the following day, my back aching from sleeping directly on the iron deck. I had slept in my filthy work clothes, as had everyone else over the past few days. The odors of sweat and coal that had accumulated on my skin had begun to bother me. Since our temporary sleeping area had no showers, those of us who occupied the place had not bathed for a number of days. To get some fresh air, I walked topside, holding firmly to the stairway rail as the ship pitched steeply. The sea looked slightly less turbulent, and I had hope that the storm—a hurricane, we learned the night before—had blown itself out.

The next day, I noticed that the ship wasn't pitching as steeply as it had the night before. I rose from the floor and walked topside to discover that the high waves with their long overhanging crests had disappeared; the waves were not only smaller, they were almost back to the calm, gentle rolls that they had been before the storm had hit.

That day I finished my shift without struggling with the coal or acquiring any aches or pains. Since the weather had improved, my shiftmates and I returned aft to our regular sleeping quarters, and I was even able to eat a full meal for the first time in four days. These, I felt, were true achievements.

CHAPTER 4

ARRIVAL AND DEPARTURE

On Friday morning, a few days after the storm had passed, we spotted several seagulls trailing our ship, probably looking for food. They were a welcome sight, as we hadn't seen other living creatures since we left the Mediterranean. Also, the appearance of the gulls indicated that we were getting closer to land. Kostas, Stelios, and I completed our shift that day, knowing that it would be our last before we arrived in Baltimore.

After lunch that afternoon, Kostas went to take a nap while Stelios and I went topside to enjoy the sunshine. As we watched some hungry seagulls that were following our ship, Stelios asked with a smile, "My friend, are you planning to dedicate your life working on ships and becoming a slave of the sea?"

"Well, I don't know," I said. "I like the sea but the storm we went through scared the daylights out of me." I paused and added, "It's hard work, but I like the companionship of people like you and your brother. If we run into another storm on our way back from Baltimore, though, I may have to give up on making a life at sea." I was careful not to indicate that I was not intending on being aboard the *P. Margaronis* when it left Baltimore's harbor.

"The sea is vicious and cruel," Stelios said. "She has no mercy for the ships that plow its oceans or for the humans who man them. Stay long at sea and you become addicted to it. Then it's difficult to break away. You end up being a slave to the waves. You don't want to spend your life that way, my friend. You aren't the seafaring type; you're a young man who belongs ashore. I know. I've watched you." Stelios turned and looked me straight in the eye. "Do you know what I would do if I were your age? Something I should have done long ago on my first voyage to America: leave the ship in Baltimore and stay ashore, where you could start a new life."

I didn't know what to make of this advice. Why was an older member of the crew telling me to abandon the ship when it arrived in America? A thought filled me with alarm: Could Stelios have been assigned to observe or, more properly, spy on the behavior and attitude of crew members and report findings to the captain? I had heard stories, before I left Greece, that some captains kept spies on their ships. If Stelios was indeed an informer, it made sense that he would pay particular attention to young and unmarried crew members like me because we were the most likely to desert. I decided it would be best for me to say nothing about my plans. I said, "I have not made up my mind as to what I want to do in life. I may pursue the sea as a profession, or I might return to school and learn a technical skill. It's too early to tell."

Stelios, as if he had not heard me, continued: "Think, Spiro. Don't ruin your youth by working as a slave on a freighter. The sea is brutal and has no mercy for the young or the old. You saw what we went through the past several days. We were lucky for two reasons: we had an experienced captain and a good ship that fought the sea courageously. Do you know how many times I have thought of quitting this dreadful job? And look at me. I always come back. Don't ask me why. I am thirty-eight years old, I came to sea at about your age, and I have nothing to show for it. I am still a fireman. I can't go any higher because there is no higher position level for firemen. Once a fireman, always a fireman.

"Please, Spiro, don't say anything to Kostas about what I've said because he might not approve of my advice. I like you and I consider you a brother. My advice to you, Spiro, is sincere. I don't want you to sacrifice your life to the sea and the Greek merchant marine."

I thanked Stelios but did not otherwise openly react to what he said. That afternoon, as I laid down to rest before supper, I decided that Stelios was probably not an informant and had given me honest advice. Even so, I knew the consequences of being wrong on this point were too great. The captain would lock me up if he knew I planned to desert. I decided not to reveal my plans to Stelios or to anyone else on the ship.

I did, however, think that Stelios could help me without me revealing my plan to him. Later that day, as we were preparing for dinner, I began to ask him hypothetical questions about America.

"Stelios, how can someone leave the ship and go into a strange country when he has no place to go, doesn't speak the language, and has no money? What would you do? Where would you go? Besides, you and Kostas would be without a helper if I left. Who would then help you below?"

"Don't worry about Kostas and me," he said. "Someone from the deck will fill in your slot. As far as going into an unknown world, it isn't difficult. First, don't stay in Baltimore. The place to go is New York City, where many Greeks own restaurants and there are several Greek churches where you could get some help. The Greeks in America have always given help to newcomers from the old country."

Curiously, I asked Stelios, "How could one purchase a ticket at the railway station if he can't speak English and has no money?

"It's very simple," he said, and added, "The only phrase of English you would need to say at the ticket window is 'ticket for New York.' And by the way, the trains operate very frequently between Baltimore and New York. And as I remember, the ticket cost is about three dollars, and I have five dollars to give you, should you accept my advice."

I didn't give him any impression that I was going to take his money or accept his advice. Luckily though, I had eight dollars with me that my father had given me.

I rolled the words around my mouth. I had learned a little English from Harry Apostol, but these words were new to me and I felt that I needed to practice them.

That afternoon I was resting in my bunk below when the ship's engine slowed down. Suddenly, someone topside hollered, "Land ahead!" I jumped up immediately and ran up the stairs; sure enough, I could see America.

Everyone from below came topside to have a glance at the American shore, as the ship was heading toward the entrance to Chesapeake Bay. After Stelios and I had admired the American countryside from the ship's stern, I went below to my cabin to see what I'd be able to take with me when I left the ship. I'd dress warmly and take my notebook, the Royal Hellenic Air Force pilot's manual I had found in one of the shops at Tatoi Aerodrome, and my eight dollars. I would secure my documents under the brown turtleneck sweater I would wear under my jacket. I could not carry any more for fear that I might cause suspicion.

After dinner that night, Stelios said, "Let's go to my cabin and have a drink to warm up and celebrate our arrival in America."

Kostas and I agreed, and in Stelios's cramped room, we sat on the floor and Stelios opened a bottle of brandy. That evening, we talked about our journey up to that point and the storm. After a while, I stood up to stretch my cramped legs and felt somewhat dizzy. I was not used to drinking such strong alcohol, and I knew then that I was ready for bed. I said goodnight to the two brothers and went to my cabin, took off my shoes, and crawled into my bunk with my clothes on.

At 2:00 a.m., I awoke, my head buzzing, and immediately noticed that the ship's engine was silent. The ship was standing still. I jumped up from my bunk, peeked through the small porthole and saw the lights from the city of Baltimore. It dawned on me that we were in port.

I said to myself, "Spiro, you have arrived at your new home, America."

At once I put my shoes on and my jacket over my shoulders and swiftly walked topside without disturbing anyone or making any noise. I wiped the sleep from my eyes and stared at the lights for a few minutes. America! I had finally made it! I started to cry as I never had before. I couldn't believe what my partially opened eyes were seeing. I will never forget the view of Baltimore from the ship.

ESCAPE TO AMERICA

When I woke up Saturday morning and went on deck, the scene was much different from the quiet I had experienced the night before. The *P. Margaronis* was moored by its two anchors and by a steel cable connecting the ship's stern to a nearby buoy near a small island. The water was full of activity. Several ships were anchored near us, and others were entering and leaving Baltimore Harbor. In the daylight, I could see the large buildings that made up the city's center. What a thrill the sight was!

While I was admiring Baltimore and its harbor, Stelios appeared topside and said, "Good morning!" He walked over to join me. "Isn't this view splendid, Spiro? But wait. This is nothing compared to New York City, with its huge skyscrapers, especially when they are lit at night. That's a view you would never forget." Stelios pointed to the small island adjacent to where our ship had anchored. "That's Fort Carroll. I visited it when I was here before with another ship."

Kostas joined us, and we all had breakfast below. When we returned topside, Stelios told us that a deck sailor had passed the word around that the ship might remain anchored in the channel next to Baltimore Harbor for a few days because our berth in the harbor was occupied by another ship. While we waited for our berth, customs and immigration authorities would be coming aboard to check the ship's papers, cargo, and the credentials of all crew members.

At about 10:00 a.m., we were called to gather outside the galley and wait until we were summoned one at a time to proceed into the officer's dining room, where the American officials waited to question us. I can well remember when one of the uniformed officials asked me my name and my birthplace and whether I had any relatives in America. At the same time, another official looked at my merchant marine papers with my photograph. After a brief conversation between the officials and our radio operator, who had been acting as translator, the Americans told me that I was free to go.

After my interview, I asked Stelios why the Americans questioned us.

"It's routine procedure," he explained. "They look at your photograph to make sure that it is you and not someone else. If you had said that you had relatives in America, they would want to know their names and where they live. That way, if you should leave the ship and stay ashore for good, the authorities would know where to look for you. In the old days the American authorities didn't ask such questions. But in recent years, many crew members from ships of various nations have deserted their ships and stayed in America for good. Nowadays, the authorities scrutinize all crews thoroughly to identify each crew member aboard a ship and to detect, if possible, potential deserters. If they suspect an individual, they can force the ship's captain to retain that individual aboard the ship while in port."

"What happens to a crew member if he leaves his ship and stays ashore for good?" I asked.

"Well," he said, "that individual is considered to have jumped ship."

"Assume that you get away from the ship clean and stay in America a year or so. What happens then if the authorities catch up with you? Do they put you in jail?" I asked.

"Oh, no," he said. "They simply pick you up and retain you somewhere until they can arrange your passage back to your homeland. But, if you are lucky, you may avoid them, stay in the country, and establish yourself. If you marry an American woman, you could qualify to gain citizenship. America is full of men who left their ships, stayed ashore, and prospered as citizens of the country."

At about noon, the port officials left the ship. They had told the captain that the ship's crew could visit Fort Carroll, if they wished. After lunch, eight of us, including the two brothers and me, took a small boat to Fort Carroll Island. What a feeling I had when my feet stepped on American soil for the first time!

That night after dinner, Stelios and I went topside to watch the city lights. He came close to me and whispered, "You see, Spiro? The railway station is in that part of the city." He pointed about northwest from where we stood. "When we go ashore," he said, "I'll show you how to get to the station."

Sunday, our day off, finally arrived. I woke up early that morning with tremendous excitement. I washed up and put on my clean clothes and the rubber-soled dress shoes I had purchased in Athens for the trip. Since it was chilly that early in the morning, I wore my brown turtleneck sweater. It was quiet aboard the ship, as everyone was still asleep. I went topside and could hear only the cries of several seagulls flying overhead. No doubt they were looking for their morning meal.

The weather was pleasant. The sun was just coming up into the clear blue sky over the eastern horizon. I could feel the morning breeze cooling my face. As I reached the ship's midsection, I looked over the side and noticed a man holding a bundle of newspapers under his arm, climbing up the accommodation ladder. When he reached the top deck, he walked toward the officer's dining room and was met outside by the steward. They both walked into the officer's dining room.

I looked below to where the visitor had tied his small boat at the bottom of the ladder. The boat was powered by a tiny outboard motor and had a big pile of newspapers stacked neatly in its stern. I realized that the man was a newspaper vendor who sold papers to the various ships anchored outside the inner harbor. I looked around. No one else was on deck, and I could hear only the banging of pots and pans emanating from the galley. The cook was up, evidently preparing breakfast.

Eventually, the newspaper vendor came out of the officer's dining room. He was alone. He walked briskly into the galley where the cook was. After a minute or so, he came out of the galley and headed for the accommodation ladder to descend to his boat below. He was about halfway down, when my instinct began shouting at me, "Move! Move now, Spiro! This is the opportunity you have been waiting for!"

I leaned over the guardrail and whistled softly to the man below, just as he was ready to sit down in his little boat. He looked up; I took a dollar out of my pocket and showed it to him. I pointed at it, then at myself, and then pointed ashore. He looked around quickly and then waved at me to come down. My heart was in my throat. I thought of my things astern and knew that I could not leave them; I waved back to the man below trying to signal him to wait a minute. He seemed to understand. I ran to my cabin and picked up the flying manual and my notebook. Putting them under my sweater, I grabbed my hat and jacket and ran on deck, jumping the steps four at a time.

On my way topside, I almost ran straight into the cook, who was emerging from the galley. By this time, I was out of breath. I came to a complete stop in front of the cook, certain that I looked like a guilty man. The cook asked me, "What's the matter, Spiro?"

"Oh, nothing," I said. "That newspaperman. I want to buy a paper."

The cook said, "That guy didn't bring any Greek papers aboard. He only had English papers."

"Oh, yes," I said. "I can read English. I studied the language at school in Athens."

"Well," the cook said, "you better run below to catch him before he pulls away." The cook went inside the galley.

I ran to the accommodation ladder as fast as I could. Luckily, the newspaperman was still there. When I reached the bottom of the ladder, I jumped into his little boat and gave him the dollar with a smile. He started the little outboard motor, and we sped away from the ship.

My heart was still thumping fast. I feared that someone might see me from the ship's deck. For a moment I felt that the little boat wasn't traveling fast enough, but I didn't know how to tell the boatman to go a little faster. Evidently, luck was with me because about five or so minutes after we left, I turned around and looked at the ship and I still couldn't see anyone on deck. Just a few minutes later, the little boat reached the American shore.

The man maneuvered his craft to the docking platform as I prepared to step ashore. He said something in English that I couldn't understand, but I took him to mean that I should jump when the boat came close to the platform. After I jumped onto the dock, he pulled away to continue his newspaper peddling on other ships. I thanked him in Greek, and he waved.

There I was on American soil! After all my planning, I had done it. No one was around, but some automobiles passed by on the roadway just beyond where I had landed. As I climbed some steps to what appeared to be a shoreline road, I regained my composure. I turned around for one last look at my ship, anchored well inside the estuary of the Patapsco River, and I said good-bye.

"Thank you, Stelios and Kostas. I will never forget you. You were the best friends I had on the *P. Margaronis*."

Then I walked westward, hoping to find the railway station.

NEW YORK BOUND

Somehow I found my way through Baltimore. I twice asked for directions using the few words of English I knew, and eventually I ended up at the train station. For a moment, I stood in front of what I took to be the ticket counters, tired, hungry, feeling somewhat miserable— my feet were hurting from walking with my new rubber-soled shoes—and frustrated. Was this where I could buy a ticket?

I saw a man wearing what appeared to be a railway company uniform standing close to the wall. I went to him and asked, "Ticket for New York?" Although I didn't understand the reply, I did understand when he pointed to a line just opposite from where I was. I thanked him in Greek, which puzzled him, and got into line.

As I approached the window, my heart started to pound. I placed my seven dollars on the counter and told the man behind the window, "Ticket for New York." The man gave me a ticket, took four of my dollars, and gave me some small change back. He also said something that I assumed was about the train, but again, I didn't understand his words. Picking up my change and the ticket, I moved away from the counter. With the help of some train officials, I eventually found the gate for the New York train, had my ticket punched, and climbed aboard the coach. I collapsed into a window seat. What a relief to sit down and rest my feet!

I was so tired that I fell into a doze, only to wake up as the train started moving. The train made stops in Philadelphia and Trenton before we reached New York. After night had fallen, the train finally began to slow down once more, as it entered an underground passageway. At that moment, the conductor came through the coach to collect our tickets, saying loudly, "Next stop is New York, New York." Minutes later the train came to a stop.

I followed the other passengers and found myself inside a huge hall full of people walking in all directions. Tired, hungry, and somewhat scared, I stopped and looked around for a moment, trying to find my bearings and decide where to go. Eventually, I found myself outside the station, which opened onto a boulevard with automobiles and big buses traveling in both directions. It was dark now and many buildings and stores were lit up. I looked to my left and saw nothing but tall buildings. I looked to my right and saw only more tall buildings. Suddenly I started to cry like a little boy who had lost his mother in a crowded place. I had accomplished not just a dream but an impossibility.

Forcing myself to focus on what to do next, I dried my face and started to walk to the right on the sidewalk until I reached the intersection. I looked up and read the street signs at the corner: Thirty-fourth Street in one direction and Eighth Avenue in the other. I made my way through streams of pedestrians and cars, crossed Thirty-fifth, Thirty-sixth, and Thirty-seventh streets and found myself at the corner of Eighth Avenue and Forty-second Street. I stopped for a moment to catch my breath as I viewed the most beautiful panorama I had ever seen. Both sides of Forty-second were filled with tall buildings, all bedecked with arrays of bright lights, as far as I could see. As I stared, I thought of Stelios, my shipmate aboard the *P. Margaronis*. "Wait until you see New York at night when it's all lit up," he had said, and he had been so right. The splendor of that view has remained with me all my life.

I stood on the corner of the busy intersection—again with tears in my eyes—as I thought about my next move. The lights and buildings were pretty, but they wouldn't keep me warm at night or give me food to eat. I decided to return to the railway station to reassess my situation. As I walked back, I saw a flash of familiar colors out of the corner of my eye. At first I thought that they were an illusion. I turned and saw two flags in front of a lighted awning: one had the red, white, and blue of the American flag, and the other displayed the blue and white of the Greek flag. When it was safe, I dashed across the avenue toward the flags.

The flags hung over the entrance of a movie house, which was playing the first movie ever made in Greece, *Voscopoula: The Shepherdess*, which I had seen in Athens a few months earlier. I looked closely at several large photographs of the film displayed at the entrance to the theater. As I stood there, two men stopped behind me and began to talk in Greek. A miracle, I thought. I immediately swung around—startling them—and asked, "Are you Greeks?"

The older one, who must have been about forty and had a well-trimmed moustache, replied, "Yes, from the island of Cyprus."

"Do you know anything about this movie?" the other fellow asked me.

"Oh, yes," I said. "I saw it in Athens a few months ago."

"You did?" the older one remarked.

"Yes," I said. "I saw it two times."

"You see?" the youngest said to the older. "This fellow saw it twice, so it must be good."

"Did you just come from Greece?" the older one asked me. Before I had a chance to reply, he said with a smile, "the way you are dressed you must be a crew member off a ship."

I decided I had to trust them and briefly told them about my jumping ship and my desire to remain in America. "I thought I could wander in the streets until I found a Greek church," I told them.

"No, my friend," said the older man, "the church can't help you. You come with us. We live in Brooklyn." The men decided to put off seeing the movie until another time and, instead, took me to their home.

As we started to walk toward the subway station, the older one introduced himself as Christos Argiriou and his companion as his younger brother Lambis. Christos was a chef at a restaurant in Brooklyn; Lambis worked as tailor in a department store in Manhattan. Christos was married and had a five-year-old boy, and Lambis lived with their mother. Christos offered to let me stay with him and his family for a few days. He even offered to contact an employment agency on my behalf. I thanked Christos for his generosity and told him I would certainly pay him back once I found a job.

After we had been on the subway for some time, the train came to a stop at Flatbush Avenue. We walked four or five blocks down the street outside the station and then turned onto a side street. We stopped at a tall apartment building, about five or six stories high.

"This is where I live," said Christos. "Lambis lives farther up the street."

We exchanged farewells with Lambis and then entered the building. We took the elevator to the fourth floor. There, I met Mrs. Lillian Argiriou, who, as it turned out, did not speak Greek. Through her husband, she made me welcome in their home and asked if I wanted something to eat. Did I ever!

"When I get to work tomorrow," Christos said as I enjoyed the sandwich his wife had prepared for me, "I will call a friend I have who manages an employment agency that specializes in jobs at restaurants. I think it will best for you to work in a Greek restaurant because such a job will not require that you know English. But as soon as you get settled and have a job, you should start taking English classes at night school. The employment agency, by the way, will charge you a small fee—twenty dollars or so. When they find you a job, you will pay them with your wages."

I told Christos that I would pay him back for whatever he spent to get me settled. He told me not to worry about that. He then asked if I had any ambition as far as the profession I wished to pursue in this country. I told him I wanted to become a pilot.

"Ah," he said. "You will have to go to school. Here in Brooklyn we have Floyd Bennett Field, a naval aviation field and civilian airport. I am certain they must have a flying school there. Maybe next Sunday, on my day off, we can visit the airfield and find out what is out there."

That night, Mrs. Argiriou made me a bed of blankets on the floor of their son's bedroom. Little Nicos was asleep by the time I had finished dinner. After thanking my saviors, I crawled into my simple bed near Nicos's crib. As I closed my eyes, I thanked God for the miracle that happened to me that night.

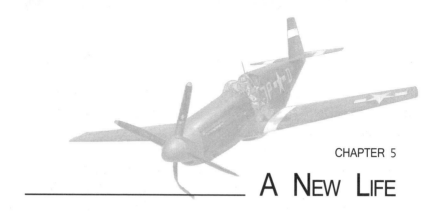

A NEW LIFE

In the days that followed my arrival in New York, I visited a supermarket (something that did not exist in Greece at that time) and struggled through the *New York Daily News*, mainly looking at the pictures. Since Christos went to work during the day, my main companions were his wife and son, Nicos. Lillian and Nicos were nice and tried hard to understand what little English I could speak.

During my second evening in the Argiriou's house, Christos came home with good news. He had found a job opening at a bakery on Broadway uptown. He asked if I had any experience as a baker, and I told him I had worked at a friend's bakery in Athens, helping to remove the fresh-baked bread from the oven.

The following morning, Christos and I left the house early to take the subway to the Apollo Employment Agency in midtown. As we exited the subway station at the Forty-second Street and Broadway, I saw yellow taxicabs, buses, and other vehicles trying to dodge the people crowding the streets.

"Where is everyone going?" I asked, a bit bewildered by the commotion.

"To work," said Christos.

When we arrived at Sixth Avenue, we made a left turn toward the employment agency. We climbed the stairs to the second floor of the old two-story building and walked down the hall to the agency's offices. There we met Manolis, the agency's owner and manager. "Have you worked in a bakery before?" Manolis asked me in Greek.

"Yes," I replied.

Manolis told me that the job was mine and then explained that I needed to pay him a twenty-dollar fee for finding me the job. He would take five dollars up front, which Christos paid and then expect the rest in five-dollar installments every two weeks. Manolis gave me the name and address of the bakery I would be working in:

Hatchis Restaurant, Bakery, and Bar, 149th Street and Broadway, uptown. Mr. Manolis told me that Hatchis was a Greek man. He would pay me fifteen dollars a week and provide my meals. Manolis also gave me an envelope to present to Mr. Hatchis when I arrived at the bakery.

After we left the agency, Christos took me to the Forty-second Street subway station and gave me detailed instructions on how to find the Hatchis's bakery and how to return to his home in Brooklyn. He also gave me his telephone numbers both at work and at home. Christos wished me luck, gave me a bunch of nickels, and put me on the Broadway train going uptown. I soon found myself in front Hatchis at 149th Street and Broadway.

I was rather impressed by the exterior of Hatchis's establishment. The restaurant and bakery covered a large space from the corner of 149th Street and around on the Broadway side. The windows, doors, and overhead signs were tinted black glass with large and small gold lettering, which apparently described Hatchis's business and key products.

As I entered the Hatchis's place through the restaurant's big glass door, I found myself in a well-decorated dining room with leather booths and a red velvet décor. A man in his thirties wearing a black jacket, white shirt, and black bow tie approached me and said something in English. The man appeared to be Greek, so I told him in Greek that my name was Spiro and that I was sent from the Apollo Employment Agency to see Mr. Hatchis about a job in the bakery. The man introduced himself as Peter, the headwaiter, and took me to an office in the back.

"This is Mr. Hatchis," Peter said in Greek, introducing me to a short, chubby, balding gentleman with a black moustache, who was sitting in a leather chair behind his desk. "This is Spiro," Peter said, "from the employment agency."

Mr. Hatchis rose from his chair and extended his hand. We shook hands, and I handed him the envelope I was given at the agency.

"Yes," he said. "They called me to let me know that you were on your way."

He asked me where I lived and if I had any experience in a bakery. I told him I lived in Brooklyn and described my work back in Greece. The boss seemed satisfied.

"You'll do for the job. What I want you to do here is to assist in the bakery during the morning hours and in the afternoon help behind the soda fountain. Then in the evening go in the kitchen and help there. You will work from 8:00 a.m. until 8:00 p.m. Do you think you can do that?"

"Oh, yes, Sir, I certainly can," I said.

"Alright," Mr. Hatchis said, "you can start right now."

Peter took me to the bakery shop, which was redolent with the smell of freshly baked pastry, and introduced me to the two bakers, who were wearing white clothing and white caps on their heads. Mr. Kostas Zapos was happy to learn that I had already worked in a bakery and welcomed me to the shop. He gave me a white apron to put over my street clothes and told me to help Mihalis Kontos, the other baker. My first task at the bakery was to butter trays in preparation for baking pastries.

I learned fast and soon progressed to more interesting work. I was introduced to the wonders of the basement, which was stocked with flour, molasses, chocolate syrup, eggs, butter, and various other groceries, as well as liquor and wine, which were stored in a separate, locked room, and perishable goods, which were stored in a huge walk-in refrigerator. While we were in the basement, Mihalis introduced me to Kostas Alexandrou, the chocolate candy and ice cream maker.

The two bakers worked from 5:00 a.m. until 2:00 p.m. After the bakers left for the day, my job, per Mihalis's instructions, was to clean up the shop and mop the floors in both the shop and the front showroom. When I finished cleaning, I brought certain supplies up from the basement for the bakers' to use the following morning. Mr. Zapos listed, thank God in Greek, the items on a small blackboard hung on the wall above his bench.

On my first day, just before I went down to the basement to pick up the next day's supplies, Mr. Hatchis walked into the shop unexpectedly.

"How are you coming along, young man?" he asked.

"Fine, Sir," I replied.

He looked around the shop and inspected the machinery, benches, floors, and said, "Excellent. After you have something to eat, if you haven't yet, go to the soda fountain to assist Jimmie there until about 6:00 in the evening."

As Mr. Hatchis said this, Jimmie walked into the shop to meet me. Mr. Hatchis introduced us and then returned to his office. I shook hands with Jimmie, and he said, "After you are through here, wash up, pick up a clean apron, and meet me at the soda fountain."

I did as I was told. Jimmie Varelas was a Greek American who spoke some Greek with an accent. I liked him right from the start. I worked with Jimmie until 6:00 p.m. that first day and then sat down to have my evening meal. After dinner, I moved to the kitchen to help the regular dishwasher with the day's pots and pans. I finished my first day on the job at about 8:30 p.m. While I rode the subway back to Brooklyn, I realized how lucky I was to have found a job in America after only three days.

The next day, I arrived at Hatchis Bakery just before 8:00 a.m., had some coffee, and ate my first Danish pastry. What a delicacy! I followed the same routine on my second day at work and began to enjoy what I was doing. By late afternoon, I found myself working hard with Jimmie at the busy soda fountain, washing soiled glasses and keeping the counter clean.

About a week later, on a Sunday, while I was working at the soda fountain, the headwaiter, Peter, came over to speak to me. He knew that I had a place to stay with my "uncle," but he had a spare room in his apartment and was willing to rent it to me. I accepted his offer immediately. Not only was the apartment close to the bakery, the rent was only three dollars a week. I moved in the next day, after bidding farewell to Christos and his family and thanking them for their great kindness.

FIRST FLIGHT

I had been on the job about a month before I was able to follow up on Christos's suggestion that I check out Floyd Bennett Field. I persuaded Jimmie to accompany me on our day off—a good thing because I had no idea how to get there.

After Jimmie asked a passerby for directions, we took the subway and a connecting bus to the field in Brooklyn. As we approached the airport, I saw some small airplanes in the sky and became excited. For a moment, my thoughts flashed far away to Kolonos and the time I spent at Tatoi.

When the bus arrived at Floyd Bennett Field, we got off and walked into the administration building. Jimmie pointed out a sign that read, "Floyd Bennett Field, a Military Installation, Shared with the Airlines and Civilian Airplane Operators." After nosing around inside the building for a while, we stepped outside onto the flight line, where we spotted a twin-engine aircraft parked nearby. The word "American" was painted on the plane's fuselage above the small windows. Jimmie asked a man standing by what type of aircraft it was and was told that it was an airliner, the Douglas DC-3.

We started to walk leisurely along the flight line toward the hangars on the west side of the field, watching some small airplanes taxiing away in preparation for takeoff. As we reached the first hangar, Jimmie spotted a big sign in the front of the hangar that read, "Learn to Fly. Joe Agliata Flying School." We walked over to the hanger and

45

asked one of the mechanics where the Agliata Flying School was. The mechanic pointed to a door inside the hangar. We went through the door and found ourselves in an office. A woman greeted us, and Jimmie asked her if we could see Mr. Agliata.

She said, "He's flying with a student, but he's due to land at any moment."

I told Jimmie to ask the woman if it would be all right for us to look at the airplanes in the hangar while we waited.

"Please do," she replied.

While we were looking at the many small airplanes in the hangar, I spotted two biplanes that resembled those that I had seen at Tatoi Aerodrome. One was painted red and the other was yellow. The red one was a Waco and the yellow a Travel Air, a mechanic told us. Jimmie asked him if I could sit in the Waco's cockpit, and he said that was OK. The moment I got into the roomy cockpit, my thoughts flashed back to Tatoi Aerodrome, where I used to climb into the cockpits of many of the Royal Hellenic Air Force airplanes. I lightly touched the controls and imagined that I was up in the air, flying around the clouds.

My daydreaming was interrupted by the noise of a small yellow airplane that taxied in and stopped by the side of the hanger. After the engine was shut down, a man in his thirties, whom I assumed was Mr. Agliata, and his student, a man about my age, stepped down and started to walk through the hanger toward the office. A few minutes later I jumped down from the Waco's cockpit and, with Jimmie beside me, headed for the office. We walked in and waited for Mr. Agliata to finish a discussion with his student. About twenty minutes later, when the student left, Mr. Agliata emerged from his office and signaled for us to come in. Jimmie introduced me to Mr. Agliata and told him that I was interested in learning to fly.

"You've come to the right place," he said, "but first you need to obtain a student pilot certificate from the Civil Aeronautics Authority (CAA) and a physical examination from a CAA-designated medical examiner." He gave me an application for the certificate and also told me how much he charged for lessons. "If you wish to train here at my school, there is an initial fee of twenty-five dollars. Dual flying—that's flying with an instructor—costs twelve dollars per hour. When you fly solo, the cost drops to eight dollars per hour. The initial fee can be made in two payments."

The flight school, Mr. Agliata told us, had four other instructors on staff, as well as a ground school instructor, and kept five airplanes available for both flying instructions and solo flying.

"One good thing about my flying school," Mr. Agliata said, "is that we don't require a student to attend regular classes or fly every day. You take your lessons at your own pace and pay the cost of flying as you go. We do require, however, that you schedule your flying at least two days in advance, so that we can accommodate everyone.

"For a private pilot's license, you will need about thirty-five to forty flying hours, with twenty of those in dual instruction and the rest in solo flying. After you have accumulated some twenty-five to thirty hours, we will schedule you to take the written examination. You will also have to pass a flight check for a private pilot's license. Simply put, you will have to demonstrate to an examiner your ability to fly an aircraft safely."

Mr. Agliata handed a small booklet of several pages to Jimmie, who passed it over to me. "You'll find everything you need to know in there, our school curriculum. After you have received your private pilot's license, you can upgrade to a limited commercial license. Of course, you would first have to accumulate the required flying hours for this license."

Moreover, Mr. Agliata pointed out, I would have to learn English so I could understand the instructor's directions and satisfy the CAA requirement that all pilots must speak English fluently.

Jimmie and I thanked Mr. Agliata for his time, and I asked Jimmie to tell him that I was definitely interested in signing up with his school, as soon as I learned some English. We were just about to shake hands and say good-bye to Mr. Agliata, when he asked Jimmie to find out if I would like to fly around the field with him for a few minutes while he went up to check an instrument in one of his airplanes. I gratefully accepted his offer. We climbed into the yellow Piper J-3 Cub and taxied out to the western part of the field to take off on the grass, away from the concrete runway. Mr. Agliata stopped the J-3 Cub, applied the brake, and revved up the engine to check the magnetos.

From the moment Mr. Agliata pulled away from the hangar area, I watched him like a hawk as he prepared for takeoff and then lined the plane up into the wind. Within seconds we were up in the air. What a thrill to be up in an airplane for the first time in my life! I wanted to shout out with joy but I held back; after all, I wasn't alone up there. I couldn't believe that I was up in the air at last.

I could see all around me: Brooklyn, the calm sea beyond, and, at a distance,

New York City with its hundreds of skyscrapers. For the first time I experienced the profound feeling of freedom known to anyone who has flown and looked down to see the whole world in a new and incomparable scale. Even after thousands of hours in many different aircraft, the flight in that little yellow plane remains a peak experience. I knew, at last, that in the sky was where I really, truly belonged.

After Mr. Agliata landed the plane, Jimmie helped me fill out the CAA application for a student pilot's certificate. As we left the flight school, I promised my future instructor that once I had learned enough English, I would return to sign up for flying lessons.

"Good. I'll be waiting for you," he said with a smile.

LEARNING ENGLISH

When I returned to my room in Peter's apartment, I glanced at the flying school's curriculum booklet, but I couldn't make any sense of it. I realized that the biggest obstacle to my goal would be learning the English language. I wanted to go to night school, but I knew that my working hours prevented me from doing that at the moment. I lay awake through most of the night, trying to find a solution to my problem, until an idea came to me. Why not try to teach myself English?

I purchased a pocket-size Greek-English dictionary and a Greek-English book for beginners. With these tools I embarked on a crash-training program. My first goal was to learn ten English words a day. My second was to learn short sentences. I would repeat the words and sentences, pronouncing the English as best I could, until I had memorized them.

I started to buy the *New York Daily News* occasionally, and with my dictionary, I, at first, translated the headlines of short articles and, then, the articles themselves. Every night, before I went to sleep, I prepared my assignment for the following day. On my way to work every day, I practiced the daily assignments by repeating the words and sentences as many times as possible. Even when I was washing dishes, pots, and pans over the sink in the kitchen, I repeated the English words. And as I walked down to Riverside Drive by the Hudson River after work, I practiced loudly, laboring to master the pronunciation of each word I added to my vocabulary. I also listened to the radio in my room, absorbing the cadences and intonations of this new and entrancing language.

During my busy days at the bakery and in every spare moment, I worked on learning English. Within a few months I could understand conversations I over-heard and what people said to me, but I still could not reply, and while I understood the separate words in a written sentence, I could not make sense of the whole. Still, I kept plugging away.

A short time after my first flight, I went back to Floyd Bennett Field and flew with Mr. Agliata in one of his J-3 Cubs for thirty minutes, just to look at the world from above. While we were in the air, he tried to explain something to me in English, but I couldn't understand him. I pretended that I could, however, to give him the impression that I had almost mastered enough English to begin lessons with him. After landing, he tried to explain something else, but I could pick up only a few words and phrases. I knew then that my autodidact approach to English was not working; I had to take English lessons.

With Jimmie's help, I found a school in a building near 153rd Street and St. Nicholas Avenue. I signed up for the beginners' class on Mondays (the day I was off), for fifteen dollars a month, three hours a week, from 6:00 to 9:00 p.m. My first class was that evening.

Once I had signed up, I headed for Floyd Bennett to buy two important aviation books that Mr. Agliata had told me to pick up: *Civil Aeronautics Administration (CAA) Rules and Regulations* and *Pilot's Power Plant Manual*. These books would supplement the Royal Hellenic Air Force aviator's manual that I had brought with me from Greece. I studied them diligently, mastering the English pronunciation of various words associated with airplanes.

When I picked up my books from Ms. Mary, Mr. Agliata's secretary, she re-membered that she had received my student pilot's permit. She opened a drawer, pulled out an envelope, and handed it to me. Inside I found CAA student pilot's permit number 79714, which had my name on it and the statement, "Authorized to fly as a student pilot only." Elated, I thanked Ms. Mary for her trouble, and left for uptown with my two books in hand and the student pilot's permit in my pocket.

I went to night school once a week and also continued my own learning pro-gram. As the days rolled by, I realized that my English class was teaching me to speak English the proper way, to read different texts, and to discover more about the American way of life. It didn't bother me that English came to me slowly and that I pronounced many words with a Greek accent. I soon learned an important lesson: if you want anything badly enough, are willing to do whatever it takes, and never give up, you will succeed.

LEARNING TO FLY

A few months into my English study, I felt confident that I was ready to start taking flying lessons. In early August, I took and easily passed my CAA physical examination. On August 10, 1938, I signed up to attend the Joe Agliata Flying School and found, to my delight, that Mr. Agliata was going to be my regular instructor.

Before I was allowed to fly, I had to join three other students, who were about my age, in a class with the ground instructor, Jack Elliot. Mr. Elliot explained the theory of flight and introduced us to basic airplane mechanics. After we had spent almost two hours in ground school, Mr. Elliot dismissed us to go for our flying lessons. Before we left, he told us that what he had covered that day was simply an introduction to the subject and that he intended to delve deeper in future sessions.

I was on my way to the flight line when I spotted the yellow Piper J-3 Cub in which I would fly that day. The J-3 Cub was a small training aircraft used extensively at flying schools at that time. It had a 50 horsepower continental engine and cruised at around 60 to 65 miles per hour. Its landing speed was about 40 miles per hour. The J-3 Cub had only a hand brake, and the pilot depended upon the tailskid to slow the aircraft on the ground after landing.

As I admired the little yellow flying machine, Mr. Agliata showed up to take me up for my first lesson. He first explained to me the steps a pilot must follow in preparation for a flight, emphasizing the walk-around and close inspection of the airplane's external surface. As we settled into the small tandem cockpit—he in the back seat and I up front—he slowly showed me the procedure for starting the engine. He explained the taxiing technique, the takeoff position, and the takeoff itself. He stressed the importance of looking around for other aircraft while taxiing on the ground. When we reached the takeoff position, he showed me the procedure for checking the engine. We received the green light from the control tower, and the J-3 Cub took off into the air.

During my first flying lesson aloft, I learned about straight and level flight, normal and steep turns, climbing and descending turns, stalls, and emergency landings. Joe executed each maneuver and then turned the controls over to me so I could practice the exercise. Surprisingly, I had little difficulty executing each maneuver Joe asked me to demonstrate. The J-3 Cub cut through the air with swiftness and grace.

After we had completed most of the hour's instruction over the sea in the vicinity of Floyd Bennett, we returned to the field and prepared to land. Joe entered the traffic pattern and demonstrated a touch-and-go landing. He let the plane's wheels briefly touch the ground and roll for several yards before we went up again. When we became airborne, he turned the controls over to me and said, "You fly the airplane, Spiro, and try to make a landing like I did. Do you think you can do it?" he asked.

"You bet," I replied, confidently.

With Joe's guidance, I entered the downwind leg, and I had my eyes fixed for the green light from the control tower. When I saw the green light, I reduced power and dropped down to about two hundred feet as I was turning into the final approach. I guided the yellow Cub down with power off and made my first, rather bumpy, landing. After the airplane had slowed down, I taxied it to the school's hangar; Joe took over to park the J-3 Cub. When we jumped down from the airplane, he said to me, "Spiro, are you sure you never had any flying lessons before?"

"No, Sir," I said. "I never had."

"You performed like a student with several hours of lessons. You shouldn't have any problems getting your license."

I left Floyd Bennett and made my way toward the subway, elated. I couldn't believe that I had been able to start taking flying lessons just five months after my arrival in the United States.

By late November 1938, however, after I had completed my sixth lesson, I found myself in an awkward position: I was short of money. I simply wasn't making enough to cover food, rent, and transportation, in addition to the flying lessons. And even with Christmas around the corner, I could not send a few dollars to my family in Athens. I decided that I needed to reevaluate my priorities.

First and foremost, I would have to limit my flying for the time being. I would not abandon flying all together but allow more time to pass between each lesson. I considered dropping out of my English class to save the fifteen-dollar monthly fee, but then I realized that improving my English was essential to my future in America. From my weekly paycheck, I started to put away a certain amount for flying and a portion for personal needs. I started to save the rest of my check, so I'd have a few dollars in case of an emergency. With my new financial plan in place, I pressed on with my life in America.

51

CHAPTER 6

EVERY SILVER LINING
HAS A CLOUD

I had met Ms. Elli, Mr. Hatchis's youngest daughter, when I first came to work at the bakery in April, and our relationship since that initial meeting had been proper, even distant, until one day, when I was helping Jimmie behind the soda fountain, our eyes locked across the distance between the fountain counter and the main cashier's booth. I tried to shrug the glance off and go on with my work, but when I looked up again, I saw her piercing eyes still focused on me. I quickly looked away because the last thing I wanted was to start flirting with her. A relationship with the boss's daughter was out of the question—it would lead to nothing but trouble for me. Still, we exchanged several significant glances in the days that followed.

My relationship with Elli began, surprisingly enough, when her father took Elli, Elli's cousin Martha (who also worked at the bakery), Jimmie, Peter, and me on one of his frequent late evening drives to Van Cortlandt Park. On our way to the park I ended up in the front seat, pressed closely against Elli. That night she looked elegant, smiling, and radiant. As we rode side by side, I could feel her heart pounding.

At the park, I had the opportunity to study Elli while she strolled ahead of me. Her walk was graceful and quietly seductive. She was at once a delicate and strong young woman, and I felt an almost irresistible attraction to her. I sat with Jimmie and Martha on a bench opposite from where Elli was sitting with her father and Peter. Elli and I looked at each other and smiled. Part of me was thrilled to have her attention, but part of me knew I needed to avoid becoming too close to her.

On the way back to 149th Street, I sat in the back of the car and ceded the front seat to Jimmie. I thought it best not to sit too close to Elli again, at least not in her father's presence. When I went to bed that night, tired from the long hours at work and the drive to the park, I could not stop thinking about Elli. I knew that I was falling for her already, but I was almost certain that if her father found out, I would lose my job.

Avoiding Elli at work soon became impossible. Each time we were thrown together by circumstances, a certain current of excitement passed between us. It was inevitable that these chance encounters would lead to an arranged meeting. That came sooner than I anticipated when I was down in the basement one day picking up supplies when Elli came over and said, "I have been waiting to ask you something, Spiro."

"Yes, Elli," I said. "What is it?"

"How would you like to go for a walk down to the river on the Hudson Parkway tonight?"

"Elli," I said, "I don't get off work until after 8:00 p.m. It will be too late for you. And I don't think we should do that. Someone might see us and tell your father."

"Oh, don't worry about that. No one will see us. It will be dark. Please, Spiro," she said, "I want to see you."

That night after work I took my first step down the slippery slope. I rushed to the basement to wash up and change clothes. Then, I dashed up to 150th Street and Riverside Drive where Elli was waiting for me. We held hands as we crossed Riverside Drive and came to the walking path by the West Side Parkway. We stopped there in the darkness of the night. No sooner had I approached her, than she embraced me and kissed me passionately.

After that first date, we continued to see each other clandestinely. I was hesitant to move things forward, but Elli was persistent. Quickly, I realized that I needed to convince Elli that it would be better if we broke off the relationship. But I simply couldn't do it, and Elli certainly didn't want our affair to end. In fact, we grew bolder.

One day we took a ride to Central Park in Elli's father's green Buick. We found a perfect spot for lovers, under a tree, away from the bright sun and people passing by. While lying on the grass, I told Elli about my love for airplanes, my desire to become an aviator, and my arrival in Baltimore. I explained how long it would take for me to earn a license, given my finances.

"Why, Spiro," she said, "if you need some money to pay for your flying lessons, I could help you. I have some money of my own and I could give you five hundred dollars to finish your training, if that would be enough."

"Elli," I said, "I can't take your money."

I was appalled at the thought. I told her that I intended to become an aviator but would pay my way by working hard and saving money.

"Well, I want you to know that I would be very happy and pleased to help you fulfill your dream," she said.

"You are most generous and thoughtful," I told her and kissed her cheek.

After that day in the park, I began to think of Elli as an intimate friend, and as winter neared, our clandestine relationship continued. I sometimes passed up the opportunity to fly in order to be with her. We went to the movies, drove to Central Park, and occasionally took nighttime walks by the river. Soon, my attachment to Elli had become deeper and more serious than I had initially wanted.

After a sleepless night in early 1939, I concluded that I must make a choice between becoming a pilot and continuing my romance with Elli. The choice was not easy. I decided to break off our relationship. I avoided her for days until she confronted me in the basement one morning while picking up supplies.

"Spiro," she said, in a low and angry voice, while looking directly into my eyes. "You have been avoiding me. I want to know why. Is there something wrong?" she said.

I explained to her that I was concerned that I had been neglecting my ambition to become an aviator because of my relationship with her. She was angry but somewhat understanding.

"I realize," she said, "that I have taken up your time, but once you catch up with your flying, can we go out again?"

"Certainly. I am sure we can do that," I replied.

She seemed to accept this and, as she started to walk away she leaned over, kissed me on the cheek, and said, "Remember you promised."

As Elli kissed me, Martha, who had come to the basement to pick up some candy, passed by unexpectedly and saw us. She blurted out "Excuse me!" and hurried away. I was surprised by the intrusion and immediately began to imagine the consequences it could have.

"I don't like the idea of Martha seeing you kissing me," I told Elli.

"Oh, don't worry," she said. "Martha and my sister Clementine know about us." Still, when we parted, I knew I was in deep trouble.

In early April 1939, the sky fell on me. On a Saturday afternoon Mr. Hatchis told me to meet him in his office. The moment I walked in and closed the door, he looked straight into my eyes and said, "Young man, today is your last day of work here. I will not need you any more after today."

For a moment, I felt paralyzed and speechless. Then I said, "Why, Mr. Hatchis? Don't I do my work right?"

"No," he said, "your work is fine. I just don't need you any more."

He gave me the pay due me for my work up to that day. Then he stood up from his chair, walked around his desk, and opened the door, gesturing for me to leave. Stunned, I walked out of his office and through the dining room and soda fountain with my head down. Although I realized I would likely lose my job because of my relationship with Elli, I didn't know what to say or do in the moment it happened. I had not seen Elli that day and wondered if her father had sent her away because he was planning to fire me.

On my way out that evening, I said good-bye to my friend Jimmie, who told me to call him sometime. I was heartbroken. I had lost my first job in America, and I had lost the affection of the first girl I had fallen for in this new world.

HUNTING FOR ANOTHER JOB

The morning after I was fired, I woke up and lay in bed for a while, trying to comprehend what had happened. Still in a state of shock, I wondered whether Peter was aware of my termination and would let me stay here until I found another job. I jumped off my bed, took a shower, got dressed, and walked into the kitchen to find Peter and his wife enjoying Sunday morning breakfast.

Peter invited me to join them for breakfast and immediately asked about my termination. He had known about my relationship with Elli. He tried to buck me up, assuring me that with my work ethic and energy, it would not be long before I had a job at another bakery, and he was kind enough to let me stay in my room at his house for as long as I wished.

How would I find another job? I planned to return to the Apollo Employment Agency to seek help from Mr. Manolis. My first visit to the agency was a disappointment. No openings were available, Mr. Manolis told me, for a job either at a bakery or as a dishwasher in a restaurant. I returned to the agency every morning, hoping an opportunity would present itself.

After looking for a job for what seemed like an eternity, the agency offered me a temporary job as a dishwasher in a restaurant near Fulton Street in Brooklyn. I took the work out of desperation, because I was running out of money. I had to commute to Brooklyn from uptown every day, and I returned home at night dead tired. A few days into my employment in Brooklyn, I heard about a rooming house on Seventeenth Street off Third Avenue that rented rooms for four dollars a week. On my next day off, I visited the house and immediately rented a room.

The regular dishwasher, who had been sick, returned to the restaurant to claim his old job back on June 20, about two months after I started working. This put me out of work again, and I immediately began a new job search. On June 26, I spoke to Mr. Manolis again. Surprisingly, he offered me another temporary job, for the summer months, at the Blue Mountain Lodge, a resort place in Peekskill, New York, about a forty-five minute train ride from Grand Central Station.

I hated to leave New York City, but I took the job for several reasons. The pay was sixty dollars a month, including room and board so I wouldn't have to pay train fare to and from the lodge. Also, I would save $180 over the three months of work, enough to fly several hours and still have enough money to live until I found another job.

Blue Mountain Lodge was a sanctuary for wealthy New Yorkers, who spent their summers in the woods away from city life. It could accommodate more than two hundred people in its cabins, which were scattered throughout a vast wooded area.

At Peekskill, I learned that in the mornings, I'd help the maintenance man on the premises repair the wide assortment of electrical and mechanical equipment that made the resort run properly. In the evenings until quite late at night, I would help the chef, a pleasant Yugoslavian fellow who spoke some Greek, by cleaning the kitchen and washing the pots and pans. Although my work at the lodge was somewhat tedious, I was happy to work with the invariably pleasant resort workers. And the atmosphere throughout the lodge was agreeable.

During that summer at Peekskill, events on the world stage became more and more tense. On September 1, 1939—during my last month working at the lodge—Hitler's Germany invaded Poland. England, France, Canada, Australia, and New Zealand promptly declared war on Germany. The press, as well as the U.S. government, reported that Hitler had a master plan, not only for Europe but for the world. Even though the American government had announced that it would remain neutral in the conflict, I, like most people, had the feeling that, sooner or later, the United States would be catapulted into a war that it wasn't prepared for.

Hitler's invasion of Poland made me think seriously about the days ahead. I pressed on with my plans. I would continue my study of English and my flying lessons so that I could obtain an aviator's license as soon as possible. During September, I spent every one of my days off at Floyd Bennett Field.

At 10:30 a.m. one Saturday afternoon, Joe Agliata and I left the ground and headed for the local flying area. After some basic maneuvers, Joe had me do a spin, some lazy eights, some stalls, and an emergency landing. We then returned to the field and made two touch-and-go landings. On my third approach for a landing, Joe said, "After you land this time, pull to the right side of the field and stop."

I made my third landing, and after the little Cub had slowed down, I did as Joe had told me. Joe jumped out of the J-3 Cub and said loudly, "Ok, Spiro, take it up, fly over the sea, make some turns, then come right back and land the way you did before. OK?"

"By myself?" I said, as my heart began to thump faster.

"Yes," he replied. "You are ready. Get going!"

As Joe pulled away from the aircraft, I opened the throttle slowly, made a turn, and taxied down to the take off spot of the field, behind another small airplane. Slowly, I went through the before takeoff checklist, and when I received the green light from the control tower, I lined up the yellow Cub and opened the throttle to full power. In seconds, I was airborne.

I immediately wanted to yell in triumph and delight, but I waited until I was over the sea. I shouted at the top of my lungs. Even though I knew that it was impossible, a small part of me hoped that the waves of the sea would carry my voice all the way to Kolonos, where my friends could hear me.

After flying around over the practice area for a few minutes, I returned to the field and entered the landing pattern. On the downwind leg, the tower gave me a green light and I maneuvered the aircraft for the landing. I crossed the field boundary on the final approach, about fifty feet above the ground. When I was a few feet above the grassy field, I cut the power and let the yellow Cub float for a short distance before it touched the ground in an ideal three-point landing. After the J-3 Cub had slowed down, I taxied slowly to the spot where my instructor was waiting for me. He smiled and said, "Spiro, that was a faultless landing. Bravo!"

I was now ready to proceed with the more advanced flying lessons. I thanked Joe for his help in getting me ready to fly solo and told him that I would always remember the day I first flew by myself. Leaving Floyd Bennett that day, I had high spirits.

On October 1, I left the Blue Mountain Lodge. When I arrived in New York City, I went straight to my old rooming house on Seventeenth Street and, fortunately, secured my old room. I had time and money to spare before I started looking for another job, so I decided to visit the Army recruiting station at 39 Whitehall Street. I wanted to fly for the military, should America enter the war. I was hardly in the door before I found out that I would not be able to join because I was not an American citizen.

I was back at square one, at Mr. Manolis's. He found several temporary jobs for me before he secured a permanent position at a bakery on Third Avenue on January 20, 1940. During my first day on the job, I discovered that my work at this bakery would be similar to my duties at the Hatchis's bakery.

One of the two bakers in the shop was a Greek-American fellow named James Stratakos. As time went by, James and I became friends and I got to know his family. When I visited the Stratakos' apartment one day James asked me about my interest in airplanes. I told him that my ultimate goal in life was to become an aviator. "Working at restaurants and bakeries is part of the means to get me there," I told my curious friend. I also mentioned the progress I had made with flying by taking lessons at the Agliata Flying School.

In early April 1940, I met Louie, a friend of James who lived in Union City, New Jersey, and was visiting New York one Sunday. The three of us had lunch together, and during the course of the conversation, James told Louie that I was learning to fly airplanes. When Louie heard that I was paying twelve dollars for an hour for flight instruction, he told me that he had a friend who was flying out of Westfield Airport in New Jersey and was paying much less than that.

"The cost of flying is much cheaper in New Jersey than in New York. You should take Spiro to Westfield some day and check it out," Louie told James.

The following Sunday James and I drove to Westfield in his father's car. The airfield had a landing strip about three thousand feet long and a red barn that had been converted to a hangar. The property had at one time, it seemed, been a farm. In a small office inside the barn, we met a man named Johnny Hilton, who was about twenty-eight years old. He was an instructor pilot and owned two planes, a J-3 Cub and a Porterfield 65.

"The cost to fly dual in the J-3 Cub is eight dollars an hour. Solo is six dollars per hour," he told me. "Flying the Porterfield 65, the cost per hour dual is ten dollars and solo, seven dollars an hour." I could not believe my ears. The prices were much cheaper, as Louie had promised.

I decided to try to find a job in Westfield so that I could move out to New Jersey and fly out of the Westfield Airport.

At work the following day, I took some time off during lunch and dashed up to the employment agency to check on job possibilities in New Jersey. I explained to

Mr. Manolis that I wanted to move to New Jersey so that I could take flying lessons at the airport in Westfield. After looking through his big black ledger, he found an opening for a dishwasher at a restaurant in Newark and for a pantry man at the Park Hotel in Plainfield. A pantry man prepares and dishes out salads, coffee, appetizers, and desserts for waiters, who serve the customers in the dining room. The job in Plainfield paid sixty dollars a month and included room and board. Plus, when we looked at a road map, we saw that Westfield was closer to Plainfield than to Newark. I told Mr. Manolis I'd take the job.

Mr. Manolis prepared a letter for me to give to Mr. Albert W. Stender, the manager of the Park Hotel in Plainfield, and told me where I could catch the Jersey Central Railroad train for Plainfield.

I returned to the bakery and told my boss, Mr. Nicos, that I'd decided to take a job in New Jersey. Mr. Nicos wished me well—not only with my new job but with flying. James had evidently told him my reason for leaving.

On my last day at the bakery I said good-bye to Mr. Nicos and James and dashed to Floyd Bennett to say farewell to Joe. I left New York the following day, with sadness in my heart but with a resolve to always remember the city I had learned to love. After a short ferryboat ride across the Hudson from Battery Park to Jersey City, I boarded the train to Plainfield.

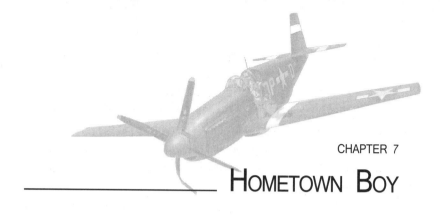

CHAPTER 7

HOMETOWN BOY

The Park Hotel was an impressive, six-story red brick building at Arlington and Seventh Street. It was the only large hotel in Plainfield and had some 125 rooms. It was located in the center of the finest residential section of the small and peaceful town. The interior was even more magnificent than the exterior; it was tastefully decorated, with greenery and large paintings adorning the white walls.

On the morning of my arrival at the Park Hotel, as I made my way across the plush carpet toward the reception desk, I was quickly intercepted by one of the hotel bellboys, who took me to the manager's office. Mr. Stender was a good-looking, cigar-smoking gentleman with blond hair who appeared to be in his early forties. I introduced myself and handed him the letter from the employment agency.

"Oh, yes," he said amiably, "I've been expecting you. I requested from the agency a young man to fill the vacant pantry man's job. Have you ever worked as a pantry man in a hotel?"

"No, Sir," I replied. "I've worked in bakeries as a helper and in restaurants as a dishwasher. But whatever this pantry man's job is I am certain I can master it, if you are willing to give me a chance."

"I like your attitude and I am going to hire you," Mr. Stender said with a smile. "Let me take you in the kitchen then and introduce you to the chef."

Mr. Stender led the way to the kitchen, where we found the chef, who was dressed in the typical white chef's attire, stirring something in a big pot over the stove.

"Ernest," Mr. Stender said, "this is Spiro, your new pantry man, just hired. This is Chef Ernest Hoffer, your boss."

The chef introduced me to Walter, his assistant, and Walter walked me over to the annex, a two-story building separate from the main hotel building. The rooms for the hotel employees were on the second floor of the annex. The building's first floor was part storage space and parking area for about a dozen cars.

On the way to the annex, I thought about the three men I had met at the hotel. Mr. Stender, Chef Hoffer, and Walter were all blond, and while they spoke English well, they spoke it with an accent not unlike my own. I realized that they must be of German descent. Given my less than enthusiastic opinion of Germany at the time, I hoped this would not be a problem.

My room, I was pleased to see, was fairly large, clean, and nicely furnished. I quickly changed clothes and made my way back to the kitchen. As I entered the kitchen, I noticed again that the space was huge and well lit, with big windows all around. The working areas were roomy and clean. Cooking tools, pots, and pans were hung in an orderly fashion above a steam counter by the huge cooking stove. The pantry and the dishwashing station were away from the main kitchen. Next to the cooking area in the kitchen was the employees' dining room. As I approached the chef, he looked at me and said, "You changed already?"

"Yes, Sir. I don't like to waste time," I said.

"Good," he said. He opened a drawer, pulled out a long white apron, and said, "Put this on."

He told Walter to watch the stove, and he and I went to the pantry to go over my duties.

"A long time ago, I worked with a Greek cook in New York named Steve. You sure look like him. You remind me of him very much," said Chef Hoffer.

From then on, instead of calling me Spiro, the chef called me Steve. As time went by, everyone at the hotel came to call me Steve, not Spiro. I liked it and even began introducing myself to others as Steve.

Chef Hoffer, after reviewing my duties as pantryman, showed me how to make coffee in the pantry's large coffee pot each morning for the dining room. He also taught me how to serve the desserts; prepare and plate the salads, including shrimp and crabmeat cocktails; and shuck oysters and clams, ingredients in many of the hotel's appetizers. After my brief lessons, I was on my own.

I started to work behind the pantry as if I knew what I was doing. With some help from Walter at lunch and dinnertime, I managed to make a bowl of green salad, serve seafood cocktails, and give out desserts. I felt that my first day was a success and that I would quickly become comfortable in my new position. The hours were long but not much longer than those for my jobs in New York, and the Park Hotel seemed like a pleasant place to work.

A week later, on my first day off, I thought about the various tasks and items I handled when working behind the pantry. The job was full of details and required swiftness to stay ahead of the cooks' and waiters' demands. To keep track of everything, I thought I might develop a plan, with a chart or two, to show the overall function of my job. To this end, I wrote down each of the items I handled behind the pantry, where each item was stored, and what was required to prepare them. For oysters, for example, I wrote, "Stored in refrigerator. Rinse shells before opening and serve six to an order. Sauce on the side. Open about three-dozen of each kind for lunchtime and five dozen for dinner." I also wrote down the sequence of my daily tasks, starting with making coffee, which was always the first chore every morning, and ending with the evening cleanup. By the time I finished, I had several pages of instructions and charts.

Once I had created my lists, I was able to analyze my job so that I could increase my efficiency. By the time I was finished with my first month on the job, I had refined the pantry's operation to the point where I felt that I had conquered the pantry man's area of responsibility. I had worked out a system of completing so many tasks so fast and at the same time that no one could figure out how I was doing it. During my days off, the chef had to use two men in the pantry to do the chores I did alone. In creating my system, I had learned things about organization and management that would stand me in good stead in years to come.

Even though I had not flown in a while, I had continued to read and study aviation. And when I was settled in and satisfied with my pantry man's job, I started to look for a way to get to Westfield Airport so that I could start flying again. Since there was no train service between Plainfield and Westfield Airport, I decided to buy a small used car. After searching all the used car lots in Plainfield, I found a neat 1930 two-door Ford Sport Coupe for seventy-five dollars cash. I had learned to drive at the Blue Mountain Lodge, but I still needed to earn a driver's license. I went to the local Department of Motor Vehicles to take a driver's test, and thirty minutes later, I drove away with a registered car and a New Jersey driver's license.

On July 18, 1940, I drove to Westfield Airport and visited Johnny Hilton. We went up in his J-3 Cub, and Johnny found me fully qualified to fly solo. Now, Johnny told me, I needed to fly by myself to build up time in the airplane and confidence in my flying skills. When I had enough hours in and was ready to take the flight check, we could fly a few hours together to cover some of the maneuvers I could expect during the check ride.

I continued to fly at every opportunity—not only on my day off but also during my midday breaks. I'd drive to Westfield, fly around for a while, and then rush back to the hotel in time to prepare for dinner. At night, or early in the morning, I'd read the daily *Plainfield Courier News* to keep informed of the aerial struggle between England and Germany. Too often, the reports portrayed a gloomy situation. The war in the air between the Allies and the Axis was vicious, with no quarter given on either side. The Luftwaffe, with its large bomber formations escorted by ME-109 and 110 fighters, was stepping up its assaults on shipping in the English Channel, as well as on London itself. Using the blitzkrieg tactics that Germany had employed so successfully in Poland, these sorties also attempted to destroy military installations—particularly aerodromes—in southern England. The Royal Air Force (RAF) Air Defense, with its Hurricanes and Spitfires, although massively outnumbered by Germany's Luftwaffe, fought bravely in defending England.

Meanwhile, my efficient operation in the pantry had evidently attracted Mr. Stender's attention. He eventually raised my wage to eighty-five dollars a month and gave me other duties in addition to my work in the pantry. I often ran errands, such as preparing for on-site catering parties and delivering foodstuffs from the kitchen to Mr. Stender's residence, in the hotel's station wagon. On certain occasions, Mr. Stender entertained city officials and friends at this house, and he'd ask Chef Hoffer to send me over to help.

One day he surprised me with an unbelievable offer during a trip to the Watchung Country Club. He told me that he wanted to see someone like me in hotel management and that he was willing to pay for me to take a course in hotel operations and management at Cornell University. When I completed the course, I could return to the Park Hotel and be a manager at one of the hotels he hoped to acquire in Newark or Trenton. I thanked Mr. Stender for his generous offer but ultimately declined the opportunity because I was committed to becoming an aviator. Mr. Stender said he admired me for my dedication, and assured me that if I ever changed my mind, I should keep his offer in mind.

My flying instruction at Westfield Airport continued without interruption. I completed a number of dual flights with Johnny and flew cross-country as well. I loved navigating through the air and observing the activities of life on earth from above. On December 4, 1940, I passed the written examination for the private pilot's license, but I procrastinated when it came to completing my flight check. Although Johnny was certain I'd pass the check, I was nervous. I couldn't believe that only a couple years after I had left Greece I was so close to earning my pilot's license.

On February 27, 1941, a man with the power to destroy my dream of becoming an aviator walked into the kitchen at the Park Hotel. The man, who was well dressed and stern looking, spoke to the chef by the steam counter, while I went about my business, paying little attention to the visitor. Suddenly, however, he turned, walked toward the pantry, and called my name. I looked up. He reached in his pocket and brought out an official-looking badge.

"I am from the Immigration and Naturalization Service [INS]. You must come with me," said the man.

"Come with you where?" I asked, a bit nervously.

"To Ellis Island," he said. My nervousness turned into almost paralyzing fear.

"May I change my clothes?" I said in dismay.

"Yes, of course," he said, "but I must come with you, and I must warn you that I am armed, so don't try anything."

The man followed me to my room, where, still in shock, I dressed in street clothes. We walked to the train station and caught the train to Jersey City. While on the train, the immigration official began asking questions.

"How did you enter the United States?"

I told him the truth. I had been a seaman and had left my ship in Baltimore Harbor back in 1938. I had overstayed the time allowed a seaman in the United States according to international law and became an illegal alien. We spent the rest of the trip in silence. Upon arrival at Jersey City, we took the ferryboat to Ellis Island.

While on the ferry, the man began to speak again, this time in a more friendly tone.

"Everybody who comes to the United States on this coast must pass through Ellis Island. You didn't, but you may still have a chance to clear the matter up with the immigration commissioner. I don't know what the authorities will do with you, but you have one thing in your favor. The government can't send you back to Greece because your country is being threatened by Hitler's armies."

I was struck by this man's sympathy. I did not expect it from a government official; Greek officials and police tended to be much more harsh. We approached the island's dock and disembarked the ferry. I was shown into an office where two men in uniform and a woman, apparently an interpreter, began to interrogate me in Greek. They asked me my name; when and where I was born; when, where, and how I had entered the United States; whether I was a communist or belonged to the Communist Party; and why I had left my ship in Baltimore. I decided that the best course of action was to be completely honest. I poured my story out to these officials, and the lady translated my words to them. I told her that since it wasn't possible for me to become a military aviator in Greece under General Metaxas's dictatorship, I had decided to leave Greece for America, the land of freedom and opportunity. Since my father had little money and didn't know anyone in America, my only hope in achieving my goal was to work on a merchant ship until I found the opportunity to leave it and stay ashore when the ship had docked into an American port. I also told her about my ambition to fly airplanes and that I had already accumulated about fifty-five hours in the air.

After the three of them discussed my situation, the lady turned to me and said that I must put in writing—in Greek or English—what I had just told them. She took me to another room, where I was given a pen and a writing tablet. I sat down and started to write, detailing my reasons for coming to America and for deserting my ship. I handed in three pages of text to the interpreter and then was taken to a dining hall full of people, where I was given something to eat. After dinner, I was taken to a dormitory, where I was given a numbered bunk in which I spent my first night on Ellis Island.

The next day, I was escorted to the INS director's office. When I entered the office, the first person I saw was my boss, Mr. Stender. He was sitting across from the director, who was behind a large, mahogany desk. I stood there for a moment, frozen. Then I realized that Mr. Stender must have come to rescue me.

As I stood at attention, the director said, "Young man, we cannot send you back to Greece now because your homeland is about to be overrun by the Germans and Italians. In view of this, your status has been changed to that of a refugee. You will be issued a working permit that will allow you to remain in the United States and seek employment wherever you wish. In the meantime we are releasing you in the care of this gentleman here." He pointed to Mr. Stender. "Mr. Stender has guaranteed the immigration authorities that you will not become a burden to the United States."

At those words, Mr. Stender arose from his chair, and we both thanked the director for his kindness and generosity. We walked out of the building and began the return trip to Plainfield. While on the road, I told Mr. Stender that I couldn't find words to thank him for what he had done for me.

He then said to me, "Don't feel bad, Steve. I was in the same predicament when I first came to America. I was working as a waiter on the SS *Bremen*, operating between Hamburg and New York. One day I got tired of the seaman's life and left the ship in New York City, the same way that you did in Baltimore. After a period of time, the immigration authorities finally caught up with me. They kept me in New York, instead of sending me to Ellis Island.

"I didn't want them to deport me directly to Germany because it would have been much more difficult to get a visa and return to the United States as an immigrant. So, I told the authorities that I would leave the United States on my own and found another job on a German ship and returned to Germany. Later on, I applied for a visa. It took some time, but eventually I was able to get the visa and return to New York. I found a job at a nightclub and that's where I met my future wife, Erna. We got married, saved our money, and eventually were able to buy the Park Hotel.

"So, as you can see, you and I went through the same experience," Mr. Stender continued. "When I learned from Ernest that an immigration representative came to the hotel and took you away, I knew how you felt because I had been there. Now you are free and everything will be fine."

I thanked Mr. Stender again as we were approaching the outskirts of Plainfield. When we reached the hotel grounds, Mr. Stender parked the wagon by the annex. I told him I'd be indebted to him forever for his kindness and rushed into my room to change clothes. Without delay, I ran into the kitchen and reported to Chef Hoffer. He was happy to see me back.

Once I returned from Ellis Island, I began to keep track of the events in my homeland. On April 6, 1941, Germany invaded Greece in an attempt to alleviate the humiliating defeats that the Greek army was handing the Italians in Albania. Three days after Germany invaded Greece, they captured Thessaloniki. Just two weeks after that, faced with the Italian and German combined forces, the Greek army surrendered. And finally, German troops entered Athens on April 27, 1941.

I was infuriated by the reports and worried about my family, especially my big brother Yannis. Yannis was serving in the Greek army, and without doubt he was in combat against the Italians and Germans. To relieve my frustration and anxiety and keep my mind off of my powerlessness to change the situation, I flew more during the months of May and June than at any other time. Then, on July 22, 1941, Johnny Hilton made arrangements with a CAA district flight examiner named Roy D. Rudy for me to go to Caldwell Wright Field in upper New Jersey and take my flight check.

I flew the Porterfield to Caldwell Wright Field, where Mr. Rudy was waiting for me. After a more than hour-long flight with the CAA examiner, who had me demonstrate for him almost everything in the book, I made a smooth landing and parked the aircraft by the administration building. I shut down the engine, and as we stepped down from the aircraft, Mr. Rudy shook my hand and said, "Mr. Pisanos, congratulations. You are now a full-fledged pilot. You can fly anywhere. You can carry passengers, but not for hire."

I was issued private pilot's license #97342, which was signed by Mr. Rudy and countersigned by C. E. Bell, Associate Aero Inspector, CAA. I thanked Mr. Rudy and took off for Westfield. While in the air, I felt like the happiest man on earth; I had achieved my long-sought dream in America.

Once I earned my license, I spent time aloft whenever I had the opportunity. I felt that the pieces of my life were finally falling into place. But that happiness was offset by the news from Europe. On the Eastern Front, the German army had captured Smolensk and had continued on toward Leningrad. The Germans were only three hundred miles from Moscow. The Luftwaffe had bombed the Russian capital on two consecutive nights. On the Western Front, the RAF was conducting nightly bombing raids on Berlin, while Germany retaliated by bombing London. In my homeland, the Germans had completed the invasion of Crete and had turned over the occupation of Athens to the Italians. According to reliable sources, the occupation of Greece had brought with it misery and serious food shortages. Widespread starvation had hit the country, particularly Athens, where people were being forced to eat cats and dogs out of desperation. As a result of the occupation, I had lost contact with everyone that I knew in Athens, and the tensions caused by the war were spilling over to the United States. Fights between Greek and Italian Americans occasionally erupted in Chicago and New York City.

During one of my days off in the latter part of August 1941, I found a chance to become more personally involved in the war effort. At a lunch with Johnny and two other flight instructors at an Italian restaurant in Westfield, our conversation turned to the war. One of the instructors, Ray, said to me, "Spiro, according to the press, your countrymen are really going through hell, suffering in the hands of the Germans and Italians."

"Yes," I said. "I saw the report in the *Plainfield Courier News* the other day. If only I could get there to fight the bastards."

Bill, the other instructor pilot, said, "Don't worry, Spiro. Before you know it, we'll be in the war, and you can fight them then."

"But, Bill, that won't help me," I said. I told them that I had tried to enlist in the U.S. Army when I was in New York but the army wouldn't take me because I wasn't an American citizen.

Ray said, "Spiro, in wartime, policies change. If we join the fight, they'd take you in with open arms."

I was skeptical but did not argue. After lunch Johnny stopped me on my way to my car and asked whether I was serious about fighting in the war. When I replied that I was, he suggested I look into joining the British Royal Air Force. I could join the RAF here in the United States, he told me. Despite official U.S. neutrality, the U.S. government was allowing the RAF to quietly recruit civilian pilots in America.

"They've approached me, but I can't go," said Johnny. "I've got a wife and three children, and I can't leave them. But you're single and have no obligations; you'd be perfect."

He urged me to visit the RAF's makeshift office, which was on the thirteenth floor of the Waldorf Astoria Hotel on Park Avenue in New York City.

"I don't know the room number," Johnny said, "but that shouldn't be difficult to find out. Outside the hotel room door, I believe there's a sign that reads, 'Clayton Knight Committee.'" He pulled a piece of paper from his pocket and wrote the details down for me.

I thanked Johnny for the information and drove away thinking about this possibility. At the same time, I thought about my German friends at the Park Hotel: Mr. Stender, Ernest, Walter—the people I worked with and admired so much. What would they think? In the end, the thought of Germany's army killing my friends and family, destroying my place of birth, trumped my reservations about the reaction of the Park Hotel staff, and I made my way to New York, taking my newly acquired CAA pilot's license and logbook with me, to visit the Clayton Knight Committee at the Waldorf Astoria Hotel.

When I arrived at the office on the thirteenth floor, I found the walls adorned with photos of airplanes and famous aviators. I came face to face with the office secretary, a young, attractive woman with dark, wavy hair, wearing a navy-blue skirt and white blouse. She asked if she could help me.

"Yes," I replied. "I was told to come here and inquire about joining the British Royal Air Force Volunteer Reserve."

"Oh, just a moment, please," she said. Then she stood up and went through a door to an adjacent office.

A few seconds later, she came out from the other office and beckoned me to follow her. She introduced me to Squadron Leader George Greaves of the RAF, who shook my hand firmly as the secretary left the room.

"Sir," I said, "my name is Spiro Pisanos. I am a private pilot with about 170 hours of flight time, and I wish very much to join the RAF."

Before responding, he asked me to sit down and tell him where I had heard about the office. I told him about Johnny's advice, and he asked, "But you aren't American?"

"Oh, no," I said. "I am Greek. Flying airplanes has been my life's ambition, ever since I saw a Gloster-Mars flying over Athens while I was walking to school."

"What a coincidence," Greaves said. "I flew the Mars after my graduation from flight school. I was also involved with transferring a squadron of those planes over to an aerodrome outside of Athens. I can't think of its name."

"That was Tatoi," I said, smiling from ear to ear.

"That's it! Tatoi Aerodrome."

We talked briefly about Tatoi before returning to the business at hand.

"Do you have your license and logbook with you?" he asked.

"Oh, yes, Sir," I said and handed him the large envelope I had with me.

He examined both of the items carefully and said, "You'll do, Mr. Pisanos. Greece is our ally, so it should be no problem that you aren't American." After I had filled out the necessary forms, the squadron leader told me I was qualified to join the RAF as a volunteer reserve.

"The Clayton Knight Committee will consider your application and you will be informed of your status in due time by this office."

A few days later I spoke to Johnny about my experience in New York. I asked him what the Clayton Knight Committee was exactly and why it was allowed to open offices in the United States for the purpose of recruiting American civilian pilots to fight in the war against Germany. Wasn't the United States bound by the Neutrality Act? Johnny explained that the story behind the Clayton Knight Committee was long and complicated and involved high-level citizens and government officials of three nations, Canada, Great Britain, and the United States. The mechanics of the recruiting system in America were not publicized because of the Neutrality Act, but still the network was enormously effective at successfully recruiting hundreds of American civilian pilots for the RAF, without surrendering their American citizenship.

CHAPTER 8

FLIGHT PLAN FOR WAR

"**M**r. Pisanos, this is Squadron Leader Greaves in New York," said the voice on the phone. It was November 2, 1941. "I just want to inform you that you have been accepted to join the RAF, and I'd like for you to visit New York for a physical examination. I have arranged for you to take your physical next week, on November 6 at 2:00 p.m. Will you be able to make it?"

"Yes, Sir."

Early on November 6, I arrived at the Waldorf and was surprised by the sign on the door to the suite, which now read "Canadian Aviation Bureau." I was quickly shown into Squadron Leader Greaves' office.

"Mr. Pisanos, so nice to see you," he greeted me, and shook my hand as we went into his office. "Well, Mr. Pisanos, as I told you on the phone last week, you have been accepted to serve in the RAF. I am terribly sorry for not getting to you sooner."

It turned out my acceptance in the RAF had been delayed because the British had to conduct a background check on me—in Greece. Greaves informed me that Great Britain actually had people in occupied Greece who could undertake a background check of an individual, if necessary.

Greaves briefed me on arrangements he had made for my physical that day and told me that he would contact me later in the week to give me additional instructions. As I was preparing to leave, I asked, "Excuse me, Sir, but that sign on the door outside your office . . . What happened to the Clayton Knight Committee sign?"

"Oh," he replied with a smile, "we changed the title of our activities. The new sign is more appropriate given our mission here in the United States."

I accepted his explanation at face value and said good-bye.

I passed my physical, and two days later, Squadron Leader Greaves called me again to inform me that he had scheduled me for a 2:00 p.m. check ride on

November 10 at Flushing Airport in Queens, with Mr. Otto Hanslik at the Aero Services Hangar. November 10, the day of my twenty-second birthday, was calm with a glorious blue sky. I arrived at the airfield promptly, just before 2:00 p.m. When I walked into the hangar of Aero Services at Flushing Airport, I asked a mechanic who was working by a yellow biplane where I could find Mr. Otto Hanslik, and he pointed to a door by the side of the hangar. I found Mr. Hanslik at a desk just inside the door.

I introduced myself, and Mr. Hanslik asked me to sit down for a moment while he went upstairs to slip on his flight suit. While I waited for him to change, I admired the yellow biplane, a Stearman, that two mechanics were preparing to push out of the hangar. The mechanics confirmed that I would be flying this plane that afternoon, and I wrote down the Stearman's serial number (NC8828) for my logbook. Then, I asked one of the mechanics about Mr. Hanslik. He told me that his boss had flown as a fighter pilot with the U.S. Air Service in World War I; he had flown Spads in France.

As I was talking to the mechanic, Mr. Hanslik appeared wearing a gray coverall, helmet, and goggles. He was carrying another set of gear and told me to put it on. The coverall fit like it had been made for me, and the helmet and goggles were somewhat worn out but usable for the flight.

Mr. Hanslik asked me if I had flown a Stearman before and I told him no. He assured me that it flew much like other biplanes. After we strapped on our parachutes, Mr. Hanslik told me to get in the front cockpit; he would fly from the rear. He helped me strap myself inside the small cockpit and pointed to the engine and flight instruments, including the innertube, which we would use to communicate.

I put my helmet on, connected the innertube to the helmet, and told Mr. Hanslik that I was ready. He started the engine, the mechanic pulled out the chocks, and we taxied away from the hangar area. In the meantime, I glanced at the instruments in the cockpit to become familiar with their locations. I was familiar with all of the Stearman's instruments except for the artificial horizon, a gyroscopic instrument that allowed the pilot to see the true horizon when he flew through a cloud or at night. The J-3 Cub and the Porterfield 65 I flown previously didn't have this instrument.

When we were cleared for takeoff, Hanslik taxied the Stearman a little farther, lined it up against the wind and said, "Go ahead. You make the takeoff."

I grabbed the stick gently with my feet on the rudder pedals and pushed the throttle wide open. The aircraft began to roll down the grassy field.

"Keep the aircraft straight, and I'll help you, if you need me to," Mr. Hanslik said. Fortunately, I had no difficulties keeping the Stearman straight.

Suddenly, the aircraft became airborne and Hanslik remarked, "That was a good takeoff, young man. Now, head north, climb to 4,000 feet, and cross the East River. As you climb, make a couple of left and right climbing turns."

After we had crossed the East River, he asked me make some steep turns. He demonstrated a roll for me and asked me to complete a roll to the left and one to the right. My rolls weren't as smooth as the one he had made. He had me do a loop, a wing over, and power-on-and-off stalls. He then said, "Let's go back to the field."

As I was heading for the airport, he cut the biplane's power to idle.

"You just lost your engine," he said. "What are you going to do?"

I immediately looked around and spotted an open field ahead. I told him that I was going to put the plane down in the field.

"Go right ahead," he said. I turned the powerless aircraft toward the field I had in sight, and as I neared the ground, I tried to convince myself that it was just another approach for a landing. I maneuvered the aircraft accordingly to land in the field. As I prepared to land, I noted that the wind had changed and further adjusted the Stearman. My altitude, I thought, was OK. When I turned the plane into the final approach, Mr. Hanslik cut into the innertube and said, "You have your engine back, let's head for the airport now."

Relieved, I opened the throttle and started to climb. I turned the aircraft around and headed for the airport. I made my turn into the final approach, about one hundred feet above the ground, and as I crossed the edge of Flushing Airport, I cut the power and let the aircraft float a little. Then, as the wheels were about to touch down, I slowly raised the nose and let the Stearman settle into a three-point landing. When the plane had slowed down, Mr. Hanslik took over and taxied the plane to the hangar area.

After we had jumped down from the plane, I thought Mr. Hanzlik was going to say something about my performance. Instead, he only said, "Let's drop our helmets in my office and have some coffee."

We left our helmets and headed for the coffee shop around the corner from the hangar. On the way there, Hanslik remained mute. I began to fear I had not passed the check ride. But after we ordered our coffees, he reassured me. I had done well for someone who had never flown this type of aircraft.

"With the additional military training you'll receive in California, you'll be alright. You passed the check."

In the days that followed, I flew every afternoon to build up my flying time. Then, on November 18, 1941, Squadron Leader Greaves called again to inform me that I had been assigned to Squadron Number 16 at Polaris Flight Academy in Glendale, California. I was to report there on November 24 for further training. He was going to mail me some advance cadet pay, as well as the airline ticket for my travel to California.

Telling Mr. Stender I was leaving was one of the most difficult moments of my life, but he was, characteristically, understanding.

"Steve, I admire who you are and commend you for what you have accomplished in such a short time," he said. "I want you to go there and give them hell, especially Hitler and his Nazi pals. I have never approved of Hitler's ideas, even when it all started in 1933. Although he's winning now, I am as certain as the sun rises every morning that he is taking Germany to ultimate defeat. You go there, Steve, with my blessings. Give the Nazis hell because they have ruined Germany, the place where I grew up. But Germany is still in my heart, so please be kind to her."

As he finished his speech, Mr. Stender came around his desk and hugged me like a father would embrace a son leaving for the battlefield.

"I want to wish you all the luck in the world, Steve, and I want you to come back because you belong here with us in the Park Hotel," he said warmly.

I left Mr. Stender's office with tears in my eyes and went back in the kitchen to reveal the news to Chef Hoffer. The chef was most surprised and said, "Why on earth would you want to go to war, Steve?" He looked me in the eyes. "War is evil— people get killed in wars."

I didn't know quite what to say because I had not thought of war in that way before. I had made up my mind to go, and that was that. As I started to leave the kitchen for the pantry, the chef added in a low voice, "I hate to see you leave, but you do what you think is right for you, Steve." He walked away, clearly disappointed by my decision to leave.

The news of my joining the British RAF and my departure from the Park Hotel spread quickly. Mr. Stender had evidently passed the word to every hotel resident, the Plainfield mayor's office, the editor of the *Plainfield Courier News*, and the chief of police. The newspaper dispatched a reporter and a photographer the afternoon I resigned to meet me at work, interview me for a story, and to snap some photos. My story and the photos appeared in the paper the following day, and so the entire city of Plainfield became aware of the Greek pantry boy at the Park Hotel who had joined the British RAF and was going to war to fight the Nazis.

Hotel residents, customers, and some strangers whom I had never met came to the hotel to see me. Some even came back into the kitchen, wanting to meet me, shake my hand, and wish me luck. Telephone calls both from people I knew and strangers, expressing congratulations and good luck, also came in all day long. I received calls from local Greeks who invited me to join them with their families for dinner before my departure. I even received calls from Greeks as far away as New York City, all wishing me good luck and a safe return. The Greek newspaper in New York City, *Atlantis*, carried an article with my photo telling its readers about my decision to join the RAF to fight for freedom. I also had a visit from my good friend James Stratakos, whom I had told about my upcoming departure.

On my last day in Plainfield, I went to Westfield Airport to say good-bye to my instructor and to other pilots and mechanics in the barn. I told Johnny that I'd always remember him because he was responsible for the journey on which I was about to embark. Our farewell was as emotional and demonstrative as a relatively reserved Brit and a relatively expressive Greek could bear.

That night, Mr. Stender gave me a farewell dinner at the hotel's dining room. We enjoyed a sumptuous meal and talked about the hotel, the war, and my upcoming part in it. As we stood up to leave at the end of the meal, a number of hotel guests in the dining room approached us, wanting to shake my hand and wish me luck. It was as if I were one of their own, a hometown Plainfield boy going off to war. After the final good-byes and hugs from my dining companions, I left to say good-bye to others with whom I had worked.

It was late afternoon on November 22, 1941, when I left Plainfield for Newark. I was happy because I was going to become a military aviator; I was sad because I was leaving a place that I considered my home in America. Ultimately, though, I knew that I was making the right decision and that I could not pass this chance up. As I left for California, tears rolled down my cheeks.

POLARIS FLIGHT ACADEMY

I flew out west on a DC-3 and eventually found my way to Glendale and Grand Central Air Terminal. After asking for directions, I found my way to a small, shed-like building with a sign above the door that read, "Polaris Flight Academy." When

I went inside I saw a husky, dark, curly haired fellow standing behind a counter.

When I introduced myself, he smiled and said, "I'm Johnny Buckley, the school's director of operations. Welcome to Polaris. I've been expecting you." He handed me a sheaf of papers that looked like forms and informational fliers. "You'll be billeted at the cadets' dormitory on the other side of the field. The facility has its own dining hall where you'll get all your meals. Now that I have you checked in, you are free for the day, but tomorrow there will be a briefing at 8:00 a.m. for all cadets of Squadron 16. You can turn in your forms then."

A station wagon took me to the other side of the terminal, where the dormitory was. After checking in, I was assigned to share a room with another cadet. I dropped off my things in my new room and headed to the dining room for lunch. There I met my four classmates who had already checked in: Bob Hage, Kenneth Peterson, Mike Gilormini, and Ted Huntington. I also met the cadet I was going to share a room with, Victor France of Squadron 15. France had just landed from a flight and joined us at our table. After lunch, we newcomers had the chance to ask Cadet France particulars about the school, its curriculum, the flying part of the program, and, of course, night activities in town.

The Barrel, a cocktail lounge on Sondra Street within walking distance of our dorm, was apparently popular with cadets. That evening, France and I walked over to the place, and I had a chance to ask him what he thought of the school overall. He was much impressed, he told me, with the organization and training.

"They are doing their best to teach us the military version of flying. If you follow their guidance, you shouldn't have any problems, but don't try to be a smart ass like a guy we have in my class. When it comes to the ground school, just study the assignments, take some notes, and review the publications they give you, and if you pay attention you'll be OK."

The following day, November 24, 1941, I had an early breakfast with several of my classmates, and at 7:45 a.m., the entire class of cadets from Squadron 16 walked in groups of twos and threes across the field to the operations shed for Mr. Buckley's 8:00 a.m. briefing.

"Before I begin my briefing," he said, "I would like for each one of you to stand up and introduce yourself. Tell us where you came from. Start with the first row, right there," as he pointed to Cadet Bell.

This was the class of cadets in Squadron #16 at the Polaris Flight Academy, as we introduced ourselves to Mr. Buckley on the morning of November 24, 1941:

Bell, V. R., Lyon, Kansas; Erickson, J. N., North Dakota; Gilormini, M., Guaya Nilla, Puerto Rico; Goin, M. M., Liberty, Nebraska; Greenway, H. J., Kewanee, Illinois; Gring, P., Santa Barbara, California; Hage, R. L., Great Falls, Montana; Mims, S. L., Jacksonville, Florida; Kirschner, C. M., St. Joseph, Missouri; Peterson, K. D., Mesa, Arizona; Schmitt, L. J., Kansas City, Missouri; Whitfield, W. T., Monroe, Louisiana; Ziesmer, R. Jr., Minneapolis, Minnesota; Huntington, T., Pasadena, California; and myself, Pisanos, S. N., Plainfield, New Jersey.

"We certainly have quite a group in this class," Mr. Buckley said, "and I want to welcome every one of you and wish that your stay here at Polaris will be pleasant and memorable. Squadron 16 is one of the largest classes we have had so far. Allow me, also, to congratulate all of you gentlemen for having joined the greatest air force in the world, the RAF. Let me cover briefly a few points about Polaris and how it all began, so you know something about the school you were selected to attend."

Mr. Buckley told us quite a bit about the history of the Clayton Knight Committee, as well as a little bit about the history of Polaris itself. He then briefed us on the current organization of Polaris.

"The chief of Polaris is John 'Poppy' Bryan, and I am the director of operations. There are others in the chain of command here and I am sure you'll get to know them as you go along with your training. Be advised also that there are four squadrons presently under training at Polaris: 15, 16, 17, and 18.

"Please don't labor under the illusion that you are on a vacation while attending this school. You are here to improve your skills as pilots, and you'll be expected to work hard to get through the heavy workload the school has designed for you, a program that normally takes several months to complete."

Mr. Buckley explained that we would be at Polaris for ten weeks, and our training would be in two phases: ground school and flying. The first phase consisted of some 240 hours of instruction on the theory of flight, aircraft and their engines, air navigation, map reading, meteorology, and Morse code, and ten hours each in the Link trainer. The flying portion would involve ninety hours of dual and solo flying in three different types of aircraft: PT-13s, BT-13s, and AT-6s, including ten hours in a Harlow and in a Stinson Type-O aircraft. We would practice normal flight maneuvers, aerobatics, formations, cross-country flying, aerial navigation, simulated emergency landings, and night flying. Our days would run from 8:00 a.m. to 5:00 p.m., and usually we'd fly in the morning and attend ground school in the afternoon. As a squadron, we would select a squadron cadet captain, who would select his own co-captain; these cadets would be the spokespeople for squadron concerns.

"That, gentlemen, concludes my briefing, unless you have any questions," Mr. Buckley said. "If not, you are dismissed for the rest of the day. Before you depart for the other side, though, proceed to the supply section at the end of this building and get your blue coveralls and flying equipment. Also, don't forget to check the bulletin board at your dormitory daily."

I picked up my two flying coveralls, an army khaki sweater, a leather helmet, goggles and gloves, a leather flying suit, two books on air navigation and meteorology, and a Weems protractor from the supply section. The supply clerk reminded us that we were required to return all of these items once we finished the course. After all of us had retrieved our issued supplies, we gathered in front of the operations shed, fell into a pretty haphazard formation, and marched as much like soldiers as we could to the west side of the field. There, we selected K. D. Peterson as our captain, and Pete selected S. L. Mims as his co-captain.

On November 26, 1941, I had my first flight with my assigned instructor, Ted Airheart, in a Stearman PT-13. He had me practice some air work and complete a few takeoffs and landings. The Stearman, built by the Boeing Aircraft Company, was a biplane primary two-seater trainer in tandem. It was well built, ideal for acrobatic maneuvers, and had been widely used as a trainer for the U.S. Army Air Corps and the U.S. Navy. All of the Stearmans and the other aircraft we used at Polaris had USAAC, not RAF, markings.

I found the husky Mr. Airheart a pleasant and capable instructor. He gave precise critiques on the completion of each of my flights. And he loved acrobatics. After my second flight with him, he sent me up solo, on December 1, 1941. As I became airborne over Los Angeles that cloudless and calm day, I felt elated. I hadn't been able to get into the Air Force Academy in Greece, but through a weird set of circumstances, here I was, flying solo over Los Angeles in a U.S. airplane, training to be part of the British Royal Air Force.

I flew toward the practice area and climbed to 5,000 feet. I did some stalls, loops, rolls, and wingovers, then returned to Grand Central and landed the yellow biplane without difficulty. Mr. Airheart was waiting for me at the spot where I was directed to park the Stearman. He came over to greet me and said, "That was a helluva three-point landing, Mr. Pisanos. How did it feel to be up there alone?"

"Fantastic!" I told him gleefully.

I continued to fly with Airheart in the days that followed, learning a method of flying that was strikingly different from civilian aviation. All of my maneuvers were

77

expected to be crisp and sharp. When I asked Mr. Airheart, he admitted that one of the school's primary goals was to train us out of our civilian flying habits.

THE DAY THAT LIVES IN INFAMY

On Sunday, December 7, Vic France and I took the two sisters we had been dating, Paula and Eileen, for a ride down to Santa Monica. We had spent the previous night at their home in Hollywood. At about noon, as we began to look for a place to have lunch, we noticed that the people of Santa Monica seemed to be walking around with dazed expressions on their faces. Paula's Chevy needed some fuel, so she decided to pull into a station up ahead. As she stopped at the pump, the attendant came over to serve us and asked Paula, "What'll it be, lady?"

"Fill'er up," replied Paula. "And can you tell us why the folks in town seem so bewildered?"

"Haven't you heard?" the attendant asked. "The Japs attacked Pearl Harbor this morning."

We were all shocked. The attendant explained that the attack had destroyed quite a few of our ships in port and killed many soldiers and sailors. Rumor was that the West Coast would be Japan's next target.

Vic paid for the fuel and told Paula to drive us back to Grand Central immediately. When we arrived at the school grounds, we went immediately to the cadet lounge, where everyone had gathered around the radio to listen to continuous bulletins from Washington about the Japanese attack. The radio announcer read from a report that said the initial evaluation of the damage inflicted on Pearl Harbor indicated there were about 2,400 casualties. Eighteen warships had been sunk at their berths, and more than 180 aircraft were destroyed on the ground.

That night, almost all the cadets, including France and me, sat by the radio listening to bulletin after bulletin from Washington and London. President Roosevelt had requested a declaration of war against Japan from Congress. It was well past midnight when we broke up the gathering in the lounge and retired to our rooms. As we turned the lights off that night, France said angrily, "The bastards will pay for all the damages, and they'll pay dearly. You just wait and see."

The following day, the United States declared war on the Axis powers: Japan, Germany, and Italy.

The Japanese attack on Hawaii forced our school officials to accelerate the pace of our training. Naturally, those of us in the four squadrons who were transitioning from civilian to military-style flying were anxiously looking forward to completing our training and moving on to the war in Europe. However, the acceleration of our training, plus the civilian air traffic into and out of Grand Central and the arrival of the newly produced Lockheed P-38 fighter aircraft at the field, had created enormous traffic congestion, both on the ground and in the air. Rumor had it that Polaris might move from Glendale.

That rumor proved to be well founded. Just shy of two weeks after the Pearl Harbor attack, we packed our possessions and headed for War Eagle Field in the Mojave Desert. We traveled in a convoy of four Greyhound buses loaded with cadets, mechanics, and school staff. Other buses and trucks soon followed. After a few hours on the road, we arrived at War Eagle Field, just a few miles west of the small sleepy town of Lancaster. There was gleaming white snow on the peak of Mount Baldy, the sky was cloudless, and it was cool outside. The only thing we knew about Lancaster and the surrounding area was what we had seen from the air: the landscape was dotted with roaming coyotes and sagebrush blown around by the wind. There were no nighttime activities, and of course, there were no lounges like the Barrel. But judging from the flight activity overhead, this place appeared to be even busier than Grand Central Air Terminal.

The military-style barracks at War Eagle were newly built with bunkbeds. They were roomy, clean, and comfortable. Each unit could accommodate twenty cadets, and all of Squadron 16 was lucky to be housed in the same unit. I took a lower bunk, and Bob Hage occupied the one above me.

Our new lifestyle in the desert was entirely different from the one we had had at Grand Central. We were flying in wide-open spaces, doing acrobatics and low-level flying without any complaints from townspeople. Some of us even chased coyotes while on solo flights. The atmosphere at War Eagle was totally military. We lived in military barracks, had our meals in a typical military mess hall, and met more men in uniform, RAF cadets from the Commonwealth. A bugle sounded every morning to let us know that it was time to wake up.

After I finished my training in the PT-13, a biplane I fell in love with, I checked out on the BT-13, a sturdy aircraft built by Vultee, a two-seat tandem-enclosed cockpit low-wing monoplane with a Pratt & Whitney R-985, 450-horsepower engine. This basic trainer was excellent for acrobatics, but it was extremely noisy. Once I was familiar with these two aircraft, I had a check ride with an instructor named Mr. Jack Barnwell. It was my fourth successful check ride in a row.

My roomate and friend, Vic France had completed his training and Squadron 15 cadets had deployed for England.

Christmas and the New Year came and went. I began to fly the AT-6 all-metal advanced trainer with a 600-horsepower Pratt & Whitney, R-1340 Wasp engine, a delightful machine to fly. Most of our training with this aircraft was devoted to acrobatics and formation, but some of the instructors occasionally tried to show us some dogfighting maneuvers. We covered all the aspects of stunt flying—loops, split-S's, slow and snap rolls, spins, wingovers, Immelmans, and other tricky gyrations. Mr. Airheart explained that the objective was to learn not only how to execute those maneuvers but also to gain confidence in our aircraft. In addition, he would occasionally have me practice some techniques used in combat flying.

Soon, my name appeared on the board for my final check ride—with none other than my sponsor, Squadron Leader Greaves, who had arrived from New York to do some flying with us cadets. My flight with him went better than I expected. I executed all my maneuvers, including an emergency landing, with precision. Midflight, the squadron leader cut my engine off and asked what I would do since I had lost power. I told him that I would make a dead-stick landing on the dry lakebed we had just passed.

"Go ahead and show me," he said. I turned the plane around and headed toward the dry lake for the landing. Evidently, my quick maneuvering and low approach to the lake were acceptable because the squadron leader said, "You have your engine back, Cadet Pisanos. Let's return to the field now."

After an almost-perfect three-point landing, I taxied in and parked the AT-6. I shut down the engine, we jumped down, and Squadron Leader Greaves said, "Mr. Pisanos, let me congratulate you for a good flight, and keep up the good work!"

This praise warmed my heart. I felt a huge debt of gratitude toward both the squadron leader and Mr. Airheart. I knew that without their help, I would still be back at the Park Hotel, with no chance of getting into the war.

After we cadets from Squadron 16 graduated, we were given a week's leave and told to arrive at the Royal Canadian Air Force (RCAF) Moncton station in Canada no later than February 29, 1942. We turned in our issued equipment, picked up our travel vouchers and some other documents, were paid, and then were free to leave the school grounds. It was evening when Mike Gilormini and I left Los Angeles on the Union Pacific Challenger for New York via Chicago. We were the only two from Squadron 16 who elected to travel to the East Coast by train. I was not going to pass up the opportunity to see as much as I could of what I hoped would someday, officially, be my beloved country.

RETURN TO NEW YORK

My trip across the country was long, but still a great adventure. After we left Los Angeles, the Challenger sped northward. The next few days were pleasant and comfortable, as the train took us through California's Donner Pass and Reno and, from there, across the Great Plains to Chicago. We then took the New York Central Limited, a faster train with silver cars. This shorter ride from Chicago to New York was even more comfortable than our trip from Los Angeles, largely because the tracks had been welded together, making the ride smoother. The morning after we left Chicago, the train crossed the Harlem River into Manhattan and soon arrived at Grand Central terminal on Forty-second Street and Park Avenue.

Gilormini was staying with his uncle in Brooklyn, so he and I parted ways at the train station, agreeing to meet there for our trip to Montreal in the late afternoon on February 28. I had $170 in my pocket, so I checked into the Astor Hotel, my favorite hotel on Times Square. After lunch, I took a long walk, had an early dinner, and returned to the hotel. By now I was feeling the effects of the long train journey. As I fell into a deep sleep, I recalled looking at the huge white building from the outside, admiring its architectural design. "Now I am a guest at this fine hotel and am looking down on Times Square. How things have changed in such a short time."

The next morning, I put my coat on and went for another walk, reviewing a list the places I wanted to visit and things I wanted to do before departing for Canada. When I reached Columbus Circle and turned onto Central Park South, my thoughts flashed back to the days I had spent there with Elli. In the evening I had dinner at my favorite Italian restaurant, which was on Broadway next to Jack Dempsey's famous restaurant. After dinner I walked down to Forty-second Street and was most surprised to see the movie *The Dawn Patrol* showing at one of the New York movie houses. As memories of Kolonos flooded into my mind, I decided to see the film once more.

I spent the next day with James Stratakos, whom I had listed as my next of kin in my military papers. I also visited Joe Agliata at Floyd Bennett Field. When he learned where I was going, he was delighted by my progress and my decision to get into the fight. He wished me luck and a safe return.

On one of my remaining days in New York, I passed a restaurant with a sign over the door that read, "Platanos Genuine Greek Food." Unable to resist the smell of a Greek kitchen, I walked in and was welcomed by a man at the register. With a menu in his hand, the man showed me to a table. On our way to the table, he looked at me closely and said, "You must be Greek."

"I am," said I, "and you?"

"I am George Platanos from Sparta."

"Sparta?!" I exclaimed. "That's where my father was born!"

Our conversation was interrupted briefly when the man was called into the kitchen. When he returned to my table, he said, "Will you leave it up to me to offer you one of my best dishes?"

"Yes, of course," I said. "I'll accept it, whatever it is."

"I am certain that you won't be disappointed." He called one of the waiters, gave him the order he had written on his tablet, and sat down at my table. We began to talk. He, of course, wanted to know what I was doing in New York. When I told him that I had joined the British RAF to fight the Germans, he was most surprised.

"You mean to tell me," he said, "that you are going to fly an airplane and fight the Germans from the air? The bastards, they killed two of my younger brothers who were serving in the Greek army on the frontier between Yugoslavia and Greece. How I wish I could be there to fight them personally! But, now that you are going to fight the Germans with an airplane, please kill as many as you can for me, Mr. Pisanos, and I'll be indebted to you forever."

"I will," I promised him.

After I had finished my Greek coffee, I went to pay my bill at the register. Mr. Platanos refused to accept payment for my meal: the most delicious roast leg of lamb with roasted potatoes I had ever enjoyed. I insisted, but he refused, and I was forced to capitulate. When I thanked him, he shook my hand and said, "Go, my boy; and may the force of the wind be with you always."

I had never heard that sort of blessing before, and I said so.

"You have not?" he replied, "and you are the son of a Spartan? That, my boy, is an ancient Spartan traditional blessing, given by parents to their warrior sons before battle with the Athenians, long ago. Evidently, your father didn't come from the mountains of Sparta, where the irresistible force of the wind is part of daily life. When I left our small village in the mountains as a young soldier in 1912, I went off to fight in the Balkan War and my father gave me that very same blessing. As a son of a Spartan, you should remember this blessing, my boy." I shook his hand and said goodbye to a fine Spartan warrior.

CHAPTER 9

OFF TO WAR

In the afternoon of February 28, I checked out of the Astor and met Gilormini and Ted Huntington at Grand Central Station. I had expected Gilormini, but not Huntington. It turned out he had changed his mind about going directly to Canada from the West Coast. Moreover, K. D. Peterson, Bob Hage, S. L. Mims, C. M. Kirschner, and W. T. Whitfield had also changed their plans and were going to join us. We had only a short wait in the station until the others arrived and then we all boarded the train. The train departed on time, and as it sped northward in the darkness of the night, we sat around drinking Mims's whiskey and talking.

When we arrived in Albany around midnight, uniformed U.S. Immigration officers boarded the train. "Gentlemen, your nationality, please, and where are you bound for?"

My heart began to pound fast, and I began to worry, thinking that the officer would ask me for a passport, which I didn't have. The only identification cards I had with me were my New Jersey driver's license, my draft board and alien registration cards, and my working permit. As I thought frantically, my friends all said that they were U.S. citizens. When the officers looked at me, I said I was a Greek national, traveling with the group. Just as I finished, Peterson intervened and said, "We are all pilots, have joined the RAF, and are traveling on military orders on our way to England."

The officer replied, with a smile, "You mean you boys are going to fly Spitfires? I wish I were going with you." He bid us good luck and closed the door to our compartment.

At about 6:00 a.m. on February 29, the train pulled into the Montreal station. We disembarked and walked into the busy train station lounge, where we spotted two military policemen, one in a gray-blue RCAF uniform.

We told the policemen who we were and where we were going, and they escorted us to an office where we had our travel vouchers validated and were also told that the train for Moncton, via Quebec, would be departing at 8:30 a.m. from the same track on which we had arrived. We took the time to have a light breakfast at the station, and then we leisurely boarded the train. Around 8:30, the train pulled out from the Montreal station for the final portion of our journey to Moncton.

On our way to Quebec, we talked about crossing the Atlantic Ocean and our chances of arriving in England without encountering any interference from German U-boats. We were all aware of the damage that the German submarines had inflicted on Allied shipping. While some of us felt that we would be rescued if our ship was torpedoed, we were not sure what we would do if we ran into trouble.

By the time we reached Moncton, an RCAF training facility and reception stop for military personnel destined for overseas, it was late evening. We checked in, had a bite to eat at the mess, and then were taken to the bachelor officer quarters (BOQ). On the evening of our second day in Moncton we found that our duties there were quite simple: Roll call, marching on the parade grounds every morning, and lectures on crossing the Atlantic on a troop ship were certainly much less hectic than our training in California. At dinnertime, we met some RCAF and RAF officers at the mess. When they learned who we were, they treated us like we were officers. We spent that night chatting and drinking until the wee hours of the morning, laughing and exchanging stories with our new comrades.

At breakfast on the morning of March 4, an officer approached our table and told us that we were to report to the personnel office at 9:00 a.m. We hurried over to the office and found that the ship we were booked on for our voyage to England was in port. We would take a train to St. John and embark there, rather than in Halifax. Before we left, we were briefed on our voyage and were given a few details on what to do if a U-boat attacked our ship.

After a long trip, our train reached the harbor in late afternoon on March 5. Everywhere we looked merchant ships were being loaded with war supplies, provisions, and troops. A good number of these ships would be part of our convoy to England. We disembarked the train and marched as a group a few hundred feet, stopping by a huge vessel named the SS *Orbita*, which appeared to have originally been a passenger ship.

When we boarded the *Orbita* we discovered that the eight of us would be accommodated in two small cabins on the second deck. The cabins were not big enough for four of us, much less our belongings. But since we were on a troop ship and not on a luxury liner, we simply accepted the situation without fuss.

We had just settled in our tiny cabins when we had to rush to the top deck wearing our life preservers for an abandon ship drill. When we reached topside, we stood in the freezing cold to listen to a lecture by a crew member. "Calmness and order," he told us, "were essential should we run into trouble and have to abandon ship." The lecture did little to alleviate our nervousness.

It was early morning on March 6, 1942, when the *Orbita* pulled out of St. John's Harbor and joined about ten other ships to steam toward the Atlantic. When our small convoy had reached the ocean, it merged with a larger group of ships that had come out from other Canadian ports, all carrying troops and war supplies destined for England. The merger created a convoy of some forty ships, which was protected by destroyers and other small warships, including some that displayed the U.S. flag.

On our third day at sea, the ship's military commander, a Canadian colonel, read us cadets a cable sent by Squadron Leader Greaves, saying that we had all been appointed as pilot officers (POs) in the RAF volunteer reserve. We, of course, were happy about this news. And, in fact, from that day on we had our meals in the officers' dining room.

It took our convoy exactly fifteen days to cross the North Atlantic. The trip was uneventful except for a single incident. On our fifth day out, an escorting destroyer was forced to launch two depth charges well south of the convoy's perimeter path, in response to what turned out to be a false alarm.

Shortly after a deck sailor first spotted Ireland's northwestern coast in the distance, the huge convoy began to break up as some ships headed for Cardiff and Liverpool.

"The *Orbita* is going to Glasgow," the deck sailor told us.

After we had passed through the North Channel, the sea that separates Scotland from northern Ireland, in late afternoon on March 21, the troop ship *Orbita* was the first ship to dock inside the harbor of Glasgow.

An RAF officer met us on the ship. We retrieved our belongings, disembarked our floating home, and boarded an RAF bus that took us to the railway station for our overnight trip to London. When we arrived at the railway station we were taken to the platform for our train, *The Flying Scotsman*, which would take us to London. The RAF had reserved a first-class compartment for the eight of us. It was pitch black outside when we left the station. Glasgow and the surrounding areas were under total blackout so that the Luftwaffe couldn't spot the towns from the air. Being unable to see anything—not even a single light—through the train window felt weird to me. The lights inside the train itself were severely dimmed, covered in a cloth gadget the shape of a funnel and pointed downward. This made walking through the corridors a little difficult, as we found out when we left our compartment for the dining car.

After dinner, we returned to our compartment, which was a bit cramped, and settled down for the long night ahead. We were all tired from the voyage across the North Atlantic and talked little. Shortly, I closed my eyes and drifted off to sleep.

PILOT OFFICER, RAF

The Flying Scotsman arrived in London early on the morning of March 22, 1942. An RAF pilot officer named Mitchell met us at the station. We retrieved our gear and walked to an RAF bus outside the station. As we settled into our seats in the bus, Pilot Officer Mitchell briefed us on our schedule of events.

When the bus pulled away from the station, fog hung over the city, but I could tell daylight was on its way. As the bus drove through the streets of London, we could see some of the destruction the Germans had caused with their day and night bombing during the Battle of Britain in 1940. Buildings and houses were demolished right down to the ground and entire streets were blocked by debris. I wondered how the people of London had been able to cope with the continuous waves of German bombers that had pounded their city without mercy.

Pilot Officer Mitchell helped us check into The Regent Palace Hotel and told us to have our meals in the hotel's dining room charged to our rooms. He also told us that he would be by around 9:00 a.m. tomorrow to pick us up for our visit to the Air Ministry. We said good-bye to Pilot Officer Mitchell and headed for the dining room, had a good breakfast, and hurriedly went to our rooms to wash up and get some sleep in real beds, a luxury we had missed since we left Canada two weeks ago. The bunks on the *Orbita* weren't all that bad, but the night we had spent on the train had taken the energy right out of us. My hotel bed was blissfully comfortable, and I went to sleep the minute I pulled up the covers.

On our second day in London, Pilot Officer Mitchell showed up just after we had finished breakfast. Together, we boarded the bus and headed for the Air Ministry. On arriving at RAF headquarters, we were directed to a personnel office, where we filled out a stack of forms that confirmed our commissions in the RAF Volunteer Reserve. At another office we received our first month's pay in English pounds, an amount that was equal to eighty-five dollars. It felt good to have some spending money in our pockets.

We didn't take an oath or swear allegiance to the Crown. We merely signed a paper stating that, as officers in His Majesty's Service, we were to serve the RAF faithfully, to obey our superiors, and to respect and comply with the service's rules, customs, and regulations. When we finished these formalities, Pilot Officer Mitchell took us to Austin Reed to be fitted with our RAF uniforms. After we had our measurements taken at Austin Reed that afternoon, some of the men hit the bar. Pete, Hage, and I skipped the bar and took a short walk around Piccadilly Circus and down to Haymarket. Just before dark, we returned to the hotel, had a drink at the bar, and went to dinner.

The following day, we returned to Austin Reed, signed some papers, picked up our uniforms, and put them on. Mine was a perfect fit. After thanking the expert tailor who had taken our measurements, we walked back to the hotel, hardly believing that we were actually wearing RAF officers' uniforms. I told my friends that we would now have to be careful how we conducted ourselves in public.

"Not only that," Pete added, as he turned back to face the others behind us, "we should also salute anyone who extends a salute to us, whether we know how to or not."

By 12:30 p.m., we had packed, had lunch, and checked out of our hotel. We caught the 2:00 p.m. train from Waterloo Station to Bournemouth. On arriving at the beautiful coastal city of Bournemouth, we were billeted at the Royal Bath Hotel.

Our days in Bournemouth were filled with a few daily chores, which were not very taxing. We were up early each morning and reported to the Metropole Hotel after breakfast for role call. Then, we assembled for a short march through some streets in town. After the daily parade, we had mail call and checked the bulletin boards at both the Metropole and at our hotel for any announcements. In the afternoon, almost every day, we assembled at a theater around the corner from the Metropole Hotel to listen to new orders, lectures, and other announcements. There, we were also frequently entertained by small troupes from London, which were part of the program to prevent the hundreds of RAF personnel in Bournemouth from becoming bored while waiting for their assignments.

We also gathered at the theater to listen to visiting speakers, civilian dignitaries, and high-ranking officers, who spoke mostly about the Allied war effort. One of the visitors was the distinguished Lord Hugh Montague Trenchard, marshal of the RAF, who had been a fighter pilot with the Royal Flying Corps during World War I. An impressive and forceful personality, the marshal was known as "Boom" because of the loud voice he used when he wanted to press a point. Lord Trenchard, as we learned from his lecture, was the one who had molded the RAF into what it was when the war broke out in 1939. His main goal was to provide the RAF aircrews with as much training as possible. He told us "to serve in the RAF is to serve in one of the finest air forces in the world. You should be proud and you should never forget this. As young pilots you should train yourselves well, and when you are up there fighting the enemy, you should always be aware of the Hun in the sun."

On April 15, 1942, twenty days after our arrival in town, Mims and I had checked the bulletin in our hotel as usual. On the board, we saw both of our names, along with Whitfield's, among those being posted to the Cosford RAF Station to attend officer training school (OTS). Cosford was near Litchfield Park, a few miles north of Birmingham. Those of us affected by the alert visited the center's headquarters to learn the particulars of our assignment, and we were told that in about two days we would depart for Cosford. Two days later, thirty officers, including Mims, Whitfield, myself, and two others from the United States who had been trained in Tulsa, Oklahoma, were on our way to Birmingham.

The weather was lousy on the day of our departure. On the train to London I gazed at the passing English countryside with a somewhat jaundiced eye, as the drizzle continued to fall and the soot from the coal-fired locomotive stuck on the window of our compartment. As I stared outside over the misty countryside, my thoughts were far away in Athens, the place of my birth. How wonderful it would have been if my parents could have seen me now in my RAF uniform. I wanted to write to them about my life in wartime England and how much I loved being in the Royal Air Force, but there was no way to send mail to Axis-occupied Greece. I could only hope that I would survive the war and be able to tell them about my success in person.

OFFICER TRAINING AND FLIGHT SCHOOL

The curriculum at Cosford was divided into two phases: outdoor activities and classroom lectures and presentations. The field training was broken into two segments: calisthenics before breakfast and squad drilling, including marching, command orders, saluting, and parading, after breakfast. Pistol firing was introduced during the later part of the course. This training kept us busy, and the daily exercise not only made us fit but also prompted us to retire early each night.

The classroom sessions were always held in the afternoon. The first lecture we heard was about the RAF's present organization and equipment, customs, traditions, rules and regulations, uniform, salutes, and grades and ranks, in relation to the other services of Allied nations. The part of the lecture that impressed me most, and which I have remembered ever since, was about the Royal Air Force's history.

England's air force was born on April 1, 1911, when an air battalion of the Royal Engineers was first established. A year later, in April 1912, the Royal Flying Corps (RFC) was formed and absorbed the air battalion into its organization. The RFC then was split into two entities: a naval wing and a land-based wing. Later on, the naval wing became the Royal Naval Air Service (RNAS). In April 1918, the RFC and the RNAS merged to form the Royal Air Force (RAF), the largest air force in the world.

By November 1918, when the armistice ending World War I was signed, the RAF had some 190 operational squadrons at home and overseas, some 27,000 officers, and over 263,000 other ranks. It had 22,600 airplanes of all kinds and 103 airships that operated from some 700 aerodromes in England and overseas. In 1936, the RAF Volunteer Reserve (VR) was established to augment its strength—no doubt in preparation for the clouds of war that had begun to appear on the horizon.

Upon completion of our training at Cosford, at the end of May 1942, our group of thirty New Zealanders, Canadians, South Africans, British, Australians, and Americans was assigned to the 5(P) Advanced Flying Unit (AFU) at the Tern-Hill RAF Station in Shropshire. Tern-Hill was located west of Birmingham, and since we were close to our new station, an RAF bus transported us there. At Tern-Hill, we attended flight training that was quite unlike the Polaris flight training back in California. Instead of flying American training aircraft, we flew British planes such as the Hurricane and Milemaster III. The Hurricane was a one-seater that had been used extensively in the Battle of Britain. The Milemaster III was a great pleasure to fly because it resembled the AT-6 I had flown at Polaris. It was easier to fly than the AT-6, however, with its 850 horsepower engine and wide landing gear.

Flying the Hurricane was an adventure all of us at Tern-Hill were looking forward to. On June 14, 1942, I spotted my name on the bulletin board; I was scheduled to fly the Hurricane the following day. I had studied the pilot's manual and had spent a few hours in the Hurri's cockpit and felt that I was ready. The

89

following morning, after an early breakfast, I rode a truck to the flight line with the other pilots scheduled to fly that morning. We were dropped off by the pilots' hut to check in and pick up our parachutes. The sergeant behind the counter said to me,

"Sir, you are flying Hurri number Y7168. Flying Officer Hutchinson is by the aircraft waiting for you. Your call sign for this flight is Penguin-13."

"Many thanks," I said to the sergeant while slinging my chute over my shoulder.

I found Mr. Jack Hutchinson and saluted him. He saluted back and remarked, "You'll have a good day to fly up there. The blue sky is waiting for you."

The crew chief took my chute and placed it in the cockpit as I started the outside aircraft inspection, with Mr. Hutchinson following closely behind. Then I dropped into the Hurricane's cockpit. Mr. Hutchinson closely observed every move I made inside the cockpit. With his help, I strapped myself in and prepared to fly. I adjusted my seat and rudder pedals, put my helmet on, plugged into my oxygen tank, and connected the radio. Then, cautiously, I went through the cockpit checklist I had memorized before firing up the Merlin V-12 power plant. Mr. Hutchinson jumped off the Hurricane's wing, and said, "Good luck, Mr. Pisanos!"

There I was, alone, in the cockpit of the Hurricane, the most powerful flying machine I had ever sat in, facing a daunting array of switches, knobs, handles, dials, buttons, and instruments—more than I had ever dealt with before. I began to feel the sweat running, first on my face, then down my spine. I looked at the crew chief, who was standing by, waiting anxiously for my signal to start the engine. I gave him a thumbs up, indicating that I was ready. He replied aloud, "All clear."

"Contact," I said and pressed the starting button. The propeller began to turn slowly until suddenly, with a loud roar, the Merlin engine caught. The Hurri vibrated a little at first, but a few seconds later, it started to run smoothly.

On my signal, the crew chief unplugged the starter trolley and pulled it away. I gave him the signal to pull the chocks, and I saw Mr. Hutchinson give me a thumbs-up send off. The crew chief signaled that all was clear ahead. I opened the throttle slowly, and the Hurricane responded without hesitation. I began to taxi toward the end of the runway, zigzagging all the way, since the long nose of the Hurri prevented the pilot from looking straight ahead.

At the end of the runway, I pulled off by the taxiway, applied the brakes, and checked the engine. It sounded good. I went through the pre-takeoff checklist I had memorized and glanced at the instruments. I was ready for takeoff.

"Hello, Tern-Hill Control, this is Penguin-13, ready for takeoff."

"Roger, Penguin-13. You are clear for takeoff," Control responded. "Watch out for traffic east of the aerodrome."

"Roger, Control," I replied.

I taxied onto the runway, lined up the Hurri, and applied the brakes. At the same time, I revved up the engine to full power and then released the brakes. Immediately, I felt the enormous 1,280-horsepower Merlin engine pulling me forward with a tremendous jolt. The Hurricane at first swung a little to the left, then to the right, but I was able to correct this with the rudder. By this time the tail came up, the nose dropped down, and I had the runway ahead in full view.

As the Hurri rolled down the runway, I kept it straight with gentle rudder corrections. Finally, after a short takeoff roll, I pulled the stick back and the Hurricane became airborne gracefully. As I crossed the aerodrome boundary, I took my hand off the throttle and placed it on the stick. Then, with my right hand, I reached for the handle to raise the undercarriage. I was astonished by the stick's sensitivity; the Hurri began to bounce all over the sky. I realized I had to be gentler with the stick when I switched hands to work the gear.

I was satisfied after a quick check of the instruments that all was A-OK. I then reduced power and started to climb. My heart was beating fast with excitement and nervousness. More sweat crawled down my face, and my mouth was completely dry. In no time I was at 20,000 feet, an altitude I had never reached before. I leveled off and started to look around; I had no idea where I was. The aerodrome from which I had taken off had disappeared, and things on the ground looked like tiny specks. I was going higher and faster than I ever had before. I adjusted the throttle to cruising air speed and started to enjoy the wonders of the sky.

After I had cruised around for a while and had found my position in relation to the aerodrome, I felt confident enough to try some acrobatics. I stalled the plane with both power on and off. I rolled left and right and then went for a loop. I dropped the Hurri's nose down, and in no time I was clocking 380 miles per hour. I pulled the stick back smoothly and opened the throttle to full power. The Merlin engine responded enthusiastically, and the Hurri came over the top beautifully. I rolled over, then did some dives and pullups, and ended with wingovers. After all of these gyrations, I felt confident with the Hurricane and decided to return to the aerodrome to see if I could land the machine without smashing it into the ground.

"Hello, Tern-Hill Control. This is Penguin-13. Request landing instructions. Over."

"Roger, Penguin 13. You are cleared to land. Runway 27, report on downwind," Control replied.

When I joined the local traffic pattern, I went through my pre-landing check on the downwind leg and reported my position to Control. I opened the canopy, and as I turned toward the base, I dropped the undercarriage and flaps. I checked the gear, which was down and locked. As I entered the base leg, I cut my power slightly and let the Hurri drop down. On the final approach, I let the machine glide on its own. When I crossed the aerodrome boundary, the runway was just ahead, wide open. Then, just a few feet beyond the beginning of the runway, I checked my air speed—ninety-five miles per hour—and prepared to touch down. I pulled the throttle back to idle and waited a few seconds for the Hurri to lose its final flying speed. When that happened I gently pulled back the spade-grip stick and held it there for a three-point landing.

The Hurri jolted a bit as it settled down onto the runway. I let it coast for a while and then started to work the brakes smoothly. Once the Hurri had slowed down, I taxied to the end of the runway, zigzagging all the way to the flight line. Finally, with the assistance of the crew chief, I parked the Hurri on its assigned stall, where Flight Officer Hutchinson waited for me.

He climbed onto the left wing, leaned over the cockpit, and helped me unbuckle my straps. When I took off my helmet, he said, "Congratulations, Spiro! You made it! And your landing was a perfect three-pointer."

Eventually, I accumulated twenty-five hours of flying in the Milemaster and Hurricane at Tern-Hill, and on June 19, 1942, I completed the course. When I received my course completion papers, I noticed two entries therein. One had been made by Flying Officer Piston, the chief instructor. He wrote after my last check ride, "Very keen and is determined to do well." Wing Commander Mark Lowe, the commanding officer of No. 5(P) AFU, made the second entry: "Above average." I knew that I was almost ready for combat.

CHAPTER 10

GATHERING OF EAGLES

On June 20, twenty men from our class of thirty departed Tern-Hill for our new assignment to the 41 Operational Training Unit (OTU) at Old Sarum Aerodrome, near the historic town of Salisbury in southern England. Among the group destined for Old Sarum were the five Americans: Pilot Officers Joe Dingwall and Bill Swain, who had been trained in Tulsa under the RAF American Training Program, and Mims, Whitfield, and me, from Polaris.

Since we didn't have to report to our new duty station until the following evening, the five of us, along with some others, spent the night in London at the Eagle Club's dormitory, an old Victorian-style house that provided accommodations for Americans serving in the RAF. The next day, we took a train from Waterloo Station to Salisbury, where we discovered that Old Sarum was a beautifully landscaped grass aerodrome that was known as the Army Cooperation College. The school was equipped with three types of aircraft: Harvard AT-6s, Mustang P-51As, and Tomahawk P-40s, all American-built machines.

Our first day of instruction at 41 OTU began with a briefing on Army and RAF tactical organizations and procedures used by the RAF in the support of ground forces in the field. The briefing covered methods and techniques used in low-level reconnaissance missions; weapons, armaments, and tactical vehicles used by the Army in the battlefield; low-level targeting, location, and identification and the use of a special code to report exact geographical position; and, finally, the search for a target from the air. The flying syllabus we followed included how to check the aircraft before the flight, local orientation, low-level cross-country formation, acrobatics, aerial dogfighting using a cine camera, and the art of attacking railroad stock, moving and stationary, particularly destroying locomotives. All these training missions were first conducted in the Harvard aircraft along with an instructor, then repeated by the student while flying in the AT-6, P-51, or the P-40.

I had studied the Mustang, but before my first flight, I devoted some time sitting in the cockpit, teaching myself to locate, with my fingertips and while blindfolded, the most essential gadgets, from left to right. I practiced this process until I had become fully familiar with the machine. I asked Pilot Officer Dingwall to watch me one day. He wasn't impressed and said, with a smile, that the exercise was a waste of time. I disagreed. My instructor, Flight Officer Coddington, had said once at the mess, when we were discussing low-level flying, "When flying on the deck below treetop level at 400 miles per hour, you don't dare to take your eyes from the outside environment to look at an instrument or locate a switch inside the cockpit. Your eyes must be glued to your surroundings at all times. And that, my friend, is the secret to survival while flying on the deck."

The Mustang was a formidable flying machine for ground strafing. It was equipped with a 12-cylinder V-1710 Allison engine that produced some 1,150 horsepower. Its armament was comprised of either two .50-caliber and four .303 machine guns or four 20-milimeter cannons. The aircraft carried more internal fuel than its rival fighters. Its top speed was 390 miles per hour at low altitudes, greater than any other RAF fighter.

In the early morning hours of July 9, 1942, a cloudless and brilliant day for flying, I was the first in our group to fly the Mustang, after a briefing by our instructor. I took the Mustang up to 10,000 feet and put it through several gyrations. Then, I dove the aircraft toward Salisbury Plains and, down on the deck, at some 350 miles per hour, zigzagging below the treetops. I was in the air for more than an hour before I landed back at Old Sarum.

I continued to fly the Mustang, and the more I flew it the more confident in it I became. I eventually felt I could hurl the machine into any imaginable maneuver and recover easily. The American-built aircraft could not outmaneuver the British Spitfire but could outrun it on the deck, at extremely low altitude. It had the ruggedness of an army tank and a firing platform that could cause substantial damage to targets on the ground. As long as the coolant system wasn't punctured or the body and wings didn't suffer catastrophic damage, the Mustang would bring you home.

At Old Sarum, I also flew the P-40 Tomahawk, but I didn't find that machine as impressive. Its engine had a tendency to overheat easily. Although I flew the P-40 several times during training, I avoided it as much as possible in favor of the Mustang. During the forty-six training flights I had at 41 OTU, I accumulated some sixty hours in the air, nineteen in the AT-6, four in the Tomahawk, and thirty-seven in the Mustang. By the end of our training, the others in my group and I felt confident that we could handle all three of the airplanes with skill.

Still, accidents happened. On the afternoon of July 26, 1942, Pilot Officer Dingwall was killed while flying a Mustang on a low-level reconnaissance training mission. Eyewitnesses close to the accident site informed the station authorities that the aircraft was flying extremely low over the terrain and plowed into a hillside. Dingwall was the first American close to me to die in an aircraft accident during my time in the RAF, and his death was a terrible shock. I realized then that I needed to keep all of my aviation skills as sharp as possible; I needed not just to avoid enemy fire but also to fly my plane as well as possible at all times.

268 SQUADRON RAF

On July 28, 1942, most of us received our assignments to RAF army cooperation squadrons throughout England. I was posted to the 268 Army Cooperation Squadron at Snailwell RAF Station in Newmarket, and at the end of July, I said good-bye to my Old Sarum classmates, to the school staff, and to the ground crews who maintained the aircraft. After a pleasant train ride to London, I caught a taxi to the American Eagle Club; spoke directly to Mrs. Mary Dexter, the woman in charge of the club; and reserved a bed at the dormitory by Knightsbridge. On my way out of the dormitory, I almost collided with my old Polaris classmate and friend K. D. Peterson in the company of a squadron leader. The two men had Eagle Squadron patches on their shoulders.

"Pete, you rascal," I exclaimed as we hugged each other at this unexpected meeting.

"Oh, say, Spiro, this is Sqn. Ldr. Chesley Peterson, commanding officer of 71 Eagle Squadron. This is Plt. Off. Spiro Pisanos, my classmate from Polaris," KD told the squadron leader, "the guy I was telling you about."

I had heard of Chesley Peterson but had never before had a chance to meet him. I shook his hand, and the three of us walked up to the coffee shop. As we sat down, the squadron leader said, "So, you are the Greek fellow KD speaks highly of."

Before I had a chance to answer, KD broke in and said, "Hey, Spiro, you don't want to go to war flying Mustangs. You should join one of the Eagle Squadrons and fly Spitfires. Squadron Leader Peterson is looking for some new pilots, and he could use you."

"We sure can," Squadron Leader Peterson said, "since you are a Polaris graduate. Do you want to come to Debden?"

"Yes, Sir, I do," I replied. "I have wanted to fly the Spitfire ever since I left Polaris."

The squadron leader said he would try to have me transferred from the 268 Squadron to the 71 Squadron. I gave him my name, rank, and serial number, and thanked him for his help in advance. When we finished our coffee, Squadron Leader Peterson had to leave. KD and I retired to the lounge, where we sat and talked about the days we spent at Polaris and our voyage crossing the North Atlantic to Glasgow. Later on, KD had to leave to return to base.

The next day I awoke with a great feeling of elation because I was on my way to report for duty at an RAF fighter squadron. On the train ride to Newmarket, the cloudless, sunny sky helped me appreciate the peaceful, green, rolling hills of the English countryside, the people working on the farms, and the victory gardens, as the train sped through the countryside. After arriving at Newmarket, I caught an RAF van to Snailwell Aerodrome in the outskirts of town. As the van was cruising inside the aerodrome on its way to the squadron headquarters, I noticed a number of Mustangs parked along the way. After a short ride, the van finally stopped in front of a building identified as the headquarters of the 268 Army Cooperation Squadron, RAF.

When I entered the building, I went straight to the adjutant's office, where I introduced myself to a flight lieutenant.

"Welcome aboard," he said, as he checked me in. "Your two class-mates from OTU, Bill Sinclair and Chappy Chapman, are already in."

He gave me a short briefing about the squadron, before taking me to the commanding officer's office to meet the squadron's boss, Wing Commander Andy Anderson.

I saluted the wing commander and said, "Sir, Pilot Officer Pisanos, reporting for duty."

"Welcome to the squadron," said the wing commander. He told me that I'd be assigned to the B flight under Flight Lieutenant Ben Griffin, whom I would meet later. Griffin would show me around the squadron and explain squadron policy, tactics, and standard operating procedures. Before leaving the wing commander's office, he told the adjutant to ar-range for a transport to take me to the billeting office in town, a private residence that the RAF had taken over for the duration of the war. The same transport that had brought me to the aerodrome earlier took me into town.

My billet was an impressive three-story building that appeared to be a huge villa. When I walked into the foyer, I was impressed with the building's interior appearance. It had a huge dining room, a large lounge, and a bar stocked with many kinds of liquor. I was given a room fur-nished with two beds and with its own well-decorated tile bathroom. One of the beds was already occupied by Chappy Chapman, my class-mate from OTU.

Since the 268 Squadron had been recently equipped with sixteen Mustangs, some of the assigned pilots were undergoing a crash training program to learn to fly the new machines. Chapman, Sinclair, and I jumped into the training at once, and in a short time we learned takeoffs and landings in two-, four-, six-, and twelve-aircraft formations; tail chasing, acrobatics, and low-level reconnaissance; and air-to-sea and air-to-ground attacks.

On occasions when we flew as a single- or two-aircraft element, we'd jump at Spitfires flying at low altitudes in the vicinity of Cam-bridge, probably from the stations of Debden and Duxford, the two nearby aerodromes with Spitfires. Above 10,000 feet, our Mustangs couldn't compete with the Spitfires, but below that level we could leave them in the dust.

In the middle of August, the squadron deployed to Weston-Zoyland Camp for two days of air-to-air firing practice, the last part of our training before we new pilots could be declared combat ready. The camp provided a high-wing Westland Lysander aircraft for target towing, and we made aerial deflection attacks from various angles with live ammunition on the towed drogue. I enjoyed this part of our training the most. On two occasions I shot the drogue off into the sea, and after my second success, Wing Commander Anderson said to me, "That's enough firing training for you, Mr. Pisanos. Let the others do some practice before the camp runs out of drogues."

After two days of extensive aerial firing practice, the squadron returned to Snailwell and was declared operational the following day. On August 20, I flew my first combat flight with three other aircraft over the North Sea to Holland. I flew in the number two position to Flight Lieutenant Griffin.

As we crossed the enemy coast into Holland, Griffin and I separated from the other element and headed south. We penetrated into enemy territory low over the ground, looking for targets of opportunity. We were directed to attack passenger train locomotives and all cars on freight trains. We flew for several minutes on a north-south pattern a few miles along the Dutch coast but did not see anything worth attacking. As we headed back over the North Sea, however, we ran into two patrol boats flying the German flag heading north.

"Blue Two," my flight leader radioed. "Let's make a quick pass at them, but be careful—they probably have plenty of firepower. You take the first one, and I'll go after the other."

"Roger, Blue One," I replied.

I turned sharply right to place my Mustang in a position to approach the leading boat from the west, at a ninety-degree angle. I pointed the nose of the Mustang directly at the leading patrol boat. I could see that Griffin had already engaged the other patrol boat and had hit it several times. At about 350 yards and closing fast, I opened fire with everything my Mustang had. As I passed to the right of the patrol boat, I observed pieces of debris flying from the target. I dropped down and flew a few feet above the water, zigzagging to avoid being hit by the return fire from the two boats. I could see tracers from their guns splashing in the water to my left and right, but none of the rounds hit my plane. The zigzagging must have paid off.

When we were well west of the two boats, my flight leader called on the radio: "Blue Two, are you all right?"

"Yes, I'm OK," I replied.

Eventually, we landed back at Snailwell. After parking our aircraft, I walked over to my flight commander's Mustang and we both had a look at his aircraft, which he thought may have been hit by the German boats. We found no damage. Our two comrades who had flown north of our route had returned without finding any worthy targets.

On my next mission, I had the chance to fire at a prime land target: a locomotive. Chappy strafed it first, and then I opened fire with all my guns. As I flew past the locomotive and turned slightly to the right to avoid some flying debris, I saw a big explosion with rising smoke. I heard Chappy on the radio saying "Did you see that?"

"I sure did!" I exclaimed.

"Let's get out of here, now," he said.

We crossed the enemy coast on the deck and headed for home. As we were pulling away, we could still see the rising smoke from the burning locomotive. We landed just in time to beat a rolling bank of fog that was moving in from the west. That night Chappy and I had a drink at the bar to celebrate the destruction of our first locomotive.

AN UNEXPECTED CALL

A few days later, when we were grounded because of heavy fog, I was called to the phone.

"This is Pilot Officer Pisanos," I said.

The caller answered in accented English. "This is Wing Commander Yannis Kinatos of the Royal Hellenic Air Force, calling from Claridge's Hotel in London. I am the air force aide to King George II of Greece, currently in exile," he said.

The wing commander, in both English and Greek, said that he had learned from the Air Ministry that I was assigned to the 268 Fighter Squadron, and because I was a Greek national, he was going to request my release from the RAF so that I could be sent to Egypt. There, he said, I would join a Hellenic Air Force Spitfire squadron that the Greek exiled government was trying to organize, with the help of the RAF. He asked me to come to his office at Claridge's Hotel at the earliest opportunity, so that he could provide me with more details.

My initial reaction to this news was anxiety. I had no idea what the exiled Greek air force had in mind for me and didn't know how I could avoid joining the group. But I had no choice; I had to go to London and tell this man that I had no desire to leave the RAF and that I wasn't interested in going to Egypt.

When I explained my situation to Flight Lieutenant Griffin, he said, "I'd suggest that you dash off to London tomorrow before your countrymen take you away and make you an Egyptian."

He gave me a big smile, which failed to reassure me.

The following day I caught an early train to London to visit Kinatos. I found Claridge's Hotel in town and his room on the fourth floor. When I entered the room, I faced a middle-aged man with partially gray hair, wearing the royal Hellenic Air Force blue-gray uniform. I saluted the wing commander and introduced myself. He offered me a seat by his desk and began asking me questions. He wanted to know my full name, my birthplace, my school in Greece, and my flight school. He again explained how the exiled government was planning to form a Hellenic Air Force squadron equipped with Spitfires, provided it could locate enough Greek pilots.

"Sir," I said when he finished his speech, "I don't know what to say. I have requested to be transferred to the 71 Eagle Squadron in the RAF, and I believe they are in the process of taking action on this matter." I had hardly finished when the wing commander broke in.

"You mean to tell me that you aren't interested in joining the Greek squadron?"

"In a way, no, Sir," I said. "I want to stay here in England with the

RAF and eventually, when the war is over, return to America and become a citizen of that country. I do not wish to go to Egypt or join any Hellenic Air Force squadron."

Once I had explained myself, I asked to be excused from Kinatos's office.

"You are welcome to go," the wing commander said in an icy tone. "I don't know what the king will have to say about this. I am certain we will pursue this matter further."

I saluted the commander and left his office expeditiously. I immediately caught a taxi and headed for the Eagle Club.

To my vast relief, when I asked Mrs. Dexter that afternoon how I could get in touch with Squadron Leader Peterson at Debden Aerodrome, she replied, "Laddie, you wouldn't find him there because he is here in town. I'll get him on the phone for you at the number he left with me."

She dialed the number and handed the phone to me.

"Hello, Sir, this is Pilot Officer Spiro Pisanos. Do you remember me?"

"I sure do," he said. "Did you get your assignment to the 71 Squadron?"

"No, Sir, not yet, but a problem that just came up could probably block my move from the 268 Squadron. I'd like to see you, Sir, and get your advice. Is it possible that we could meet somewhere, Sir?"

"Sure," he said, "Why don't you meet me at the lobby of the Regent Palace Hotel at about noon? We could have lunch there, and you can brief me then."

I was waiting anxiously in the hotel lobby when Squadron Leader Peterson walked in just before noon. We greeted one another and shook hands.

"I am surprised you haven't heard anything about your transfer. Fighter Command personnel assured me that they were going to take care of it when I talked to them in early August. I'll check again upon my return to Debden the day after tomorrow. Now what's the problem you wanted to talk to me about?" he asked.

I explained to the squadron leader exactly what had taken place at Claridge's. He saw how upset I was and assured me that the Hellenic Air Force would not be able to take me without my consent. The RAF had trained me and wanted to keep me. The squadron leader would go to Fighter Command himself and make sure I was posted to the 71 Squadron.

Toward the end of our lunch, the squadron leader told me, "By the way, I am not the commanding officer of the 71 Squadron anymore. I have turned the squadron over to Gus Daymond, a highly qualified leader. He is well liked by the pilots and cares about his people."

"And you? What are you going to do now?" I asked, a bit dismayed by Peterson's change in status.

"Well," he said, "all three Eagle Squadrons will be transferred to the 4th Fighter Group of the U.S. Army Air Force and remain at Debden. The group will be commanded by Col. Edward Anderson, and he and General Hunter of 8th Air Force Fighter Command have asked me to be the group's deputy for operations." The transfer would take place at the end of September or early October.

After lunch, I thanked Peterson for the meal and his efforts to transfer me into the 71 ES. As we prepared to leave the dining room, the squadron leader said, "The men who attended Polaris Flight Academy with you and who are now assigned to 71 and 133 Eagle Squadrons speak highly of you and feel that you should be at Debden as well. I'll see what I can do to get you there."

I walked away from the Regent Palace feeling that despite the Greek military's efforts, Peterson would keep me in the RAF. As I took the train back to Newmarket, I prayed that my transfer would be arranged as soon as possible, before the Hellenic Air Force started putting pressure on the RAF. I feared that the king of Greece might personally demand that I be assigned to the squadron in Egypt, even though it really didn't exist. I knew that as long as I was a Greek national the Greek government had a claim on me.

In the days that followed, I flew a number of missions during which I had the chance to fire my guns against enemy targets in Holland. I fired at locomotives, coastal shipping, and other targets of opportunity, such as a military camp we strafed one day while the soldiers were lined up for lunch. But, I became increasingly puzzled by the fact that we had not encountered a single enemy aircraft during the several missions we flew over enemy territory. We itched to go on some missions over France, but it was not our sector, so we had to be content with flying over Holland, hoping someday we'd run into some Luftwaffe fighters and shoot it out.

I waited breathlessly for news about my possible move to Debden. Finally, one day at the beginning of September, Wing Commander Anderson informed me about my immediate reassignment. I told him that the Hellenic Air Force in exile had threatened to move me to a Greek squadron in Egypt and that strings had been pulled to get me into the 71 Eagle Squadron at Debden to block the exiled Greek government's attempt to claim me.

"I hate to see you go, Mr. Pisanos," my commanding officer said. "Griffin has reported that you have adapted well to combat operations. I have no choice in your transfer, but I do wish you the best."

The next day I said farewell to my friends in the squadron, including Chappy, who dropped me off at the railway station with my duffle bag while on his way to the aerodrome.

"Let's keep in touch, Spiro," Chappy said, as we shook hands. "If you get a chance, fly into Snailwell with your Spit and I'll fly into Debden with a Mustang."

"It's a deal," I said.

71 EAGLE SQUADRON RAF

Debden Aerodrome was a prewar facility with two runways in an approximate orientation, east-west and north-south. It was used extensively as a fighter aerodrome during the Battle of Britain and was now used exclusively by the 71 Eagle Squadron.

The pilots in the 71 ES, as well as those in the other two Eagle Squadrons—121 and 133—were all Americans, except for the few English pilots who were attached to the squadrons for short periods. These Americans had come from across the United States and were a cross section of the U.S. population. Some were single and a few were married. They were students, teachers, clerks, social workers, locomotive engineers, factory workers, mechanics, department store workers, commercial pilots, and taxi drivers.

When I entered the 71 Squadron's headquarters building, I found

Squadron Leader Peterson standing by the door of his office, talking to a tall, husky RAF wing commander, who apparently was about to leave. Squadron Leader Peterson noticed me and waved for me to come forward.

"Come on over, Spiro," he said, "and meet Wg. Cdr. Duke Woolley."

Pete told the wing commander I had just arrived on station to join the 71 Squadron.

"Good to have you aboard," said the wing commander as he excused himself, telling Peterson that he'd see him at the mess later in the evening.

After the wing commander had gone, Pete invited me into his small office and said, smiling, "I am glad to see you here, Spiro. You made it at last." He lit his pipe and added, "But let me tell you what it took to get you here."

Pete had decided to take on the might of the Royal Hellenic Air Force, such as it was, and went to see Squad Leader Pete Wyckham at Fighter Command, who was responsible for personnel assignments. Wyckham had resisted the Greek demand that the RAF release me and was backed up by his superiors, who felt that to give away a trained fighter pilot for an assignment to a nonexistent air force squadron didn't make sense. Fighter Command did some fast maneuvering before a representative of the Greek government in exile visited the Air Ministry to personally ask for my release from the RAF.

"Since you're here now, they will have to call us in order to get you," my benefactor told me. "And they will be in for one hell of a fight which they won't win!"

I thanked Peterson profusely for everything he had done for me.

"Steve," Pete said, "think nothing of it. It was my job, as commanding officer of the squadron, to get pilots that I felt would contribute to the fighting and spirit of the organization. Now you go and get settled, and I'll see you this evening at the mess. There you'll meet Squadron Leader Daymond and some of your friends."

The officers' mess that evening was crowded. Quite a few pilots from the 133 Squadron had come over from Great Sampford, the nearby satellite base of Debden, to have dinner because the accommodations at their base were somewhat primitive. My friends from Polaris, K. D. Peterson and Dick Braley, were among the visitors, along with Squadron

Leader Carroll McColpin, the commanding officer of the 133 Squadron, Don Blakeslee, Bob Smith, Don "Snuffy" Smith, Ervin Miller, Joe Bennett, Leroy Gover, Don Nee, and a few others who were scattered throughout the lounge.

K.D. introduced me to a big-framed guy named Don Gentile, when he walked into the lounge. Gentile was a pilot of 133 ES who had attended Polaris in California in an earlier class. He was about six feet tall and well built with broad shoulders. Although Gentile was from Ohio, he had black wavy hair and a Mediterranean olive skin. His father had left Italy for New York at age seventeen. From the moment I met Gentile I liked him. We became the best of friends at Debden Aerodrome.

Squadron Leader Peterson and Squadron Leader Daymond walked into the lounge shortly after I had met Gentile with drinks in their hands. Peterson spotted me standing by the fireplace with K.D. and Gentile and walked over with Daymond, a young dynamic man with piercing eyes. Daymond was slim with black hair and had a well-trimmed mustache that made him look a little older than his age.

Peterson said, with a smile, "Steve, this is Squadron Leader Daymond, your commander."

I shook hands with my new commanding officer and said, "It's a great honor for me, Sir, to join the 71 Squadron, and my gratitude goes to Squadron Leader Peterson for making it possible to have me reassigned here."

"We are glad to have you, Steve," Daymond said. He and Pete excused themselves and walked away to join Wg. Cdr. Duke Woolley, who had walked into the lounge.

I asked Bob Boock, a fellow Polaris graduate, how Squadron Leader Daymond was as a commanding officer, and he told me that Daymond was one of the best, an absolutely fearless fighter in battle. He was already an ace, with eight victories to his credit, and he had been with the 71 ES since it was organized in November 1940.

I made my first visit to the dispersal with Vic France, who was also in 71 ES, and he filled me in on the Spitfire, the squadron, and how they operated in combat. The 71 ES was equipped with eighteen VB Mark Spitfires, powered with Rolls Royce Merlin engines of about 1,470 horsepower. Even though the squadron periodically lent aircraft to the two other Eagle Squadrons for training and operational missions, 71 almost always had twelve Spitfires ready for missions.

The VB Mark Spitfire was equipped with two 20-milimeter Hispano cannons with 120 rounds each, and four .303-inch Browning machine guns with 350 rounds for each gun. The maximum speed of this model was 365 miles per hour at 19,500 feet. Its fully loaded weight was 6,785 pounds, light when compared to other fighters. It had a rate of climb of some 4,750 feet per minute and an operating ceiling of 35,500 feet, but it was a little sluggish at that altitude, France said.

The Spitfire also had a rear view mirror installed outside on top of the windscreen, so that the pilot could spot anyone who might attempt to jump his aircraft from behind. The aircraft was not suitable for night flying because of the blue flames and sparks that came out from the engine exhaust system and interfered with the pilot's night vision. Despite this, the Spitfire was one of the best fighters over the European sky during World War II.

The 71 ES had about twenty-five pilots, including the commanding officer, each assigned to one of two flights, A and B, each with nine aircraft. The two flight commanders at the time I reported to the squadron were Flt. Lt. Bob Sprague in A flight and Flt. Lt. Oscar Coen in B flight. In battle formation the squadron flew in three sections of four aircraft each, in line astern with the assigned colors of red, white, and blue. The commanding officer led the squadron in the white section, and the two flight commanders, or alternates, flew in the red and blue sections. The squadron's aircraft markings, as assigned by Fighter Command, were XR, followed by a letter of the English alphabet for each aircraft.

Vic France then introduced me to the airmen who handled the squadron's operational matters, and I learned that I had been assigned to the A Flight under Flight Lieutenant Sprague, who had appointed Plt. Off. Howard Hively to assist me in my checkout on the Spitfire. France showed me around the dispersal and pointed out the pilot's status board for the A and B flights. And this is how the board looked:

PILOT'S STATUS BOARD

71 EAGLE SQUADRON RAF
SQUADRON LEADER GUS DAYMOND
COMMANDING OFFICER

A Flight

Flight Lieutenant Robert S. Sprague

Flying Officer Richard D. Mcminn

Flying Officer Stanley M. Anderson

Flying Officer Walter J. Hollander

Flying Officer Alfred H. Hopson

Pilot Officer Duane A. Beeson

Pilot Officer Victor J. France

Pilot Officer James C. Harrington

Pilot Officer Anthony J. Seaman

Pilot Officer Howard D. Hively

Pilot Officer Robert L. Priser

Pilot Officer Eugene M. Potter

Pilot Officer Spiro N. Pisanos

B Flight

Flight Lieutenant Oscar H. Coen

Flight Lieutenant Thomas J. Andrews

Flying Officer James A. Clark

Flying Officer John F. Lutz

Flying Officer William B. Morgan

Flying Officer William T. O'Regan

Flying Officer Gilbert G. Ross

Flying Officer Hubert L. Stewart

Pilot Officer Robert A. Boock

Pilot Officer Raymond C. Care

Pilot Officer Henry L. Mills

Pilot Officer Gordon H. Whitlow

Flight Sergeant Vernon A. Boehle

Hively, I learned from France, had acquired the nickname "Deacon" because he occasionally imitated a deacon giving a sermon in the officers' mess. Hively was a great personality imitator and, in addition to the deacon character, did a hilarious imitation of my old hero, Baron von Richthofen. Using a short stick cut from a broom and sitting on a chair on top of the piano in the lounge, Hively mimicked the Baron flying his Fokker triplane during battle. Hively's facial expressions and mock thick German accent made for a hilarious act. Everybody at the station loved him.

Hively and I became friends, and he taught me much about the way the squadron functioned. But my real education in operational flying was from my flight commander, Flt. Lt. Bob Sprague.

"First of all," Sprague told me one day, "the policy in the squadron is teamwork. Individualism in aerial combat doesn't pay. When we are flying over enemy territory, you want to stick close to your flight or element leader. Don't ever leave the formation to go after an enemy aircraft unless someone is covering you. If for some reason you get separated from the formation, like when the squadron is pounced by a superior enemy force, your first aim should be to join up with another aircraft in the squadron or any aircraft from a squadron in the wing. If you can't join with someone, head for home as fast as you can, but don't fly straight and level. Bank your aircraft left and right, check the sky around you, and watch the direction from the sun. You must learn to turn your neck sharply to look above, below, and behind your aircraft. At all times your maximum lookout effort, however, should be devoted to the area behind your aircraft.

108

"If you go after an enemy aircraft, hold your fire until you are close to the target. But, here again, watch your tail, as a friend of the guy you are after may be behind you.

"Should you get jumped while wandering over enemy territory, break into a steep turn against the attacker and try to break up his angle of attack. If the attacker sticks around for a fight, do the best you can to fight your way out.

"You'll be flying in the number four position in the section until you gain some experience. Then you'll move up front slowly.

"If, during a mission, the squadron leader decides to attack an equal or superior enemy force with the entire squadron, the squadron will move into a line astern formation for the attack."

Sprague followed this lecture with a review of the chart posted on the wall, which outlined the different missions the squadron flew:

Rodeo: sweeping over enemy territory

Circus: escorting a small force of twin-engine bombers to a target, normally in France

Sweep: conducting an offensive sweep over enemy territory, with your squadron or with one or two other squadrons

Rhubarb: strafing specific targets, fixed or mobile, or looking around for targets of opportunity (usually conducted by two aircraft)

Convoy Patrol: providing protective cover to shipping convoys over the English Channel or the North Sea (usually conducted by two aircraft)

Ramrod: escorting heavy bombers deep into enemy territory

He also mentioned that our squadron did not usually participate in ramrod missions because the Spitfires lacked long-range capability.

After he briefed me on these basics, my flight commander sent me off on my first flight in a Spitfire. With Hively at my side, I grabbed a parachute and walked to the first Spitfire at the dispersal with the marking XR-K. I walked around this beautifully built Supermarine Spitfire and then climbed on the wing and stepped into the small but comfortable cockpit. Hively climbed up and stood on the wing by the cockpit. Carefully, and with Hively observing every step I made, I buckled my parachute, then strapped myself in the seat and started my memorized checklist, BTFCPPUR: brakes, trim, flaps, controls, petrol, pressures, undercarriage, and radiator. After I had connected the oxygen to my facemask and switched the radio to the tower frequency, I was ready to start the engine.

Hively jumped down from the wing, and I gave a thumbs up to the crew chief, who was standing by the battery cart. "All clear," he said. I pressed the starting button and after the propeller turned a few times the engine burst into life. The engine temperature started to rise slowly. I gave the crew chief the signal to pull the chocks, and he raised his hands and pointed the way out. I called the control tower and was cleared to taxi.

I opened the throttle slightly, and the Spitfire, with its Merlin power plant, started to move forward. I taxied on the perimeter taxiway, zig-zagging for visibility as I had done when I flew the Hurricane and the Mustang. I parked the Spit at the end of the runway and checked the engine. When I received clearance for takeoff, I pushed the throttle to full power and let the Spitfire roll gracefully down the runway.

Hively had told me to "watch the torque, the nose, the stick," and I followed his advice. This kept me busy and I began to feel the sweat on my forehead. The Spit was now accelerating down the runway with a tremendous roaring speed. I made minor corrections with the rudder to compensate for the torque caused by the propeller's rotation. At 100 miles per hour, the Spit flew off the runway and leapt into the air. I raised the gear, closed the radiator and canopy, and started to climb.

I continued climbing past 10,000 feet from Debden toward the north. At 25,000 feet, I leveled off and was surprised at how fast I was traveling through the air. The Spitfire was, indeed, a much more agile aircraft than the old Hurricane, just as my instructor had told me at Tern-Hill. From 25,000 feet, I could pick out Debden and Duxford aerodromes, which looked like small specks on the ground. I could see London in the far distance, protected with a mass of flying barrage balloons. To the east, I could see Newmarket and Snailwell Aerodrome, the home of the 268 Fighter Squadron, where I was first posted out of OTU.

110

Once I had settled in, I put the Spit into some gyrations to acquaint myself with what it could do. First I performed a few stalls. The aircraft responded beautifully, wanting not to stall but rather to continue flying. I did two barrel rolls, one to the left and one to the right. I went for a loop, pushing the nose down and, in no time, clocking over 400 miles per hour. Gently then, I pulled the stick back and, at the same time, pushed the pitch control and throttle forward. The Spit came over the top beautifully. I rolled over at the top of the loop and remained in level flight.

After a while, I descended in the vicinity of Debden and received clearance to land. I flew over the fence at about eighty-five to ninety miles per hour. When I was about to make contact with the runway, I cut the power. Seconds later, I touched down in a three-point landing. I let the Spit roll down the runway for a while and then gently applied brakes, keeping in mind the Spit's narrowly spaced landing gear. I turned off of the runway and taxied to the dispersal, where Hively was waiting for me.

For the next few days I practiced many exercises in the Spit: formation takeoffs and landings; air-to-air combat maneuvers; attacks in the air; and, finally, two-aircraft tail chasing using the gun camera, including air-to-ground firing over the Wash (a shallow area of water off the coast, northeast of Debden). Then, I started to fly on convoy patrols and, later, on missions across the English Channel to France. Fighter sweeps and escorting light bombers were the primary missions that kept the 71 ES busy.

It seemed that during September, more and more U.S. Army Air Force personnel arrived at the aerodrome in preparation, I guessed, for the forthcoming transfer. At the same time, rumors about the transfer were circulating. I heard that the air force bosses in England were planning to break up the three Eagle Squadrons and send some of the most experienced pilots to the fighter groups that would soon begin to arrive in England from the United States. Squadron Leader Peterson was adamantly opposed to this move. In fact, it was said that Peterson told Gen. Carl Spaatz, the commanding general of the 8th Air Force, that the Eagle Squadrons would rather remain in the RAF than be broken up and distributed to the USAAF. Shortly after this rumor circulated, the 8th Air Force issued a statement that once the transfer had occurred the three Eagle Squadrons would remain intact. I also heard that every one of the Eagle Squadron pilots would have to take a physical and be interviewed by a special 8th Air Force board that was ready to convene in London. Of course, no one objected to these requirements. Each one of us pilots would be transferred into the USAAF with the equivalent rank he held in the RAF. And any American pilot could choose to remain in the RAF. Few elected to do so. Pay in the USAAF was about three times what we were making in the RAF. In addition, once we transferred, we'd receive a $10,000 life insurance policy and a $150 uniform allowance.

Squadron Leader Daymond finally passed the word that the transfer would take place and that all pilots of the 71 Squadron should proceed to London, two or three at a time, and take care of the interview and the physical. In a few days most everyone from the squadron, except for a few—including me—had gone through the process in London. Because I was not an American and feared that transferring from the Eagle Squadrons into the USAAF was reserved for American citizens, I delayed my trip to the city. Then, on the morning of September 23, I encountered Squadron Leader Peterson. The squadron leader stopped me and asked, "Have you been to London for the interview yet, Steve?"

I said no.

"You'd better get down there to go through the interview and your physical," he said.

"But, Sir, do you think they'd take me into the U. S. Army since I am not an American citizen?" I asked.

"Yes, they will, because they need every one of us from the three squadrons," Pete said firmly. "Get to London pronto."

I got another swift kick in the rear during breakfast, when Flight Lieutenant Sprague walked in and said, as he looked me in the eyes,

"Steve, you get your ass to London at once, and I mean now. Get the physical and interview out of the way."

I knew that Pete had spoken to Sprague to urge me to go. Even with that sort of encouragement, I felt uncertain about my fate as I rode on the train to London.

I was about to walk into the office, in a building on Grosvenor Square, where the interviews were being held when I ran into Bob Priser and Gordy Whitlow, my two squadron mates, as they were coming out of their interviews. The two pals, graduates of Polaris Academy, had been in London on a short leave and evidently had decided to have their interviews while in town. They both said that the colonels who were running the interview were friendly and that I should not worry.

Once in the office, I was ushered into a small conference room, where I faced three Army Air Force colonels sitting behind a long table. The one in the middle asked me to sit down, introduced himself as Colonel Henry Stovall, and introduced the other two colonels. I was so anxious that I didn't catch either of their names and saluted blindly. I felt like a deer trapped in car headlights.

The question came when they heard my accent. "Are you an American citizen?"

My reply, of course, was no. I gave a brief recap of my background.

"Do you intend to return to the United States to live after the war?" the colonel in the middle asked.

"Sir," I said, "even though I am not an American citizen, I wish with all my heart to join the American air force and fight the Germans for America alongside my friends. My ultimate desire, Sir, is to return to the United States if I survive this conflict and become an American citizen."

The colonel in the middle looked at the other two for a moment and then directed his gaze at me. "Young man," he said, "I am impressed by your ambitions. Based on your RAF rank, would you accept a commission as a second lieutenant in the USAAF?"

"Do you mean, Sir, that I'd also be able to transfer into the Army Air Force?" I asked, as my heart pounded.

"That's correct," Colonel Stovall said. "We are going to need every one of you boys in the Eagle Squadrons."

I had made it! It was clear sailing from there on. I completed and signed a number of papers and passed my physical. By noon, I was out of the building and on my way back to Debden. While in the mess that evening, I was delighted to give the good news to Peterson.

"Sir, you are looking at a future second lieutenant of the USAAF."

"You see, I told you they'd take you," Pete said. "Now if only we could make you a U.S. citizen."

On September 29, 1942, the three Eagle Squadrons were officially transferred to the USAAF. The military ceremony at Debden, held in a light drizzle, was an occasion for us to feel proud; we were leaving one great air force and joining another. Representatives of both air forces gave speeches and showered us with expressions of appreciation, laudatory thanks, and salutes. I listened closely to what was said during the changeover ceremony, and two comments have remained with me ever since. The first one was made by Sir William Sholto Douglas, the head of the Fighter Command, who paid tribute to the departing American volunteers: "It is with deep personal regret that I, today, say good-bye to you, who it has been my privilege to command. You joined us readily and of your own free will when our need was greatest." The other remark that hit home came from Gen. Carl "Tooey" Spaatz, the commanding general of the 8th Air Force, who said, "The operational experience of the Eagle Squadrons is a most valuable asset to the fighter units of the American air force. I welcome you with great sincerity."

It was clear that we, the RAF-trained pilots, were going to play a key role in the air war against Germany. The USAAF bosses were aware of the achievements of the three Eagle Squadrons: seventy-three and one-half enemy aircraft destroyed in the air; of that number, forty-five aerial kills, fifteen and one-half probably destroyed; twenty-four and one-half damaged credited to the 71 Eagle Squadron alone. The 71 Eagle Squadron produced four aces: Chesley Peterson, Gus Daymond, Carrol McColpin, and William Dunn.

The fight against the Germans was no piece of cake for the Americans. Of the ninety-three volunteers who served in the 71 ES the day it was formed (not including the British pilots who were attached to the squadron), twenty-five had been killed in action. Eighteen were killed

113

in accidents, and eleven had become POWs. A handful had been posted to other RAF squadrons, and those who were lucky to survive became members of Uncle Sam's air force. Those of us who had survived the struggle in the skies over Europe continued to fight Germany's Luftwaffe, inspired by memories of our beloved RAF and its people, who were forever in our hearts.

After the ceremony, an airman from the mailroom gave me a letter from the Air Ministry, addressed to Flying Officer Spiro N. Pisanos. At first I thought someone had made a mistake on my rank, but when I opened the letter, I discovered that the Air Ministry had promoted me to the rank of flying officer in the RAF Volunteer Reserve. "What a going-away gift," I thought.

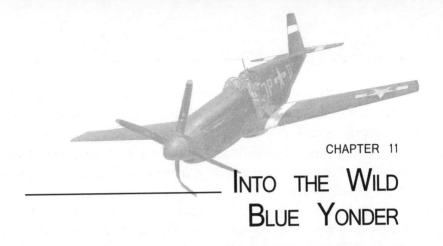

CHAPTER 11

INTO THE WILD BLUE YONDER

The 4th Fighter Group, the organization that absorbed the three RAF Eagle Squadrons into the U.S. Army Air Force, was one of the greatest fighter units in American aviation annals. By the end of the European conflict in May 1945, the 4th Fighter Group had destroyed more enemy aircraft—1,016 in the air and on the ground—than any other U.S. or Allied organization in Europe or the Pacific. This achievement was attained in large part because of the group's outstanding leadership, but teamwork, aggressiveness, dedication, and courage were also essential.

Once the Eagle Squadrons were officially transferred, the first order of business was their metamorphosis into U.S. units. The 71 ES became the 334 Fighter Squadron (FS) of the U.S. Army Air Force and was placed under the command of Maj. Gus Daymond. The 121 ES became the 335 FS and was placed under the command of Maj. James Daley. The 133 ES became the 336 FS and was placed under the command of Maj. Carroll "Red" McColpin. Col. Edward Anderson, a thirty-nine-year-old fighter pilot and able administrator with an extremely pleasant personality, presided over the 4th Fighter Group as a whole. Brig. Gen. Frank "Monk" Hunter, chief of the 8th Fighter Command, who had chosen Anderson for the command, gave verbal orders to Colonel Andy in simple terms: "Lead these seasoned ex-RAF warriors into battle against the Luftwaffe, and destroy it."

Colonel Andy was given a most capable fighter pilot and aerial tactician to assist him on operational matters, Sqn. Ldr. Chesley Peterson, who was promoted to lieutenant colonel and assumed the title Deputy Group Commander. Colonel Pete was highly respected and admired by all at Debden. He was, without doubt, the most experienced fighter pilot to come out of the three RAF Eagle Squadrons, an ace with six RAF-confirmed victories.

By arrangement between the RAF and the 8th Fighter Command, Colonel Anderson was given authority to retain Wg. Cdr. Duke Woolley, a capable tactician and proven RAF combat commander with eleven victories to his credit. The wing commander, who had led the three Eagle Squdrons into battle, led the 4th Group for a while to make the transition easier. Then Woolley and Colonel Pete began alternating leading the 4th Group on operational missions. Upon Woolley's departure, the burden of leading the 4th Group fell on Colonel Pete alone.

On the few occasions when Wing Commander Woolley or Colonel Peterson did not lead escort or strafing missions, they assigned alternate squadron commanders to take their place. Squadron commanders often turned over their command to flight commanders. And, similarly, flight commanders could turn over their command to element leaders. Passing command opportunities down the ranks was an RAF tradition designed to allow pilots to gain experience leading fighter formations into combat.

Our leaders were assigned a tough task. They had inherited from the RAF a bunch of irregulars who didn't even know how to march in a military formation. They showed us how to salute, wear our new uniforms properly, behave on the station and in public as American officers, and adhere to U.S. military customs, bit by bit. Our bosses were American instead of British. We had generals leading us instead of air marshals—generals who had started in the aviation field with the U.S. Army Air Service when it was in its infancy in 1918.

Because no American fighter aircraft were available to equip the newly formed 4th Fighter Group, London and Washington agreed that the group would retain, for the time being, the Spitfires that were assigned to the three Eagle Squadrons. We also kept our own personal flying equipment, including parachutes, flying suits, Mae Wests, helmets, and ground support equipment, and a good number of RAF administrative and maintenance personnel. The small cadre of American maintenance personnel initially assigned to the group worked side by side with their RAF counterparts and, immediately after the transfer, painted the American markings over the RAF roundel on each one of our Spitfires. We retained, for the time being, the RAF aircraft letter designations: XR for 334 Squadron, AV for 335, and WD for 336.

The conduct of the air war after we had transferred into the USAAF was business as usual. The flying procedures and tactics we used remained the same as those we had been trained for and had employed while in the RAF. We continued to fly convoy patrols and fighter sweeps, to escort small numbers of light RAF bombers, and to conduct low-level rhubarb missions as before.

The area of our operations also remained the same: the coastal areas of northern France, to the south as far as the cities of Lille, Amiens, and Rouen and to the west as far as the Cotentin Peninsula. However, as when we were under RAF command, the 4th Group, with its three Spitfire-equipped squadrons, was prevented from operating deep in enemy territory because the Spitfire's radius of action was only 175 miles out and back from the point of takeoff and the Luftwaffe's fighter strength at the time was far superior in number to the combined RAF and 4th Group Spitfire Squadrons.

In October 1942, the German air force had concentrated more fighters (ME-109s and FW-190s) in northern France than in any other area in Western Europe. Some of the Luftwaffe's top aces were with the Schlageter JG-26 unit at Abbeville Aerodrome and with other units scattered at aerodromes throughout northwestern France.

On typical fighter sweeps, the moment we crossed over Dover, climbing toward the French coast and maintaining radio silence, our 11th Group controller would report the approach of enemy aircraft to our leader: "Hello, Blackjack Leader. Neptune calling. You have bandits in a force of approximately fifty, climbing from the south and heading your direction."

Our leader would acknowledge the message, and minutes later, we would get another report: "Blackjack Leader, from Neptune, bandits appear to be in the force of seventy-five plus, climbing from the west and heading in your direction."

These reports would often be followed by another: "Hello, Blackjack

Leader. This is Neptune. Bandits in the force of eighty-five plus, climbing from the east in your direction."

In short, we would often have over one hundred German fighters rising to meet our challenges; nevertheless, the presence of the 4th Group and the other larger RAF fighter force kept the JG-26 boys from Abbeville and the other Luftwaffe units from the surrounding German bases in check. They kept their distance, and we kept ours.

118

Our superiors, however, encouraged us to press on whenever possible to harass the Luftwaffe, in the air and on the ground.

"We must ultimately destroy the enemy fighter force if we are to gain air superiority over Europe," General Hunter told us in our lounge one evening, during one of his frequent visits to Debden.

As the end of October approached, Don Gentile and I decided to take a few days' leave to visit London, to have some fun, and to check on the reports that the London clothiers had begun to receive shipments of ready-made U.S. Army uniforms. As it was, all of us were still wearing the RAF uniforms because the army uniforms were not available at the time we transferred to the USAAF.

After we arrived in London and checked in at the Regent Palace Hotel, we dropped our gear in our room and walked to the American Eagle Club coffee shop for lunch. There, we treated ourselves with hamburgers, french fries, and cokes. As we were munching our burgers, we decided it would be fun to catch a train for Bournemouth, our old stomping ground, in the morning.

That afternoon, before we left London, we visited the Austin Reed Clothiers to see if the American army uniforms they were expecting had arrived. It turned out that the store had received the uniforms just two days earlier. We were fitted for our new uniforms, and because the trousers and jackets needed some minor alterations, we told the tailor we'd be back to pick everything up in two days. He assured us that our uniforms with their accessories would be ready then.

Early in the morning the next day, Gentile and I caught the train to Bournemouth, where we spent our leave dancing in nightclubs and dining at the RAF Royal Bath Hotel. Our uniforms were ready for us when we returned to London, as promised.

On October 20, 1942, 334 Squadron experienced its first casualty. We lost Lt. Tony Seaman over the English Channel during a convoy patrol mission. Seaman's wingman, Lt. Alfred "Hoppy" Hopson, reported on his return to Debden, "We were on our last lap over the convoy when Tony called me on the radio to tell me that his engine was acting strange. I told him that we should head for home to check it out. Suddenly, Tony's Spitfire exploded in the air in front of me. I screamed at Tony to get out, but he gave no response, and the Spitfire plunged straight into the channel in a ball of fire. I switched over to the Air Sea Rescue channel, gave "Mayday," and circled the spot where Tony's Spit went in. I saw no sign of Tony on the surface of the sea; the aircraft had sunk immediately, evidently with Tony still in the cockpit."

While coming to terms with the loss of Seaman, we continued to fly on missions when the weather permitted. During November, the 4th Group, along with some RAF squadrons, flew escort missions to northern France for RAF medium bombers and, frequently, small numbers of the newly arrived American B-17 heavy bombers. We also flew some diversion sweeps for RAF bombing raids in northern France. Of course, convoy patrols continued to be the daily bread and butter for all three squadrons. In addition, we flew a few rhubarb missions inside the French coast, looking for locomotives and other military targets. To me, rhubarb missions were a great adventure because I never knew what lay ahead. I could run into a flak tower unexpectedly, and if I wasn't flying below treetop level, I was a sitting duck for the flak tower gunners.

As the days rolled by, I had my share of flying but not as much as I wanted. As the newest pilot in the squadron, I had to fly in the most undesirable spot in the formation, the "tail-end Charlie" position, for a good number of missions. No one wanted to fly as a tail-end Charlie because in an attack against an enemy formation the tail-end fighter barely had the chance to fire his guns and when the enemy bounced the squadron the tail-end position was always the first to be shot at. A formation leader could prevent the loss of a tail-end Charlie aircraft by ordering the pilot to weave and bank from left to right, to the point where the pilot's neck would have to rotate almost 180 degrees each way, to cover the sky behind, below, and above the formation. The time I spent in the tail-end position not only trained my neck to swivel as necessary for a fighter pilot but also gave me experience that built my confidence for the days ahead.

On November 26, our squadron experienced its second casualty when we lost our beloved flight commander, Capt. Bob Sprague, during a training accident. Sprague was always anxious to learn his pilots' strengths and weaknesses in aerial combat. To accomplish this, he conducted a tail-chasing exercise with almost every pilot, paying particular attention to the newly assigned pilots. His tail-chasing system consisted of two phases. He would take each pilot up to 30,000 feet in a two-Spitfire element. Before takeoff, he'd brief the pilot about the exercise, and when he gave the signal, the pilot would fly 300 to 500 yards behind him and follow him.

"Just stick behind me and try not to lose me," he'd say. "If I do a loop, you do a loop. If I roll, you roll."

Sprague would start with some smooth maneuvering, and then he would launch into loops, rolls, Immelmans, wingovers, and then a split S.

During the second phase of the exercise he would jump the pilot and ride his tail. Captain Sprague, like any other attacker, preferred to come down from the sun, to make it more difficult for his victim to spot him. If the pilot was alert and spotted him early, he could turn sharply into him and break up his attack.

The day Sprague was killed, he was checking Lt. Jim Harrington. A preliminary investigation revealed that the wooden propeller of Harrington's Spitfire had made contact with something during the flight. Harrington had been following Sprague's Spitfire closely during the maneuvering and tail chasing, when Captain Sprague, perhaps unintentionally, cut off his power. Harrington's propeller had struck the tail section of Sprague's Spitfire, and the captain never replied when Harrington urged his teacher to abandon his aircraft. Sprague's Spitfire likely went into a violent spin after it was hit, making it impossible for him to leave the cockpit. He was missed by all in the 4th Fighter Group.

A couple weeks later, on December 12, 1942, I attended a debriefing on an escort mission for sixteen B-24s assigned to bomb the aerodrome at Romilly, France. Major Daymond had led the group of thirty-six Spitfires and seemed angry when he returned to base. Using the map on the board, he explained to us what happened on the mission.

"First of all," Daymond said, "we didn't meet the B-24s over Hastings, our rendezvous point. I was going to return to base, but the controller from the 11th Group directed me to proceed to the target, as the bombers were early for the mission and had gone ahead without us. We set course, at once, for Le Crotoy, then flew to Abbeville. Still no B-24s. As I turned back to return to base, I spotted the B-24s north of Disemont. After we caught up with the bombers, still over French territory, the group took position over the B-24 formation and provided escort to within ten miles of the English coast."

Bombers often arrived early or late at rendezvous points prearranged with escorting fighters during the early days of the USAAF bombing campaign, but as complaints began to mount from both RAF and 8th Fighter Command and as the bomber group commanders gained experience, communication between the fighters and the bombers began to improve. Nonetheless, the task of escorting fighters became rather difficult when a group of bombers was upward of thirty minutes late to a rendezvous point. The fighters could not protect the bombers if we used too much of our fuel waiting for them to arrive.

At the end of December 1942, large numbers of B-17s and B-24s began to arrive in England from the United States' arsenal, in preparation for the daylight-bombing offensive against Hitler's European fortress. At that point the bosses at the 8th Air Force were confronted with a dilemma: they did not have a suitable long-range fighter that could provide escort to the bombers on distant targets for the daylight raids. The only aircraft available for escort duty at the time were the RAF Spitfires, including the three squadrons of the 4th Fighter Group, the only USAAF unit in England.

Some of the planners at 8th Bomber Command, including Gen. Ira C. Eaker, who had taken command of 8th Air Force from General Spaatz, believed that the heavily armed B-17s and B-24s, flying in close box formation, could defend themselves without fighter escort. The Flying Fortresses and Liberators could drop their loads on their targets and return to England with minimum, if any, losses. This reasoning turned out

121

to be wishful thinking. At the beginning of their bombing runs in northern France, small numbers of B-17s and B-24s were provided close escort by RAF and 4th Fighter Group fighter squadrons in their short-distance bombing raids. In these types of bombing raids, the bomber losses were minimal and were caused mostly by flak.

As the war progressed, American bombers continued to arrive in England in larger numbers, and bombing raids were extended to cover targets deep into enemy territory and well beyond the Spitfire's radius of action. During the unescorted part of a bombing run, Luftwaffe fighter pilots flew in for the kill, using their agile aircraft and skills to attack the invading bombers.

I flew my last mission of the year in the late afternoon on December 31, a day with low clouds and light drizzle that restricted visibility considerably. The weather made patrolling over the large, spread-out convoy of some fifty merchant ships difficult, but the mission was critical. The conditions presented an ideal situation for a single JU-88 to fly inside the cloud deck, drop down over the channel, hit one or two of the ships, and then sneak back into the clouds. Vic France and I provided aerial cover to the northbound convoy armada without incident, circling overhead in a racetrack pattern for almost forty minutes. As darkness approached, Control released us to return to Debden. We left the convoy area and hurried home to clean up for the big New Year's Eve party the officers' mess was preparing for us.

GOOD-BYE SPITFIRES

In the first half of January 1943, I flew six missions, the first four of which were routine convoy patrols over the English Channel and the North Sea. Convoy patrols were the most unpopular and boring missions, but they were essential to the war effort and Great Britain's survival. My last two missions were on the same day, January 13.

In the morning, I was one of thirty-six Spitfire pilots to provide close escort to twelve RAF Bostons on their way to St. Omer, where the RAF bombers were to attack the Fort Rouge Aerodrome. We rendezvoused with the Bostons halfway across the English Channel, provided escort to the target, and brought them back to the French coast. There, an RAF

122

wing took over to bring them home. Six additional RAF squadrons had flown diversionary sweeps earlier to prevent German interference with the Bostons' mission. Because of this massive aerial coverage, we encountered no opposition during our mission, except the usual flak from the French coast, which greeted us on the way in and on the way out.

That afternoon, after we climbed out of our cockpits, had a quick lunch, refueled our planes, and took off again to provide withdrawal support for seventy-two B-17s that had bombed the aerodrome and a railway center at Lille, France. Colonel Peterson led the group on this mission, also with thirty-six Spitfires, twelve from each squadron. Nine RAF squadrons from Biggin Hill and North Weald aerodromes also provided close escort at various stages of the mission. Some of the RAF Spits went on diversionary sweeps in support of this mission.

After the group returned to Debden, during the debriefing, Colonel Pete reported that someone had sighted four FW-190s near Calais, but the group had not made contact, as the enemy aircraft kept their distance from the bomber formation and its protective umbrella. However, south of the target area, the colonel said, there must have been a big fight; he and other pilots had seen many crisscrossing contrails at high altitude.

Later, we learned that the 8th Bomber Command had lost three B-17s on the mission. Two had collided in the air as they were turning away after they had dropped their bombs, and one was brought down by flak over Lille. The participating RAF squadrons had lost two Spitfires in a dogfight but had also shot down several FW-190s. All of the 4th Group aircraft had returned safely from the mission, except for the Spit flown by Lt. Leicester Bishop of the 336 Squadron, who encountered engine trouble and crash-landed with a dead engine at Manston Aerodrome. Bishop wasn't hurt in the crash.

While we were flying these missions with our Spitfires, rumor had it that the 4th Group was destined to convert to the American-built P-47 Thunderbolt. At first nobody knew when the transition would begin and those in higher headquarters denied it, but on January 15, the rumors were proved correct. Major Daymond informed all of the 334 Squadron pilots that the squadron was being taken off operations to become the training squadron on the station. In the days that followed, P-47s were delivered to Debden, almost on a daily basis. We didn't all train at once, however; some of us from the 334 Squadron were attached temporarily to the other two squadrons on the station to fill the slots that were vacated by pilots who had begun to train with the P-47. I, among others, was sent to the 335 Squadron.

On January 20, 1943, Bob Boock and I, flying 335 Squadron Spits, were cleared to go on a rhubarb mission to Le Touquet, France, to strafe any military installations we could find in the area. As I followed Boock on the takeoff roll, my engine inexplicably quit. I had already become airborne and had raised the landing gear, so I had no choice but to crash through the defense perimeter barbed wire at the aerodrome's edge. Luckily, the aircraft didn't catch fire, as I had turned the switch off just before the crash, but it was damaged badly. The left wing had broken off at the point where it joined the fuselage.

I immediately unstrapped myself, unbuckled my parachute, and climbed out of the cockpit of the wrecked machine. I fought my way swiftly, on hands and knees, through the thick barbed wire. Eventually, I was able to walk away on my own, shaking. Once I had put some distance between myself and the wrecked Spitfire, I became so dizzy that I collapsed. An ambulance and fire truck arrived on the scene, and the men helped me up. As I stood, I began to feel better.

I was lucky. Apart from some cuts on my hands and face, incurred while I tried to crawl through the barbed wire, I was not injured. When I was released from the dispensary, I went straight to my room to lie down for a while. I must have fallen asleep because when I awoke it was past noon. The short nap evidently had helped to relax my nerves, and I felt much better. When I went to the lounge, I learned that Vic France had taken my place on the mission, and Boock and France were able to destroy a locomotive before returning to base. I was sorry not to have gone on the mission, but I felt lucky to be alive.

The next day, I went to look at my wrecked Spit in the hangar. The fuselage, resting on a stand, was being inspected by the Rolls Royce resident engineer, a civilian whom I had seen frequently at the mess but had not spoken to. On seeing me, the engineer offered an explanation for my crash. He retrieved a small, thin, curved tube line, about a foot long, from the top of the engine and handed it to me.

"That's what deprived the engine from attaining full power with a wide-opened throttle. This vacuum line evidently broke after you had applied full power—perhaps from fatigue or vibration. The break prevented the vacuum pressure necessary for high-pitch manifold pressure, which the engine needs to attain full power for takeoff. What you had, after this line broke, was low-pitch power, and the Spit couldn't take off in low-pitch."

As the days went by, the P-47 training program had reached full swing, as more and more training missions were flown every day. Some of the pilots who had flown the P-47 at high altitude were still skeptical about the "monster's" potential, in comparison to the agile Spitfire's. They felt that the Thunderbolt was too bulky for dogfighting maneuvers. Others, however, felt that in due time we'd find out how to use the aircraft, and everything would fall into place. Actually the record proved that the Thunderbolt was deadly effective in the air and equally effective attacking targets on the ground. By the end of the war, pilots flying the "monster" had shot down more than 3,700 German aircraft and destroyed more than 3,300 on the ground, along with thousands of locomotives, railroad cars, and armored and transport vehicles.

By the end of January 1943, twenty-four pilots from the three squadrons had been checked out on the P-47 and were involved in the advanced stages of the training program. By this time, also, the 334 Squadron had received more than twenty-five brand new "Jugs." The conversion program was progressing nicely, but not without accidents: two of the training aircraft were damaged, but the pilots escaped injury.

On February 1, 1943, we had our first casualty with the P-47. Lt. John Mitchellweis of the 336 Squadron was killed while on a training mission. His aircraft caught fire as he cruised at 5,000 feet. He bailed out successfully, but unfortunately, when he deployed his parachute, it separated from his body. He was killed instantly when he hit the ground. This accident, of course, forced every pilot on the station to double-check his parachute for tightness.

In the afternoon of February 27, Colonel Pete led our group, flying

Spitfires, on a close escort mission for twenty-four RAF Venturas on a run to bomb an armed raider that had docked overnight in the small harbor of Dunkirk. The mission was supported by an additional eight RAF Spitfire squadrons flying diversionary sweeps within a seventy-mile radius of Dunkirk. Bob Boock, Duane Beeson, and I were flying in Colonel Pete's White Section. We met the Venturas over Beachy Head, and Colonel Pete positioned the group to protect the bomber formation over the top, left, and right flanks. We stayed in that position almost all the way to the target area.

The bombing was accomplished from 14,000 feet altitude, and the Venturas dropped 500-pound and 150-pound bombs. But the armed raider must have left port during darkness because it wasn't there when we arrived over the harbor. Still, the bombs the Venturas dropped devastated the small harbor, completely destroying its docks. The bombs also hit a small, slow-moving ship, that caught fire.

We were met with heavy flak over Dunkirk, but no one was hit. As we were turning away from the target area to head for home, the 11th Group operations controller reported that an unknown number of enemy aircraft were approaching from the south at 30,000 feet. We never saw the enemy aircraft and encountered no interference on our way home. We assumed that the reported bandits were intercepted or tangled up by RAF Spitfires, as we could see many contrails well south of our position over the English Channel.

We stayed with the Venturas until we crossed the English coast, at which time we left the bombers and headed for home. All Spitfires landed at Debden safely.

The next day, the 334 Squadron dropped all of the Spitfire aircraft from its inventory. By this time, all of the pilots who had been assigned to transition to the P-47s had completed their thirty hours of required training. Col. Pete told us that evening that we needed at least one squadron operational with the Thunderbolt as soon as possible in order to challenge Hitler's air force with the new machine.

I was still flying Spitfires. On March 1, Boock and I took off on a convoy patrol. Immediately after I became airborne, I felt complete loss of power from the engine. I quickly turned off the switch, pointed the

126

nose of the Spit down, and headed straight ahead to land on the remaining part of the runway. I knew from the speed I had that I wasn't going to be able to stop the aircraft on the runway, even if I applied the brakes gently. The aircraft ran off the runway pavement, and as the wheels hit the muddy grass at the end of the runway, the Spitfire nosed over, causing the propeller to strike the ground. I wasn't hurt and was able to jump down from the cockpit. I wasn't even shaken up; I was angry as hell to have experienced my second Spitfire mishap. The damage to the aircraft was light, although the propeller and engine had to be replaced.

127

I was driven to the 335 dispersal. Since no other pilot was around at that moment to take my place, I was given another Spitfire to go on the patrol mission. Boock was circling overhead waiting for someone to join up with him. I hurriedly started the engine, taxied out, and took off on the east runway. After circling the aerodrome once, Boock and I headed for the English Channel. Boock was shocked when he realized I was the pilot in the replacement aircraft. He couldn't believe that I had gotten back up in the air so soon after the accident I had just experienced.

While we flew over the channel, looking over the northbound armada of some forty freighters, I pounded my head, trying to figure out what went wrong with the engine. Was it the same problem I had experienced before? Or perhaps I had forgotten to check something. The mission proceeded as planned, and in the afternoon, after Boock and I had returned to the base, I visited the 335 Squadron hangar and found Mr. White, the Rolls Royce engineer. He told me that he could not get the engine to start and would have to return it to the factory so that their experts could determine the cause of the accident. Because the Spit was not damaged in the crash, it was fitted with a new engine and a new prop and was flown away from Debden with the other Spitfires that were slowly being transferred out. I never found out what had caused the engine to quit during that second incident.

On March 10, 1943, the 334 Squadron was able to scrounge up enough combat-ready pilots to pull together its first operational mission with fourteen Thunderbolts. Under the command of Colonel Peterson, the squadron took off from Debden at 3:15 p.m. and set course to sweep the area from Walcheren Island to Blankenberge and out over Ostend, cruising at 27,000 feet. The squadron encountered heavy flak throughout the area, but no enemy aircraft were seen anywhere and none were reported. All of the Thunderbolts returned to Debden and landed safely. That night Colonel Anderson, our group commander, who had just flown his first combat mission, bought the drinks at the bar. The Thunderbolt was now baptized for combat.

The next day Lt. Frank Fink and I flew a convoy patrol mission. We arrived over the convoy area in the English Channel, just east of Dover, in time to relieve two other Spitfires from an RAF squadron. The armada of merchant ships was about forty-five strong. After we had been on station about fifteen minutes and had completed our second turn around the convoy, flying in an easterly direction, I scanned the sea surrounding the convoy and the sky around our two Spitfires. Suddenly I spotted a black dot on the eastern horizon, above a low cloudbank that covered the entire eastern part of the channel. I kept my eyes on that dot as we continued to fly eastward and soon realized the dot was the silhouette of an aircraft. I called Fink on the radio, pointed to the silhouette, and told him that the dot looked suspicious.

"Let's go check it out," replied Fink. I called Control to report the sighting and that we were going over to investigate.

"Dammit, Frank," I hollered as we approached the aircraft, "it's a JU-88!"

This was the first enemy aircraft I had seen up close since I had arrived in England. The JU-88 was a light twin-engine bomber with a 300-mile-per-hour top speed the Luftwaffe used extensively against shipping in the English Channel and the Atlantic. I called "tally ho" on the radio as I turned to the right to get into position for a shot at the German. Fink, on my left, followed me, but the enemy pilot must have had his eyes on us because he made a sharp left turn, dove into the cloudbank, and disappeared. Fink and I circled a couple of times over the spot where the 88 had gone in, thinking that the pilot might attempt to come out of the clouds and make a run for the convoy, perhaps from a different direction. But we had no such luck. We then decided to return to the convoy area, until we were relieved.

The next day, we flew two missions. In the morning, Major Blakeslee, the commanding officer of the 335 Squadron, led the 335 and 336 squadrons on a withdrawal support mission for some seventy B-17s that had been bombing the rail yards at Rouen. I flew in Major Blakeslee's White Section and had Vic France as my wingman. We took off at 12:15 p.m. and set course to cross over Beachy Head at 10,000 feet. Then we climbed to 23,000 feet and crossed into France near St. Valery. Approximately five miles inland, we sighted the bombers as they were turning away from the target. The bombing had left one of the biggest smoke clouds I had ever seen rising from what had been the rail junction of Rouen.

Just as we sighted the bombers, pilots of the 336 Squadron reported five bandits south of Dieppe flying at about 27,000 feet. We all turned our eyes in the direction of the five reported bandits and prepared for a fight. Unfortunately, the reported bandits turned and flew away from our area, but we could see contrails south of our position, probably near the RAF diversion Spitfires that had been mixed up with the yellow nose FW-190s. Our intelligence showed that the Richthofen unit that flew the yellow nose 190s was one of the most experienced Luftwaffe fighter units. Almost every pilot in the unit was an ace. Apparently, it operated out of the Triqueville Aerodrome near Le Havre.

As we approached the bomber formation, we took our positions. The 335 Squadron was top cover and weaved above the bomber formation, and the 336 Squadron split into two sections and positioned themselves to the left and to the right of the B-17 formation. Above and south of the B-17s and 4th Group's protective fighters, there must have been some five or six other RAF Spitfire squadrons providing high-altitude cover for the B-17s. As we flew near the French coast, the German ack-ack guns sent the usual flak our way. There must have been many antiaircraft batteries, all firing skyward at the huge B-17 formation and its escorting fighters, but we all slipped across the French coast without any hits.

When I was almost halfway across the English Channel, I noticed some oil leaking from my engine, partially blocking my vision through the windshield. Thinking that it was a small leak, I didn't pay too much attention to it, but the moment we pulled away from the bomber formation, north of Beachy Head, and set course for Debden, the oil leak worsened to the point where my windshield was completely covered with black oil and I had difficulty seeing in front of me. I knew then an oil line was either loose or broken. I had to land, I thought, before my engine froze. I radioed Major Blakeslee to tell him about my problem, and he was able to see my aircraft from his. He immediately ordered me to land. Having West Mailing Aerodrome in sight, I pulled away from the formation, and after contacting the control tower, I opened the canopy and landed the Spit with my head leaning outside. I taxied to the end of the runway, zigzagging all the way. While on the taxiway, I noticed that the oil pressure needle was at zero. I stopped the aircraft and shut down the engine, and then jumped down from the cockpit. To my great surprise, I found the entire fuselage covered completely with black oil. I would never have made it to Debden. I reported my aircraft's condition to 335 Squadron operations, and the squadron sent someone with an aircraft to pick me up.

About two hours after my return to Debden, Major Blakeslee led the group again on a rodeo mission to France, and I was assigned to fly as his wingman. The 335 Squadron would rendezvous with the 336 Squadron, which had deployed early to Martlesham Heath, near Dover. We took off from Debden at 3:45 p.m. and headed for Dover, flying low on the deck. After we had rendezvoused with 336 Squadron, Major Blakeslee moved the two squadrons in a line astern formation. We climbed and set course to cross into France. The 336 Squadron broke away and proceeded to patrol the area between Dunkirk and Audruicq-Calais at 15,000 feet. Major Blakeslee, with 335 Squadron, changed course, and we began to patrol the area between Dunkirk and St. Omer at 14,000 feet. We were surprised not to see a single enemy aircraft during this patrol, only the usual flak.

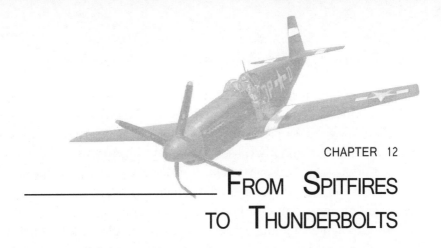

CHAPTER 12

FROM SPITFIRES
TO THUNDERBOLTS

On March 15, on landing from a convoy patrol, I was told that my temporary duty with the 335 Squadron was over and that I was to report to my squadron so that I could start training with the P-47. Upon returning to my squadron, I found a P-47s pilot's manual and studied it while waiting to attend the short ground school course. I wanted to learn everything about the operational procedures for, capabilities of, and limitations of the P-47 before I spent time in the cockpit.

The Republic-built fighter was the largest and heaviest American single-engine fighter aircraft introduced to the European theater in World War II. The aircraft was equipped with a Pratt and Whitney turbocharged eighteen-cylinder (R-2800-21) engine that produced some 2,300 horsepower. Its unique turbocharger used compressed air to give the engine extra power at high altitudes. It had a four-bladed propeller twelve feet long. Its internal fuel capacity was 305 gallons, which gave the aircraft a 205-mile radius of action. With a 108-gallon external metal fuel tank, the aircraft could fly more than 375 miles from base. The P-47's armament was eight .50-caliber machine guns, four on each wing, with 425 rounds for each gun.

Despite its formidable firing platform, some of the pilots from the first group who had been checked out on the new aircraft had expressed some skepticism about the qualities of the Thunderbolt as a fighter versus the Luftwaffe's ME-109 and FW-190 swift fighters. Some felt that the monster could do no more than dive away from anything that threatened it. But, as pilots accumulated more time in the air with the Jug, their initial displeasure disappeared, especially when they discovered the Thunderbolt's maneuvering capabilities and control responsiveness at high altitudes.

The P-47 wasn't a problem-free aircraft. We had many mechanical misadventures that initially caused some real concern among the bosses and the pilots who flew the machine. There were radio problems, oil leaks, smoke in the cockpit, and sudden bursts of fire in the air. In addition, we had inoperative turbochargers and crankshaft failures. The R-2800-21 engine's ignition system caused unacceptable radio interference during transmissions, whether you were contacting a ground station or another aircraft.

Small oil leaks, especially in radial engines, were normal, but the R-2800-21 engine's secured oil lines would loosen or break down, causing heavy oil leaks, and its spark plugs would blow completely out from cylinder heads. This saturated the engine and windshield with black oil, completely blocking the pilot's forward vision, and if the oil reached the hot exhaust pipes, a fire was inevitable.

The P-47's engine crankshaft was another major problem. It seemed the crankshaft wasn't getting proper lubrication, especially at high altitudes, so every P-47 had to be ferried, a few at a time, to a depot at Burtonwood for the necessary modifications.

Once these problems were corrected and the pilots had learned how to use the aircraft, the P-47 was a much better flying machine than we initially thought. It was true that the P-47 was heavy and couldn't climb like the Spitfire or the German fighters, but it was maneuverable at high altitude and could challenge anything up there. In addition, the Jug could outrun all of the planes the Germans had at the time. In a dive, the Thunderbolt allowed its pilot to position the aircraft on the tail of a diving opponent and press on for the kill. The Jug could also take punishment and still bring its pilot home. A good number of the 4th Group pilots who were approaching the end of their transition to the P-47 were convinced that the fighter could challenge the Luftwaffe squarely at high altitudes.

On March 17, 1943, I started the P-47 ground school along with the others who had returned from duty with the 335 Squadron. The course lasted three days and consisted of lectures, presentations, and diagrams showing the frame layout, engine, and systems. All of the instructions were presented by the Republic and Pratt and Whitney technicians on the station. In addition to the presentations, we spent considerable time in the aircraft's cockpit learning about its instrumentation and controls.

Although I had studied the manual well, I was determined to learn the arrangement of knobs, switches, buttons, and levers in the cockpit by heart, just as I had at 41 OTU with the P-51A Mustang. On March 22, after Jim Clark gave me a thorough cockpit check, I strapped myself in the P-47, taxied out, and took off with a tremendous roar. I was airborne in no time. The Jug's wide landing gear made the takeoff a piece of cake.

I took the aircraft up to 20,000 feet and played around for a while, making stalls and acrobatic maneuvers, and was extremely pleased with the way the P-47 flew. I returned to Debden and landed using the Spitfire approach method. That afternoon, I went up again, this time taking the Jug up to 30,000 feet. I made some spins, loops, and rolls and then put the Thunderbolt into a dive of a little more than a forty-five-degree angle to feel it out. The downhill acceleration made me feel as if I was flying a rocket as the airspeed indicator moved higher. I was clocking over 550 miles per hour when I zoomed up into the blue sky with tremendous satisfaction. By the time I landed my confidence that the Jug could be used successfully against the Luftwaffe at high altitude had grown significantly.

On March 23, the remaining 334 Squadron pilots returned from their duty with the 336 Squadron and immediately started ground school in preparation for flying the Jug. In the meantime, those of us who had returned from duty with the 335 Squadron and had completed Thunderbolt training continued with the P-47 training program developed by the 4th Group. The pilots who had been trained earlier helped the latecomers with their Thunderbolt check-out and training.

The 4th Group training syllabus for all new P-47 pilots required that before we could be declared combat ready, we had to accumulate thirty flying hours around several exercises, including check out, transition, acrobatics, combat maneuvers and tactics. Dogfighting using the gun camera, formation, and aerial target shooting with live ammo, including air-to-ground firing at the wash area were all part of the exercises. By far, the most fascinating and exciting part of our combat training in the squadron was the dogfighting. We used various tactics and maneuvers to learn the Thunderbolt's promising dogfighting capabilities. Frequently, two pilots would take their P-47s up to 30,000 feet in formation and then break up to meet each other almost head-on.

The objective of this exercise, of course, was to get on the tail of other aircraft and make a hit using the gun camera. In this exercise, a pilot could use any maneuver or take any action necessary to achieve his objective. Getting on the tail of an adversary is strenuous and difficult, especially at high altitude, where, to keep alert, a pilot must breathe pure oxygen continuously. In combat, a pilot's legs and hands are shaking as he centers his gun sight and presses the trigger for the kill. And, of course, the opponent he is trying to hit may be an experienced air warrior or a better pilot than he is. In aerial dueling, there is a cardinal rule; it doesn't matter how good or skillful or knowledgeable a pilot is—there is always someone out there who is better than you.

The exercises and maneuvers we went through in the air with the new aircraft forced us to stay alert in the sky. While dogfighting with my friends, I learned to search the sky without disregarding my tail, something many of us do when we fly over enemy territory. We became better at anticipating and spotting enemy aircraft hidden in the sun, and we practiced judging when it was appropriate to drop swiftly behind an adversary for the kill.

When we were on the ground, we practiced clay pigeon shooting, an exercise directly connected to aerial fighting. Lt. Duane Beeson, one of the sharp shooters in our squadron, had inherited the additional duty of squadron gunnery officer and was in charge of this training. Beeson would use a snap machine to launch clay pigeons into the air, and a pilot, using a double-barreled shotgun, would try to blast the decoys out of the sky. The objective of this unique exercise was for the fighter pilots to maintain their proficiency in deflection shooting, an important aspect of aerial combat.

On April 3, 1943, the squadron was involved in an incident that almost cost Maj. Oscar Coen—who had taken over command from Major Daymond—his life. The 8th Bomber Command had sent a B-17 bomber to Debden for a fighter-bomber affiliation exercise, to allow the bombers to become familiar with the P-47. Four P-47s from 334 Squadron, flown by Major Coen, Capt. Tommy Andrews, and Lts. Jim Clark and Bruce Morgan, were to take off and follow the B-17, which was scheduled to rendezvous with a small group of other B-17s from its parent bomb group. The P-47s were to fly around and make passes on the bombers from different angles so that the gunners and other crewmembers aboard the B-17s would have a good view of the Jug, which, from certain angles, resembled the German FW-190 fighter.

While on the exercise, Major Coen experienced some engine difficulties. Both Morgan and Clark told him that his turbocharger appeared to be on fire. Coen quickly decided what to do. He opened his canopy, exited the cockpit, crawled onto the left wing of his aircraft, and jumped away from the burning P-47. As his parachute opened, he caught his arm in the parachute harness, badly fracturing his shoulder. Luckily, he managed to reach the ground without further injury. The abandoned P-47 exploded in the air before it hit the ground.

The incident took place northeast of Alconbury RAF Station, and Morgan was able to land there to request assistance. The station sent Morgan with an ambulance to the point where Coen had come down in his parachute. After a checkup by medics at the RAF station, Coen was driven to Debden with his right arm in a sling. Captain Andrews was appointed acting commanding officer of 334 Squadron while Coen was recuperating.

On April 15, 1943, a group of RAF ferry command pilots arrived at Debden to take away the last of our Spitfires. Some of the pilots in our squadron, including myself, were heartbroken to see our Spitfires fly away. I vividly remember how we stood outside the dispersal watching the Spitfires take off, one after the other.

In late afternoon that day, Colonel Pete led a group of P-47s from 334 and 335 squadrons, augmented by eight P-47s from the recently arrived 78th Group, on a fighter sweep at 30,000 feet from Furnes, Belgium, to Cassel, France. Pete held a preflight briefing 4:00 p.m., and takeoff was set at 4:50 p.m. I had a practice flight scheduled for that afternoon and was at the dispersal before the group was to take off, when Colonel Pete walked in.

"Tommy," Pete said to Captain Andrews, "I want an aircraft with a

135

good radio."

Andrews looked around, and his eyes locked with mine. "I think QP-K has a good radio," he said. "Isn't that right, Spiro?"

"Yes, Sir," I replied. "QP-K has a damn good radio!" I had flown the plane that morning.

I surrendered my plane to Colonel Pete and was left without an aircraft for my training flight. The 4th Group of two squadrons with twenty-four P-47s was to fly a sweep across the English Channel to challenge the Luftwaffe. At 4:50 p.m. as scheduled, those of us who were not flying came out to watch the P-47s take off in twos. In less than two minutes, the twenty-four Thunderbolts were off the ground. Colonel Pete set course for Furnes and was expected to reach the enemy coast at 5:30 p.m. at 30,000 feet.

As the group faded away over the southeastern horizon, several of us jumped on the squadron's Jeep and headed for group operations to listen to the radio channel we had there. As prearranged during the briefing, Colonel Pete put the two squadrons in line astern battle formation, and they swept the area inland, passing northwest of Furnes and then down to Cassel, before returning to base.

Those of us gathered by the radio at Group Operations sat in complete silence as we waited to hear conversations among the pilots on the mission. Suddenly, the silence on the radio was broken when the 11th Sector controller cut in and alerted Colonel Pete that a gaggle of bandits was approaching his position from the northeast at 27,000 feet. Colonel Pete acknowledged the bandits and told the group to keep an eye on them. After some anxious waiting by the radio, we realized that Colonel Pete wasn't going to allow the German formation to pass behind his group, and he, no doubt, would have to make a move as they came closer. Colonel Pete's voice came back on the radio and said, "OK, guys, I'll make a right turn and go after the bastards. White Section will make the attack. Blue and Red sections, cover us, and Greenbelt squadron, provide top cover."

"There seem to be only eight to ten mixed 190s and ME-109s," said someone else on the radio.

The radio chatter indicated that the Germans sensed the mass of P-47s was about to attack and, deciding to try out the American newcomers,

136

turned to face the Thunderbolts. A mix-up ensued, but from the chatter, we couldn't determine what exactly happened. The events moved too quickly and the static on the radio prevented us from hearing every word. Finally, after a long while, the P-47s from the mission began to appear overhead in singles, twos, and fours. When we heard the first P-47 overhead, Vic France, Deacon Hively, and I left group operations and walked to the tower to watch the returning aircraft land.

The last P-47 to land was QP-W, flown by Jim Clark, who confirmed to Group Intelligence that Dick McMinn and Stan Anderson had gone down. They hadn't heard anything from McMinn, but they knew Anderson had been hit and was going to bail out. Neither pilot was found. It seemed that Colonel Pete had to bail out also over the English Channel, close to the Belgian coast. Tommy Andrews and Bud Care saw Pete's aircraft splash into the channel and Pete's parachute hit the sea's surface. They quickly circled the spot where the chute had splashed down and transmitted "Mayday" on the emergency channel. Andrews said that after a few minutes the Air Sea Rescue (ASR) controller told him that they had a fix on the spot where Pete had gone down and that an ASR Walrus was on its way for the pick up.

We didn't hear a word about Pete's fate until much later that evening. We had gathered in the lounge when, we heard from Hawkings Aerodrome that the colonel had been picked up successfully and flown to Martlesham Heath for a night's hospitalization for his badly bruised face. Apparently, he had bailed out because of engine trouble. He was due to return to base the next day.

On the evening of April 16, Don Gentile and I, along with several others, were standing by the piano in the lounge drinking American beer while Clark, Andrews, and Care tried to reconstruct the mission they had been on the day before. To our surprise, Colonel Pete, wearing sunglasses to hide his black eyes, despite the darkness outside, walked into the lounge with a drink in his hand. On seeing him, we spontaneously burst into cheers. As he joined our circle by the piano, more pilots from the other two squadrons as well some from the 78th Group surrounded us. After a sip of his drink and some prompting by Clark, Colonel Pete said, "I will always remember the mission where I almost bought the farm. After I spotted the Germans, if you remember, I told you guys in the formation to keep your eyes on the bandits, but when I saw them approaching and realized they would pass to our right and below, I felt that we were in the ideal position to jump them.

"Since I was in front when I gave the signal and turned right to go after them, I closed in behind the 190 at the tail-end Charlie position and lined up on his tail. Apparently the Germans were just waiting until we got close to them, and they immediately broke up their formation, all going off in different directions. The 190 I was following and closing in on fast made the mistake of going into a dive. I followed him all the way down, and, in fact, I was closing on him so fast with my Jug that I thought I would overshoot the bastard.

"When I was within about 200 to 300 yards of him, I opened fire and bang! Pieces of metal began to fly off his aircraft, followed by black smoke. I knew that I had nailed the guy. He was still diving when I broke the pursuit and started to climb and head for home. I had no idea what had happened to Stan Anderson, who was my wingman.

"I started to climb in a northwesterly direction, hoping that I would find someone to join up with. Just as I had reached about 8,000 feet over the channel, not too far from Ostend, my engine made a terrific bang and the upper part of the engine cowling flew over my head. At that moment, I thought that two, maybe three, or even more cylinders must have blown off the engine because it started banging violently. Then, suddenly, I lost power. The engine appeared to be frozen up; everything had gone dead.

"I decided to glide the crippled Jug as much as I could toward England and bail out at a lower altitude. I looked at the altimeter after I had glided down for a while, and I remember it read about 600 feet over the channel. I released the canopy, unbuckled myself, and rolled the aircraft over so that I could fall away from the cockpit. When I left the aircraft in that upside-down position, I was about 300 to 400 feet above the sea's surface. I pulled the rip cord when I was well clear of the aircraft, but somehow the chute did not open fully by the time I hit the water, so I was falling unusually fast. I remember that when I hit the water, it was with a tremendous bang, head first.

"When I struck the water, I felt like I had a couple hundred pounds of lead tied on my back. I don't know how deep underwater I went. I remember, though, that when I opened my eyes it was dark all around me. My parachute topside acted as a float, evidently, keeping me from sinking deeper. I immediately wanted to swim to the surface—I desperately wanted to breathe. When I finally reached the surface, I took the deepest breath I can remember. Had I stayed below a little longer, I don't think I would have survived. Then I took stock of the situation. I felt like someone had punched my head a thousand times. But, despite the pain, I started to work on my dinghy. I unhooked my parachute harness and pulled the dinghy away, inflated it, and crawled onto it. What a relief! The water was unbelievably cold.

"Then, after a couple of hours, maybe more, when I was full of anxiety about the coming darkness, a Walrus flew overhead and spotted me. The old thing landed perfectly, taxied a short distance, and with help from the crew, I climbed aboard. The flying boat took off for home. Mind you, these guys came very close to Ostend and the Germans to rescue me. They certainly saved my butt. I doubt I would have survived through the night with the water that cold. I remember I was shivering badly when I was helped aboard the Walrus."

When Colonel Pete had finished telling us the ordeal he had gone through, he looked around and spotted me.

"Hey, Spiro," he said with a smile, "your kite had a good radio all right, but a lousy engine." We all laughed.

On April 23, 1943, word came down from squadron personnel that I had been promoted to first lieutenant. Vic France and Don Gentile pinned the silver bars on my uniform that day. Later that afternoon, my roommate, Capt. Donald Willis of 335 Squadron, left Debden for an assignment to the 8th Fighter Command headquarters, and Gentile became my new roommate. After Gentile moved in with me, we started to go to London more often on forty-eight-hour passes. Sometimes France would join us and lined up dates for us with beauties from the Windmill Theater. Almost daily Gentile and I ate in the dining room together or shared a drink at the bar. We'd go to movies on the station and accompany one another to briefings before missions. We even began to pray together at the chapel before taking off on a mission. As the days went by, Don and I forged an imperishable friendship.

CHAPTER 13

BECOMING AMERICAN

On May 3, 1943, after an early breakfast, Gentile and I headed for our dispersals to fly on the early morning training flights. Don and I were to do some tail chasing as we had talked about in our room the night before. The sky was cloudless, and the waters from the small rivers and canals sparkled here and there with the brilliant reflection of the rising sun. We had nearly unlimited visibility.

At 8:00 a.m. sharp, Gentile rolled down the runway for takeoff, and I followed behind. After I had caught up with his P-47 a few miles out of Debden, at about 2,000 feet, I closed in and locked my Jug to the right of his aircraft, and we started to climb in close formation toward the Wash. By the time we had reached our destination, we were at 27,000 feet, still in close formation.

As we arrived over the practice area, Gentile pulled ahead. I slowed down and fell behind by about 300 yards. We then started our training exercise with a wide barrel roll and then went into a split S. As he came down from his second maneuver, he reversed direction. After he had dropped a few thousand feet, he zoomed straight up and then rolled over. After a short, level flight, he dove down again and went into a loop. We continued this maneuvering for some time. I must admit that it was challenging to follow my roomate's twisting and turning, trying to shake me off his tail, for so long, but I was able to keep close behind his aircraft.

After about thirty minutes of dogfighting, we switched places, and I took the lead as Gentile took his position behind me. We were about 28,000 feet in the air. Just as I was about to begin maneuvering to shake Mr. Gentile off my tail, Debden Control called on the radio and advised me to return to base immediately. I peeled away from my roommate and headed back to base, wondering what this could be about. Control had never recalled an aircraft from a training mission. For a moment, I wondered whether the king of Greece had asked the American authorities for my release from the USAAF. And then I worried that the American authorities had discovered that I was taken into the U.S. Army Air Force erroneously.

When I arrived back at the base, Colonel Peterson and Captain Andrews were waiting for me.

Peterson told me to get into his car, and I was convinced that something was wrong. When we reached the group's headquarters, we went inside to Colonel Pete's office. I sat down in the chair he offered me and the colonel picked up the phone. "This is Colonel Peterson. Will you connect me with the American embassy in London, please?"

These words confirmed my fears, and my anxiety only increased as he waited to be connected with the embassy. I could feel the sweat dripping down my spine and my heart beating faster than normal. Finally, Colonel Pete said, "This is Colonel Peterson from the 4th Group. Will you please connect me with the ambassador's office?" When the ambassador came on the line, Pete said, "John, I have the young lieutenant here in my office, and I think you should talk to him directly."

He handed the phone to me. For a moment, I didn't know what to say or what to expect, fearing that the Greek government in exile had gone to the U.S. embassy for my release from the U.S. Air Force.

"Yes, Sir, Mr. Ambassador?" I said nervously.

"Lieutenant," the ambassador said, "how would you like to become an American citizen today?"

I couldn't believe my ears. "What?" I said, trying to cover my confusion. I looked at Colonel Pete, who was smiling as he lit his pipe. I sat there, holding my breath with the phone in my hand.

"Lieutenant," the ambassador said, "are you still there?"

"Yes, Sir," I responded. "It would be a pleasure and a great honor. But, Sir, I thought I had to wait until the war was over and return to America for this."

"No," the ambassador replied, "we are going to make you an American right here today, so you'd better hurry and get to London as soon as possible. There will be a ceremony this afternoon, but you need to be here early to meet an officer from the Immigration and Naturalization Service [INS], who will administer the oath of allegiance during the ceremony." He asked me if I knew how to get to the embassy in London.

"Yes, Sir," I replied. "It's at Grosvenor Square."

"Good," he said. "When you get to the embassy tell the people in the lobby to direct you to my office."

"Yes, Sir," I said and handed the phone back to Colonel Pete.

142

"Yes, John," Colonel Pete said on the phone. "Yes, I'll get him down there immediately, and John, I want to thank you for this. Yes, he sure looks happy and excited. Thanks, again, John." He put down the receiver, looked at me with another smile, and said, "Were you surprised?"

"Surprised?!" I said. "You have no idea the agony I went through between receiving the request from Control to return to base and speaking to the ambassador. I thought that I was going to be turned over to the Greek air force! How did this happen?"

Colonel Pete explained: "Do you remember the day you returned from your interview in London for the transfer, and you told me that Colonel Stovall had accepted you into the U.S. Army Air Force? I told you that the next step would be to make you a U.S. citizen. That, my friend, stayed with me. I talked to Gen. Jesse Auton [our wing commanding officer] and Gen. Frank Hunter, who told me he would check with Washington. But nothing came of his inquiries.

"In mid-March, I attended a social event in London at which Ambassador Winant was present. I told him about your background and asked him about making you a citizen. I even told him that I was willing to be your sponsor. The ambassador told me that, a few days before, he had received a news release about the Nationality Act, which was recently passed by Congress. This act, the ambassador told me, allows non-U.S. citizens who serve in the U.S. armed forces at home and overseas to become U.S. citizens simply by taking the Oath of Allegiance given by an INS officer.

"The interesting part, the ambassador told me, is that they were planning to initiate the program of naturalizing noncitizens in the U.S. armed forces here in England, since there are quite a few people in that category now on British soil. The ambassador said that you could be the first one to go through this unusual process. Early this morning he called me in my quarters to tell me that the INS officer arrived in London yesterday evening. Since the officer expects a heavy workload, he wanted to get started immediately on his duties."

I thanked Colonel Pete for his generosity and told him I was deeply indebted to him for keeping me out of the Greek air force, finding a place for me in the 71 ES, and arranging for me to become a U.S. citizen. "I just don't know how on earth I am going to repay you for all this," I told him. He said no payment was due to him.

When the train pulled into Liverpool Street Station that morning, I jumped down onto the platform and rushed through a crowd of people to find a taxi. I didn't have to wait long in the queue outside. In less than fifteen minutes, I was sitting in a taxi, and some forty minutes later, I was dropped off at the American embassy on Grosvenor Square.

I had to show my ID to enter the building. As I entered the lobby, I stopped at the information desk to ask for directions to the ambassador's office. I took the elevator up a few floors and knocked on the ambassador's door.

I entered and introduced myself, and the ambassador rose and extended his hand.

"I am Ambassador Winant, and this is Dr. Henry Hazard of the Immigration and Naturalization Service," the ambassador said, pointing to the white-haired man.

He went on to explain to me that the INS planned to hold the naturalization ceremonies in military installations since all of the people who were to gain citizenship were military personnel. Dr. Hazard had made arrangements to have the ceremony at the European Theater of Operations (ETOUSA) headquarters building on the square at 2:00 p.m. I left the office with Dr. Hazard to prepare for the ceremony.

After we left the ambassador's office, Dr. Hazard and I went to the Public Information Office (PIO) at ETOUSA and met Maj. Samuel Gumble, the man in charge. The major told me that the ceremony would take place in a large conference room that would be quite crowded and that the ambassador, as well as some prominent Americans who lived in

London, members of the press, and war correspondents, would be present. In view of this, he told me I should be prepared to answer questions the newspaper people would probably ask, but I should be cautious and avoid giving out sensitive information.

After this briefing I went down to the conference room with Dr. Hazard, where he administered the Oath of Allegiance and I repeated in front of some one hundred people. Dr. Hazard then extended his hand and said, as he looked into my eyes, "Lieutenant, you are now a citizen of the United States of America. Congratulations." He turned to those who had gathered inside the conference room and said, "Gentlemen, may I present to you Lt. Spiro Pisanos, who has just been naturalized as a U.S. citizen on foreign soil."

The ambassador was the first to come forward to congratulate me. Then, the members of the press and war correspondents in uniform surrounded me and showered me with questions.

"Lieutenant, how do you feel now that you have become a Yank on British soil?" one of the English reporters asked.

"Great, and I am extremely happy and proud," I told him. "I'll never forget this day as long as I live."

As the crowd began to thin out, two gentlemen approached Dr. Hazard and me: the legendary Edward R. Murrow of CBS and Ben Lyon, an American actor who was then living in London and appearing in a show at the Palladium Theatre with his wife, Bebe Daniels. The men shook my hand and congratulated me. Mr. Lyon told me he was proud to see me being naturalized as an American in London and admired me for having flown with the RAF.

"Gentlemen," Mr. Lyon said to me and Dr. Hazard, "here is my card with the address of my residence in the Mayfair area, not far from here. Tonight, around 8:00 p.m., my wife and I are having a cocktail party for some close friends, and I want to dedicate this party to you, Lieutenant. Will you gentlemen join us with our friends this evening? It would be a great pleasure to have you both."

Dr. Hazard immediately declined, as he had to catch a train that evening. I told Mr. Lyon that it would be my pleasure to attend.

Dr. Hazard and I then went to Maj. Gumble's office to complete some INS papers.

"Your certificate of naturalization," Dr. Hazard told me, "will be mailed to you from Washington at the address you put down on the forms you completed just now." Then he gave me a wide grin and said, "By the way, Lieutenant, did you know that Ben Lyon played a British aviator in the Royal Flying Corps in Howard Hughes's World War I movie *Hell's Angels*? I'm glad that you accepted his invitation; I am sure you'll enjoy talking to him."

In fact, I hadn't realized Mr. Lyon was the star of *Hell's Angels*, and I was astonished by the news. *Hells Angels* was one of the three World War I aviation movies that had initially captured my heart and made me fall in love with the airplane. I was now very much looking forward to the night's party.

After I said good-bye to both Dr. Hazard and Major Gumble, I caught a taxi in the square and headed for the Regent Palace Hotel, hoping to secure a room for the night. I checked in for the night without difficulty and rested for a while in my room, since I wanted to be fresh for the party.

At 8:00 p.m. sharp a taxi dropped me in front of a huge apartment building in the Mayfair area. I went up to the floor the Lyons lived on and could hear the sound of a party in full swing as I approached the open door to their apartment. Mr. Lyon spotted me, broke away from the circle of people he was with, and came over to greet me.

"Come in, Lieutenant," he said with a smile. "Come in and meet my friends."

Mr. Lyon waved over his wife, who looked beautiful in her long, white dress. She greeted me with a smile.

"Lieutenant," Mr. Lyon said, "this is my wife Bebe Daniels. The lieutenant is the new American I spoke to you about," Mr. Lyon said to his wife.

"It's a pleasure having you in our home, Lieutenant, and congratulations on becoming an American citizen today," she said. "Please make yourself at home and get a drink."

Once Mr. Lyon had introduced me to his wife, he asked for the attention of his guests and said, "Ladies and gentlemen, may I present to you Lt. Spiro Pisanos, who, on this day, became an American citizen on British soil. He was naturalized this afternoon here in London, and I am dedicating this little gathering in his honor." After warm applause from his guests, Mr. Lyon escorted me to the bar, introducing me to some of his friends along the way.

"You know, Sir, we have met before," I told Mr. Lyon.

"We have? Where?" he asked, puzzled. Before I could open my mouth, he came right back and said, "It must have been in Hollywood or New York City."

"No," I said, "it was Athens, Greece, my birthplace."

"But I've never been to Greece," he replied.

"Yes, you have," I said, "in the motion picture *Hells Angels*."

He smiled, and I told him *Hells Angels* had played a part in my decision to become a military aviator.

"How amazing, Lieutenant," Mr. Lyon said, "to hear that Mr. Hughes's movie contributed so much to your love of flying. My God, you certainly accomplished your boyhood dream, first as a fighter pilot in the RAF and now a pilot in the U.S. Air Force. What a great achievement on your part!"

That night Mr. Lyon introduced me to Charles Sweeny, the British World War I veteran who had initiated the recruitment of American civilian pilots into the Royal Air Force. I, of course, knew who Mr. Sweeny was before we were introduced. I told him that he was mentioned often around Debden, particularly by Colonel Peterson.

The party continued until past 10:00 p.m., but I decided to leave early along with some other departing guests. Mr. Lyon was busy talking with some friends, so I said my good-bye and thanks to Mrs. Lyon.

"We enjoyed having you, Lieutenant," she said. "I want to wish you good luck, and promise me you will be careful when you are flying against the Germans."

As I assured her I would be as careful as I could, Mr. Lyon noticed I was preparing to leave and came over.

"Sir, the ceremony I went through today to become an American was, of course, a significant event, but to have had the opportunity to meet you, one of my aviation idols, on this day . . . well, I can't find the words to express how I feel. I will always remember you, Sir, and how we met, and thank you for inviting me to this wonderful party," I told Mr. Lyon as we shook hands.

146

"Lieutenant," Mr. Lyon said, "I am glad to have met you and, above all, am very pleased that you are now an American. Good luck in the war, and when you are flying up there against the Huns, give them hell for me."

When I woke up the following morning and went to the lobby to pick up a paper before breakfast, I found my face on the front page. The caption below the photo read, "Greek in the American Air Force Is Naturalized as a Yank on British soil." The photo showed Dr. Hazard administering the oath to me.

A little past noon, I walked into the dining room at the officers' mess back at Debden and was greeted with a huge roar of applause. Gentile rose from his table, hugged me, and said, "Congratulations, buddy. That's a good photo of you in this morning's *Stars and Stripes*. You now belong to Uncle Sam!"

Colonel Pete and Colonel Anderson also congratulated me and invited me to have lunch at their table, where I had the chance to tell them about my meeting with the ambassador, the ceremony, the party, and my introduction to Mr. Charles Sweeny. I thanked Colonel Pete again for everything he'd done for me.

Later in the afternoon Vic France, my friend, asked me what I was going to do to celebrate becoming an American. I told him I had nothing planned, but, in fact, I had a surprise for my friends. I arranged with the mess officer to buy drinks for everyone at the bar that night. When we arrived at the bar that evening, we found that the mess boys had posted a sign, about ten by three feet, in color, that read, "Tonight all drinks are on Steve Pisanos, American." As the night wore on, the bar served not only my friends from Debden, but visitors from the 78th Fighter Group from nearby Duxford Aerodrome, 8th Fighter Command, and a good number of RAF officers. We all drank, sang, and made noise, and many toasts were made in my honor. I shook more hands than I had at any other time in my life.

The next morning, I woke up, washed and shaved, and went downstairs with Gentile to have breakfast. As we sat down at our table, the mess officer walked into the dining room and handed me a piece of paper, the bill for the bar expenses from the night before. The damage? $275. It was well worth every cent.

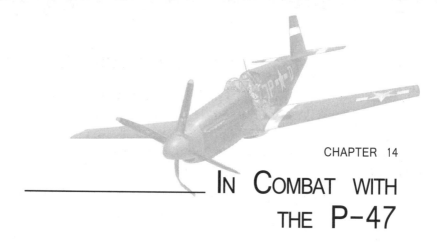

CHAPTER 14

IN COMBAT WITH
THE P-47

On May 9, 1943, I was one of several pilots at Debden who were declared combat ready in the Thunderbolt. Three days later, I flew on my first Thunderbolt mission, as a wingman to Captain Andrews, on a fighter sweep to Dunkirk. Unfortunately, the good weather that we had enjoyed until takeoff turned sour, and as we approached the enemy coast, we were advised to abort the mission and return to base.

My disappointment at the mission's cancellation was soon replaced by elation. Captain Andrews called me at the dispersal after we had returned from the mission to tell me that he had assigned a new P-47 with the marking QP-D to me. The aircraft was brand new and had been delivered to the squadron only two days before. It had just come out from inspection.

I flew QP-D a few times that afternoon, when the weather had improved, to become familiar with my new aircraft. It performed magnificently, and I really started to fall in love with the Thunderbolt.

On May 19, we learned that Colonel Peterson was being transferred to the 8th Fighter Command's headquarters. Pete had flown more than 200 missions and had seven enemy aircraft destroyed to his credit, six while he was in the RAF and one while he was with the USAAF. I knew everyone at Debden would miss Pete, but I was certain I'd miss him more than anyone because he had helped me so much in the past. To me, Colonel Pete was not only my commander in the RAF and the USAAF, but also a friend and a brother.

To replace Colonel Pete as deputy commander for operations, Colonel Anderson appointed the indefatigable commanding officer of the 335

Squadron, Maj. Don Blakeslee. All of us at Debden were looking forward to having our new boss lead us against the mighty Luftwaffe, and the chance for that came sooner than we expected. On May 21, we were instructed to have an early lunch and be in the briefing room shortly afterward.

Major Baldwin, our group's intelligence officer, had recently rearranged the 4th Fighter Group briefing room with the assistance of the intelligence officers from the three squadrons. On the center wall of the room was a giant board, left over from the days when we were in the RAF, displaying a map of Europe extending as far as east as western Russia and as far south as northern Africa. Berlin was marked with a red circle. The map was covered by thin Plexiglas that could be written on with grease pencils. The known locations of enemy air force units and heavy and light flak areas, including areas we were supposed to avoid flying over, were clearly marked across the map. The outbound and return courses of each mission were also plotted so that during a mission briefing the pilots could have an overall view of where they were going.

In addition to the map, the room was cluttered with small models of almost every enemy and Allied aircraft. Photos and posters reminding all who entered the room to be on their toes adorned the walls. One poster read, "Remember, Walls Have Ears"; another one read, "Don't Talk to Strangers"; and another one, "Remember, If You Go Down in Enemy Territory, Your Aim Should Be to Avoid Capture. But If You Are Captured, Give Your Captors Your Name, Rank, and Serial Number and Nothing Else. Escaping Should Always Be in Your Mind."

When Colonel Anderson walked in, followed by Major Blakeslee, on the afternoon of May 21, all of us who had congregated in the briefing room stopped talking and jumped up as Major Baldwin, who was standing by the door, called us to attention. Colonel Anderson, while on his way up front with Major Blakeslee, ordered us to be seated. And Major Blakeslee leaped onto the platform and, with a pointer in his hand, started the briefing.

"This afternoon, gentlemen, the 4th Group, with three squadrons of thirty-six P-47s, will take part in a rodeo mission to Ghent." He pointed to the map on the board. "We'll cross the enemy coast over Ostend at 31,000 feet, proceed inland to Ghent, then to Zwevezele, and back to Ghent on the way out.

"About the same time, the RAF will be conducting a bombing mission west of the area we are going to patrol, with B-26 light bombers escorted by Spits. Other RAF Spitfire squadrons will conduct diversion sweeps prior to and after our patrol of the area. So, be aware that a bunch of Spitfires will be operating west of the area of our operation, possibly going in and coming out.

"If the Germans decide to deploy reinforcements to the area where the B-26s are bombing, in all probability they will fly out from southern Holland or Belgium. It will be our aim to stop those bastards from interfering with the RAF's bombing mission.

"We'll be controlled by 'Corby' on Channel C. Emergency will be on Channel D. I'll be flying with the 336 Squadron. Start engines at 1:00 p.m., and H hour is 1:10 p.m.. Squadrons will use assigned call signs, and I'll be Horseback Leader. If I have to abort for any reason, Major Gilbert Halsey will take over.

"The 334 Squadron will follow 336 on takeoff and 335 will be last. Takeoff and assembly will be normal, and after all aircraft are airborne, we'll climb out in a V formation, with 334 to the left of 336 and 335 to the right. Use the clock system to give positions and directions but be certain about what you have to say before you press that radio button." The major emphasized this point. "If you encounter trouble with your aircraft and you need to return to base, give your call sign, turn back, and head for home or land somewhere if you have to. If you have an emergency, switch to Channel D so that ASR can get a fix on you.

"I want radio silence all the way. Unless it's necessary for you to report something, keep your mouths shut. I want radio discipline, gentlemen. Do I make myself clear on this? Get the courses to where we are going and back and the various times from the board, and don't forget to turn on your IFF [Identification Friend or Foe system] after takeoff."

We synchronized our watches and then stood at attention while the bosses walked out of the briefing room. Everybody rushed outside to catch rides to their dispersals. Several of us bummed a ride on Captain

Andrews's Jeep, while others caught a ride in a squadron truck that was waiting outside to take the pilots to the dispersal. As our Jeep sped toward the dispersal, the captain remarked, "Maybe this will be the day we can have some action."

This is how the pilot's board looked when Capt. Andrews posted the names of the pilots who were going to fly on this mission."

WHITE SECTION

Captain Andrews	QP–Y
Lieutenant Pisanos	QP–D
Lieutenant Whitlow	QP–H
Lieutenant Macfarlane	QP–N

BLUE SECTION		**RED SECTION**	
Captain O'Regan	QP–X	Lieutenant Hopson	QP–I
Lieutenant Douglas	QP–Q	Lieutenant France	QP–E
Lieutenant Morgan	QP–U	Lieutenant Priser	QP–L
Lieutenant Care	QP–R	Lieutenant Boehle	QP–O

Lieutenant Beeson spare with QP–K

I picked up my parachute, Mae West, and helmet, and as I began to walk toward my aircraft, Captain Andrews, who was behind me, said, "Spiro, you stick close to me, OK?"

"Yes, Sir," I replied.

The weather was the best we had had for several days: a cloudless sky, normal temperature, and good visibility. Just before engine start time, complete silence draped the aerodrome. Nothing moved along the perimeter taxiway. I looked at the clock. It read 1:00 p.m., the time to start engines.

My eyes were fixed on Andrews's P-47, and when I saw the propeller of his aircraft turning, I signaled to my crew chief that I was ready to start my engine. He signaled back the all clear. I pressed the starting button and after the propeller blades turned around twice, the R-2800-1 power plant responded with the sound of a thunderclap. Two or three coughs later, the engine started with a little roughness but settled down to smooth running in a few seconds. A minute or so later, Captain Andrews signaled that he was pulling out. When he passed in front of me, I followed his P-47 on the taxiway. The rest of the 334 Squadron aircraft were following behind.

Major Blakeslee had taxied onto the runway with his wingman and was waiting for the time to start rolling. The remaining 336 Squadron P-47s were parked on the taxiway and on the grass west of the runway and were ready to follow the leader's roll. The 335 Squadron aircraft were parked behind the 336 Squadron.

At exactly 1:10 p.m., Major Blakeslee began to roll down the north runway with his wingman. Just before the first two P-47s became airborne, two more 336 Squadron aircraft began to roll down the runway, and two more taxied into position. While we were waiting for the remaining 336 P-47s to take off, we checked our own engines. Then, when the last two 336 aircraft were rolling down the runway, Andrews taxied onto the runway and positioned his aircraft well to the left. I followed him, lining QP-D up to the right and a little behind Andrews's P-47.

A few seconds later, the flagman, a pilot standing just off the runway on the left side of Andrews's aircraft, dropped the red flag—the signal for us to begin our roll for takeoff. Andrews looked at me and gave me a thumbs up. I returned the gesture, and the two of us started to roll down the runway, picking up speed rapidly. Just before we had reached the end of the runway we were airborne.

I raised the gear and flaps, closed the canopy, switched on my IFF, and followed Andrews's aircraft as he started to turn left. When all 334 P-47s had become airborne and joined up, Captain Andrews maneuvered the squadron to the left of the 336 Squadron, and Major Blakeslee made another wide left turn around Debden Aerodrome to allow space for the 335 Squadron to join up.

Finally, all three squadrons were west of Debden and in position, and Major Blakeslee started to climb on course toward Ostend. As I followed Andrews's aircraft, I glanced at the instrument panel from the corner of my eye every so often to make sure that all was well. We passed 18,000 feet over the English Channel, maintaining complete silence except for some radio static and the humming of engines. When I glanced at the altimeter again, it read 27,000 feet, and I could see the enemy coast below.

Our silence was interrupted by our leader: "Hello, Corby. This is Horseback Leader, Angels Three-One. Over."

"Roger, Horseback Leader. Receiving you loud and clear. Out," replied Corby Control. The group crossed into Belgium over Ostend at 31,000 feet and made a slight turn to the right to head for Ghent. Then, just before reaching Ghent, Corby Control came back on the radio.

"Hello, Horseback Leader, you have a gaggle of bandits about ten o'clock low flying on a southwesterly direction. Over."

"Roger, Corby. Have bandits in sight. Horseback out," Major Blakeslee replied.

When Corby Control reported the bandits' appearance, I looked in the ten o'clock direction, and there they were—a few small specks way out toward the east, becoming larger as they approached us. Since the 334 Squadron was on the left side of the formation and closest to the enemy, Horseback Leader directed Pectin Squadron to deal with the approaching bandits. Captain Andrews led our squadron in a left turn, heading toward the bandits. But when the German leader of some eight to ten FW-190s saw us closing in, almost head-on from above, he broke up his formation. And the 190s scattered in all directions.

"OK, White and Blue sections going down. Red Section, stay up for cover," said Captain Andrews as he started to dive on the scattered 190s. Bud Care and Bruce Morgan from Blue Section were the first to break away from formation and go after the Germans. The White Section was still intact and in a diving turn.

Captain Andrews spotted two 190s below and ahead of us in a line abreast, flying away in the direction from which they had come.

"Let's go get those guys before they get away," he said over the radio.

As we closed in on the two fleeing 190s, they decided to split up. One veered to the right and the other to the left. Whitlow and MacFarlane must have gone after the 190 that veered right because when I turned my head to check behind us, they weren't there. Evidently, they had broken away without saying anything.

"Follow me, White Two," said Andrews.

"I'm behind you. Go," I said, as I fell back a little. Andrews closed in on the 190 he was after, until the clever German pilot cut his power abruptly and snapped his aircraft into a steep left turn, forcing Andrews to overshoot him. Having gone by the 190, Captain Andrews slammed his P-47 into a steep left turn, forcing me to pull up in a wingover to keep my eyes glued on his aircraft. Andrews's turn was so steep he must have experienced a high-speed stall. His P-47 flipped over on its back, fell down, and began turning in what appeared to be a flat spin.

"Tommy," I said on the radio, "are you OK?"

"Dammit. I screwed up. Go after him, Spiro, and I'll catch up with you," he replied.

I took my eyes away from Andrews's aircraft, turned my plane to the left, and dropped down with full power, trying to catch the 190, which was still trying to get away. I gained some distance with my full-power dive. I must have been about 400 yards out and behind the 190 when the guy started to turn left. I tightened up my turn and was able to slide inside his turn. I must have been about 250 to 300 yards behind him, and I thought that I had the 190 in a perfect position for a deflection shot. I pressed the trigger and gave him a short burst to make sure that I wasn't wasting my bullets. Every one of my bullets flew to the right of the 190. I tightened my turn more and gave him a long burst. Bang! Smoke started to pour from his aircraft. "I must have hit his engine," I thought. I could see something like a piece of cowling fly off the 190.

The smoke was getting heavier and the 190 suddenly stopped turning. I had him now in the center of my gunsight. I gave him another burst and still the only thing I could see was more smoke and no fire of any kind.

"'Ata boy. You nailed him. He's smoking badly," Andrews, who had finally caught up with me, said. "I'm behind you, White Two. Go on and finish the bastard."

The 190 appeared to have slowed down as I was closing in, and when I pulled up to his right, I could see the whole aircraft was engulfed in smoke. As I watched the smoking aircraft, its canopy blew off.

I thought the pilot was going to jump, but nothing happened. The pilot was still in the cockpit. Was he wounded and unable to move? For a moment I considered turning back, since we were flying deeper into Belgium. Andrews, probably thinking the same thing, cut into the radio and said, "Let's turn around, Spiro. The guy is done. He has to jump."

I then joined Captain Andrews and the two of us headed for Ostend, our exit point. As we crossed Ostend at 24,000 feet, Andrews spotted another P-47 closing in from our left. We kept our eyes on it until we could make out its markings. I was pleased to see that it was QP-R, the Jug flown by Bud Care.

We were halfway across the English Channel when we started our descent. We crossed the English coast, and in less than thirty minutes, we landed at Debden. While we were taxiing in, more P-47s from the mission appeared overhead.

During the debriefing, I reported my encounter with the FW-190—my first encounter with the enemy—to Lt. Ben Ezzell, our squadron's intelligence officer. Since I had not seen the 190 pilot abandon his aircraft or crash, I claimed the machine as one FW-190 damaged, based on the rules of combat. Captain Andrews added that he saw the German machine smoking badly and that the pilot had released his canopy, no doubt intending to bail out. But neither Tommy nor I had seen the German leave his aircraft. Based on this observation, Ezzell raised the claim to probably destroyed.

Lt. Bud Care, who was standing behind us waiting to be debriefed, told Lieutenant Ezzell that when he and Lieutenant Morgan went after an FW-190, which he too overshot, they were jumped by two other 190s that had come out of the sun. That was when he had gotten separated from Lieutenant Morgan. He then heard Bruce saying that he was hit but that he was okay and that he was going to bail out.

At that moment, Vic France, who had just landed and walked in to be debriefed, told Lieutenant Ezzell that he too had heard Bruce Morgan saying that he was hit, but that he never came back on the radio, and he never heard from either Lieutenent Whitlow or Macfarlane. He did, however, see two parachutes floating down but had no idea whose chutes they could have been.

On our way to the mess after our debriefing, I asked Captain Andrews what had happened to him when he overshot the 190 and flipped over.

"It was stupid of me not to have slowed down when I saw that I was closing in fast on the guy," Andrews said. "When I realized that, it was too late. Then, when I attempted to tighten my turn to stay close to the 190, I flipped over and found myself in a flat spin. Very foolish on my part." He was mad at himself for having missed the chance to nail the enemy.

By 2:35 p.m., all of the aircraft were in, except those flown by Lieutenants Whitlow, MacFarlane, and Morgan. We waited all afternoon but received no word on their fate. Lieutenant Ezzell, who stayed by the phone all afternoon, hoping to find out what happened to the three pilots, could give us only the results of the day's mission. "Three of our aircraft are missing. One FW-190, probably destroyed by Lieutenant Pisanos."

Later on, however, this claim was raised to one FW-190 destroyed, based on Lieutenant France's report on this mission. Figher command assumed that one parachute was that of Lieutenant Morgan and the other was the pilot of the FW-190 Lieutenant Pisanos had hit.

Days later, we learned from the Belgian Underground, through London, that both Whitlow and MacFarlane had been shot down and killed near Ghent. Morgan had bailed out and was injured on reaching the ground. The Germans had captured him as he was trying to hide in a wooded area.

During the remainder of May, I flew three more missions: a rodeo to Knokke, during which I was again wingman to Captain Andrews; another rodeo to Knokke, Zwevezele, and Roulers; and a circus mission to Walcheren Island and Eeklo-Maldegem. On this last mission, I flew as wingman to Major Blakeslee. Although we spotted enemy aircraft from afar on all three missions, the Germans kept their distance.

Beginning with the rodeo mission we flew to Blankenberghe on June 7, we operated with sixteen P-47s in each squadron instead of the twelve we had flown in the past. On a ramrod mission we flew to Niueport-Thielt and Eecloo on June 11, the 4th Group broke the record in 8th Fighter Command when it became airborne with forty-eight P-47s in five minutes. The landing upon the completion of that uneventful mission was completed in four minutes with the same number of aircraft.

The 4th Group managed to take part in fourteen missions in June: eight rodeos and six ramrods. I was lucky to participate in seven of those missions, and on two occasions, I was wingman to the boss, Major Blakeslee. I did not fire my guns on any of these missions. Others in the group, however, did have the opportunity to score and added five more kills to our group's tally: three ME-109s and two FW-190s. The 335 Squadron destroyed an ME-109 and two FW-190s, the 336 Squadron got an ME-109, and the 334 Squadron destroyed one ME-109, probably destroyed another, and claimed one as damaged.

157

The Thunderbolt was slowly making a name for itself, and because of the popularity of this unique fighter, generals, congressmen, and high-ranking U.S. government officials continuously swamped Debden Aerodrome. They all wanted to see the 4th Group in operation and to talk to its pilots about being the first to employ the Thunderbolt against the Luftwaffe. In addition to these distinguished visitors, reporters from newspapers and magazines from all over the United States, looking for stories about the air war to take back to America, invaded Debden.

Another group of journalists also visited Debden: American war correspondents. U.S. newspapers and wire news agencies had assigned these people overseas specifically to cover the Anglo-American progress of the war in the air against Germany. They could be identified by the U.S. Army officer uniforms they were authorized to wear without insignia of rank. Instead their uniforms were adorned with a patch on the shoulder that read, "U.S. War Correspondent." Under certain conditions, a war correspondent could fly on a mission as an observer aboard a bomber aircraft in order to get a story.

One day in the beginning of July, Vic France and I left the dispersal about midmorning and headed for the mess. As we walked into the empty lounge, we ran into a war correspondent who introduced himself as Walter Cronkite of United Press International, who was stationed in London. Mr. Cronkite asked if we were Thunderbolt pilots. When we said we were, he asked if we could spare a few minutes to answer some questions. Since we had time before our afternoon flight, France and I agreed. Mr. Cronkite pulled out a pad and fired away.

"You fellows here," he said, "flew Spitfires with the Eagle Squadrons while in the RAF. Now you are flying a heavier and larger fighter. How would you compare the P-47 with the Spit?"

Leiutenant France looked at me and then said, "You're talking about two entirely different fighters. The Spitfire is a 7,000 pounds aircraft and was designed and built as a defensive fighter. It's capable of fighting enemy aircraft from the ground up to 35,000 feet. In this role, it's superior to any Allied or enemy fighter. I doubt that the Thunderbolt would have performed the mission of air defense as well as the Spitfire did during the Battle of Britain.

"The Spit is an excellent fighter for point defense but limited for escorting bombers beyond a few miles inside the northern coastal areas of France. It can't hold enough fuel. The Thunderbolt, in contrast, is a rugged offensive fighter twice the weight of the Spitfire. Its airframe can take heavy punishment, but its best performance is at high altitudes. It can outdive and outzoom any of the existing Allied or enemy fighters. The Thunderbolt does well, also, in escorting bombers because it operates at high altitudes where maximum efficiency is achieved with its turbocharged engine.

"But the Thunderbolt, like the Spitfire, has limitations because of its fuel capacity. The 8th Bomber Command has begun to carry the air war into Germany's heartland with the B-17s and B-24s, and neither the Spitfire nor the Thunderbolt can provide escort all the way to targets deep inside Germany. Even with external fuel tanks, which we expect to receive soon, the aircraft would not be able to escort the bombers to distant targets like Berlin."

Mr. Cronkite asked me what I thought of Lieutenant France's comparison, and I told him I fully agreed with my friend's remarks. "If we are to destroy the German air force, as our bosses say, we need to have an escort fighter with the Spitfire's maneuverability, high-altitude handling, good rate of climb, high speed, and adequate firepower. But it must carry enough fuel to accompany the B-17s and B-24s anywhere in Germany. Unfortunately, such a fighter does not exist in our inventory at present."

"Have you boys had the chance to bring down any enemy aircraft with the Thunderbolt yet?" Mr. Cronkite asked.

"Not me," Vic replied, "but my smart-aleck Greek friend here has, and it was on his first mission with the Thunderbolt."

Mr. Cronkite turned to me and said, "You must be the man Lieutenant Hively told me about. Would you like to tell me how it happened, Lieutenant? Could you describe for me how a fighter pilot feels when he gets behind an adversary and is ready to fire his guns?"

"When you are chasing an enemy aircraft in the sky and trying to get in a position behind your foe for a quick kill," I said, "you are in an entirely different world, especially when the enemy pilot is aware that you are locked in on his tail. Out of desperation, the guy up front will try violent maneuvers to shake you off his tail, especially if he's an experienced air warrior. Normally, that won't work because you have the advantage. You're glued onto his tail and ready to blast him out of the sky, and you are as determined to bring him down as he is to shake you off his tail. The aerial duels happen too fast for you to think and worry. Luck, concentration, guts, and accurate shooting are of paramount importance as you aim to destroy the enemy in front of you.

"You trail your foe while rotating your head left and right to check your tail for any enemy aircraft. Your heart is pounding fast, and you begin to feel dryness in your mouth. Your body is sweating, and your arms and legs are trembling. Your muscles become tense, and your neck starts to ache as you hold your finger on the trigger, ready to fire your guns. You now feel sweat dripping on your forehead and down your spine as you begin to open fire against your foe, and by a great stroke of luck you may get a direct hit. Suddenly, the enemy machine will begin to burn from the bullets' impact. You are still trembling, exhausted, and drenched from the sweat on your skin, but you can't relax yet.

"As you pull away from the area and head for home, you start to experience the effects of your accomplishment—you have just killed another human being. Then, slowly, as you get closer to base, your mind and body return to normal. You approach the landing field with a little extra speed, and you perform a roll to signal those on the ground that you have downed an enemy aircraft. You land, and the flight surgeon approaches you while you are still in the cockpit, with a shot of whiskey to calm your nerves and to wet your dry mouth."

"Very interesting, Lieutenant," Cronkite said, "but tell me, being a Greek national, how on earth you ended here in the 4th Group?"

France and I invited Mr. Cronkite to join us at lunch, and I told him my tale in the dining room. After lunch, we said good-bye to the reporter and headed for the dispersal to prepare for our training flight.

On July 16, after what seemed like an endless stream of talking, promising, complaining, and waiting, we finally received external fuel tanks for our Thunderbolts. With the several hundred ugly, British-made, two-hundred-gallon unpressurized drop tanks fabricated from corrugated paper and some other durable material, we could begin to escort the bombers deeper into Germany. The tanks were designed to be carried under the belly of the P-47, and when you looked at a Jug that was fitted with a tank, the plane appeared to be pregnant. During trials, we discovered that the tank when fully loaded had a small clearance to the ground. If you happened to bounce a little during taxiing, the bottom of the tank could scrape the pavement. Also, once you became airborne with the belly tank, the lateral stability of the aircraft was off balance, even with only a half load. We tested the tanks for proper feeding and also released them over the sea by the wash area, to make certain the release button in the cockpit worked. Surprisingly, we experienced only a few occasions when the tanks either didn't feed properly or couldn't be released. After the testing was completed, Fighter Command decided we would operate our P-47s with only one hundred gallons of fuel in the drop tank because of the lateral stability problem.

Our first escort mission to Germany was scheduled for July 28, 1943. After a precise and detailed briefing that morning, the 4th Group, in planes using the ugly belly tanks, took off at 10:40 a.m., assembled over Debden, and set course for Emmerich, Germany, where it would rendezvous and provide withdrawal support for B-17s returning from hitting targets inside Germany. The bombing mission involved three B-17 wings scheduled to hit two separate targets: a fighter components factory in Kassel and an FW-190 facility at Oschersleben.

Maj. Gilbert Halsey led the group and flew with the 335 Squadron. Capt. Spike Miley led the 336 Squadron and had as his wingman our thirty-nine-year-old group commander, Col. Edward Anderson, who had insisted on coming along on the mission. Captain Andrews was leading our squadron, and I was flying as wingman to Deacon Hively in Red Section's tail-end Charlie position. Capt. Hoppy Hopson was up front in our section with his wingman, Lt. Jerry Montgomery.

Out of the forty-eight P-47s that took off on that mission, seven had to abort because of propeller problems, drop tank malfunctions, and other mechanical issues. The remaining planes started to climb into the cloudless and calm sky, crossing the enemy coast without interference, except for the usual coastal flak batteries. At 11:32 a.m., when we had reached 25,000 feet over Westhoofd, the group leader, gave the signal to drop belly tanks. We crossed the Rhine River and arrived over Emmerich at 11:47 a.m., but no B-17s were in sight. We continued toward Leerdam and spotted a group of B-17s, but they were not the aircraft we were looking for.

The group continued for several more minutes and finally spotted a large formation of B-17s, at a distance and to our right, flying toward us. Major Halsey made a wide starboard turn to line up behind the B-17 formation, which was being shadowed by a large bunch of enemy fighters on its port side, about 6,000 to 7,000 feet above. Halsey immediately maneuvered the three squadrons in position to cover the bomber formation. The 335 Squadron settled on top, 336 took the port side, and 334 covered the starboard flank.

The Germans held their distance but flew parallel to our course. All eyes in our group were glued on the enemy above and south of the bomber formation. Suddenly, Halsey cut into the radio and said, "Here they come, guys. Keep your eyes on the bastards."

The Germans started to dive down from the sun.

Captain Miley turned into the Germans as they approached the bombers on the port side and cut them off. A section or two from 335 Squadron joined the melee. On the starboard side of the B-17 formation, where the 334 Squadron was cruising, everything was quiet, until a couple of ME-109s dashed under the bombers from the port side. Captain Andrews directed Lieutenant Mills's Blue Section to go after them. I stayed in my position, checking the sky, especially the starboard side of the bomber formation, for any threat.

There must have been forty to fifty ME-109s and FW-190s swarming across the sky on the bombers' port side, firing from a distance against the formation. Parachutes began to pop out from one of the B-17s that appeared to have been hit. The machine began to smoke and then more chutes opened and started to float downward. Someone cut into the busy radio channel and screamed, "Did you see that goddamned 109? The pilot fired his guns at one of the floating parachutes!"

"Somebody get that sonovabitch," said another.

At that point, the enemy fighters appeared to be pulling away from the bombers, but a few were still firing rockets from a distance. The smoking B-17, from which the parachutes had dropped, suddenly exploded in the cloudless sky. Chunks of the aircraft began to float down in flames. After a while, the Germans stopped firing altogether and flew away from the area.

We stayed with the bombers as they crossed over Belgium and up to the middle of the English Channel, and then we broke away and headed for home, landing at Debden around 1:00 p.m., just in time for lunch. Immediately after lunch, Group Intelligence called a special briefing for all pilots to evaluate the mission. The group tally for the day was nine enemy aircraft destroyed, one probably destroyed, and six damaged in a running air battle with the Luftwaffe over German territory. The 336 Squadron lost one pilot, Lt. Hank Ayres, who, as we learned later, had bailed out but had been captured by the Germans.

That afternoon, some of us returned to the briefing room to receive decorations, presented by Brig. Gen. Ross Hoyt from the 8th Air Force headquarters. I received my first oak leaf cluster to the Air Medal for number of missions flown. During the presentation, Colonel Anderson extended his appreciation to the pilots who took part in the first P-47 mission to Germany. He pointed out that the 4th Group was the first organization to use the new belly tank, the first organization to penetrate into Germany with a fighter aircraft, and the first fighter group to fly a distance of 575 miles out and back from our base.

"For this," said Colonel Anderson, "I congratulate you and the men on the ground who made it possible for us to fly that distance and fight

THE HOUSE WHERE I WAS BORN - 87 PETRAS ST., KOLONOS, ATHENS

MY FAMILY— L-R: STAMATIS, CHRISOULA, ATHINA (MOTHER), JOHN, GEORGE, SPIRO, NICHOLAS (FATHER), AND MIMIS

THE GLOSTER MARS BRITISH-BUILT BIPLANE FIGHTER OF THE GREEK AIR FORCE
THAT MADE ME FALL IN LOVE WITH THE AEROPLANE - ATHENS, GREECE, 1932

MIMIS VIMAKIS - MY SCHOOLMATE AND
CLOSEST FRIEND IN KOLONOS, 1936

FLT. LT. GERASIMOS GAVRILIS OF THE
GREEK AIR FORCE WHO HELPED ME WHILE
I WAS VISITING TATOI AERODROME TO
WATCH THE AEROPLANES FLY - ATHENS,
GREECE, 1932-36

BY MY J3-CUB AGLIAYA FLYING
SCHOOL, FLOYD BENNETT FIELD-
BROOKLYN, NEW YORK, OCT. 1938

BY THE KAPRALOS COFFEE SHOP AT THE
TOP OF THE HILL OF KOLONOS, JUST ABOUT
THE TIME I ATTEMPTED TO STOW AWAY ON
THE ITALIAN LINER *REX* THAT WAS BOUND
FOR NEW YORK – 1937

THE PARK HOTEL, MY HOME IN PLAINFIELD, NEW JERSEY – 1940

RAF CADET SPIRO PISANOS BY A STEARMAN 13 BIPLANE. POLARIS
FLIGHT ACADEMY - GLENDALE, CALIFORNIA, 1941

P/O STEVE (SPIRO) PISANOS
RAF REDISTRIBUTION STATION,
BOURNEMOUTH, ENGLAND ON MY
WAY TO OTU - APRIL 1942

S/Ldr Chesley Peterson, my guardian, protector and mentor who took me into the 71 Eagle Squadron and who arranged to have me naturalized as an American citizen in wartime London - 3 May 1943

Me, P/O Spiro Pisanos when I reported for duty with the 268 RAF Fighter Squadron, Snailwell Aerodrome - Newmarket, England July 1942

Me, P/O S. Pisanos on the wing of a Spitfire just after my transfer into the 71 Eagle Squadron in the RAF - Debden, England Sept. 1942

IN THE COCKPIT OF 334TH FS SPITFIRE JUST BACK FROM
A STRAFING MISSION OVER FRANCE - OCTOBER 1942

MY P-51B ON ITS BELLY WHEN I LOST MY ENGINE ON A MISSION TO BORDEAUX,
FRANCE, MARCH 5, 1944, AND WAS FORCED TO CRASH LAND IN OCCUPIED FRANCE.
NOTE THE GERMAN SOLDIER GUARDING THE AIRCRAFT.
(PHOTO COURTESY OF THE FRENCH RESISTANCE)

PHOTO TAKEN JUST AFTER WE WERE TRANSFERRED FROM THE
RAF INTO THE USAAF AND WERE FITTED WITH OUR NEW UNIFORMS -
LONDON, ENGLAND, 1942

TAKING THE OATH OF ALLEGIANCE FOR MY AMERICAN CITIZENSHIP,
FROM DR. HENRY HAZARD, SPECIAL EMISSARY FROM THE U.S. DEPT. OF
JUSTICE. HQ ETOUSA LONDON, ENGLAND, 1943

DURING A BRIEFING (FRONT ROW, RIGHT), ON OUR FIRST ESCORT
MISSION INTO GERMANY WITH OUR P-47S - DEBDEN, 1943
(PHOTO COURTESY OF LIFE MAGAZINE)

L-R: LT. STEVE PISANOS, LT. MIKE SOBANSKI AND LT. COL. DON BLAKESLEE,
DEPUTY 4TH GROUP COMMANDER, AFTER RECEIVING DECORATIONS - DEBDEN, JAN. 1943

IN THE COCKPIT OF MY P-47 QP-D UPON MY RETURN FROM AN ESCORT MISSION TO FRANKFURT, GERMANY WHERE I HAD A DOUBLE VICTORY. DEBDEN - 29 JANUARY 1944

MY ROOMMATE DON GENTILE (R) CONGRATULATING ME AFTER I WAS AWARDED THE DISTINGUISHED FLYING CROSS (DFC) - DEBDEN, 1943

LT. VICTOR FRANCE, MY FIRST CLOSE FRIEND AND ROOMMATE AT POLARIS FLIGHT ACADEMY. WE WERE ALSO SQUADRON MATES AT 71ES AND 334TH FS AT DEBDEN, 1942-44

THE CAFÉ IN THE VILLAGE OF EPINAY IN OCCUPIED FRANCE WHERE I WAS TAKEN, FIVE DAYS AFTER MY CRASHLANDING, MARCH 5, 1944. IT WAS OWNED BY M. GIBOURDEL.

IN THE VILLAGE OF LA BARRE-EN-OUCHE. THE HOUSE OF M. GOYER, WHO PICKED ME UP AT THE CAFÉ AND BROUGHT ME HERE TO LIVE FOR 15 DAYS BEFORE I WAS MOVED TO PARIS. TODAY THE PLACE IS A GARAGE.

CLAUDE GOYER TODAY, THE SON OF M. GOYER. HE WAS AROUND 10 TO 12 YEARS OLD WHEN I STAYED IN THEIR HOUSE AND GAVE HIM MY SILK ESCAPE MAP IN MARCH 1944

FRANK SPEER, A FELLOW PILOT OF
THE 334TH FS - DEBDEN, 1944

THE INCREDIBLE COL. DON BLAKESLEE WHO
COMMANDED THE 4TH FG TO GREATNESS. THE WWII
AERIAL LEADER WAS ADMIRED BY THE TOP BRASS IN
THE 8TH AIR FORCE IN ENGLAND AND RESPECTED
HIGHLY BY THE GERMAN LUFTWAFFE, 1941-44

JOHNNY GODFREY (L), ME, AND DON GENTILE BY THE WING OF A YP-80
AT WRIGHT FIELD, MID-1945

ME AND GABBY GABRESKI (L), AMERICA'S LEADING ACE IN EUROPE DURING WWII, WHILE WE WERE STATIONED AS TEST PILOTS AT WRIGHT FIELD OHIO -1945

THE LOCKHEED BUILT YP-80 JET FIGHTER I FLEW AT MUROC LAKE DURING THE AIR FORCE'S SERVICE TEST PROGRAM. NORTH BASE MUROC, CALIFORNIA, 1945

MAJ. RUSS SCHLEEH (L) CHIEF OF FIGHTER TEST BRANCH, CONGRATULATING ME AND CAPT. DON GENTILE UPON OUR RETURN TO WRIGHT FIELD FROM THE YP-80 SERVICE TEST - MUROC, CALIFORNIA, MAY 1945

ALBERT W. STENDER (L), THE OWNER OF THE PARK HOTEL IN
PLAINFIELD, NEW JERSEY, THE FINEST BOSS I HAD IN AMERICA, MEETING
MY WARTIME BUDDY, CAPT. DON GENTILE (R). PLAINFIELD, 1945

SOPHIE AND ME ON OUR WEDDING DAY ON JUNE 30, 1946 - KANSAS CITY, MISSOURI

CELEBRATING AT THE KAROLOS TAVERNA, MY RETURN TO KOLONOS AND ATHENS
AS A MAJ. IN THE USAF, WITH MY BOYHOOD FRIENDS AND FRIENDS OF MY FATHER,
AFTER BEING AWAY FOR 14 YEARS - KOLONOS, ATHENS, 1952

GETTING READY
TO FLY THE F-102 AT
TYNDALL AFB WHILE
SERVING IN ADC, 1963

LT. COL. STEVE N. PISANOS,
USAF OPERATIONS OFFICER,
57TH AIRLIFT SQ., RECEIVING MY
FIRST LEGION OF MERIT FROM
GEN. JOHN P. MCCONNELL,
CHIEF OF STAFF USAF -
CAM RAHN BAY, VIETNAM,
NOV. 29 1967

TAKING OVER COMMAND OF THE
457TH AIRLIFT SQUADRON FROM
COL. WILLIAM MASON, COMMANDER
OF THE 483RD TACTICAL AIRLIFT
WING - CAM RAHN BAY AIR
BASE, VIETNAM, MAY 1968

AT MY OFFICE IN ATHENS, GREECE AS
CHIEF OF THE USAF SECTION WITH
THE MISSION FOR AID TO GREECE -
ATHENS, GREECE, MAY 1971

L-R: Lt. Col. Jack Bray, Brig. Gen. Chuck Yeager, and Col. Steve Pisanos celebrating the 50ᵀᴴ Anniversary of the USAF Test Pilot School - Edwards AFB, California, Summer 1995

After I was inducted into the "American Combat Airman" Hall of Fame, at the Heritage Museum - Midland, Texas, Sept. 2003

the enemy, destroying nine of his aircraft with the loss of one of our own. To me, the mission this morning was a significant one."

That night, we all gathered by the bar to celebrate the success of our first mission to Germany. At some point, Major Baldwin walked in and told us to join him in the lounge. We all picked up our drinks, moved to the lounge, and sat down in our comfortable leather chairs and couches to listen. Major Baldwin said he had just gotten off the phone with his counterpart at 8th Bomber Command, who told him that on the mission to Germany this morning the bombers had lost twenty-three B-17s. Fifteen of those bombers had been lost from one bomb wing.

"The bombers," Baldwin said, "met heavy enemy opposition in the air during the part of the mission when they flew into and out of the target without escort. Flak over the two targets also brought down a number of B-17s, and they were hit not only by machine guns but also by cannons, floating bombs, aerials mines, and rockets that were mounted under the wings of some fighters.

"The B-17 gunners claimed the destruction of some sixty-six enemy fighters, but command is reevaluating those claims.

"The morning mission to Germany was costly for the 8th Bomber Command, but without doubt, the U.S. Army Air Force left a mark on the Luftwaffe, showing American fighters over German soil."

CHAPTER 15

ESCORT TO GERMANY

By mid-1943, three USAAF fighter groups had employed the P-47: the 4th, 56th, and 78th. With a force of some 150 Thunderbolts, 8th Fighter Command began to conduct almost daily missions, from fighter sweeps and diversions to escorts of small numbers of B-26s and B-17s over northern France, Belgium, and western Germany.

Given the P-47's radius of action, which was well beyond the Spitfire's, we could provide a protective umbrella to the bomber formations all the way to their short-distance targets across the English Channel, remain with the bombers over the target area, bring them back to a point, and then turn the escort over to RAF Spitfires for the final leg of the trip back into friendly territory. Once the Thunderbolt entered the escort business, however, the bombing planners at 8th Bomber Command slowly began to extend their selection of targets deeper into enemy territory, well beyond the P-47's radius of action. To meet the 8th Bomber Command's new challenge, 8th Fighter Command established a procedure whereby on distant bombing missions, one or two P-47 groups would rendezvous with the bomber formation somewhere over the channel or over enemy territory and escort the big friends up to a point on the way to their target, at which time the escorting P-47s would break away and return to base. From that point on, the bombers would proceed to their target without escort, relying entirely on their own protective firepower to defend themselves against attacking enemy fighters. Once the bombers dropped their bombs on the target, they'd turn around and head for home. At a predesignated point, the returning B-17s would rendezvous with another P-47 group for the withdrawal support to friendly territory, normally halfway across the channel or up to the English coast.

Between the inbound escorting fighters' termination of their escort duty and the arrival of the withdrawal support P-47 group, the Germans hammered the B-17 formations with everything they had at their disposal: single- and twin-engine fighters and JU-88 and Dornier bombers, using cannons, rockets, and aerial mines that were dropped from above and ahead of the bomber formations. The German pilots' attacks against the bombers were made with determination, but when the withdrawal support P-47s appeared to be closing in to protect the returning B-17s, the Germans ceased their harassment of the bombers and flew away. Any German fighter pilots who remained behind for another pass at the now-protected bombers had to deal with the escorting P-47s.

When a damaged B-17 had fallen behind the main formation box, the Germans would keep up their harassment on the helpless bomber until it was brought down, unless the escorting P-47s arrived on the scene in time to protect the straggling aircraft. If the bomber could keep flying, the P-47s would escort it home.

The Luftwaffe had a good number of fighter pilots, however, who would attempt to attack a bomber formation even if it was well protected by escorting fighters. Those pilots were, without doubt, the Luftwaffe's best. They were courageous and skilled. They were determined and willing to make a run for a kill, whatever the odds.

In 1943 the German air force was still manned by masterful tacticians, and even though they had been defeated by the RAF during the Battle of Britain, Hermann Goering's men continued their operational training, preparing the Luftwaffe pilots to achieve and sustain absolute air superiority over much of the European continent. Until the Allies had a fighter that could escort the bombers deep into German territory, the German air force would continue to sustain that superiority.

In the meantime, the 8th Air Force bombing planners continued to dispatch B-17s well beyond the P-47's radius of action, and the losses of bombers continued to mount. These missions, of course, caused concern that spread from England to the halls of the Army Air Force's headquarters in Washington, D.C. The Army Air Force warned the 8th Bomber Command to restrict unescorted missions, to no avail. Between

165

April 17 and August 17, 1943, in only seven bombing raids, 187 bombers and 1,870 trained crew members were lost. In every one of these seven missions, Spitfires and Thunderbolts provided fighter escort only part of the way inbound and outbound.

The Germans had discovered that a frontal attack by a flight of two or four fighters, coming in on line abreast, was the best method for assaulting a B-17 formation. From experiments, they learned that if they closed in on a bomber formation quickly from the front, they had a better probability of killing the pilots in the leading and adjacent B-17s and damaging some of the bombers' engines. They had also learned that the front gun turret of the B-17 was equipped with only one .50-caliber machine gun, not a heavy weapon that could cause much damage to a swift attacking fighter. Further, a frontal attack could cause sudden disorder within a formation, even as the bombers closed in on their target. When 8th Bomber Command learned that the Germans had discovered the B-17's weakness in the front, they installed another .50-caliber machine gun on the nose turret. Still, frontal attacks continued on the unescorted American bomber formations throughout the war.

The Germans would also use one or two heavily armed FW-190s to attack close B-17 box formations from high above. While barreling downward at high speed, the 190s would aim to hit the leading B-17, a strike that would often either kill the pilots in the cockpit or create an explosion. The Germans expected the mortally wounded bomber to then collide with one or two adjacent B-17s, creating a disturbance in the formation. Other fighters in the area would then join up and further harass the loosened formation before it reached its target.

To attack B-17s with escorts, the German fighter leaders used a third method. They would dispatch a section or two of their fighters as a decoy to shadow the bomber formation, with the intent of luring some escorting P-47s away from their positions. If the trick worked, the remaining German fighters would attack the bombers at the spot the escorting P-47s had left unprotected.

Understanding this tactic, Major Blakeslee's philosophy was to protect the bomber formation at all cost. He always emphasized this point by saying, "If German fighters are cruising along in the vicinity of the bomber formation, leave them alone as long as they don't bother the bombers. But if they decide to close in with the intent of attacking the bombers, we would then have to deal with them."

THE AIR OFFENSIVE AGAINST GERMANY

Low clouds, drizzle, and fog curtailed our flying activities in early August 1943. The gloom prevailed across most of southern England and the continent, grounding even the seagulls. We had two ever-present enemies to deal with: the Luftwaffe and the weather.

While the weather had hampered 8th Bomber Command operations, the bombing planners, along with their RAF counterparts, continued to formulate plans to increase the bombing activity on targets deep inside Germany. The RAF Bomber Command wanted to continue its night offensive operations on German targets, while the 8th Air Force bombers decided to extend their daylight campaign. The German aircraft industry would be the number-one target for both forces. Ball bearing production facilities and oil and synthetic rubber factories were the Allies' second-tier targets. As they devised this plan, the Allied decision makers agreed that, before we begun any large-scale bombing of German targets, we had to destroy the Luftwaffe's fighter force, as its threat to the daylight bombers had increased considerably with Germany's industrial ability to produce—as reported by intelligence—1,000 frontline fighters a month.

Realizing that the American bomber squadrons wanted to continue their daylight raids inside Germany, Gen. Frank Hunter, chief of 8th Fighter Command, reminded the bombing planners that the P-47, even with its external fuel tank, would not be able to escort the B-17s to distant targets. The P-38, a twin-engine escort fighter, was expected to arrive in England soon, but although it had a better radius of action than the P-47, it wouldn't be able to escort bombers to targets as distant as Berlin. The planners at the 8th Bomber Command, however, were willing to accept the high bomber losses. Daylight raids deep into enemy territory were on the upswing, and the losses of B-17s continued to mount.

The first escort mission the 4th Group pilots were able to fly after early August's gloomy weather was on August 12. It was a withdrawal support effort for a task force of 250 B-17s returning from a bombing run on targets in the Ruhr Valley. At exactly 8:15 a.m., the group leader in the White Section and his wingman rolled down the runway. The rest of the group followed, and all the P-47s became airborne on time and without any problems.

A few minutes later, the three squadrons assembled in an impressive formation west of Debden and headed for Sittard, Germany, where we would rendezvous with the returning bombers. We crossed the enemy coast between Knokke and Flushing at 9:12 a.m. at 23,000 feet. As we passed Antwerp, the group leader gave the signal to drop our belly tanks. As usual, I turned on my gun sight and gun switches at that point. So far, all was calm in the totally cloudless sky.

At about 9:25 a.m., we arrived over Sittard at 29,000 feet. The group leader broke radio silence, saying, "Big friends straight ahead. Get ready and watch out. We're over the Krauts' domain."

As we approached the five boxes of B-17s flying westward, we saw a large swarm of mixed ME-109s and FW-190s approaching from the east, maneuvering for position to jump on the rear box of the bomber formation. We couldn't count the number of enemy fighters, but many were scattered in gaggles all over the eastern sky. We settled into our defensive positions, with 334 on top of the bomber formation and spread out, 335 to the port, and 336 to the starboard side.

Suddenly, eight to ten enemy fighters came from behind and above to bounce Captain Clark's Green Section. At the same time, about six to eight more ME-109s started their dive, aiming for our Red Section. Captain Hopson, our section leader, was the first to spot the diving bandits as they barreled down with the sun behind them. Hoppy immediately cut into the clattered radio and screamed, "Pectin Red Section, break, break now."

Hoppy broke violently to his left, and I broke frantically in a steep turn to the right, trying to face whoever was after us. I started to maneuver my Thunderbolt to escape the awkward predicament I was in. I looked in all directions, trying to reorient myself. My heart was throbbing fast. The ME-109 pilot who had come after me had zoomed upward when he saw that I had made a violent turn into his line of flight, perhaps to reposition his fast-moving machine for another attack. He never came back.

As I turned around and around, I found myself in the middle of a big melee of P-47s and enemy aircraft. Everyone was twisting, turning, climbing, and falling crazily, and out of the corner of my eye, I could see tracers flying all over. It seemed that everyone, friend and foe, was trying to get into an advantageous position for a kill. I continued to twist, looking above, below, and behind my tail to make sure that no one was after me. Because I was turning my head back and forth so fast, I began to feel pain in my neck and sweat pour down my spine.

As I banked into a sharp left turn, I spotted a P-47 below me at about 1,000 to 1,500 feet, flying westward and being followed by an ME-109 with blazing guns. I could see the 109 shooting at the P-47, but all of the shots fell short.

"My God," I said, "that pilot had better do something."

I called the P-47 on the cluttered radio channel without knowing who the pilot was. I screamed, "P-47 flying west, look out for 109 on your tail firing at you!"

I heard no response, so I chopped my throttle to slow down a bit and let the 109 go by. After he was well ahead of my position, I pushed the throttle and dropped my aircraft down to maneuver behind the 109. As I dropped, I passed through the enemy's prop wash that shook me up a little but didn't stop me from preparing to fire my guns from about 200 yards out.

Up to this point, the 109 pilot had not seen me, perhaps because his attention was on the P-47 he was after. I opened my throttle a little to maintain my distance behind my prey, and to keep away from his prop wash, I dropped my aircraft a little below the swiftly moving 109. Just as I was ready to press my gun button, the ME-109 pilot spotted me and banked sharply to the left. It was too late. At that moment, I had opened fire, and he flew into my firing line. I must have hit something near the engine and around his cockpit because heavy black smoke and flames engulfed the German aircraft as it spun out of control. The pilot made no attempt to abandon his doomed machine. One of my bullets, I thought, must have hit him.

I followed the burning 109 down to about 17,000 feet. I then pulled away and started to climb, hoping to find some of my friends to join up with. I was climbing and banking sharply left and right, looking behind me the whole way, when I spotted an FW-190 below. I reversed direction with a wingover and made a sharp diving turn to the right. This placed my aircraft behind and above the 190, about 800 to 1,000 yards away. With my dive and full throttle, I was closing on him fast. I must have been about 300 yards away when I opened fire from above. I saw some puffs of smoke rising from the 190, and the pilot immediately snapped his aircraft violently, maneuvering into a split S and pulling away fast with his dive. It wasn't wise to follow him down on the deck, I thought, so I abandoned my chase and started to climb, again hoping to find my friends. No one was around, so I decided to fly away—fast. I pushed the throttle wide open and pointed the nose of my faithful Jug in a shallow dive toward England and home.

I crossed the enemy coast, descending with a tremendous speed, weaving and checking my tail all the way. When I was halfway across the Channel, I could see the English coast way ahead, and this brought some relief from the fear that was still with me. Finally, I spotted other P-47s in the distance flying in my direction, and I slowly began to calm down.

I crossed the English coast, still coming down fast. At 5,000 feet, my plane's reserve fuel light came on, and I decided to land at the Framingham RAF Station to refuel. I parked my Jug by the control tower and jumped down to go inside to call Debden. Captain Andrews answered, and I told him that I had landed for refueling, that I was OK, that I had shot down an ME-109 and possibly damaged an FW-190, and that I would be home soon.

After my aircraft was refueled, I took off for my short trip home and landed at Debden. Lieutenant Ezzell immediately debriefed me. I told him about my engagements with the ME-109 and the 190 and that I was claiming an ME-109 destroyed and an FW-190 damaged. I also told him what had happened to my section after the Germans had jumped us.

Later that night after dinner, Major Baldwin told us that the group on today's mission had destroyed four enemy aircraft and damaged one. The 334 Squadron destroyed three, including my ME-109, and Lieutenant Padgett of the 335 Squadron destroyed one. The bombers had lost twenty-five B-17s, almost all of them during the period they were without fighter escort.

Four days later, on August 16, we flew a target support mission for a group of B-17s that were bombing Le Bourget Airport and other targets near Paris. I was the wingman for Deacon Hively on that mission, and when we arrived over the French capital and took our position to protect the bombers, we were jumped by a large bunch of ME-109s and FW-190s. The attack developed into a violent melee.

As Hively and I were twisting and turning, trying to find an opportunity to fire our guns, he spotted two 190s below our altitude that appeared to be flying away from the brawl. We dove our Jugs after them, but as we closed in on the two fleeing 190s, they spotted us and broke away, one to the left and the other to the right. Hively went after the guy on the left, and I followed the one to the right as he was heading south of the city. After some turning and tumbling around, I finally nailed the guy, and he went down in flames. By that time our squadron and the B-17s had left the area, so I turned around and headed for home. I was lucky to run into Hively well northwest of Paris at my altitude. He confirmed that he too had clobbered his 190, and we headed for home in close line abreast formation.

We were the last of our group to return from the mission. Lieutenant Ezzell debriefed us and filed our two claims—two 190s destroyed.

"That's good," Ezzell said. "This brings the tally for the group up to ten enemy aircraft destroyed."

In the evening, however, as we were celebrating our victorious day, Lieutenant Ezzell approached me at the bar and said, "Steve, I am sorry, but your gun camera didn't record your engagement today. The armorers who checked the camera discovered that it was jammed. So unfortunately your claim was turned down."

I was disappointed, of course, but I knew darn well that I had blasted the 190 out of the sky. That day the group scored nine enemy aircraft destroyed with one loss: Lt. Joe Mathews of 336 Squadron, who bailed out because of engine trouble. We learned later that Mathews evaded capture on his landing in enemy territory and was helped to safety by the French resistance.

The next day's mission to Regensburg and Schweinfurt involved two task forces of 315 B-17s and was the biggest and costliest mission to date for the 8th Bomber Command. The 56th and 353rd groups were assigned to escort the 1st Task Force in the morning as it bombed the Messerschmitt factory at Regensburg. After the bombing, the task force was to proceed to bases in North Africa. The 4th and 78th groups were to escort the 2nd Task Force in the afternoon as it bombed the ball bearing facilities around Schweinfurt and then return to England.

Lieutenant Colonel Blakeslee, who had been promoted at the end of July, was leading our group; Capt. Abe O'Regan was leading our squadron; and I was flying in the Red Section. The 4th and 78th groups took off at about the same time, at 2:55 p.m., and headed for Eupen-Düren, the point of our rendezvous with the B-17 task force. When we arrived at Düren, we discovered that the task force had gone by, and we had to catch up with the B-17s a few miles beyond the rendevous point, just as a gaggle of enemy fighters arrived to attack the force.

When the Germans spotted the approaching armada of P-47s, they abandoned their plans and flew away. We took our positions over and around the B-17 formation and provided escort to a point well southeast of Düren. Then all 4th group fighters turned around and headed for home, landing at Debden at 3:45 p.m., disappointed at not having tangled with the Luftwaffe.

In the evening while at the mess, we learned that the 56th Group had flown two missions. After they had returned from their morning mission, they flew again in the afternoon as the withdrawal support for the 2nd Task Force. During the mission, they had entered a fight with the Germans and shot down seventeen enemy aircraft. Lieutenant Colonel Blakeslee was furious when he heard the news. But the real disappointment came when we learned that the bombers had lost sixty B-17s and 600 trained crew members during their two missions that day.

A few days after this blow, on August 20, we learned that Lieutenant Colonel Peterson was returning to Debden to take over command of the 4th Group, as Colonel Anderson had been promoted to brigadier general and was taking command of the 67th Fighter Wing. A week later, we learned that Brig. Gen. Frank Hunter was being reassigned and that he would be replaced as the chief of 8th Fighter Command by Maj. Gen. William Kepner.

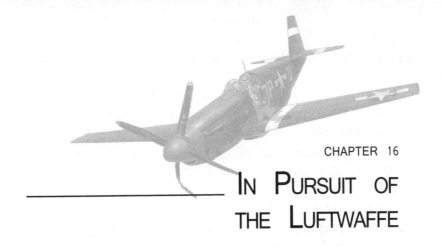

CHAPTER 16

In Pursuit of
the Luftwaffe

"Gentlemen, first let me assure you that I am extremely pleased with the way the 4th Fighter Group is fighting the Germans in the air. As I see it, however, it is of paramount importance that we continue to pursue the Luftwaffe not only in the air but on the ground as well."

Maj. Gen. Bill Kepner, our new boss at 8th Fighter Command, made this comment during his first visit to Debden. The short talk the general gave after dinner to the large gathering of 4th Group pilots in the officers' mess was reassuring and to the point. In few words, General Kepner told us that we must continue to defy the Luftwaffe's control of the sky over Europe so that our bombers could reach their targets safely and destroy Hitler's industrial war-making machinery. General Kepner closed by saying, "I am confident that the 4th Fighter Group will do its best to achieve this objective."

The general's comments inspired a new zeal in the 4th Fighter Group pilots, which endured until the end of the conflict in Europe. September was now with us, and we looked with optimistic determination for some action. Ground crews had been working day and night, installing brackets on our P-47s to carry the new, metal 108-gallon external fuel tanks that our group had received. The tanks would extend the Thunderbolt's radius of action to some 375 miles from base.

At the same time, an interesting but somewhat disturbing intelligence report that would to some degree affect air operations over Germany came out of 8th Fighter Command. The report, addressed to all fighter group commanders, said, "Since the 8th Bomber Command has stepped up its daylight raids on targets inside Germany and American escorting fighters have begun to appear over German soil in large numbers, the Luftwaffe has been, for some time now, moving large numbers of fighters from other areas, especially the Eastern Front, into the interior of the Fatherland in preparation for the defense of Hitler's industrial complex."

The report revealed that the Luftwaffe had already moved 600 ME-109s and FW-190s, as well as more than 200 twin-engine day fighters.

"Flying crews can expect these skillful German pilots to attack the American daylight bomber formations and their escorting fighters from any angle imaginable and to use many different weapons without considering how well the bomber formations are protected by their own guns and escorting fighters. These elite Luftwaffe pilots are going to try to break up the escorting fighter formations first, then make their assault on the bombers at all costs," concluded the report.

The 4th Group pilots were skeptical.

"So what. Let the bastards come," remarked Deacon Hively, as we finished reading the report at the dispersal. Despite our bravado, we knew that even with our new external fuel tanks we would be unable to provide escort to the bombers all the way to distant targets inside Germany.

The outcome of unescorted missions was less than gratifying. As noted previously, the American bombers were left on their own to deal with the increased Luftwaffe menace outside the P-47's radius of action. The bomber crews were forced to defend their own formations using concentrated crossfire against the skillful, determined, and stubborn enemy. Many B-17 crews expressed their concern for their own safety, and they were not the only ones to complain. Generals and RAF air marshals had been saying, publicly, for months that a new type of long-range escort fighter was needed to successfully take the fight to Hitler's homeland.

Finally, we saw signs that our complaints were being heard. One day, General Kepner informed all of the group commanders that the 55th Fighter Group was being equipped stateside with the Lockheed-built twin-engine P-38 Lightning and that the group was expected to deploy to England soon.

"And there is something else also shaping up in the pipeline," Colonel Pete told us one evening at the lounge. "They're coming up with a new fighter that will be far superior to the P-38 and P-47, a machine that can be used for long-range escort."

September came and went fast, and most of the few missions we flew were simple milk runs. On September 26, on our return from our last mission of the month—a B-17 escort to Les Andelys in northern France— I taxied into the dispersal area only to find a P-51 Mustang with a four-bladed propeller parked on the grass across from my stall. The Mustangs I had flown in RAF OTU and the 268 Squadron had been equipped with a three-bladed propeller. "What do we have here?" I wondered.

When my crew chief, Sgt. Paul Fox, climbed on the wing to help me unstrap, I asked him about that new aircraft.

"I don't know, Lieutenant," he said. "A pilot flew it in after you all had left on the mission and parked it right there."

When I arrived at the dispersal hut, I asked the operations sergeant about the parked Mustang, and he referred me to a captain from Fighter Command, who was waiting in the hut. The captain introduced himself as Capt. Jack Miller. He told me that the strange plane was the P-51B Mustang that was equipped with the Packard-built Rolls Royce Merlin engine. It was a fighter with lots of fuel. The aircraft was on loan to the 4th Fighter Group for its pilots to fly and evaluate from an operational standpoint.

After I stored my chute, I walked over to the parked Mustang to have a closer look. As the other pilots parked their P-47s, they too came over to check out the slick new fighter. We all admired the olive-green painted Mustang with great enthusiasm.

"You know, guys," Hively said, "I'll bet this is the aircraft Colonel Pete mentioned that night at the lounge."

At the beginning of October, the Mustang was released by maintenance for flying. I was more familiar with the machine than anyone else at Debden. When Captain Clark saw my RAF logbook, with some eighty flying hours on the P-51A from OTU and my short tenure with the 268 Squadron, he was surprised indeed.

On my first flight in the souped-up Mustang, I took the aircraft up to altitude and flew around for about fifteen minutes until I was satisfied with the way the engine sounded. I dropped down on the deck and decided to make a pass over Debden, clocking some 450 miles per hour.

175

As I passed over the aerodrome, I zoomed up and rolled to the left and to the right. Then I went into a loop. I pointed the nose of the Mustang at the aerodrome again and buzzed the place a few times.

Jim Clark, Colonel Pete, Deacon Hively, Duane Beeson, and Vic France came over from the dispersal to see me as I was getting off the Mustang. They all eagerly inquired what I thought of the machine. I told them that without doubt it was one of the finest aircraft I had flown.

"Better than the Jug?" Hively asked.

"Yes, better than the Jug, the Hurricane, the Spitfire we flew in the RAF, the P-40, and the P-51A. Wait until you fly it, and you'll see for yourselves."

Beeson, France, and Hively each went up after I had and had nothing but praise for the North American Aviation-built machine. When Hively came down from his flight, he said, "Greek, you can have my Jug, and I'll take the Mustang."

"Sorry, Deacon," I said, "you're a little late." We grinned at each other like boys with a new toy. Unfortunately, Fighter Command took away our new Mustang only two weeks later, after a good number of 4th group pilots had had the chance to fly it.

In the days that followed, we were confronted with the approaching winter, but despite the low clouds, fog, and drizzle, we managed to fly a mission here and there. On the morning of October 8, we deployed with forty-eight P-47s to refuel at Shipdham RAF Station, and then we proceeded on a ramrod penetration support mission to Bremen, Germany, escorting some 180 B-17s in three box formations. Lieutenant Colonel Blakeslee led the group, and Captain Clark led our squadron. I flew in the second element in Captain Clark's White Section, and this time I had a wingman, Lt. Vasseure Wynn, to watch and protect my tail if we became involved in a scrap.

At 2:19 p.m., we met the bombers over Tessel Island, immediately dropped our tanks, and took up our positions over the well-spread-out bomber formation. The 334 Squadron was assigned to cover the rear group of some sixty B-17s. We had just settled over the B-17s when Captain Clark warned that about thirty bandits had been spotted approaching our position from the south, well above our altitude.

As the Germans came closer, it appeared that they were heading for the rear box of the bomber formation. The other two boxes were well ahead. Captain Clark told us to keep an eye on the bandits above as they maintained their altitude. Minutes after his initial warning, Captain Clark cut into the radio and said, "Here they come, Pectin Squadron. Be ready to break when I give you the signal."

At first, we thought that the enemy was after the bombers, but we soon realized that we had been duped. Fifteen of the ME-109s ignored the bombers and headed straight for our squadron. Their plan was obvious: break up the escorting fighters and open the door for more of the enemy, half of whom remained above, to go after the B-17s.

Captain Clark came back on the radio and said, calmly, "Pectin Squadron, break hard now."

We had no choice but to break violently. Captain Clark and his wingman, Flt. Off. Ralph "Kid" Hofer, broke to the right and my wingman and I broke left. This scattered our squadron all over the sky over Meppel. I couldn't tell who was who in the melee. P-47s and ME-109s were chasing each other, hoping to get a shot. Soon my wingman had disappeared, just as, when I had been a wingman, I had found it difficult to stay with my element leader. In such a situation everyone is on his own.

As I twisted and turned fearfully, I spotted an ME-109 crossing under my aircraft, about 2,000 feet below. I pulled up and made a wingover to kill some of my speed and change direction so I could drop on the guy from behind and above. My plan worked, and evidently the 109 pilot did not spot my maneuvering, perhaps because the sun was behind me.

When I closed in within 300 yards, I tried to place the 109 in the center of my gunsight, but my hands were shaking a little and I couldn't get a lock. I told myself to settle down. I pressed the trigger, and gave the enemy a long burst of gunfire. The 109 began to smoke, and the German turned steeply to the left into a dive. Before he could get away, I gave him another burst, and this time heavier smoke rose from his engine. I thought that I must have hit his oil tank or glycol (engine coolant).

Suddenly, I saw a stream of tracers from behind just miss my right wing. Someone was after me. Fear and cold sweat came over me, and I immediately cut my throttle, pulled the stick against my stomach, and kicked my left foot all the way forward to snap around and break the attacker's aim of fire. When I came out from the maneuver, I spotted the 109 that had fired on me. He zoomed up past me and never came back.

Still, I was shaken up by the ordeal. The guy had scared the daylights out of me. I had concentrated so much on chasing the ME-109, and had disregarded the cardinal rule of air fighting: watch your tail at all times. I turned and started to climb, hoping to join up with one of my friends, when I spotted a P-47 just below me, chasing an ME-109. Immediately, I stopped my climb, turned around, and started to cover the P-47—although I didn't know who the pilot was. As I settled behind and little to the right of the P-47, I saw firing from the Jug's guns blasting the 109 out of the sky. Flames engulfed the 109, and I watched it explode in the sky.

178

The P-47 had to veer to the right to avoid the big mushroom fire from the explosion. As the Jug turned right, almost cutting in front of my line of flight, I noticed its marking: QP-B, Duane Beeson's aircraft. Before I had the chance to call Beeson on the radio, he cut in and said, "I see you, Steve. Let's join up and stay together around here."

"Roger, Duane," I said.

Beeson made another turn and headed toward the bomber formation. I followed him, placing my Jug to his right and a little behind, becoming his wingman. We stayed close to the bombers, and when the time came for us to leave the area, we headed for home.

I stayed by Beeson's wing over the North Sea and to the English coast before I noticed my reserve fuel light on. I told Beeson that I was low on fuel, and I'd better land somewhere soon.

"I'm OK and will press on," he replied. "There's Halesworth straight ahead."

I left Beeson to make his way home and dropped down in preparation to land at the 56th Fighter Group base. After my plane had been refueled, I was on my way home, and I landed at Debden at 4:10 p.m.

When Lieutenant Ezzell debriefed me, I claimed one ME-109 probably destroyed and confirmed Lieutenant Beeson's kill. Later in the evening, while I was at the bar with the boys, Lieutenant Ezzell joined us to tell me that he'd upgraded my claim to destroyed. When he and

Major Jesse Gittinger had assessed my gun film from the flight, they noted heavy smoke and flames coming from the German aircraft I had hit. This made my count four confirmed kills. If I could've counted the unconfirmed kill I had over Paris, I would've been an ace now.

A couple days later, on October 10, the 4th Group provided target support for 180 B-17s of the 2nd Task Force that were to bomb the railway yards at Münster, Germany. If clouds obscured Münster when we arrived there, the bombers were going to proceed to Ham, their secondary target. As usual, Lieutenant Colonel Blakeslee led the group, flying with 336 Squadron; Captain Clark led our squadron, and I was flying in the Blue Section with Lt. Allan Bunte as my wingman, while Mike Sobanski was leading the section. The 56th Fighter Group was assigned to relieve us on this mission.

By 1:35 p.m., we were headed toward Noordwall, climbing to 28,000 feet. The group crossed the enemy coast at 2:44 p.m., dropped tanks at 3:38 p.m., and at 4:06 p.m. rendezvoused with the B-17 formation. They were flying in a three-box formation at altitudes between 25,000 and 30,000 feet, headed toward their primary target, the city of Münster.

We soon realized that it would be difficult to provide total cover to the dispersed bombers, but by this point, we had learned to deal with such situations. Blakeslee cut into the radio and directed Greenbelt (335) Squadron leader to cover the middle box of B-17s and Pectin (334) Squadron to protect the rear box of some sixty B-17s.

"I'll be up front with Shirtblue (336) Squadron," said Blakeslee.

Captain Clark ordered our four sections to spread out to better cover the rear box of scattered bombers. White and Red sections took position over the bomber formation, Green settled on the left, and Blue covered the right flank. So far, except for some light flak here and there, we had not seen a single enemy aircraft in the space we were flying in. Eventually heavy black smoke began to rise ahead, from the bombs dropped by the first and second boxes of bombers.

As the box of bombers we were protecting reached the initial point for their bombing run, some twenty miles out, Pectin Leader cut in to the radio channel and said "Bandits, three o'clock high. There must be thirty or forty, or perhaps more."

Everybody looked in the three o'clock direction. Clark came back on the radio and said, "There seem to be 109s, FW-190s, ME-110s, and some JU-88s." The JU-88s were used frequently by the Luftwaffe to launch rockets against the bomber formations from a distance.

As the rear box of bombers approached the target, the swarm of Germans started their dive from above our formation, in preparation for a frontal attack on the bombers we were protecting. When Clark reported the coming attack, Blakeslee with 336 Squadron turned around to come to our aid.

"OK, Pectin Squadron," Captain Clark said over the radio, "let's cut the bastards off before they reach the big friends."

All four sections in our squadron came to a line abreast and spread out a little more so that we could face the attackers head-on. Captain Clark led the entire squadron in a shallow dive to intercept the Germans, who had already started their descent in a line abreast. Clark's maneuver placed our squadron some 3,000 yards in front of the bombers, on a head-on collision course with the diving Germans. When the Germans saw us in front of their path, they scattered in all directions. Some rolled over and went into split Ss. Others zoomed upward, and others turned around and flew in the opposite direction. By this time, Blakeslee with 336 Squadron had arrived on the scene to help us. We then turned and headed to catch up with the last box of B-17s, which had already dropped its bombs and was flying away from the target.

As we approached the bomber formation on the starboard side, Lieutenant Sobanski of our Blue Section spotted and reported another six FW-190s ahead and to the right of our path, maneuvering for what appeared to be another attack on the bomber formation.

"Blue Section is going down," Mike Sobanski said.

Captain Clark acknowledged Mike's report and directed the Red Section to cover the Blue Section. Sobanski, Blanchfield, Bunte, and I broke away from the squadron formation, flew toward the six FW-190s, and prepared to jump them. Suddenly, Mike screamed on the radio, "Watch out, Pectin Blue Section! Another bunch of 190s behind us! Break! Break now!"

I broke sharply to the right, cutting in front of one of the attackers from above who overshot me and zoomed upward. At the same time, I spotted tracers flying in all directions around my aircraft. They were, I thought, from another attacker, perhaps the wingman of the guy who had jumped me first. This double attack on my aircraft scared the hell out of me, and I continued to twist and turn to make certain that no one was on my tail. It was difficult to tell who was who in the fracas that had erupted, as P-47s and FW-190s were twisting and tumbling, everyone trying to get on the tail of the other for a shot.

I was coming out of a steep turn when I spotted an FW-190, just a little bit below me, going straight in for an attack on a B-17 that was flying well outside the right flank of the bomber formation. From my position it was impossible to maneuver my P-47 behind the German plane, so I decided to dive on the guy and cut him off in hopes of getting a deflection shot. With the German on my right and the B-17 on my left, I closed in fast at a ninety-degree angle to my target. I figured that I had nothing to lose by firing a deflection shot when I got closer, though I knew a ninety-degree deflection shot was difficult to execute. As our paths converged rapidly, I took a shot, hoping that he would fly through my firing line, but I missed. I immediately fired a long burst, and suddenly the German abandoned his plan to attack the B-17, rolled over, and went into a split S—diving straight for the deck. He must have seen my firing.

I found myself alone out there, deep inside Germany, and decided not to go after the guy. I figured that I could count the encounter as a victory, since I had diverted the German from making an attack on the lone B-17. I took a quick glance at the clock on my plane's dashboard and realized that it was well past the time for leaving the area. I then turned toward England with a wide-open throttle, watching my tail, knowing that I was still in danger this far inside Germany.

I had started my descent as I crossed the enemy coast, but when I was halfway across the channel, my low fuel warning light came on. I had to land somewhere. As I approached the English coast, I spotted the familiar Boxted RAF Aerodrome and put my thirsty Jug down. Unfortunately, just as I landed, some heavy fog rolled over the aerodrome and stayed there for three days. I didn't return to Debden until October 13.

Even though the October weather wasn't the best, the month was profitable for the 8th Fighter Command, and General Kepner had good reason to be happy. The groups under his command had destroyed seventy-three enemy aircraft, and we had lost fourteen P-47s. The bomber squadrons, however, didn't fare as well. They lost another sixty B-17s on the second Schweinfurt raid, plus several more in crash landings on their return to their bases in England.

Nevertheless, the losses during the second Schweinfurt mission deep inside Germany finally forced the Joint Chiefs of Staff and the Air Council, including the combined chiefs, to reevaluate their strategy and admit, somewhat reluctantly, that if daylight bombing strategies were to succeed on targets deep into Germany, the bombing forces would have to be escorted by fighters all the way to their targets. The bombing planners of the 8th Air Force suspended the distant daylight raids inside Germany for the time being and concentrated on short bombing missions across the English Channel and the North Sea, on which P-47s could accompany the bombers all the way to their targets and back.

CHAPTER 17

THE RACE FOR AIR SUPREMACY

As a result of the Schweinfurt calamity, the United States was sending us two new fighter planes. The 20th and 55th fighter groups, both with P-38J Lightnings, were being deployed to England and would soon be available for escort duty. The P-38J, a Lockheed Company–built fighter, was equipped with two Allison V-1710-89/91 supercharged engines that produced some 1,475 horsepower each. The aircraft had an operational ceiling of 40,000 feet and could attain a top speed of 433 miles per hour at 30,000 feet. Its armament consisted of four .50-caliber machine guns and a 20-millimeter cannon, all mounted in front of the pilot, which could cause heavy damage to an opponent in an aerial duel. With its 450-mile radius of action, the Lightning could provide escort to the daylight bombers on deeper penetrations than our P-47 could.

In addition, all of the newly produced P-51B Mustangs were being diverted to England. This version of the Mustang was a formidable and revolutionary single-engine fighter, with phenomenal range and great maneuverability. The new Mustang was equipped with the American-built Packard, 1,520 horsepower, V-1650-3 Merlin engine and could operate at altitudes up to 42,000 feet, with a top speed of 441 miles per hour. The P-51B was equipped with four .50-caliber guns, two on each wing, and could fly 485 miles from base using only internal fuel. With two 75-gallon external fuel tanks, the range increased to 650–700 miles, and with two 104-gallon tanks its range became much greater.

General Kepner said that this new aircraft would enable us to provide protection to our bomber formations on deep penetrations and to challenge the Luftwaffe for air supremacy in every corner of the European air space. With this aircraft, we could ultimately dominate the sky over Germany. Those of us at Debden who had had the chance to fly the P-51B hoped that it would not be too long before the 4th Group was equipped with the new fighter.

As we waited for the Mustangs to arrive, the 354th Fighter Group personnel—who had just arrived from the United States—were settling into their new home at Boxted RAF Station. Shortly after the new group arrived, General Kepner learned that the 354th didn't belong to the 8th Air Force but instead to the newly created 9th Tactical Air Force (TAF), which was commissioned primarily to conduct low-level strafing operations. The 354th was also waiting for its Mustangs, and General Kepner felt giving the aircraft to the 9th TAF was a waste of resources.

"A high-altitude escort fighter aircraft," the general thundered at a group of fighter group commanders, "and Washington wants to use it to support low-level strafing operations!"

He refused to accept Washington's thinking or compromise his position, and—surprisingly—he had his way. Gen. Carl Spaatz, Kepner's superior, agreed that the 354th Fighter Group would remain assigned to the 9th TAF but that the 8th Fighter Command would retain total operational control over the group's assigned aircraft and personnel. This arrangement freed the new aircraft for escort missions deep inside Germany.

Following a short bomber crew rest after the second raid on Schweinfurt, and despite the unfavorable weather predicted for November, the bomber planners decided to launch a force of some 566 B-17s and B-24s against the seaport city of Wilhelmshaven on November 3. General Kepner promised Bomber Command that five fighter groups, including more than 200 P-47s and about fifty P-38s from the combat-ready 55th Fighter Group, would be available for the mission. The 55th's first long-range escort mission over Germany called for the fighters to use a relaying procedure General Kepner had recently developed. Three P-47 groups would rendezvous with the inbound bombers at a point inside the Dutch coast and escort them to a point deeper into enemy territory. The P-38s, with their greater range, would take over and escort the bombers to their target. After the bombing run, the Lightnings would bring the bombers out from the target and stay with them

184

up to another point, where two groups of P-47s would make the rendezvous, take over the escort from the P-38s, and bring the bomber force back to friendly territory.

Lieutenant Colonel Blakeslee led the 4th Group on this mission, using his new call sign, Upper. Major Clark led our squadron, and I flew in the Red Section with Lieutenant Wynn as my wingman. We took off from Debden at 9:45 a.m. and, after stopping to refuel at the 56th fighter group home base, assembled south of Halesworth Aerodrome before heading out over the North Sea in an echelon-up formation. We climbed to 26,000 feet, with 334 Squadron in the up position to the right. The group had crossed the enemy coast south of Kijkduin, Holland, at 12:25 p.m., when Warmsun Control broke the radio silence to warn us to look out for bandits approaching from the southeast. Upper's reply was a simple "Roger, Warmsum." All of our eyes were aimed to the southeast, straining to find any hint of contrails, indicating the approach of enemy aircraft.

As we leveled off at 26,000 feet, with 334 Squadron to the right and about 2,000 feet higher, we were suddenly bounced from above by a group of ME-109s. Clark, who was the first one to spot the 109s coming down from the sun, gave the signal just in time for Pectin Squadron to drop our tanks and break hard against the attackers. Bob Priser and Ralph Hofer broke right, and my wingman and I broke sharply up and to the left.

My turn against the attackers from above was extremely sharp, and I blacked out for a moment. When I came to, my wingman was gone and I saw nothing but P-47s turning and twisting like mad dogs. Blakeslee with 335 Squadron tried to come to our aid, but another group of ME-109s attacked them while they were in a turn. Shirtblue (336) Squadron turned around and joined the melee of twisting, turning, tumbling, and zooming P-47s and enemy aircraft.

I saw more German fighters diving from above, and the radio screamed with curses and reports from the embattled pilots. The Germans appeared to be coming down in twos, fours, and sixes, and almost all of them zoomed upward from their dives, no doubt in preparation for another bounce. I looked around, hoping to spot Priser's aircraft or any other P-47 to join up with, but I had difficulty identifying anyone in the tangle.

I was in a steep turn trying to position myself when I spotted an

ME-109 below me. I turned my Jug around and dove toward the lonely 109. With my diving speed and full power I closed in fast on the enemy plane. I must have been about 300 yards behind the German and slightly above when I opened fire and hit him on the right wing, but the German pilot pulled up into a steep left-climbing turn and zoomed away from me. I realized the enemy aircraft must have been an ME-109G and gave up the chase. I would never have caught up with that fast-moving Luftwaffe agile aircraft. With a top speed of more than 400 miles per hour, the ME-109G could operate above 40,000 feet and was far superior in armament and maneuverability to my Jug and most of the aircraft the Allies employed.

186

I was alone in the midst of the fray, when Upper leader came on the radio and said, "All scattered aircraft return to base."

Since I could not find any of my friends, I turned around and headed westward over the North Sea. As I flew westward over the North Sea, I began to realize what the Germans had done to us. The attack on our group was meant to force us to jettison our tanks early and prevent our forty-eight P-47s from meeting the bombers. The bastards had succeeded. It was a clever trick, I thought. Later we learned that Fighter Command had recognized the trick as well and decided that if the German continued to use this tactic, they would send a squadron or two of RAF Spitfires ahead of escorting fighters to clear and patrol the path and to deal with any unexpected ambushes.

I came across the North Sea alone, but as I crossed the English coast on my descent, I spotted several P-47s converging with me on the way to Debden, where we all landed at 2:00 p.m. At the debriefing, we learned that we had shot down only one of the enemy planes and had lost Lieutenants Moon and Gallion, both from my squadron. The score of kills on the mission was thirteen enemy aircraft destroyed: nine by the 56th, 78th, and 353rd P-47 groups, which were able to complete the escort; three by the 55th P-38 Group over the target; and one by our own Lt. Alex Rafalovich. He made his kill when the Germans jumped us on our way into Holland. Although the target was completely covered by clouds, the bombers were able to use radar to complete their bombing.

Later that evening, some of the P-38 pilots from the 55th Group who had taken part in the mission visited Debden to compare notes with us. When describing the action over the target, one P-38 pilot said that the German pilots kept their distance from the bombers. The few who thought they could get away with some head-on passes against the B-17 formation were unpleasantly surprised by the circling P-38s, and many broke away from their initiated attacks. Nonetheless, four B-17s were shot down by flak and three were lost to German fighters. This was an extremely low percentage of the force of 539 bombers that reached the target. We knew that the boys at the 8th Bomber Command would be happy with the results. This mission proved that a suitable fighter escort all the way to the target would allow the bombers to get away with minimal casualties.

The group flew a number of uneventful missions through November. By the end of the month, my roommate and I had piled up so many missions that we took a few days off to relax in London. When we returned to Debden on the evening of November 30, I learned from Vic France that there had been only one kill during the three missions the group had flown while we were away. The 56th Fighter Group, however, had bagged twenty-six kills on the November 26 mission to Bremen, placing them well ahead of our group's meager tally. We were not able to close the gap by the end of November, and we ended up with only four kills for the month. The drought continued through December; I fired my guns only once that month.

On December 16, the 4th Group began to use some new tactics imposed by Fighter Command. Previously, the squadrons had flown in groups of sixteen, with sections of four airplanes each. Thus, with 334, 335, and 336 Squadrons all in the air at the same time, a typical escort force had forty-eight airplanes. The Luftwaffe's resistance, however, made it necessary to add a fifth section to each squadron, bringing the total group force to sixty aircraft. The extra sections made it easier for us to cover the bomber formations, which could extend on a line up to thirty miles long.

Each fighter squadron flew about 2,000 feet above the bomber formations, and each squadron's new Purple Section positioned itself 1,000 feet above the rest of the squadron planes to act as scouts and to report any approaching enemy. If the Germans attacked, the Purple Section would be their first target, allowing the rest of the squadron to carry out its escort duties. The tactic served us well, but we didn't find many opportunities to engage the Luftwaffe as we neared the end of 1943.

We had Christmas Day off from flying so that everyone could celebrate the holiday. We had lunch with the first three grades of NCOs. It included punch, lager, and assorted finger foods in the officers' mess. That afternoon, some sixty enlisted men from our squadron played host to about one-hundred British orphans visiting the station. The children were taken to the station theater to watch Disney movies, and after the movies, the American Red Cross treated them to cake, ice cream, and candy, while Sgt. John Cross played Santa Claus, handing out gifts to each of the orphans. After they were shown our Thunderbolts at the dispersal, the children left the station—a little happier, we hoped.

The day after Christmas we were back at work, undertaking an uneventful freelance and withdrawal support mission for the 2nd Bomber Task Force returning from Mannheim. On December 31, 1943, we flew our last mission of the year—freelance and target support for about 450 B-17s and B-24s bombing Luftwaffe aerodromes near Paris. I was flying the spare aircraft for our squadron, hoping that some unlucky pilot would drop out so I could take his place. My somewhat uncharitable desire was fulfilled when Deacon Hively—who was leading the Red Section—had to turn back because of fuel problems.

"Greek," he said on the radio, "come up and take my place. I have to turn back."

I immediately maneuvered my aircraft and dropped into Hively's slot at the head of the Red Section. Since we were early, we circled Rouen and then headed to cover the bomber armada flying toward the southern end of Paris. We had just settled over the bomber formation when Jensen Control told us to sweep the Paris metropolitan area. As we were orbiting over Paris, the bomber formation broke up into several groups south of the city and headed in different directions to bomb separate targets.

Villa Coublay and Le Bourget aerodromes, both within the Paris area, were hit and damaged heavily, though both aerodromes appeared to be empty of planes. The Germans no doubt had flown away earlier. The heavy smoke we saw throughout the outskirts of the French capital made it clear that the big friends had done one hell of a good job, and surprisingly, we had not seen any enemy aircraft while circling over Paris. When the bombers completed their runs, leaving several targets in flames, they turned around and headed for England, encountering no opposition but the ever-present flak. We made another sweep south of Paris, hoping to see some Germans, but we were out of luck. Jensen Control then released us to return to base, and we landed at Debden at 1:15 p.m.

That afternoon, we learned that fifteen more P-47s were being delivered to Debden, bringing the total aircraft for each 4th Group squadron to twenty-five. The 4th Group would now operate with seventy-five Thunderbolts. We also learned that our rival in the air, the 56th Group, had been operating for some time with more than one-hundred P-47s and all of their Jugs had been fitted with new paddle-bladed propellers, which improved the aircraft's performance, especially in climbing. We suspected this accounted for the 56th Group's success against the Luftwaffe.

The 4th Group closed the year with a less-than-stellar record of kills. In the twenty missions that our group had flown during the last two months of 1943, we had destroyed only eight enemy aircraft and lost two pilots, both from my squadron. And the miserable winter weather we had encountered over England and across the channel was more of a hindrance for us than it was for the Germans. When our bombers could not penetrate the weather to bomb Germany, the Luftwaffe had a chance to regroup.

We in the 4th Group began to fear that if we continued to experience bad weather and little enemy resistance, we'd never catch up with Col. Hub Zemke's 56th Group, even with the additional aircraft assigned to our group.

A NEW STRATEGY

The New Year brought a number of changes in the upper echelon of command, designed to accommodate the new overarching plan: to destroy the Axis forces in the air and on the ground. Gen. Carl Spaatz became the commander of the newly organized U.S. Strategic Air Forces in Europe. His primary responsibility was to coordinate the 8th and 15th air forces along with the RAF's Bomber Command in order to undertake strategic operations to destroy Germany's war-making industry from the air.

Maj. Gen. Frederick Anderson became deputy for operations under General Spaatz's command and served as chief coordinator of the two strategic air forces. Lt. Gen. Ira Eaker was transferred to Italy to take over command of the newly organized Mediterranean Allied Air Forces. Maj. Gen. James Doolittle, who had led the daring first bombing raid on Japan with B-25s launched from the aircraft carrier *Hornet*, took over as boss of the 8th Air Force. General Kepner remained as boss of the 8th Fighter Command, and the 15th Air Force in Italy remained under the command of Maj. Gen. Nathan Twining. On January 1, 1944, Colonel Pete was also assigned to the newly formed 9th TAF as director of operations and thus relinquished command of the 4th Fighter Group to Don Blakeslee.

In addition to these changes in management, we received new objectives, rules, tactics, and procedures. The strategic bombing planners began preparing to bomb targets throughout Germany, both in clear and inclement weather. When clouds obscured the targets, the American bombers would bomb by radar. The main objective for the U.S. Strategic Air Forces was the destruction of German aircraft production facilities, plants, military installations, industrial facilities, aerodromes, and anything that contributed to Hitler's war effort.

The recently arrived 55th, 20th, and 354th fighter groups, with their P-38s and P-51Bs, as well as several more groups that were on their way, were part of the Allied effort to deal with the German fighter force with increasing strength. The 8th Fighter Command also planned to change its mode of operations to support the new daylight bombing operations. The fighter groups would patrol a certain segment of the bombers' path to and from a target, forming a relay of information and protection in the air. RAF Spitfires would take the first leg of the missions. They would be relieved by P-47s, which in turn would give the escort duties over to the P-38s. Last, P-51Bs would take the bombers all the way to their targets. Any attempt by the Luftwaffe to interfere with the passing bombers would be met by fighters patrolling assigned segments of airspace.

That new escort system was not the most interesting change in strategy. After the fighters had finished their escort missions, they would be released to look for targets of opportunity on the ground—such as aerodromes with parked aircraft, rail traffic (particularly locomotives), military vehicles, and anything that appeared to be of military value—on their return leg to base. This was certainly a welcome development, as it allowed us to start flying rhubarb missions, something I hadn't had a chance to do since my tenure with the RAF.

Everyone in the squadron was excited about the new venture, even though we knew that strafing a target on the deck would be difficult and dangerous. To augment our skills, we began to practice dive-bombing, a tactic used by the Germans with their Stukas and by both American and Japanese forces in the Pacific. First, we practiced diving without bombs. Then we started to carry 500-pound bombs on the external fuel tank brackets under our fuselages. We dropped the bombs on a specially designed circled target over the wash area. Some hits were good; others, of course, were not. But we kept practicing.

Our first mission of the New Year, on January 4, was routine penetration support for the 1st Bomber Task Force, which was bombing targets in Münster, Germany. Our next mission was also routine. But on January 7, we finally ran into some trouble when we provided withdrawal support for B-17s coming out of Ludwigshafen. A gaggle of FW-190 fighters, coming out of the sun, jumped the White Section of 336 Squadron. Our leader, having just shot down an FW-190 in a fierce dogfight, had no choice but to call for help. Jim Goodson, who was nearby with his wingman, Bob Wehrman, responded promptly and rendered assistance to Colonel Blakeslee—who by then was flying a partially crippled P-47. When Captain Goodson arrived on the scene, where Blakeslee was fighting for his life against an overwhelming force of German fighters, he not only chased the Germans off the boss's tail but also managed to blast two of the attackers out of the sky.

On his way back to England, Colonel Blakeslee landed his crippled Thunderbolt at the first aerodrome he sighted, Manston RAF Station. There, the ground service crew counted seventy-one holes in his P-47. The colonel was airlifted home and forced to leave the bullet-riddled P-47 at Manston.

On January 11, the group attempted to provide withdrawal support to a force of some 633 B-17s and B-24s returning from three separate targets: the FW-190 plant in Oschersleben, the JU-88 plant at Halberstadt, and the ME-110 plant at Brunswick. However, the mission was doomed by bad weather. As we climbed over the North Sea, we could see forbidding black clouds ahead. Crossing into enemy territory, we were forced to fly through some solid dark clouds, sweating it out for a while until we broke out on top at 33,000 feet. As a result of the weather, our squadron's Green Section became separated from the rest of us and had to return to base. The other squadrons had similar problems. By the time we had reached the top of the cloud cover, almost half of our group had been forced to turn back. Finally, at 12:12 p.m., all aircraft were ordered to return to base. Luckily, we all returned safely. After we had parked our aircraft and began to walk toward the dispersal hut, the frustrated Lieutenant Hively asked, "Who in the hell planned this mission for us?"

We learned later that a good number of the bombers from the task force had to abort the mission and return to England because of the weather. Some of the other fighter groups that had been part of the big show, though, had not been affected by the weather and had succeeded in escorting a number of the bombers to their targets. Surprisingly, there had been some big fights in the air, resulting in the destruction of twenty-nine enemy aircraft.

Despite the success of the overall mission, we in the 4th Group were unhappy with our participation. Frustrated, I took Vic France up on his offer to take a few days off and head to London to blow off some steam. We didn't return to Debden until the evening of January 14.

The first person France and I ran into as we walked into the lounge on the base was one of my friends from 336 Squadron, Lt. Willard Millikan.

"Hi, Millie," I said. "What's going on around here?"

Millikan explained to us that my roommate had almost been lost on a fighter sweep in northern France that afternoon. When I heard the news, I rushed to our room to make sure Gentile was OK.

"Hey, buddy, how are you doing? Do you feel alright?" I asked, on entering the room. Gentile was stretched out flat on his bed.

"Not exactly," he replied. "I almost got clobbered on the mission this afternoon. Man, I should have gone to London with you and Vic."

Gentile told me how that afternoon, the group had flown a freelance mission to Magny-Soissons, while B-17s were bombing the V-1 sites. The group was to patrol the area south of Magny. When it arrived on the spot at 25,000 feet, it ran into a bunch of FW-190s some 3,000 feet below. The 336 Squadron was directed to bounce the Germans, and Gentile jumped into the attack with his section. During the mix-up, Gentile was separated from the others in his section.

While he was in a turn, he spotted two 190s below him, flying eastward, away from the ongoing fight. He dove his Jug after them and managed to hit the number-two aircraft. At that point, the other guy dove for the deck. Gentile followed him and finally nailed him a few feet above the treetops, but as he began to climb to return to the fight, he saw two more 190s barreling down on him fast. He cut into them to break their attack, and both initially overshot him but came around, trying to get on his tail. He managed to get on the tail of one of them and fired his guns while he was in a turn. But he missed his target, and the 190 zoomed up and flew away. Then he realized the other guy was trying to get on his tail. The two of them went around and around over the treetops, and at one time he had the German in his gunsight for a deflection shot. He pressed the trigger and nothing happened; he was out of ammo.

He and the 190 continued to turn until the German managed to get behind Gentile and started shooting. Luckily, all of his bullets went to the right of my roommate's steep-turning Jug until finally the guy ran out of ammo. The German pilot eventually caught up with Gentile and flew alongside his Jug with his long nose 190. The German looked at him, gave him a salute, and then flew away.

And that's how my roomate's butt was saved, as he was still shaking from the ordeal.

A week after my return from London, on January 21, we went out on a freelance mission near Pas-de-Calais, while the B-17s pounded Hitler's V-1 sites for the second time. I flew as wingman to Deacon Hively. We flew to the area between Amiens and Arras, and there, we found twelve enemy aircraft. Blakeslee dispatched 336 Squadron to challenge them. In the small engagement, 336 Squadron destroyed one of the FW-190s and damaged another one.

As we turned and headed for home, Hively and I were cleared to do some strafing before we reached the English Channel. In a close line abreast, we dove down at high speed, hoping to find some targets. The Arras Railway Station was deserted, so we continued on toward Le Touquet, where we would cross over into the channel. There, we found what appeared to be a heavy ack-ack battery complex, with guns pointed skyward.

Hively came on the radio and said, "Straight ahead, Greek. Looks like the guys who are shooting at us when we fly over the coast. Let 'em have it."

In the few seconds that followed, I must have emptied all eight of my guns. I pressed my firing button again and again at the exposed batteries. I could see a bunch of soldiers around the guns, either taking cover or already hit by Hively's and my bullets. We crossed over the batteries and the enemy coast traveling at high speed, zigzagging and staying close to the sea's surface.

On January 29, I was out again and had the chance to fire my guns at aerial targets, this time on a penetration support mission to Frankfurt. A total of thirteen fighter groups of P-47s, P-38s, and RAF Spitfires were covering the armada of 200 B-17s and B-24s. The 4th Group's task was to escort the 3rd Air Division deep into Germany up to a point where the 20th Fighter Group, with their P-38s, would pick up the bomber formation and provide escort to the target and back to a point where another P-47 group would provide escort home.

We rendezvoused with the 3rd Air Division bombers north of Brussels at 10:27 a.m. We took our positions over the bomber formation and stayed with them until we were northeast of Malmédy, without interference from the Luftwaffe. We left the bombers behind at 10:46, when the 20th Fighter Group showed up, and set course for home. Over Maastricht, Captain Mills, who was leading 334 Squadron, spotted a gaggle of about sixteen to eighteen aircraft at ten o'clock and below. At first, we all thought that they were P-47s from the withdrawal support group, but Mills didn't agree.

"Hell," he said, "they can't be P-47s. It's too early for them to be here."

Sure enough, when the aircraft flew closer, we saw that they were ME-109s. Captain Mills ordered the entire 334 Squadron to attack the bandits. As they passed by, we made a shallow left diving turn aiming to jump the Germans from behind and above. They, of course, had spotted us as we were coming down in full force. As we began to attack, someone reported ten to twelve FW-190s flying well behind the 109s, in the same direction and at the same altitude. We jumped the ME-109 formation and forced it to break up in all directions. P-47s and enemy fighters twisted and turned, all trying to get in position for a kill. As the melee developed, Green Leader Vic France snapped our section around violently from left to right, maneuvering for position, trying to line up behind someone. I soon discovered that my wingman, Lieutenant Bunte, missing. He must have been separated from us during the attack. I decided to stick behind Vic and his wingman, Lieutenant Blanchfield, acting as their tail-end Charlie.

Lieutenant France cut into the radio and said, "Green Section, eleven o'clock below, three bandits. Let's go get them."

I glanced in the direction France had indicated, and sure thing, there were three aircraft flying east. Without hesitation, Green Leader peeled off to the left in a shallow dive to attack the two FW-190s and the ME-109 flying in a close line abreast. As we barreled down, the three Germans seemed easy prey, but they must have spotted us because they broke their formation and tried to turn into us. The 109 I had been aiming for turned to the right and went into a dive. I pushed my throttle to full power, dropped my Jug into a right diving turn, and maneuvered to line up behind the diving 109. I wondered why the guy had decided to dive away from my P-47. That, I thought, was a great mistake.

I caught up with the 109 and was close enough to open fire as we both plowed downward at about a forty-five-degree angle. Suddenly, the 109 zoomed upward in front of me, as if to execute a loop, exposing the top surface of his plane to my line of fire. I pressed the trigger and nailed him with a long burst. My bullets must have hit his fuel lines or tanks because a ball of fire engulfed the 109. I followed the aircraft until I was sure that it was dead. When it flipped onto its back I pulled

195

away to avoid burning parts falling off the doomed 109, as it began to fall downward in flames and finally disappeared into the clouds below.

I started to climb and looked for France's aircraft or any other friendly plane. The clatter on the radio—the usual angry and jubilant curses and shouts—indicated there was a big mix-up above me. As I climbed, I spotted another ME-109 about 500 feet below me, flying away from the battle. I winged over, changed direction, and began to dive toward the unsuspecting German. With the momentum of my dive and throttle, I closed in on the lonely 109 faster than I had expected. I must have been about 200 yards behind him when I jabbed my thumb down savagely on the gun button, aiming to blast the 109 out of the sky. My short burst of firing splashed onto his right wing and forced the pilot to make a violent roll and turn toward me. His turn wasn't steep enough because I was able to drop inside and get on his tail. He tightened his turn, and I whipped my Jug around into an extremely tight turn. I could see thin contrails streaming from the tips of my Jug's wings. I kept the stick back on my stomach as the G forces pushed me down on my seat. My aircraft wheeled around on its left wingtip while I prepared to fire, but the German was a tough nut to crack. He tried everything in the book to shake me off his tail—but without success.

Finally, in one of the turns I found myself in position for a deflection shot, and I opened fire. Smoke started to rise from the 109's engine, and a huge flame followed. A split second later, the canopy flew off. The 109 banked sharply to the right, and the pilot fell out of the cockpit. He tumbled downward for a while before he deployed his chute. He was safe, but I had destroyed his 109. I was now an ace with five kills.

The mission was a successful one. We had destroyed nine enemy aircraft and lost only one pilot—Lt. Burton Wyman of 335 Squadron. The other fighter groups had destroyed a total of thirty-three enemy aircraft, for a total of forty-two enemies destroyed that day. January closed with the 4th Group claiming the destruction of twenty-nine enemy aircraft against the loss of two pilots in the ten missions flown that month. We had helped the USAAF 8th Fighter Command give the Germans a good pounding, which marked the beginning of the destruction of Goering's Luftwaffe. We went into February looking forward to even greater success.

CHAPTER 18

MUSTANGS, AT LAST

Command's weather prognosis was the same for February as it was for January: low cloud ceilings, drizzle, and fog combined with industrial haze and high overcasts with tops anywhere from 25,000 to 30,000 feet. A certain amount of doubt had to be factored into the evaluation of this prediction. The command meteorologists' reports in previous months had not been accurate because the winter weather in England was traditionally difficult to forecast. The USAAF and RAF meteorologists occasionally contradicted one another.

The soot from coal burning in almost every home and factory throughout England mixed with the thick fog and drizzle made the atmosphere pretty miserable for those who had to be outdoors. It was often impossible for us aviators to conduct successful flight operations against the enemy. Some days the visibility and ceiling were so poor that you could barely see halfway down the runway. Even the crows that roamed around the aerodrome refused to go aloft.

The task of the escorting fighters during inclement weather was always unpleasant and sometimes impossible. To make it into the clear above an overcast sky was fatiguing, and staying together took concentration. Sometimes we would not get word from Control that the bombers had aborted their mission until after we had made it above the cloud cover. In turning back, we would have to penetrate the clouds from which we had just emerged.

Although the seasoned pilots were skilled in flying with only instruments for guidance, we still had to be ready for the vertigo that often accompanied flying on instruments for a long time inside a thick overcast. It was more difficult for the pilots who had just come out of flying school. They had been assigned to operational squadrons without the necessary skills and experience to fly through the thick clouds safely. Weather-related accidents were frequent, and all too often they involved inexperienced pilots who crashed into hills while flying in the clouds or in poor visibility.

When the weather wasn't suitable for flying, we pilots would gather at the dispersal hut or go to town on a pass. On one of those nasty days, Hively, France, a few other pilots, and I were at the dispersal hut, reading through various reports, when Lieutenant Ezzell handed us "An Analysis of the P-38 and P-51B Aircraft Performance since Their Arrival in Theater." The report's focus was not the fighters' performance but the number of enemy aircraft shot down by the 55th and 354th fighter groups with their long-range aircraft. The abilities of the P-38 and the P-51B that flew on escort missions well beyond the range of our P-47s had made a stirring impression on us at Debden, in part because the 354th Fighter Group had piled up so many kills in such a short time. We felt strongly that, since the 4th Group was the oldest USAAF combat unit in England, it certainly deserved to be reequipped with Mustangs so that we, too, could fly deep into Germany.

As we read the report, Hively pointed out that the installation of the paddle-bladed propellers and the water injection system on the 56th Fighter Group's Thunderbolts had made their P-47s far superior to the aircraft we were using at Debden. At that time, though, there were no indications that the 4th Group would convert to another type of aircraft. It appeared that we were destined to keep our limited P-47s.

By early February 1944, Major Clark felt that I had enough experience to occasionally fly as section leader. Around that time, Fighter Command informed us that an enemy aircraft destroyed on the ground would now be considered a kill equally as important as an aircraft destroyed while in the air. This new classification gave us quite an incentive to strafe ground targets. Attacking targets on the deck was more dangerous than trying to shoot a moving target in the air. The strafing pilot had to be clever, use the element of surprise, and make only one pass, if he wanted to return to base and fly another day.

Late in the morning on February 13, a few of us pilots were at the dispersal, when suddenly we heard the sweet sound of the Rolls Royce Merlin engine overhead. Curious to see what the commotion was, we ran outside and saw three beautiful P-51B Mustangs, painted in dark olive green camouflage, circling over our aerodrome in preparation for landing. When the Mustangs had landed and were taxiing toward the control tower, Major Clark, France, Hively, and I jumped in a Jeep and headed for the control tower to have a look at the visiting aircraft. We guessed pilots from the recently arrived 357th Fighter Group had flown the Mustangs in. They had probably gotten lost and landed here to refuel.

We were wrong. The three Mustangs had been assigned to the 4th Fighter Group, one to each squadron. The other pilots and I cried out in happiness when we heard the news. Major Clark said, "Too bad Colonel Blakeslee isn't here to see and welcome our new flying machines."

Just before darkness that day, Colonel Blakeslee flew in from Leiston Aerodrome, where he had been helping the 357th become operational with its Mustangs, as he had done with the 354th Fighter Group. When he appeared at the mess that evening, smiling, we surrounded him. Once he had a beer in his hand, he began to tell us how he had begged General Kepner to supply our group with Mustangs. Kepner resisted at first because transitioning to the Mustang would have required our group to go off operations for at least two months. Preparations for the big bombing offensive were already under way and he couldn't afford to lose so many pilots. But Blakeslee kept up the pressure and assured the general that the transition could be completed in a short time.

"Although the general listened to my pleas, he showed no indication of sympathy," said Blakeslee. "I saw him in the hallway at the 8th Air Force headquarters one day, and he said that he was in a bind with the Strategic Bomber Command and that he couldn't spare us to go off operations. So, this last time, I told him that, if he gave us the planes, I would have you all ready to go in twenty-four hours. Even then, the general didn't say anything; he just smiled and walked away to attend a meeting. But just a few days ago, he called me at Leiston to ask if my promise to have you guys ready in twenty-four hours was still good. I told him that it was, and he told me that the planes were on their way.

"And I see we got three today, the boss said.

"Hurray," Hively shouted as he raised his glass for a toast.

Then a newly assigned pilot at the end of the bar raised his hand and said to the boss, "Sir, you mean that we aren't going to get some training on this aircraft before we go on a mission?"

"That's correct," the Colonel said with a smile. "You can get your training on our first mission out."

The first Mustang assigned to our squadron was turned over to maintenance for inspection, and short ground school classes were established for maintenance and flying personnel. Major Clark formulated a short flying training sequence to transition and check out all pilots on the Mustang. Since I had already logged many hours in the Mustang, he told me to be ready to help out with the checkout and training program.

In the meantime, the "Big Week" offensive, as it became known, was put in motion on February 19, 1944. That night, the RAF Bomber Command annihilated the German city of Leipzig with some 800 Lancasters and Halifaxes. The next day, the USAAF Strategic Air Forces fought through the cloudy skies to hit Leipzig again and moved on to destroy Berburg and Brunswick. The raids on the three cities involved more than 1,000 B-17s and B-24s from bases in England and Italy. P-47s, P-38s, P-51s, and RAF Spitfires organized into fifteen fighter groups provided escort support to the huge armada of bombers.

On February 20, 1944, the 4th Group supported the withdrawal of the first bomber task force out of Leipzig. We intercepted a gaggle of enemy fighters about to attack the bombers and destroyed four of the enemy's aircraft, while losing only one of our own. Overall, the mission was a complete success, causing heavy damage to the JU-88 and the ME-109 production lines at the Erla aircraft plant. About fifty ME-109s were caught on the ground before they could be flown away to Luftwaffe bases. Twenty-one Allied bombers were lost, most of them brought down by flak.

On Friday, February 25, 1944, the last day of the Big Week and a superb day for flying, I flew my last flight with the P-47 on a routine ramrod mission to Stuttgart, where the bombers were hitting a ball bearing factory and the ME-110 components plant at Fürth. When we landed from this mission, we found another fifteen Mustangs parked by the control tower. We now had fifty P-51Bs, all undergoing acceptance inspections and preparation for operational flying, and ferry command pilots had begun to arrive daily at Debden to fly away our faithful Thunderbolts. Our mechanics worked day and night to get the Mustangs through the required inspection. Soon they released some aircraft to the squadrons, allowing the pilots the chance to spend some time flying the aircraft.

Several missions were flown with the new Mustangs in the days that followed, and on each of them, the aircraft displayed a number of minor but annoying problems. Some of the 4th Group pilots began to regret having given up our Thunderbolts. But things began to fall in place when the local technical representatives of North American Aviation and Packard met with our maintenance people to analyze the problems we had encountered and plan for corrective action. In the meantime, we continued to fly the Mustangs, knowing that the aircraft had problems that, if we weren't lucky, might endanger us. This aggressiveness served us well, and by month's end, we had taken part in seventeen missions, fifteen with Thunderbolts and two with our new Mustangs. During those missions, the group had destroyed twenty-eight enemy aircraft and lost three of our own. Although I was proud of our total, I was somewhat disappointed because I had fired my guns only twice during the month—and had not scored any kills.

On Friday, March 3, 1944, we were scheduled to escort several hundred B-17s to Berlin. Along with two other groups of Mustangs, the 4th Group was to provide support to the bombers all the way to the target. It was our first escort mission over such a long distance. We put up forty-eight Mustangs and three spares. I was flying in the number-three position with Lieutenant Hively, who was leading the Blue Section, and had Lieutenant Blanchfield as my wingman. We took off at 9:40 a.m., crossed the enemy coast uninterrupted, and rendezvoused with the bombers near Neumunster. Eight Mustangs from our squadron and almost a similar number from the other two squadrons had to abort the mission because of various mechanical problems.

As the reduced number of Mustangs in our group settled over the leading box of the bomber formation, I noticed the weather ahead looked bad. But the mission continued. Surprisingly, not a single enemy aircraft had appeared in the sky thus far. We must have been somewhere northwest in the outskirts of Berlin when Skybird Control informed us that the big friends were aborting the mission because of the unsuitable weather over the target.

Eight pilots from 336 and 335 Squadrons, including Lieutenant Gentile, missed this message, even though Colonel Blakeslee broadcast it twice. These eight continued to follow a group of B-17s that had also missed the message that the mission had been recalled. As the eight Mustangs continued toward Berlin, more than sixty enemy aircraft of all kinds—ME-109s, FW-190s, ME-210s, and ME-110s—attacked them. Gentile later reported that the eight aircraft destroyed an equal number of German planes but lost four of their own. That evening we held an informal debriefing of the four survivors in the lounge. A number of curious pilots wanted to know how the eight Mustangs were able to repel the overwhelming number of the German attacking force.

"By rights," Gentile said, "the Jerries should have shot down every one of us up there, but they failed because they flew poorly and couldn't shoot straight. They were shooting all over the sky, often from out of range."

"We think," added John Godfrey, "that some of those guys who were flying the German machines must have been student pilots."

If that were true, we all agreed, we were well on our way to winning the war. We were all veterans of many engagements, and if we were up against students, the odds were in our favor.

The next day, March 4, we had another chance to fly to Berlin. This time the mechanical problems were even worse, and ten of us, including myself, had to abort. Some pilots encountered new problems such as windscreen frost at altitude. Colonel Blakeslee's guns jammed as he tried to shoot an ME-109 while in a steep turn. Lt. Hugh Ward of 335 Squadron went after an ME-109 in a dive, and as he reached a speed of some 550 miles per hour, his canopy blew off and hit the vertical stabilizer, separating the stabilizer from the fuselage. Lieutenant Ward managed to get away from his crippled Mustang and deploy his parachute, but the Germans greeted him when he hit the ground.

After the frustrating second Berlin mission, we blew off some steam at a big blast in the evening at the Debden officers' mess. I don't know whether we were celebrating the fact that we had flown twice to the German capital or were drinking to alleviate our frustration at the problems we were having with our Mustangs. The drinking started after dinner and continued with gambling at the billiard room. There was music and a lot of singing, as well as drinking, happening in the bar, the lounge, the hallways, and a few rooms. Deacon Hively, sitting on a chair on top of the piano with his helmet and goggles and a broomstick, did his hilarious impersonation of Baron Von Richthofen. When Hively was through with the baron act, Pierce McKennon of 335 Squadron proudly took over the piano. First, he played his favorite boogie woogie, and then, he switched to Chopin and Beethoven.

The clock on the wall above the fireplace in the lounge read midnight when Lieutenant Ezzell approached me and said, "Stevo, take it easy. You are going out tomorrow morning. Briefing at 0800 hours. Go get some sleep."

A FATEFUL MISSION

Well before sunrise on Sunday, March 5, 1944, the charge of quarters corporal knocked on the door. Gentile was up first and washed, shaved, and dressed; I followed suit. We walked downstairs to the dining room to have an early breakfast, and as I looked around the dining room that morning, I could see that most of the guys were groggy from partying the night before. I asked Gentile how he felt.

"Lousy," he said. "Don't forget to get some pure oxygen in the cockpit before engine start."

"Thank you," I said. "I was just about to say the same thing to you."

As usual, we stopped at the chapel to pay our respects to the Lord before we headed to the briefing. When we arrived in the briefing room, we learned that we were flying to the southwestern part of France.

"As you can see, gentlemen," said Maj. Jesse Gittinger, "you will be flying to two major aerodromes today: one in Limoges and the other one in Bordeaux. The Luftwaffe has been using these aerodromes for

JU-88s, which are bombing shipping convoys in the Atlantic on their way to England from Canada and the United States. Over the long run, the losses of merchant vessels in the Atlantic to these JU-88s raids have been high. This bombing mission is intended to put these two aerodromes out of commission."

After Major Gittinger covered the location of German air defense forces in the area, flak locations, and escaping and evading procedures, the weatherman presented the atmospheric conditions over England and the route to the target: "Good weather over England, with some strong winds from the north at altitude. You can expect some low clouds to the east along your route. The two targets should be in the clear and you can anticipate contrails around 29,000 feet."

Colonel Blakeslee, who was going to lead the group, continued the briefing: "The mission for today, gentlemen, is close escort and target support for the 2nd Bomb Division. The B-24s will operate at 25,000 to 26,000 feet, and we will provide cover, as usual.

"Each squadron will provide sixteen aircraft and a spare. Start engines at 8:50 a.m. and H hour is 9:00 a.m. We will assemble as usual. Our flight out will be echelon-to-starboard, with the 335 Squadron following 334, and 336 as tail-end Charlie. I'll be flying with the 334 Squadron today. 335 will follow 334 on takeoff, and 336 will take off last. We'll make landfall west of Fécamp at 9:51 a.m. and rendezvous with big friends west of Cognac at 10:58 a.m. The 334 Squadron will fly top cover, 335 will take the bombers' port side, and 336 will take starboard. Any questions?" The boss asked. There were none.

We synchronized our watches and scrambled outside for the waiting trucks and Jeeps that would take us to our dispersals. This is how the board was set up with the pilots who would fly on the mission.

WHITE SECTION		RED SECTION	
Colonel Blakeslee	WD-C	Lieutenant Hively	QP-L
Lieutenant Wynn	QP-X	Lieutenant Markel	QP-M
Lieutenant Pisanos	QP-D	Lieutenant Whalen	QP-C
Lieutenant Hills	QP-K	Lieutenant Blanchfield	QP-E

BLUE SECTION		GREEN SECTION	
Captain Mills	QP-Q	Captain Beeson	QP-B
Lieutenant Biel	QP-H	Lieutenant Lang	QP-U
Lieutenant Smith	QP-N	Lieutenant Chatterly	QP-G
Lieutenant Carr	QP-I	Captain Van Epps	QP-V
		Spare Lieutenant Smith	QP-Y

We emptied our pockets of all personal items and made a last run to the john before leaving for the flight line. Just before leaving the dispersal hut, major Clark made a few more remarks: "Remember, guys, keep radio silence, and wingmen, stay close to your elememt leaders. Good luck to you all."

When I got to my plane, I did the usual walk around check with Sergeant Fox, who also helped me settle into the cockpit. I strapped on my parachute, fastened my safty straps, plugged in the radio and oxygen, and took a few deep breaths of pure oxygen. This helped clear my lungs and head from the excesses of the night before. I then went through the before-engine start check and everything was set. At that moment, I glanced at my two devoted mechanics, Paul Fox and Jerome Byrge, who stood by waiting for my signal to start the engine. Paul and Jerome were the two trusted guys I had on the ground. They had maintained my aircraft all along when we flew Spitfires, then Thunderbolts, and now the Mustangs. I deeply respected these two men for their devotion to duty and to me, and the manner in which they kept the machine I was flying.

In fact, I have always felt that the crew chiefs, their assistants, the mechanics in the hangars, and all those who were connected to the maintenance of the airplanes we flew at Debden were devoted patriots. They were dedicated airmen who worked hard, day and night, to keep us up in the air. I strongly believe that they contributed immensely to the greatness and glory the 4th Fighter Group achieved by the end of World War II in Europe.

When Colonel Blakeslee's Mustang's propeller started to turn, I could hear the roar of the Merlin engines resonating across the aerodrome. I signaled to Sergeant Fox and pressed the starter. The propeller started to turn slowly and unwillingly, and after the usual cough, the engine caught and began to operate smoothly. At 8:52 a.m., Blakeslee pulled out and was followed by Lieutenant Wynn, his wingman. I waved good-bye to Fox, opened the throttle, and followed behind Lieutenant Wynn's aircraft. Seconds later, I glanced in my rearview mirror and saw all of the squadron aircraft on the taxiway, one behind the other.

At 9:00 a.m., the flare from the control tower was fired and the flagman on the left side of the runway dropped his red flag. Colonel Blakeslee and his wingman rolled down the runway for takeoff. After they were under way, my wingman and I followed. In a few short minutes, all forty-eight aircraft were aloft and assembled in formation west of the aerodrome, as we set course for the point of rendezvous with the bombers.

The group of forty-eight Mustangs headed south and passed over London. From our altitude we could see the south coast of England and the English Channel in the far distance. The clear blue sky and calmness made our climbing out pleasant. The white cliffs of Dover were below us and to the left as the terrain below changed from the rolling hills of southern England to the waters of the channel.

We had our first abort as we crossed into France, just west of Fécamp, at 15,000 feet. A 336 Squadron pilot advised that he would have to turn back because of a rough engine. Our second loss in the formation was more serious. Colonel Blakeslee broke radio silence to notify us that he, too, was returning to Debden with a bad engine. Major Carpenter of 335 Squadron took over to lead the group, and Captain Beeson with his Green Section moved forward to lead our squadron.

Four more pilots from the other squadrons turned back in the subsequent few minutes, all of them with engine roughness or trouble, probably caused by faulty spark plugs. Our new Mustangs had been shipped to England without spark plugs. To get the aircraft into operation in a hurry, the bosses at Command decided to use regular English-made Spitfire spark plugs. These replacements had a life of only six to eight hours in the Mustang, and this caused problems on long missions. We had learned to respect this condition and were always on the alert, especially when the symptoms appeared after we had departed on a mission. If an engine problem developed when a pilot was deep into enemy territory, he then had a problem.

Aircraft continued to drop out of the formation, one after the other. From the sixteen Mustangs that had taken off on the mission, our squadron was eventually reduced to only six aircraft. Even the spare aircraft that had taken Captain Mills's place had to turn back. Captain Beeson ended up leading the six of us on the mission in two sections of three aircraft each. I was in the Green Section with Beeson and Wynn, and the Red Section included Hively, Markel, and Carr. The other squadrons were also hit hard by aborts, to the point where the group was reduced to fewer than thirty Mustangs. Despite this, we proceeded on course to rendezvous with the bombers.

We found ourselves in quite a predicament, but I tried to keep my morale up, concentrate on staying close to Beeson, and watch out for our bombers. Our persistence was rewarded at about 11:00 a.m., when we spotted the 200 B-24s in a formation north of Cognac, cruising at about 26,000 feet. Our reduced group couldn't take its usual positions to port and starboard of the big friends. Instead, Major Carpenter instructed us to stay above the bombers. While 335 and 336 squadrons kept watch over the larger bomber segment, 334 Squadron, with only six planes, settled above the smaller segment. Shortly after the bomber formation split up, the large segment veered to the left while the smaller one continued southward toward Bordeaux. The six of us stayed with the B-24s that were headed for Bordeaux. The weather in the area was solidly overcast well east of Bordeaux, with tops at about 8,000 feet. The area to the west, toward the sea, was wide open. The bombers we were protecting approached Bordeaux from the northeast but continued south and made a wide right turn. It seemed that the big friends were going to attack their target from the south.

As we followed them on their course, I searched the sky in all directions. Suddenly, I spotted some small moving specks to the east of our position. I called Captain Beeson to report the sighting.

"Duane, nine to ten o'clock high. I think we have company. There may be eight to ten."

"Roger," responded Beeson. "I see them. Can't tell the type yet, but let's keep an eye on them."

By this time, the bombers had completed their turn and were flying steadily northward. Our six Mustangs were above and behind the rear of the bomber formation. We could see the German planes on an intercept course from the east, to the right of the bombers and us. We quickly realized the Germans, eight to ten ME-109s and a few FW-190s, were going directly for the bombers. When Captain Beeson gave us the signal, we cut in front of their approach. Our maneuver forced the Germans to break up and scatter in all directions—not upward and away as usual, but stayed at altitude. We had prevented their attack on the B-24s, and they were probably mad as hell.

I climbed steeply, trying to get closer to Beeson's plane, when an ME-109 barreled down behind Beeson's Mustang. I yelled a warning to my friend.

"I see him, Steve," Beeson said, as he swirled his Mustang around to avoid the 109's firing line. By the time I was able to approach Beeson's plane, the German had flown away. When Beeson saw me, he said that his plane might have been hit. I started to fly close to check his aircraft for visible damage, but as I maneuvered, Beeson yelled to me to watch out.

"Watch out, Steve! There's a 109 on your tail. Break hard now."

I broke sharply right, as bullets flew all around my Mustang. My turn was so tight that I blacked out momentarily. I recovered and barely avoided flipping over, putting my plane into a high-speed stall. Then I hurled my Mustang around at full throttle to pursue my tormentor. Instead of diving or climbing, my enemy had flown straight ahead, and I had him in my sight. He made a wide left turn. This allowed me to cut the corner and close the distance between us. I was on his tail now, but the German tightened his turn and forced me to readjust my course. I dropped five degrees of flaps and tightened my turn, too. When I reached within 200 yards of him, I pressed the trigger. The 109 flipped over and exploded in flame. Pieces of metal flew around me, and I maneuvered to avoid the shrapnel. As I looked below, I could see the fireball falling toward the earth.

Beeson congratulated me. We joined up in formation again, and I checked out his aircraft. His plane had indeed been hit, near the vertical stabilizer. I told him it seemed to be holding up OK.

As we set a course back to England, I spotted two 109s zooming toward us. I alerted Beeson, and we prepared for the encounter.

"Let's break when they are a little closer. I'll break left and you break right," Captain Beeson said. He was the best in the squadron at judging when to break.

The 109s were approaching us in line abreast. When they were within firing range, Beeson yelled, "Break hard now, Steve!"

I went into a steep right turn, cutting in front of the firing 109. His bullets missed me and he overshot my plane, flying overhead and going into a right shallow turn. My turn, no doubt, had saved my neck. I knew the 109 pilots didn't like to go into high-speed right turns because their aircraft had high wing loading and were likely to flip over and into a flat spin. I reversed my turn and gave chase to the 109 that had overshot me. He had stayed almost at the same altitude, possibly considering coming around for another pass on me.

I pushed the throttle forward and started my chase. Eventually, I caught up with the German, but he spotted me as I was closing in for the coupe de grâce. He went into a steep left turn and started to dive. "Mistake number one," I thought. I followed him down to about 10,000 feet, until he pulled up and tightened his turn. I put down my flaps again to make my turn tighter than his. I had the feeling my Mustang could outturn the 109. I opened up fire and nailed him with a deflection shot. Black smoke began to pour out of the enemy aircraft, and the plane curved away, as flames engulfed the engine and spread all the way back to the cockpit. I wondered what the pilot was going to do. He was still in the cockpit as the aircraft flipped over and fell through the air, crashing to the ground in flames.

I pulled up and started to climb, looking for a Mustang to join up with. And suddenly I flew very close to two Mustangs with 336 Squadron markings. One of the pilots cut into the radio and said, "Did you get that guy, QP-D? That was good shooting."

"I sure did," I replied. Surprisingly, the pilot came back and said, "Hey Spiro, this is K. D." It was my Polaris academy classmate, K.D. Peterson. Just as I was turning around to join up with them, I ran into Hively and decided to stay with him.

After a few minutes of flying on Hively's side, at around 14,000 feet he cut into the radio and said, "Greek, four 109s ahead, twelve o'clock low. They are probably looking for scattered Mustangs. Let's go bounce the bastards."

"Roger, Deacon. Go," I said.

Hively went into a shallow dive, and I followed him. I opened up into a line abreast and fell a little behind. We had the sun directly behind us and so were approaching the four Germans unseen. Suddenly, the four 109s started to split up. Two veered to the left and the other two to the right, almost in a northeasterly direction. Hively came back on the radio and said, "Greek, I'll take the two on the left, and you go after the two on the right."

I followed them for a short while, until the number-two guy I was after started to fall back from his element leader. This maneuver would make it easier for me to attack. To prevent the Germans from spotting me, I dove my aircraft below their altitude by about 3,000 feet. Then I zoomed up with full power and aimed the nose of my Mustang straight up at the number two's belly. I could see in a vivid flash the battle green camouflage of the 109's lower surface, the gray belly, and the black crosses under his wings. My rapid closure allowed me time enough for only a short burst. As I pulled sharply to the right and upward to avoid a collision, I could see hits forward on the enemy aircraft's belly. I banked to the left momentarily to observe the 109's position and was surprised to see it still flying straight toward the cloud deck. It was pouring black smoke, probably from burning coolant and oil.

I dropped down to get on the enemy's tail and finish him off. I opened fire from about 300 yards away and saw more hits, but the German dropped his nose and disappeared into the cloud deck below. I had seen smoke coming out of his aircraft, but no fire, so I couldn't be sure that I had gotten him. I pulled above the cloud deck and looked for the other 109. He was coming after me now. I kept my eyes on him as he neared. When he came close to me, I turned sharply right, causing the German to flash past me.

I came out of my steep turn, rolled over to the left, and pushed the throttle to full power to start my chase after the fleeing 109. My Mustang was streaking through the air like a rocket. As his comrade had before, this German started to turn when he saw me on his tail, but with my five-degree flaps down, I was once again able to tighten my turn. I closed on him fast in the turn at about 8,000 feet. On the second turn around, I maneuvered myself into position for a deflection shot. I waited a little longer to get closer. Then, at about 200 yards out, while still in a steep turn, I opened fire. I must have hit the 109 because smoke began to pour out of his engine. I gave him another burst and heavier smoke began to come out from his engine, spreading back to the fuselage.

As his wingman had before him, the German dove down and vanished into the clouds before I had a chance to fire my guns again. I pulled up and turned toward home, knowing that I was probably behind the bombers and my friends who, at this point, were retreating from their targets. I radioed Hively but received only a garbled response. I had no idea how much ammunition I had left, if I had any at all, and I began to worry. Being alone, I was certainly a perfect target.

I continued my northbound climb and still didn't see any of my friends. I had reached 22,000 feet over Le Mans, when my engine suddenly gave me a jolt, followed by a light vibration. I tried to ignore the roughness but couldn't. My engine's operation became even rougher, and although I could see the English Channel in the distance, I doubted I could reach it. I had the feeling that not all twelve of my engine's cylinders were firing, and I figured that my plane's spark plugs had let me down.

I kept my sore neck turning in all directions in order to watch my tail as I was flying over one of the toughest areas in the Luftwaffe's domain. I had reached the outskirts of Le Havre and the English Channel, and I could see the south coast of England in the far distance. It looked mighty good. I had decided to fly a little left of the city to avoid the flak from below when, suddenly, the roughness started again and was more severe than before. I had the feeling the engine might quit on me at any moment. "To hell with the flak," I said to myself and decided to fly straight ahead so I could reach the channel as quickly as possible. The engine started to run extremely rough, and I thought that was it for me.

I pressed the button on the radio and said, "This is Pectin 39. If anybody is receiving me, my engine is running poorly and is about to quit on me. I am coming up over Le Havre, and I don't think I'll be able to make it to the channel."

Only George Carpenter heard my broadcast. Faintly, I could hear his response. "Come on, Steve. You'll make it."

"I don't think so, George. It's going to quit on me at any moment. In case I don't make it, George, I brought down two ME-109s and damaged two more."

212

"Come on," he said again, "try to make it." But as he stopped talking, bang! The engine quit for good.

I came back on the radio again and said, "This is Pectin 39. Mayday! Mayday! I have just lost my engine over Le Havre. I'll try to glide over the channel and jump, if possible, away from the coast."

The fighter controller came on the radio and said, "Aircraft in distress, give me a long transmission, please."

"This is Pectin 39, Pectin 39. Mayday, Mayday! Pectin 39 here, I say, again, Mayday!"

As I finished the transmission, the radio went dead, and right then, the bastards below unleashed some of the heaviest flak I had ever seen on my crippled aircraft. I started to think fast about what to do. Should I try to penetrate the flak barrage and glide out to sea, and then bail out over the water? Would the ASR come out to pick me up so close to the French coast? The Germans, I thought, would probably have the first crack. That was no good. The strong winds from the north could drift my parachute toward Le Havre, making me a perfect target for the ack-ack gunners or any enemy aircraft that happened to see me. Fearing this outcome, I gave up on the idea of bailing out over the channel. I turned my plane to the south, figuring that I could bail out over France, as far away as possible from Le Havre.

I made it through the flak barrage without a scratch, but I was still afraid that some wise-guy German would come up and finish me. After gliding with my dead engine for a while, away from the coast some twelve or so miles, I began to look around for an open area to jump from my crippled machine. I passed through 10,000 feet still gliding south and began to prepare for my jump. I had never bailed out from an aircraft and hoped that 2,000 feet would be adequate.

At 2,000 feet, well south of Le Havre, I trimmed the aircraft so it could fly on its own for a while. Then I released my harness, tossed my gloves and helmet on the floor, and released the Mustang's canopy. With the wind pushing my body backward, I tried desperately to hold myself steady as I stood up. As I struggled to step on the wing, I could feel something was holding me to the cockpit. I looked down and saw the dinghy cord, which I had failed to connect to the Mae West. The plug at the end of the nylon cord appeared to be jammed somewhere underneath the seat. I pulled the cord to free it, but it wouldn't come loose. I had to sit down. I tried again to free the trapped plug by pulling at it from a seated position, but I was unsuccessful. I began to panic and sweat with fear. I considered using my escape knife, but it wasn't in its usual place on the side of my right boot. I tried to use a small knife I had in my pocket, but the blade wasn't sharp enough to cut the nylon cord. I had exhausted my options.

I tried again to dislodge the cord, pulling it to the left and right. Finally, a miracle: the plug came loose! Losing no time, I jammed it into my Mae West, stood up, and braved the wind again. This time, I was able to step onto the wing and prepare to jump. But the time I had lost trying to free myself from the cockpit had brought my plane too close to the ground to bail out. Had I proceeded with my plunge, undoubtedly I would have hit the ground before my parachute had deployed, and that would have been the end of me. I knew that my time was almost up, as I held tight by the cockpit.

I looked ahead and saw my engineless plane gliding straight for the roof of a barn, which was adjacent to the only farmhouse in the area. I held onto the longeron, bracing myself for the inevitable. For a moment, I considered getting back in the cockpit and trying to guide the Mustang away from the barn to a belly landing. But I didn't have time. I looked ahead and estimated that the aircraft was about 100 to 150 feet in the air—and headed straight for the barn.

At first I thought the Mustang would barely clear the barn, but then, as it neared the ground, I realized it would probably hit the roof. I reached inside the cockpit and pulled the stick back gently, causing the Mustang to pass just over the barn. This action, of course, killed some of the Mustang's gliding speed and I was about to crash.

I prayed and held with all my strength onto the longeron, my knees firmly against the surface of the wing. The Mustang's right wingtip scraped the ground, and its belly skidded along the soft farmland. Despite my grip, I was thrown forward and to the left, barely missing the stopped propeller. My eyes were closed as I tumbled through the air, and I never saw the ground rushing to meet me. I wondered at that moment why my life had to end this way, in enemy territory.

CHAPTER 19

Down in Enemy Territory

When I regained consciousness after the crash, I had no idea how long I had been lying on the ground. Slowly, I opened my eyes, looked up in the sky, and thanked God that I was alive. Once I regained my senses, I found myself trembling and breathing fast. I lay on my left side, as my shoulder was encased in fiery agony. Nothing else appeared to be seriously injured, although I ached all over.

Without moving my body, I raised my right hand to wipe some of the perspiration from my face. When I pulled my hand down, it was covered with blood; apparently, my forehead was cut. Slowly, I unbuckled my parachute harness to get myself free. It seemed the chute had absorbed most of the shock from the impact. I looked at my watch; it was about 1:15 p.m. I tried to stand up, but I couldn't. I felt dizzy. I leaned back, figuring that the dizziness would eventually dissipate.

When it did, I sat up. I could see my airplane, on its belly, some distance from where I had landed. Beyond my aircraft, I could see the farmhouse and the barn. A door at the farmhouse was open, but I didn't see anyone in there. The scene was peaceful, but I was in enemy territory and I was afraid. I had no way of knowing whether the Germans had spotted my plane's descent. I needed to get away from the crash scene as quickly as I could.

Again I tried to stand up, and this time, I succeeded—although my knees were shaking. It was a miracle that I was alive at all, I thought. I looked again at my plane, this time to assess the damage. It wasn't as bad as I thought, and I knew that I had to try to destroy it to prevent the Germans from confiscating it to study its engineering.

I decided to set the plane on fire, using the matches in my escape kit. I fished the matches out of the kit and emptied everything else into my flying jacket. I dragged the parachute up and into the cockpit, and managed to wet my scarf in the fuel tank. I was about to pull the D ring to expose the silk and light the match, when my concentration was interrupted by the sound of automatic weapon fire. I looked up and saw two German soldiers about 400 to 500 yards away, walking quickly toward me with their guns drawn.

"To hell with the D ring," I thought. I ducked my head to avoid the soldiers' next rounds, opened the matches, and with my hands trembling, tried to strike a match. It didn't light. I moved to pull out another match, and the box fell from my hands. The soldiers were getting much closer.

I retrieved the box and was ready to strike the second match when bullets ricocheted off the left wing, coming too close to me for comfort. I dropped everything and ran for my life. I could see a wooded area only about one-hundred yards away. As I ran toward it, I zigzagged to avoid the bullets, which I could see striking the ground ahead and to the left. At any moment, I thought, one of those bullets could cut me down. Suddenly the Germans stopped firing. I figured that they had reached the crashed Mustang.

By this time, I had reached the wooded area, and I was trying to fight my way through the thick underbrush. I looked back and could see the two Germans still walking toward me. I figured that they were old-timers because they had not tried to run. They began firing again. I turned back to the underbrush and made a last push through the bushes. I struggled to move past the thorns and finally reached the interior of the forest. I knew that the soldiers would keep after me, and I continued to run through the woods, traveling fast enough that I had to work hard to avoid the trees that surrounded me.

As I ran deeper into the thick forest, I heard sounds of shouting in German but couldn't locate their source. For a moment, I thought that I was walking into a German army camp housed in the forest. I stood still for a while, trying to regroup, but the sound of bullets hitting the branches above my head interrupted my thoughts. I dropped to my belly and tried to crawl on my stomach away from my enemy. After a few minutes, the forest was silent. I figured that the two soldiers had given up their pursuit, so I rose and began to walk again, slowly and cautiously. I tried to use my RAF escape button compass to set a course, but my hands were shaking too much to get an accurate reading.

I continued to plod through the thick woods, jumping over fallen branches and other obstructions, perspiring from exhaustion and fear that I might be captured. Finally, after wandering for what seemed like forever through the closely bunched trees, I came to an opening—the very spot I had come from in the first place! I could see my aircraft in the distance. Apparently, the soldiers chasing me had cut through the trees, widening the opening I had made by forcing my way through the underbrush. I left the forest and ran as fast as I could toward the farmhouse. I didn't look behind me, fearing that the Germans might emerge from the forest at any moment.

When I reached the area below the farmhouse, I jumped over a small fence and onto a narrow paved road. I walked down the road for a while and, as I was coming around a bend, spotted a parked military motorcycle—the motorcycle the two German soldiers had ridden to the site of my crash. Frightened that more Germans would show up at any moment, I jumped over another wire fence on the opposite side of the paved road, which put me into a different property with many scattered trees and bushes.

After a while, I came to a small creek. Figuring that I was out of immediate danger, I stopped to drink from the creek to soothe my dry mouth. I also washed the blood off my face and the few scratches I had over my forehead, neck, and hands. After my brief rest, I continued traveling. Although I came across several farms, I saw only a few animals—no people anywhere. By late afternoon, I had slowed my pace and begun to worry about finding a place to spend the night, as the sun was approaching the western horizon.

I must have traveled some twelve to fifteen miles before I came upon a cart trail and stopped to evaluate my surroundings in the light of the evening sun. I spotted a small bridge, surrounded by trees and bushes, that appeared to be in the center of a small farm. I thought that the bridge might be a good place to spend the night, so I left the cart path and walked cautiously toward the bridge.

It was indeed a good place to spend the night, so I crawled under the bridge and sat against its brick wall. My feet ached from my trek, so I removed my boots—only to find blisters on both heels. As the sun set, it turned colder, and I was forced to put my boots back on and huddle against the brick wall to try to keep warm. I fell asleep but wasn't able to rest for long. The cold woke me up. I spent the rest of the night moving around and rubbing my body to keep warm.

When the sun came up, I left the bridge and walked back to the cart path. I had to keep moving if I wanted to find someone to help me get to the Spanish border, from which I could more easily return to England. I headed south, walking cautiously through wooded areas, away from roads.

Even though the sky was clear, it was cold, and my jacket and boots didn't help to keep me warm. I was hungry and tired, but I forced myself to keep walking. Suddenly, I heard the sound of low-flying aircraft, and as I looked up, I saw about a dozen ME-109s flying eastward at about 2,000 feet altitude, probably deploying somewhere. I ducked under some bushes and waited until they had passed before continuing.

I walked through what appeared to be farmland, figuring that I could find food there, but the only plants in the field were wild dandelions. Thinking of the delicious dandelion greens I'd enjoyed in salads back in Athens, I picked a bunch of these greens and put them in my pockets. I would wash them in the next creek I came across.

As I continued through the bushes along the road, I heard a loud sound and immediately crawled under the thick shrubbery for cover. As the sound faded away, I raised my head from behind the bushes to see what it was. Rumbling down the road away from where I was, were three huge German tanks. I realized that I was walking in a direction that would have taken me toward the area the three tanks had come from. I decided to change my course and head south.

I had been on the run since dawn, and my wristwatch read just after 5:00 p.m. I began to think about finding another place to sleep. I came upon a fork in the road on one side of which was a huge haystack and said to myself, "Spiro, ol' boy, that's where you are going to spend the night."

218

I waited behind the bushes until darkness arrived and then dashed across the road toward the haystack. I dug out a hole in the side of the stack about six feet deep, large enough for my body. I scattered the pile of hay I'd removed so as not to rouse any suspicion and, with a little struggle because of my sore shoulder, managed to crawl into my improvised bedroom, feet first, to spend the night there. After I had settled in the hole, I pulled a small bunch of hay from the inside and placed it in front of my face to cover the opening.

At about 5:30 a.m., the sounds of heavy motors and shouting in German awakened me. I slowly raised my head, pushed away some of the loose hay in front of my face, and saw the silhouettes of German soldiers and several large trucks that had stopped in front of my haystack, at the split in the road. My heart began to pound and I held my breath, fearing that they would come closer to the haystack and discover me. I watched several of the silhouettes walking slowly toward my hiding place. Still talking loudly, they unzipped their pants and began to relieve themselves—just feet away from my face. They were so close to me that I could hear the sound of the urine splashing on the hay that I had scattered the previous evening.

Luckily, that was as close as they came. They soon walked back to their comrades, some of whom were looking at a road map with some dimmed flashlights. I had no idea how long they would be there, so I kept quiet and waited them out. Finally, after some minutes, they got back on their trucks and moved west along the road to the right. Once the German convoy had pulled out and the tranquility of dawn was back, I left the haystack and continued walking south toward Spain. I could feel that my energy was fading somewhat, and my feet were bloody with blisters. My shoulder was still sore, but I was not in as much pain as I had been in the day of the crash. I was hungry and would've given anything for a hamburger.

In the afternoon, I was able to rest by a shady bush, wash my feet in the cool waters of a nearby creek, and cut the tops off my flying boots, thinking that the trim would make walking easier. I buried the tops in the dirt. Then I washed my dandelions in the creek and ate them. The spot where I had stopped was not very secluded, so I decided to move on to see if I could find a more suitable place to spend the night.

Soon I came to the edge of a wooded area, not far from the spot where I had stopped to rest, and found a valley, with a few farmhouses in the far distance. As I descended into the valley, I spotted a small shack that appeared to be a place where farmers kept their tools and small equipment. It would be an ideal place to spend the night, I thought.

I looked over the shack, and behind it I found a beautiful patch of cabbage. "Holy mackerel!" I said to myself. "Food!"

I looked around to make sure that nobody was in the area, and then, I jumped into the patch, pulled a small cabbage off its stem, and returned to the shack with dinner in hand. As I approached the shack, I noticed there was a glass window on the side and a small porch. I tried the door, hoping that it wouldn't be locked. It wasn't; with a push, the door opened inward easily. A few rusted tools, some hay, and some buckets lay on the floor.

I sat on the floor and attacked the stolen cabbage. In a short time, I had eaten the whole head. Spreading the hay around, I lay down and thought about my situation. As yet I did not know how I was going to leave occupied France. Pondering this problem, I fell asleep.

The next morning, I stepped outside, checked my little compass, and headed south. It was still cold, but I knew that the sun would soon warm me.

About midmorning, I reached the top of a small hill and spotted a rather small village of maybe forty stone houses. I stood at the top of the hill for a while, looking down at the place through the bushes, debating whether to walk into or go around it. My concern, of course, was that Germans might have set up camp there. As I watched the village, I decided the place looked deserted. After some thought, I made up my mind to walk in and see if I could find someone who might be able to help me. I made it all the way to the middle of the village's lone intersection before I noticed a woman behind a thin curtain at a second floor window, looking down at me. Another woman joined her at the window. I heard the sound of a squeaky hinge, and before too long, a young man, about seventeen or eighteen years old, appeared in front of me. I froze.

The young man walked toward me and said, "Etes vous un aviateur anglais [Are you an English aviator]?"

For a moment I didn't know what to say, but the French that I had taken in school back in Athens came back to me.

"No, no," I said, "Américan. Aviateur américain."

At this, he snatched my hand and pulled me around the corner. He took me through the doorway and shut the squeaky door behind us. I found myself inside a courtyard. From there he dragged me toward another, smaller door. My companion, in a stage whisper, cried "Maman, Maman," and suddenly a large-framed woman appeared. Again, the boy said, "Maman, un aviateur Américain."

The big woman engulfed me in a bear hug, kissed me on both cheeks, and dragged me into her house. The boy fetched a bottle of red wine and poured some into a glass. The woman returned from the kitchen with a plate of ham, cheese, and a hunk of dark bread and placed it in front of me.

I began to devour the food; I barely bothered to chew. In one of the bites, I remember, I almost choked and had to drink the full glass of wine to clear my throat. After that, I slowed down a bit. Nevertheless, what the woman had put in front of me disappeared in no time. I wanted to eat some more but didn't know how to ask for seconds. What a relief, I thought, after four days of starvation. The dandelions and the cabbage I had the day before had satisfied my hunger somewhat but could not compare with the bread, cheese, ham, and wine.

When I had finished eating, the young man brought an English-French dictionary to the table, and we began to talk.

"Me," he said, "Pascal and maman, Vivien."

I introduced myself, and then opened the silk map from my escape kit. When I asked him to point out where I was, he pointed to the villages of Epinay and Broglie. He pointed to Evreux and said something about "le Boche [German]." I told Pascal I was looking to find some help so I could get to Spain.

"Oh!" he exclaimed.

Haltingly, we continued. He told me that he couldn't help me but that in the village of Epinay, which was not too far away, there might be help. He would show me how to get there.

As we talked, Pascal kept his eyes fixed on my flying jacket. He said that if the Germans spotted me with that jacket on, they would pick me up and send me to Germany. He brought me some civilian clothing: a heavy brown shirt, a pair of trousers with patches sewn on both knees, a worn-out coat, and a beret that fit perfectly on my head. I emptied the pockets of my flying jacket and changed into my new clothes.

It was past noon and time for me to head for Epinay. I said good-bye to Pascal's mother, who hugged me farewell and gave me an apple to take on the trip. After we had walked for about thirty minutes, Pascal pointed the way to the village of Epinay. I shook his hand, gave him a hug, and thanked him for his help. He waved good-bye, and I continued on to Epinay.

After walking through farmland, trees, and bushes, I reached a plateau and followed a cart path to what I thought were the outskirts of Epinay. From the path, I spotted a woman walking with her bicycle, along another path on my right. When our paths merged, I noticed the woman was good looking with dark hair. She looked at me curiously and said in French, "Are you English?"

"No," I said, surprised, "American. American aviator."

"Where are you going?" she asked in accented English. I told her about my encounter with Pascal and that I was going to Epinay to find help so I could get to Spain.

"That is the village of Epinay up ahead," she said, "but come with me. My husband speaks English, and he is returning from Paris this evening. I am sure he will be able to help you."

I decided to trust this woman, and we set off together. We entered the outskirts of Epinay and, after a short walk, arrived at a house with a garden in front. As we entered the house, she asked me to sit down and went to fetch some bread, cheese, and wine.

Later that evening, a nice-looking gentleman, about the same age as the woman, approached the house. The woman met him outside, and they had a brief exchange before coming inside. As they entered, the man greeted me with a smile.

"Hello, there," he said in perfect English. "My name is Henri. Henri Durant. My wife told me that you are an American aviator?"

222

"Yes, I am," I said. I gave him my name and rank.

"But you speak English with an accent," he remarked. I explained my past and how I had come to arrive in Epinay.

"Evidently," M. Durant said after I had finished my story, "you have gone through some hell—but you've survived, and that's what counts. What are your plans now?"

I told him I was hoping to return to England via Spain.

"It's very difficult to contact the people who normally help downed Allied airmen," M. Durant told me. "However, as you've heard already, there are some people here who may be able to help. They usually gather in a café on the other side of the village. I know a boy who can walk with you there."

M. Durant excused himself to track down my guide, and minutes later, he returned with a nice-looking man, about my age and height.

"This is André," M. Durant said. "He comes out at night only to avoid being seen by the Germans. He'll take you to the café on the other side of Epinay."

I shook hands with André, and we prepared to leave. I said good-bye to M. Durant and his wife and thanked them for their help and generosity. Then André and I walked out into the pitch darkness of the night. It was so black that I couldn't see anything beyond one-hundred feet. I had to walk with André arm in arm.

After a few minutes or so of walking in the darkness through small streets, alleys, and paths, we arrived at a small coffee shop. André had me wait outside while he went in. When he returned, less than a minute later, he guided me to the back of the building, and we entered through a door into what appeared to be the kitchen. André handed me to a husky lady wearing a white apron. He said something to her quietly, shook my hand, and left immediately through the door we had just come in.

An elderly man walked into the kitchen from the café and said, "Bon soir, mon ami [Good evening, my friend]." He conversed with the lady for a few minutes and then signaled for me to follow him. I was hustled along into the darkness again through the rear kitchen door. The man held my hand as we walked about twenty-five yards in silence to an unlit house. Quietly, he guided me through a door, turned on a dim light,

223

and took me upstairs into a room on the second floor. When we reached the room, the man said in English, "Name Aumond. You here. Friend come for you take away." Then he walked out of the room. Minutes later, he brought me a croissant and some cold slices of meat, several slices of Swiss cheese, and coffee with milk.

After I enjoyed the snack, I lay down to sleep on the room's small low bed, which was surprisingly warm and comfortable. As I lay there on my back looking at the ceiling, I began to think about Henri Durant. He couldn't have been a Frenchman as he claimed to be. He spoke perfect English, without a trace of an accent. I convinced myself that he was either a British agent or an American with the Office of Strategic Services. And what about his wife? She must have been a French woman with the Underground or the French intelligence service who had teamed up with him.

Whoever they were and whatever their connections was not my business; I was already thankful to have run into Mme Durant in the countryside.

CHAPTER 20

CONTACT WITH
THE MAQUIS

The following day, after I had had a good night's rest, a knock on the door awoke me from my slumber. I jumped off the bed to open the door, but M. Aumond Gibourdel, the café owner, entered the room before I had a chance to let him in myself. He held out a cup of freshly made coffee and asked, "Ça va bien aujourd' hui, mon ami? [Are you well today, my friend?]"

"Yes, Sir," I replied in French.

M. Gibourdel told me that a man who could help me was waiting in the room downstairs. I quickly combed my filthy hair and rushed down to meet the visitor. M. Gibourdel and the gentleman were waiting for me at a table while drinking coffee. When M. Gibourdel saw me, he waved me over to an unoccupied chair and introduced me to the gentleman, M. Goyer, a middle-aged man with the torso of someone who must have been a soldier in the French army at one time. We shook hands, and in fair English, he asked me for my name and rank. I gladly provided the information.

Over coffee and croissants, M. Gibourdel and M. Goyer discussed my situation in rapid-fire French. Although I could catch bits and pieces, I wasn't able to understand the whole conversation. When they finished, M. Goyer said to me in English, "You must come with me and we'll see how we can help you. We should go now."

We said good-bye to M. Gibourdel and his wife, and I thanked them profusely in French. We pulled away from the café in M. Goyer's Citroën without speaking. I did not know where we were going.

Finally M. Goyer said, "If we are stopped by a German road patrol or the French Milice, do not say anything. Keep your mouth closed and play dumb. Can you do that, Lieutenant?"

"Yes, Sir, I'll do my best," I replied. "What is French 'milice'?"

"They are young Frenchmen who have been hired by the Gestapo for police duty," he said. "They are hated by every patriotic Frenchman because of their collaboration with the occupation authorities."

After about twenty-five minutes, we arrived at our destination: a two-story building in the village of La Barre-en-Ouche, where my escort apparently lived. The street-level floor of the building was a country store, and the second floor was living quarters. M. Goyer took me around to the back of the building, where we climbed a stairway to the second floor.

There were two bedrooms, a small foyer, a living room, a small bathroom, and an indoor stairwell that led to the store on the ground floor. M. Goyer took me to the smaller bedroom at the front of the building and showed me where I would stay until he found out what we needed to do next. The small room was crowded with a small bed, a table and lamp, and two chairs.

"Make yourself comfortable," he said, pointing at the bathroom.

At lunchtime, his wife, a matronly woman, brought cheese, bread, wine, and apples to my room. M. Goyer, who accompanied her, stayed behind to have lunch with me.

"Stephan," he said as we ate, "you do not speak English like an American." As I had with Mr. Durant, I explained my background.

The next few days passed uneventfully. I spent much of my time in the small room, hiding from the Germans. On the fourth day, M. Goyer introduced me to his friend M. Gaston, who spoke limited English, so M. Goyer served as our translator. Through M. Goyer, I learned that M. Gaston was from the French resistance and that he could arrange for my return to England. Before arrangements could be made, however, London had to verify my identity.

I gave M. Gaston my name, rank, and serial number as he asked; place and date of birth; my address in America; my unit and the name of my commanding officer; my station and the name of my roommate; the type and marking of my aircraft; and, finally, the date I had crashed in France. M. Gaston wrote everything down on a paper, which he then folded and placed in the stocking in his right shoe. M. Gaston told me that a message would probably go to London the next night and that we should expect a response in a few days.

After the two men had left I lay in my bed with my eyes fixed on the ceiling, I wondered if giving this information so freely had been the right thing to do. M. Gaston could have been a German informant, and I might have just given a lot of information to the enemy. I knew, though, I had no choice but to cooperate with the Frenchmen if I were to have a chance of returning to my unit in England.

The next few days did not improve my mood. I heard no word from M. Gaston, and I had begun to wonder if getting involved with M. Gibourdel and M. Goyer had been a good idea. Finally, on the fifth day after my meeting with M. Gaston, as I watched the street scene below from my bedroom window, I spotted M. Goyer, limping as usual, coming toward the house. Two gendarmes accompanied him.

"This is it," I thought to myself. "He has turned me in to the French police, and they are coming to pick me up."

I began to look for a way to escape my room. I considered dashing into the bathroom and jumping out from the small window to the back of the house. But, as I opened the door to my room, the three had already climbed the stairs from the store below and were walking toward me.

"Bonjour, mon lieutenant," exclaimed M. Goyer. "Shall I call you Steve or Spiro or le Grec? [The Greek]"

"What?" I asked sharply.

"So you are the Greek, as they call you in your squadron. I know who you are now," said M. Goyer, "and these are my friends." He gestured to the two gendarmes, who leaned forward and, one at a time, hugged me and kissed me on both cheeks. I returned the greetings, somewhat embarrassed that I had considered escaping.

The two men left, and M. Goyer and I sat down in the small room. He started to share with me what had happened while I was holed up in the house.

"Four days ago, M. Gaston's people sent a message to London; last night, they received a reply. London confirmed your identity and asked that we give you as much help as we could. Now, you belong to us until it's decided by the people in Paris what to do with you."

While M. Goyer was speaking, his son, Claude, brought a bottle of wine and two glasses into the room. My guardian filled both and raised his glass in a toast to me. As we drank the wine, M. Goyer explained to me how dangerous it was for Frenchmen to help downed Allied airmen nowdays. The Gestapo had had occasional success in infiltrating the French resistance, for example, by using agents who speak English better than Englishmen and Americans to impersonate downed aviators seeking help.The Gestapo had already caught, tortured, and killed hundreds of French patriots using such methods.

He went on to tell me that getting to Spain would be difficult and risky. The Gestapo and Milice had guards on all the main roads, as well as at railway stations and on trains. Trying to walk alone to the Spanish frontier was not impossible, but it had been prohibited by London. And, at that time, no one was available to escort me from northern France to Spain because the resistance was involved in much more important work than simply providing escort to aviators. They had begun to ambush German convoys and to sabotage military installations, and in retaliation, the Germans were rounding up and killing French hostages.

M. Goyer planned to continue to house me until the situation changed. He told me that I might have a chance to fight the Germans on the ground, instead of from the air, as a member of the French resistance. He also told me that we must wait to hear from the people above him because I would likely be moved to Paris. In view of this, I would have to abandon any hope of getting to Spain.

That night, M. Goyer asked me to join his friends with him in the living room to listen to the BBC Radio news. After the regular news broadcast ended, another announcer continued the broadcast in code: "Mary had a baby girl. Mother and baby are doing well. John has left on a holiday. The birthday celebration at George's house was a success." After the others had left, I asked M. Goyer what the second broadcast was about.

"Ah, Stephan," he said, "those words you heard on the radio were very important messages for certain people, including the Maquis and British and American agents in France. They refer to forthcoming airdrops of supplies, weapons, or agents. We make similar broadcasts from France in French and in English. We have to be more careful than the British, though, because the Germans can pinpoint the location of our transmitters. We have lost many people this way."

After two weeks in M. Goyer's house, I was given French identification papers. According to them, I was Jean Claude Boyer, born in Marseilles, Department of Bouches du Rhone, on November 10, 1919. I resided at 265 rue du Lafayette, and my occupation was mécanicien de la voiture (automobile mechanic). I had a hearing impediment from my army service in the heavy artillery during the war. Although fake, the papers, having my photo, the appropriate stamps, and signatures, appeared genuine. Along with the ID card came an identité du titulaire, a certificat de travail, and a rations card.

The day I received my papers, the village doctor, named Dr. Duval, examined my shoulder. He said that he couldn't tell if it was broken but that he would arrange to have it x-rayed at a nearby clinic the next morning. M. Goyer told me that the doctor was going to give me an alibi by saying that I had climbed a tree to cut some branches and that I had fallen, injuring my shoulder. "You are, of course, to avoid saying anything. Let the doctor do the talking."

The following morning the doctor and I rode almost thirty minutes to what appeared to be a German infirmary. A German soldier guarded the gate. On seeing the guard, I became nervous. The doctor must have noticed this, as he smiled at me and said, in English, "Do not worry."

I was not reassured.

"It is all right," the doctor said. "This clinic is operated by German civilian doctors, whom I know well."

We stepped out of the car and walked to the gate. The doctor presented a paper to the guard, who saluted us and allowed us into the complex. A tall blonde man wearing a long white coat greeted us and shook hands with Dr. Duval. They indeed appeared to know one another quite well. They spoke in French, glancing at me every so often. Finally, we were ushered into a dimly lit room, where I was x-rayed.

Back at the house, M. Goyer listened carefully to Dr. Duval, who, using the x-rays as visuals, explained to him my condition. When the doctor finished speaking, M. Goyer translated: "You're lucky to have suffered no fracture. It's only a simple dislocation." The doctor reset my arm that afternoon.

At about 10:00 a.m. the next day, M. Gaston picked me up to take me on a trip to meet some of his friends. We were stopped only once by the French Milice, and although my heart was pounding, I kept my mouth shut and let M. Gaston do the talking. Evidently, the policemen recognized M. Gaston, and after a quick glance at our papers, they saluted him smartly and allowed us to move on.

We traveled through some beautiful countryside and then turned onto a dirt road, shaded on both sides by poplar trees. We drove for some time down the road, until we reached a huge three-story white villa. As I looked around at the several barns scattered across the property, I realized we had entered an immense farmland.

M. Gaston pulled into the driveway in front of the villa and stopped. He reached underneath his seat, pulled out a beret, and placed it on his head. The beret bore the Croix de Lorraine, the symbol of the Maquis. M. Gaston explained to me that he could not wear this symbol in public for fear that the Germans would arrest him, but when he visited the Maquis in private he wore it to show his identity.

As we reached the huge, carved door at the front of the villa, it opened and a big man with an athletic frame and well-trimmed mustache walked forward to meet us. He and M. Gaston embraced.

"This is Stephan," M. Gaston said, "an American aviator, the Greek American, but his French name is Jean."

The big man, whose name was M. Charles and who spoke perfect English, hugged me, kissed me on both cheeks, and welcomed me to his home. We entered the villa, and, as I looked around, I commented that the house must have been built for a nobleman.

"It might have been," M. Charles said, "but it belongs to me now."

We walked into a huge dining room and sat at the end of a long table, where some twenty-five to thirty aristocrats could have sat for dinner. A servant with white gloves appeared with a tray, three glasses, and a bottle of red wine. M. Charles filled our glasses, raised his own, and gave a toast. "Vive la France and vive la Amérique!"

We took a sip from our glasses, and then M. Gaston gave his own toast: "Viva President Roosevelt!"

Over wine, I told M. Charles where I had come from and how I had come to be in his company. In return, I learned that the chateau in which we were sitting was a cover for the Maquis. The field hands were all Maquis, working on the grounds between their sabotage and harassment missions. After we spoke for a while, I was taken to one of the barns, which had been renovated to be living quarters for the farm workers. Many bunks lined the walls, the floor was carpeted, and a large table was in the middle of the room. Two bathrooms had been built on the side of the barn.

M. Gaston rolled back the carpet to reveal a trap door on the floor. "That door," he said, "will lead you down into a basement." He rolled the carpet back. "Do you know what we have hidden in there? Automatic weapons, hand grenades, plastic explosives, and many other arms of war that we use to fight the Germans. Every day, the Maquis make another attack against le Boche somewhere in France."

As we walked outside to the front of the barn, M. Gaston pointed to other structures as well as to the woods beyond. "The RAF drops supplies for our fight in an open field beyond those woods from the air during the night," he told me.

We returned to the villa, where M. Charles had prepared a lavish luncheon. Shortly after we finished the delicious lunch, we said goodbye to M. Charles and headed back to La Barre-En-Ouche, hoping to arrive there before dark. While on the road, I told my friend that I was impressed with what I had seen and learned about the resistance that afternoon.

"Yes, mon ami, the work done by the Maquis and various other groups is good and effective. However, we are at a disadvantage because we are only poorly trained civilians fighting against a well-trained army."

I was sobered by this observation, and we said little else as we drove back to the village. We arrived there as the sun was setting. As M. Gaston dropped me off at M. Goyer's house, I thanked him for the ride to the countryside and told him that while I was in France I wanted to be part of the resistance. He accepted my offer joyfully, and we shook hands before he drove away.

Two days later, at just about noon, M. Goyer brought a woman upstairs to meet with me. She was from Paris. She was about thirty years old, had curly red hair, and wore sunglasses. M. Goyer introduced her as Mme Raymond; she was a member of the resistance. She spoke some

English with a heavy French accent and let me know through M. Goyer that I would be moved to Paris for safekeeping and I would wait until it was decided what to do with me.

PASSAGE TO PARIS

During the next few days, M. Goyer made arrangements for my upcoming move to Paris, and one day in the early morning, a huge truck, loaded with firewood, stopped by his house to pick me up for my journey. My guardian introduced me to my traveling companions, and as they sat down for coffee with M. Goyer's wife, he took me aside and briefed me on the two men I would be traveling with.

"The man with the mustache is the driver, who I don't think speaks English. The other man is Pierre Dagues, a gendarme, who knows his way around the countryside as well as the city of Paris. You'll enjoy him because he speaks some English."

As we prepared to pull out, I embraced M. Goyer, his wife, and young Claude and thanked them for everything they had done for me. M. Goyer walked with me to the waiting truck, and as he helped me climb up to the cab, he said, "Bonjour, Stephan, et bonne chance! [Good-bye, Steve, and good luck]"

Along the way, I communicated with Pierre as best I could. I was sitting between my two companions, resting my feet on a pile of burlap that covered some unidentifiable cargo. Because the seating arrangement was cramped, I kept kicking the bundle with my feet. I couldn't figure out what it was. When Pierre noticed what I was doing, he first looked away and then looked at me. *"Mitrailleuse automatique* [automatic machine guns] boom-boom, le Boche." He grinned.

"Machine gun," I said to myself. Realizing that I was riding on a main road busy with German traffic with an automatic weapon under my feet made me a bit more jittery. My two companions were acting as casually as possible, but my heart began to pound faster every time I saw a German military vehicle go by.

As we approached the outskirts of a town, I spotted a low-flying ME-109 and wondered if we were near an aerodrome. Pierre noticed my look and said, "Ville d' Evreux ici. Allemand avion de chasse, chez la

232

aerodrome de Evreux [This is the village of Evreux. German fighter planes are at the Evreux Aerodrome]." Apparently, we were near a Luftwaffe fighter base.

As we passed the aerodrome, I observed a number of parked ME-109s, including the one that had been approaching for landing. Just after we passed the aerodrome, two German soldiers, walking on the side of the road, turned back toward us and dashed in front of our truck. One of them pulled out his pistol, aimed it at the driver, and yelled harshly, demanding that we stop. My heart leapt with fear. The driver, of course, slammed the brake immediately, stopping the truck. The Germans walked to the driver's side. The one brandishing the pistol said in French, "To Paris?"

Evidently, they wanted to bum a ride. Pierre and the driver looked at each other, knowing that they had no choice. The driver motioned to the Germans to climb onto the pile of firewood in back of the truck. As we started to move again, Pierre motioned with his eyes toward the pile of burlap under my feet. Quietly, he said, "Au-dessous le bois de feu, beaucoup automatiques." I couldn't understand the first part of his comment, but the second part clearly referred to weapons. He tried again, in English. "Below the firewood, many machine guns."

He went on to explain that the weapons had been air-dropped by the British a few nights before. We were taking them to the resistance fighters in Paris. His explanation made me want to get out of the truck even more. I knew that if we were caught, all three of us would be shot immediately.

Nevertheless, we kept rolling along on the road to Paris with our precious cargo. As we continued to pass through checkpoint after checkpoint, I began to rethink the situation. The Germans on top of the firewood, I thought, were likely good security. The military patrol vehicles probably saw their fellow Germans on our truck, and let us pass. I then began to relax somewhat.

As we approached the gates of Paris, Pierre pointed out the spire of the Eiffel Tower rising into the sky in the far distance. In a resentful tone, he said, "Life in Paris is now miserable. It isn't what it used to be since the conquerors control all Parisians. Gas and electricity are available only certain hours of the day. The métro also operates only a few hours a day. There are food shortages throughout the city. Bread, butter,

233

eggs, meat, coffee, and fish are all scarce. The Germans are stealing these French staples and transporting them to Germany. There is a black market, of course, but you have to be rich to buy food from that source. Medicine is also difficult to find."

Shortly the driver announced, "Voilà, nous sommes arrivé à Porte de St. Cloud [We have arrived at the Port of St. Cloud]."

We had finally reached Paris. One of the German soldiers pounded on the cab's roof. The driver pulled close to the curb and stopped. The two German soldiers jumped down, and as they came by the driver's side, one of them said, "Thank you" in French. The other said something in German. The driver looked at them and said nothing.

We crossed the Seine River, which looked quite different from the ground, and headed toward the heart of the city. As we traveled along Avenue Felix Fauré, I noticed some concrete pillboxes and other barricades at main intersections. I also noticed that the streets and boulevards in the heart of Paris were empty, except for a few buses and automobiles and even fewer people.

A taxi with a funny trunk sticking out on its back passed us. I asked Pierre what the ugly-looking trunk was.

"Ah," he said, "that's a *gazogéne*, one of the things the Germans brought into France after we surrendered to le Boche. The vehicle burns wood for locomotion. The Germans use all of the gasoline available in France, so we have to make do with vehicles that burn firewood. Our truck uses the same system. Look at the box in the rear when you step down."

After a short drive through some back streets, the truck stopped in front of a white, three-story building. Pierre got out of the cab and went in the front door. A few minutes later, he appeared at the door and waved for me to step down and join him. I shook hands with the driver and told him, "Thank you for bringing me to Paris safely." The driver grinned broadly in return.

I joined Pierre, who said, "Stephan, this is the place where you'll stay. Come and I'll take you in."

We walked down the hallway a few steps and stopped in front of a door that was ajar. As we walked in, I came face to face with Mme Raymond, the woman who had visited La Barre-en-Ouche to interview me at M. Goyer's house a few days ago. In English, she said, "Come, Stephan. Come in."

Pierre, anxious to leave, said good-bye to Mme Raymond and me and wished me good luck. Mme Raymond gestured for me to sit down on a small couch in the tiny living room. A quick glance around revealed that my new temporary home was a small, one-bedroom apartment, with a living room, a kitchen, a bedroom at the end of a short hallway, and a cramped bathroom. In the middle of the living room was a small table with four chairs, as well as a glass cabinet with dishes, assorted glassware, and figurines.

235

After I rested for a bit on Mme Raymond's couch, she set the table for two and went to the kitchen to prepare some food. Minutes later, she winked at me from the kitchen door and said, "Sit down at the table, *s'il vous plaît* [please]." She ducked back into the kitchen and returned with dishes of sautéed meat, potatoes, and salad greens in her hands. She joined me at the table with the requisite French bottle of red wine.

That first dinner was decidedly uncomfortable. Mme Raymond and I had little in common; she spoke little English, and I spoke even less French. But during the next ten days and nights, sharing the tiny living space, we were forced to become more comfortable with each other. When I finally left Mme. Raymond's apartment, we parted reluctantly, as we had enjoyed each other much in the previous days.

An agent from the resistance, a well-dressed, middle-aged man with a nicely trimmed mustache and a black beret, appeared in the apartment one afternoon. Lucky for me, he spoke some English. His name was Claude.

"Well, my friend, first of all, I have no car, so we are going to use the métro," Claude said, as he started to prepare me for our trip to the next safe house. "On the métro, don't sit next to me but don't lose me in the crowd. When we are walking on the street, walk behind me—again, don't lose me. If we are stopped anywhere for ID check, just show your papers; if for some reason they detain you, don't tell them that you are with me. The Gestapo will stop people for ID checks anywhere and any time. If they suspect that you are one of those wanted or that a house is harboring an enemy of the Third Reich, first they knock on the door. If no one answers, they'll break the door down, and they'll turn the house upside down looking for evidence."

As we left Mme Raymond's apartment, M. Claude gave me a French newspaper to put in my coat pocket. The paper's name, *Paris Soir*, showed outside the pocket. As we walked to the métro, I was careful to stay a few steps behind M. Claude as he had instructed. We entered the station and boarded the métro for my new home.

We changed trains twice. On the second change, we had to go through a checkpoint, manned by two men in civilian clothes and four German soldiers carrying automatic weapons. When I saw the checkpoint, I panicked and tried to find a way to avoid going through. But I was already inside the corridor and two soldiers were behind me, blocking anyone who would attempt to escape. I could see that M. Claude had already passed the checkpoint and was waiting for me on the other side, and I decided to go on, even though my heart was pounding and my mouth was dry. As I approached, I realized that the Germans checking IDs paid more attention to the faces of the civilians than their papers. Evidently, they were looking for someone.

When I reached them, I mimicked the others who had passed before me. I took my papers out of my pocket, raised them with my right hand, and continued walking through. The man, no doubt a Gestapo agent, glanced at my ID and looked at me directly. He didn't say anything. Trembling, I passed him, spotted M. Claude, and followed him to the platform. There, we waited for the next train.

We boarded the train, and a few stops later, we exited the station and surfaced on the street. I backed off and stayed about fifty feet behind my escort. After walking for several blocks on what appeared to be a boulevard, we turned off into a small side street with several tall buildings. They looked residential. M. Claude stopped in front of one of the buildings and waited for me to catch up. We entered the building through the opened door and started to climb the stairs.

When we reached the top floor, my escort rang the doorbell. The door opened, and we faced a man who was about fifty years old. M. Claude said to the man, "Monsieur Marcel Delong, I presume?"

"Yes," said the man and told us to come in. "I was expecting you."

Once inside, I was introduced to M. Delong's wife, Julienne. Claude turned me over to the Delongs' care and left.

After Claude left, M. Delong said, "Come and meet one of your comrades."

He took me to a room where I came face to face with a man with light blond hair who was about my age. He introduced himself as FS Ken Scott, RAF.

"Call me Scotty," he said.

"First Lt. Steve Pisanos, U.S. Army Air Force," I told the British pilot.

Scott had apparently gone down when ack-ack gunners at Abbeville Aerodrome, which he had been strafing at the time, hit the Typhoon he was flying. Through Scotty, who spoke French almost perfectly, I learned that M. Delong was an engineer and his wife was a teacher at a grade school. Scotty and I would spend the days that followed together in a room in the Delongs' apartment. Scotty played the piano magnificently and played all sorts of English melodies when the Delongs were at work. I read some English books I had found in M. Delong's library. When we were both tired of these pursuits, we talked about our exploits, our current situation, and the war.

Often, especially in the evenings, M. Delong would join in our discussions. He spoke English well and appeared to be highly educated. He held an important position in a French company that manufactured generators and starting motors for German aircraft, and he worked at Villa Coublay, a Luftwaffe aerodrome. He also held a high-level position in the Forces Françaises del Intérieur (FFI), one of the Paris resistance organizations. He was proud of being part of a group that was fighting the Germans and bragged about the resistance fighters' successes against the occupation forces in Paris.

"Le Boche is being harassed almost daily," he told us.

Scotty and I enjoyed the many conversations we had with M. Delong. It was a pleasure to listen to him; he was an excellent storyteller. One evening, he told us, "Since you both speak some French, I might arrange for you to go out with the resistance boys and get involved in some action, killing Germans."

"I would love to do that," I said to M. Delong.

Scotty agreed: "I'll be ready anytime, as long as I have a weapon in my hands."

CHAPTER 21

THE NOTORIOUS GESTAPO

One evening, after dinner, while Mme Delong was busy in the kitchen cleaning up, M. Delong told us about the conflicts that were taking place between the Gestapo and the French Underground. A friend had told him recently that the Gestapo and the French Milice had broken into an apartment in his neighborhood in the middle of the night. They had apparently been looking for an English aviator the tenants were harboring. Of course, his friend had said, the Gestapo left empty-handed; they had either gotten a false report or the Englishman had been moved before the Gestapo's incursion.

M. Delong gave us some instructions. If we heard loud banging on the door in the middle of the night, we were to immediately sneak out onto the balcony—and be sure to close the shutters behind us. He wanted us to sleep with our clothes on from now on to be safe.

He explained to us that the Gestapo used many techniques of torture to force its prisoners to confess crimes and reveal other members of the resistance. The group beat, kicked, and harassed its prisoners, and often more than one interrogator questioned a suspect. If the interrogation techniques did not work, then the Gestapo would subject a prisoner to electric shock, in the most sensitive parts of his body or tie him up at the end of a long pole and submerge him in a pool of water until his lungs were ready to burst.

Still the French Underground continued to fight the German military machine throughout France, attacking military installations, blowing up lines of communication and storage facilities, ambushing convoys, destroying bridges, derailing trains, and killing Germans on sight when possible. The Underground was fighting Hitler's soldiers without interruption and thought their country's freedom was in sight. Even Hitler's generals, Delong told us, had admitted that the resistance had created an unacceptable annoyance for the occupation.

Several days after M. Delong had warned us to be alert, Scotty and I were awakened at 4:00 a.m. by a loud knock on the door.

"What was that?" Scotty said as he jumped out of the bed, and then in answer to his own question, he mumbled, "Somebody at the door."

"Ouvrez la porte [Open the door]. Police," the knockers commanded.

It took only a second for Scotty and me to put our feet into our shoes and dash to the balcony adjacent to our room, as we had planned. As Scotty and I stood on the balcony, trembling and out of breath, I began to wonder whether we'd be safe out there. I whispered to Scotty, "They'll look out here if they're smart. If they do, then we're sure to be on our way to a stalag [prison] in Germany. If we are lucky. And the Delongs won't be lucky."

Scotty agreed but didn't see a way out. "The way I see it, we're stuck out here," he said grimly.

"No we aren't," I insisted. "If we could jump to the next balcony, and then to a couple more along the way from this balcony, we could be far enough away that they won't be able to see us."

This plan wasn't as far-fetched as it might seem. The distance between the balconies was only about three or four feet. The jump itself wouldn't be too bad. I looked at the adjacent balcony and decided that the stunt would be less risky than staying here and waiting for the Gestapo.

I told Scotty, "I'm going to jump across, and you can follow me."

I took a deep breath to calm myself, wiped my sweaty hands, and leaped forward. I took hold of the next balcony's railing, climbed over, and found myself safely on the balcony floor, outside M. Delong's library. Scotty, who had watched me jump across, followed me without difficulty. I thanked God that it was dark so that we could ignore the five-story distance between our feet and the street below. With two more jumps we were on the Delongs' neighbors' balcony. Just as we reached it, we heard our balcony shutters slam open. Immediately, we dropped flat to the neighbors' balcony floor and listened to the voices.

"Rien ici [Nothing here]." Then, silence.

Our close call frightened me badly. I'm certain Scotty was frightened too. Our fear of being captured by the Gestapo gave us the courage to leap forward. We knew that if we were caught and sent to Germany we would die—and so would the Delongs.

We stayed flat on our bellies for quite some time on the cold floor of the neighbors' balcony. Then, we heard Mme Delong's voice calling us from the balcony of our room. "Monsieur Stephan. Monsieur Scotty."

I whispered back, knowing that the police might still be below us on the street.

"Madame, Madame, ici, ici [here, here]!"

When Mme Delong heard my whispers, she realized where we had gone. We stayed on the neighbors' balcony until almost dawn, when M. Delong crashed into his next-door neighbors' apartment in his pajamas. I don't know what he told the elderly couple, but when he and the old man with his wife in their sleeping clothes opened the shutters of their bedroom apartment and found Scotty and me standing there, trembling from the cold and fear, they were startled. Without another word to the puzzled elderly couple, M. Delong whisked us out of the apartment and brought us back to his own. After closing the door, he looked at us in dismay and said, "I've got to get you both away from here. I have already communicated through the phone with my people, using a coded message. You just wait here and someone will show up to take you both to another place."

While we were waiting in the kitchen with the Delongs, who both looked shaken up by what had happened, M. Delong said, "It was the Gestapo. When I opened the door, the two Germans, who were in civilian clothes, stormed into the hall and demanded to know where the two young men were. I, of course, pretended ignorance. They saw the slept-in bed, and I told them that I slept there. But when one of them went for the shutters to check in the balcony, I thought that my wife and I were doomed.

"When he opened the shutters and told his partner that nothing was out there, I was relieved. Then I couldn't imagine what had happened to you. For a moment, I thought you had jumped down to your death to avoid being captured. I was so relieved when my wife found you alive and safe on my neighbors' balcony."

As the sun was coming up that morning, two men from the resistance appeared at the door. They rushed Scotty and me down to the street without giving us a chance to say good-bye to the Delongs. One of the men took Scotty in his car and drove off. The other took my arm and said, "Et vous, venez avec moi [You, come with me]." He opened the door of his car for me to get in. I never saw Scotty again.

After a short drive around the neighborhood, we stopped in front of a tall apartment building. We did not go in but were met outside by a man. He greeted my companion and said to me, in English, "My name is André, and I am to take you to another safe house. I have no car, so our travel will be by foot, the métro, and the bus."

As we walked to the nearby métro station, he told me to act like we weren't together. He purchased two tickets and slipped one to me as I walked behind him.

The train ride was uneventful, and we got off at Châtelet Station. After a short walk, we turned into what appeared to be a busy alley. Pedestrians, going to work early in the morning, walked busily up and down on both sides of the street. Suddenly, panic spread through the crowd, and someone shouted, "Le Gestapo! Atention! Le Gestapo!"

Sure enough, soldiers, who had emerged from trucks parked at both ends of the streets, quickly blocked the entrance and exit of the alley. They began to direct the pedestrians down the alley toward a checkpoint at the other end.

"Damn it," my escort said, "the bastards have blocked both ends of the street. I don't want to go through the checkpoint. They might recognize my face."

I wondered what André had done to cause the Gestapo to recognize him, as we both watched the people rushing to line up. He looked around the buildings, stores, and doorways, seeking out an escape route. I followed his eyes to a manhole cover on a nearby section of the curb. He walked quickly to it, pulled what looked like a stiletto out of a hiding place next to his leg, bent down, and opened the manhole cover with his tool.

"Here," he said, "get down quick and grab the handles on the wall. Go all the way to the bottom."

I descended through the darkness until I felt the wall handles give way to the cement floor. I stepped down and waited for my escort. Before descending, he pulled the manhole cover in place behind him, and we were left in complete darkness. Evidently prepared for this, André used a small flashlight, which he had in his pocket, to light our way forward through what I now realized was a sewer. I could hear running water echoing around us.

"My friend," he said, "we are safe here in the sewers of Paris. Follow me. I know the way. For two years, while I was attending law school at night, I worked for the city sewer department. The job was lousy, but the pay was good and I got to know the layout of the entire city sewer system. It's easy to navigate below the streets of Paris, once you've learned how the system is laid out."

Soon my escort signaled that we had arrived at our destination. We ascended from the depths of the sewer, and emerged in the middle of a small square to continue our journey. After walking a few blocks, we caught the métro again and traveled farther away from the heart of Paris. We exited the métro at the Porte d'Italie Station. Boarding a bus, we went farther south of the city and got off at a stop near the Seine.

By this time, André felt that it was safe for us to talk more freely, and I asked my escort why he didn't want to go through the Gestapo checkpoint back in the city. He said that he was with the French intelligence service and that he didn't want to show his face because he had been involved in the killing of some Gestapo agents.

"I didn't want to take the chance that they knew me—so I thought that the sewer was a better option."

Shortly, we arrived at a compound with many nice homes and a huge building that looked like a hospital. An older gentleman opened the front door of a house within the compound and beckoned to us to enter. The man's name was Dr. Christian, and it seemed his house would be my new safe house. Dr. Christian's wife, Julienne, was also a doctor. I figured that if I were to get sick, I would be in good hands.

This supposition turned out to be entirely incorrect. Over the next two weeks, I learned that Dr. Christian had wanted to become a fighter pilot himself, but his bad eyesight had forced him into the army. He was not a doctor at all, but a lieutenant colonel in the French intelligence service. His wife, who was also only pretending to be a doctor, was not his wife but instead a Polish intelligence agent who had joined the French to fight their mutual enemy. I never found out whether "Christian" and "Julienne" were even their real names.

Late afternoon one day, the doctor took me out for a short walk along the riverbank and showed me a path to follow should I come out there to walk by myself. He felt that it was safe for me to walk out there in the countryside alone, but he cautioned me to stay on the path, not to wander out in the darkness, and, above all, not to talk to anyone. Walking outside became a habit of mine, and every day I strolled along the river, basking in the French sun.

One day, I walked a little farther down the path than usual. As I was turning around to head back to the house, I was startled by the familiar sound of an aircraft engine. The sound was coming from across the river, but bushes along the path prevented me from locating its exact source. I walked farther down the path and came to a partial opening between two bushes. Squeezing through, I came out at the edge of the riverbank, and I could clearly see the opposite bank of the river. I couldn't believe what I saw there: several buildings forming some sort of factory and an open area with five engine stands. On three of the stands, I could clearly see the ME-109 inline engines with their propellers. On one of the other stands was a running engine, the one that had attracted my attention.

I hurried back to Dr. Christian's house to report my finding. As I walked, I considered what I had seen. Was it an engine manufacturing facility? Or possibly an assembly plant? What did they do once an engine checked out on the stand? As I approached the compound, it hit me that the factory was an engine assembly facility. After the engines were tested, they would ship them out. Who would need serviceable engines? An operational unit, a fighter squadron at an aerodrome.

When I arrived back at the house, I told the doctor what I had seen. He told me that he would look into it.

After dinner that night I went to my room, read a little, and then went to bed, but I had difficulty falling asleep as the ME-109 engines were foremost in my thoughts. After lunch the next day, I told the doctor that I was going to walk down by the river later on to confirm what I had seen there the day before. The doctor didn't attempt to stop me but said, "Be careful and don't let anyone see you."

By the time I made it back to the opening in the bushes by the riverbank, the Germans had removed the engine I had seen running the day before from its stand. This time, only two engines were visible on the stands, but they were not running. I was a bit disappointed and walked a little further down the path, hoping to have a better view of the facility. To my surprise, I found a place where the bushes were thinned out and I had a clear view of the river beyond my vantage point on the path.

I stopped to look at a large river barge, which was tied to the opposite bank of the river well past the engine facility. It reminded me of the barges we used to strafe on the Rhine. I didn't pay too much attention to the barge until I noticed an armed German soldier walking slowly up and down the deck. The barge was low in the water, and I could see pipes and valves across its deck. Next to the barge, by the riverbank, were two small buildings resembling Nissen huts, semicircular corrugated metal structures. I realized that pipes and valves on the deck could be used only to control and transfer liquid, and the only liquid valuable enough to be guarded was petrol. Were the Germans using the barge as a storage tank? If so, trucks would drive up to it at night, load up, and deliver the petrol to aerodromes before sunrise.

I rushed home to tell Dr. Christian about this additional discovery. Yes, I told myself, the Germans had to be storing fuel for aircraft in that barge. And since the American B-17s had been bombing almost all of the Luftwaffe's aerodromes, the Germans couldn't afford to build new fuel dumps and had decided to disperse the fuel away from the aerodromes.

When I told Dr. Christian about what I had observed, he was astonished. He could not believe the Germans were carrying out such activities so close to his backyard, and he admitted that he wasn't familiar with such technical aspects of the air war. He told me that a friend of his who was more familiar with the Luftwaffe and aviation was planning to visit him in a few days. He asked me to brief this friend about the barge.

Three days later, the doctor's friend showed up in the early morning.

His name was Maurice, and he spoke both French and English without an accent.

"Lieutenant," Maurice said, "Dr. Christian told me that you have observed some interesting things down river."

"Yes, indeed," I said, and I told him what I had seen. I agreed to lead him to the area that afternoon.

After we had something to eat, M. Maurice and I left the doctor's house and started walking along the river path. Once M. Maurice had seen the barge downriver and the ME-109 engine stands across the river, he agreed that they were of some concern. He too thought that the pipes and valves arranged across the barge's deck indicated that the ship must store some sort of liquid. Although he agreed that the barge must hold something valuable to warrant the protection of an armed soldier, but he was not sure that it was petrol. Before his departure that night, Maurice assured me that he was going to take care of the barge and factory, and a few days later, Allied fighters strafed the barge and the engine facility, as well as a few more barges down the river.

On June 1, I had to move again—this time, to a place called Clichy. Jacques, the man who escorted me to my new safe house, indicated that my accommodations in Clichy would probably be temporary. After an uneventful journey, we arrived on a street with beautiful trees on both sides. My escort dropped me off at an apartment on the ground floor of a nice building. I was welcomed there by an elderly couple who spoke little English.

245

CHAPTER 22

THE HOUSE IN PANTIN

On Sunday, June 4, 1944, after I had spent two days with the elderly couple in Clichy, a woman from the Underground named Mme Colette visited the couple's apartment to inform me that I would travel by train to Brest in two days' time. Mme Colette appeared to be in her mid-twenties and spoke perfect English. She would be my escort, and on the journey we would pretend we were husband and wife. She had secured a baby from an orphanage who we would pretend was our child. Once I was in Brest, Mme Colette said, I would wait with others in a safe house until I could catch a submarine to take me back to England.

On June 6, the day I was supposed to travel, the plan for my escape to England was ditched when the Allies landed in Normandy. Paris was chaotic that day, and the German occupation forces began to patrol the streets with armored vehicles and tanks. The Underground put off moving me for a few days.

On June 12, a Frenchman took me by car to a house in Pantin, a suburb northeast of Paris. My safekeepers there were M. Louis and his wife, Mme Jocelyne. M. Louis spoke English well, but his wife's knowledge of the language was limited. They lived in a two-story building overlooking a canal. The ground floor was a coffee shop and bar, patronized by the locals. M. Louis's wife and a female relative managed the place. The couple lived on the second floor.

M. Louis appeared to be in his mid-thirties. He was good looking, with an athletic, muscular build. He was a lithographer and had owned a lithographic shop in the heart of the city, but he was forced to shut down the shop when the Germans swarmed into Paris in June 1940. At first I could not figure out what he was doing now, four years later, but after a few days with him, I realized that he and a few other men were conducting a clandestine activity in his basement.

One day, after I had lived in the safe house for a while, M. Louis asked me to join him for coffee in the coffee shop. Two men surfaced from the basement in their working clothes and sat at a table near ours. I asked M. Louis who the men were and what kind of work they were doing in the basement. He agreed to show me their operation, and after we finished our coffee, we headed downstairs. With a key from his pocket, M. Louis unlocked the door, and we both walked down several steps, finding ourselves in a long hallway. After a short walk, we stopped at another door, which he unlocked with another key, and we walked into a huge, dimly lit room. I was stunned by what I saw in the room: a first-class printing shop with three presses. Two of the machines were in full operation, monitored by a worker who I had seen in the coffee shop.

"Ah, a printing shop," I said to M. Louis loudly over the noise of the presses.

He nodded. "We print all sorts of forged documents for the Underground throughout France: identification cards, birth certificates, circulation papers, ration cards, and other papers for the benefit of the French resistance. Your forged ID card was probably printed here. We print everything except money, but if I had the right plates, I could do that easily."

We left the printing shop and moved on to another room in the basement. This room housed a complete arsenal: automatic weapons, rifles, hand pistols, hand grenades, and boxes of plastic explosives and knives.

"We kill Germans with these," M. Louis said with a smile, "and we also supply some resistance groups with weapons from this store."

A few days after my tour of the basement, M. Louis introduced me to his friends Alain and François. Alain was a daring individual, a chemist who worked for a company in Paris. He was an expert in the use of plastic explosives and lived near by Louis's house. Alain spoke English well. François loved to tell jokes. He worked in the nearby Pantin railway freight yard and was an expert in blowing up and derailing trains.

François also spoke English but not as well as Alain. Both Alain and François were tough and dedicated resistance fighters.

I soon learned that, along with M. Louis, Alain, and François had taken part in several skirmishes, sabotaging German installations, ambushing military convoys, and killing Germans on sight. At this point in the war, almost two months after the Normandy invasion, the Maquis and other resistance groups began to increase their sabotage against the occupation forces. The only weapons the French resistance employed were those that the RAF and USAAF could supply during the night airdrops. The German occupation forces, however, had heavy armor and knew how to use it against the French resistance.

From my room in the house, I had frequently observed the three resistance fighters load M. Louis's Citroën with weapons and plastic explosives and disappear into the night, sometimes by themselves and other times with one or two other men. I knew they must be going on sabotage and harassment missions against the Germans, and I wished I could go along with them. In the meantime I contributed to the cause by assisting the men at the printing shop, sorting the printed forged documents.

One evening at dinnertime, I told M. Louis that I knew how to use an automatic weapon and that I was anxious to join the fighters on their next escapade, whatever it was.

"You would like to be a resistance fighter?!" he exclaimed. He eagerly agreed to include me in the next mission.

The following day I joined Alain, François, and Louis on their drive to a farm some seventy kilometers northwest of Paris, where we would assist another resistance group to retrieve air-dropped supplies. The chief of the group briefed us on how to handle the airdrop. We visited the drop zone area in two groups before nightfall to familiarize ourselves with the terrain and surroundings. The ground-to-air signal was made up of three powerful flashlights arranged in a triangle. Each flashlight was to be wrapped in a sleeve to funnel the light upward so that the airdrop pilot could easily see where he should release the cargo. I was told that I would handle one of the three flashlights.

Just before midnight, in the splendor of the moon's brightness, we returned to the drop zone to clear the area for the airdrop. We took our positions and waited. A little past midnight, we heard the sound of an approaching multiengine aircraft. Immediately, the word was passed around to light up the flashlights. The pilot flew low overhead, making a circle over the triangle. He dropped the cargo and then flew away.

We retrieved the bundles and containers from the middle of the triangle and placed them on the three trucks the group had brought along. In no time, the entire group moved to the barn, where the goods—weapons, ammunition, and radios—were hidden under a haystack to be moved by others at another time.

One day in the latter part of July, over dinner, M. Louis asked me if I would be interested in going out with him and the other fighters on a small sabotage mission not far away from the house. I enthusiastically agreed. Three days later, in the darkness of the night, Louis, Alain, François, a man named René, and I left in Louis's Citroën for the small freight rail yard in Pantin. Our mission was to sabotage any locomotives we could find inside the yard.

The Germans used the Pantin freight station, which was about two kilometers from Louis's house, to ship goods and military hardware into and out of Paris. Although Germans guarded the yard, François, who worked there during the day, was familiar with its layout and knew how to get into the premises undetected.

Louis parked the Citroën by an alley at around 10:00 p.m., and we walked the rest of the way in complete darkness, guided by François. We snuck into the yard through a small opening between two adjoining walls. As I dropped down inside the yard, my heart started to thump. François spotted the silhouette of an unattended locomotive connected to a long freight train, waiting on a sidetrack, perhaps, to pull out at the first light of dawn. He walked around quietly to make sure there were no guards in the area. When he returned to our group, he told Alain, "You take Stephan, proceed to the open barn, and take care of the locomotive that's in the shop for repairs."

François, Louis, and René took care of the unattended locomotive on the sidetrack, placing their handbags of plastic explosives strategically throughout the machine. Alain slapped my shoulder lightly and whispered, "Allez, [come] Stephan, follow me." We both walked cau-

249

tiously into the darkness to the open barn, where we found a huge steam locomotive that was out of commission. Immediately, Alain started to work. An expert in explosives, he knew exactly where to place the plastic explosives to inflict the maximum damage to the machine.

When we neared the locomotive, Alain reached inside the small handbag I held open and pulled out one of the plastic explosives and a detonator. He placed the first batch under the boiler and then climbed the steps into the cabin from which the engineer and fireman operate the locomotive. He placed some of the explosives there. Then he jumped down and placed a third batch at a spot under the forward wheels. We both then retreated quietly to the spot where we had entered the yard and waited for our friends. We soon spotted the silhouettes of our three companions approaching.

In no time, we found ourselves outside the yard, and we hurriedly walked separately to the alley where the Citroën was parked. In less than fifteen minutes we were back at the house, well before the beginning of curfew. At exactly midnight, we heard two explosions down by the canal. The detonators must have worked. We broke open a bottle of wine to celebrate our success. Louis and François seemed happier than the rest of us. Louis said, "The commander of the resistance will be happy when he learns that the Germans have two fewer locomotives to operate their trains."

By the end of July, the resistance had learned that the Germans were going to blow up certain buildings—power plants, stations, and bridges—in the heart of Paris. They were going to do this while they evacuated the city. These plans were, in great measure, foiled by members of the resistance, who disarmed many of the explosive devices. (It should also be noted that Gen. Dietrich von Choltitz, the commander of the German occupation forces in Paris, ignored Hitler's order to burn the city.)

The Germans also planned to empty the prisons around Paris, especially the prison of Fresnes, a penitentiary south of the city, and to transfer thousands of French prisoners to Germany by train. These prisoners included resistance fighters and Jewish people whom the Germans had locked up during the occupation. To prevent the move, snipers with small arms attacked Germans in dark alleys, and in some cases, the resistance confronted small groups of Germans in daylight, forcing pedestrians to run in panic for cover. These attacks infuriated the German commander in Paris, but he hesitated to fight back, wanting to avoid further Allied retaliation. So he only warned his soldiers to be alert as they wandered in the streets of Paris.

The German forces had heavy weapons, but the French fighters in Paris and the Maquis had courage and determination even if they couldn't equal the Germans in weapons. Some of the resistance fighters, including François, had also become experts in stealing German supplies. François had managed to smuggle many supplies out of the Pantin rail yard, including train schedules; duplicate keys to offices, warehouses, and maintenance shops; and valuable railroad tools such as T-bar wrenches and crowbars used to bolt down sections of rails on the railroad ties.

The resistance used T-bar wrenches and crowbars to remove rail sections in order to derail incoming and outgoing German supply trains. I gained firsthand experience in this type of sabotage when M. Louis received orders from the FFI to help derail a freight train scheduled to depart the Pantin freight yard before dawn one day. It was a last-minute plan, he explained over dinner, because we could attack only under the cover of darkness. At twilight the four of us left in Louis's Citroën and headed for the rendezvous point with a group of eight.

We met our friends about an hour later in a wooded area northeast of Pantin. After a short meeting, we traveled an additional five kilometers and parked in another wooded area, just a few hundred feet from the main line to Nancy. We stayed in the thick forest until about 10:00 p.m., before we began our work. The men from the other group unloaded the tools from their truck, and we started to carry them down to the rail tracks. Six of us began to unscrew the bolts that held the rails on the ties, while some distance away, other men with shovels started to dig a small ditch the size of the rail sections to bury the six rails we were planning to remove from the line. In less than an hour the work was completed and we were ready to return home. The three Frenchmen and I returned to Pantin well before curfew.

The following day, Louis learned that the train had derailed around the bend where we had removed the rails. It had probably been traveling at high speed and the engineer hadn't had time to stop it. Although neither the Germans nor the Paris press had reported the derailment, the Gestapo had apparently been called in on the accident. They were furiously looking for the saboteurs, who, if caught, would doubtless be executed.

After the train derailment, Louis's group laid low for a few days. My last outing with my resistance friends was in mid-August, when we ambushed a German military convoy east of Paris on the road to Nancy. Because of continuous strafing by Allied fighters in the daytime, the Germans had begun to transport supplies and stolen French property only at night. Even in the darkness, the drivers were forced to move quickly along the roads to avoid ambushes by resistance snipers.

One day in the early evening, a man from FFI visited the coffee shop in Pantin. He and M. Louis spent considerable time in the basement, and then, after the visitor departed, Louis joined Alain, François, and me at our table for dinner. He started to brief us on the mission he had been assigned.

"We are to ambush a military convoy, probably carrying supplies and stolen goods being transported to Germany," he told us. "Our team will join up with another group of six resistance fighters, east of Paris on the road to Nancy. FFI's intelligence has indicated that the convoy is preparing to depart a military warehouse in the heart of the city tomorrow night. It's expected to consist of some six to eight large military trucks and will probably be accompanied by one or two military police motorcycles. We are to rendezvous with the other team at a designated location before we make the ambush."

Although by this time I had participated in two other small skirmishes, I had not been involved in a large enemy convoy ambush. Alain went on to describe how to carry out such an attack.

"You select the most suitable location, preferably on the bend of a road, and inspect the area for hiding and recovery after the attack. At the appropriate time, in the darkness of the night, you position specially designed spikes, painted the color of the roadbed, about thirty centimeters apart across the pavement. These will blow out the front tires of the first vehicle. The trucks will be moving fast, and the driver will have difficulty controlling his vehicle if the front tires suddenly go flat. He'll try to brake, but this won't help because the truck that's following close behind won't be able to stop in time. The result will be a huge wreck that will cause heavy damage and injuries."

Louis interrupted Alain and said, "That's the critical moment for you, then. You begin the attack using automatic weapons and hand grenades and kill anything that moves. The other drivers, or occupants who may be riding along, will attempt to take cover. This is useless because the grenades will damage whatever cover they manage to find."

253

Just before darkness the next day, the four of us filled the trunk of Louis's car with the weapons we were going to use in the attack and headed for Nancy. I carried a .38 revolver and a British automatic machine gun for the mission. After an hour or so of driving, Louis pulled off the main highway to Nancy and turned onto a dirt road. He came to a stop in a thick forest. Suddenly, six men, dressed warmly and carrying automatic weapons, appeared from the darkness of the tree foliage and walked toward our Citroën. We got out of the Citroën to greet the men; M. Louis introduced me to the group as "Stephan, l'aviateur Américain."

The chief of the group, named Armand, told Louis to have someone drive the Citroën to the hiding place on the other side of the wooded area. We unloaded our weapons from the trunk before Alain and one of the chief's men drove the car to a barn being used as the hiding place. Armand and Louis went over the ambush plan and how it was going to be carried out.

After a short while, Alain and the other man returned and joined the rest of the group. We waited.

At about 10:30 p.m., François, M. Louis, and three members of Armand's team walked down the road and placed the spikes on the roadbed. Once they returned, we took our positions. The minutes crept by slowly, and my heart began to thud faster with anxiety.

Suddenly, Armand jumped up and said in a low voice, "Attention, please." Evidently, he had heard the sound of heavy vehicles. "They are here. The bastards have arrived."

Every one of us tensed for the attack, pointing our weapons toward the eastern side of the bend. Finally, the silhouette of the first convoy truck appeared in the moonlight, followed closely by another truck. The leading truck's front wheels went over the spikes and, with a terrific bang, were ripped to shreds. The driver attempted to brake, but his truck swerved out of control and rolled over on its side. The second truck had no chance to stop and smashed into the overturned truck. Flames burst out, and they were followed by an explosion.

Only the first two trucks smashed into one another. The following trucks and a motorcycle were able to stop in time to avoid slamming into the two burning vehicles. German soldiers converged near the flames. The occupants had been able to get away from the wreckage and fall to the ground not too far away. They must have been injured.

Armand gave the signal to attack, and we stormed out of the nearby woods and swarmed at the confused Germans on the paved road, weapons blazing. As instructed by Armand, those with hand grenades aimed for the intact trucks first. Those of us with the automatics went after the men, who by this time must have realized that they were being ambushed. They tried to take cover but were quickly cut down by the rain of bullets.

I used my automatic gun to its full extent. I must have brought down six or eight of the Germans who tried to run for cover. By the time I ran out of ammunition, the ambush was largely over. Alain came to my side.

"Ça va bien, Stephan? [Are you all right, Steve?]" he asked, concerned.

"Yes, I'm all right," I said.

"Watch this," he said and tossed his last hand grenade directly on top of the still-intact motorcycle. It was blown to pieces.

In less than ten minutes, the sensational display of French guerrilla-style teamwork had six trucks and one motorcycle in shambles and twenty-five German soldiers dead. After Armand was convinced that no one was alive, we fell back into the woods to leave the scene of destruction. After a short walk through the forest and over a hill, we found the barn where our vehicles were hidden. We could still see the glare from the burning wreckage towering over the other side of the hill, illuminating the night sky.

We slept in the barn that night, catching what little sleep we could on haystacks, and said good-bye to our comrades the next morning. Then Louis drove us through country roads back to Pantin.

The attacks against the German garrison in Paris continued day and night as the city's citizens became aware of the German evacuation. German trucks and other vehicles loaded with soldiers, civilians, and stolen possessions passed through the streets of Paris in a disorderly manner, anxious to leave before the resistance fighters could block the roads.

Unfortunately, my stay at Pantin was coming to an end. At dinner one night, my host looked me in the eyes, rather sadly, and said, "Stephan, I am extremely sorry that you have to leave us."

255

The Allied command wanted all the downed airmen in the Paris area to be assembled in certain locations throughout the city. The next day, Alain would take me to a farmhouse in Bondy.

I protested this move as vigorously as I could, but M. Louis said he couldn't deny his superiors' orders. I hated to leave the people I had learned to love and admire, the people I had fought with for the liberation of their country, but I had no choice.

CHAPTER 23

THE LIBERATION OF PARIS

The following day, after a short drive through country roads, Alain and I arrived at my new safe house. I was surprised to see that the place wasn't a typical farm, but a vineyard. As we drove up, I could see a huge spread of thousands of grapevines. At one end of the property, up a hill and away from the two-lane road, was a big white two-story house, and at the opposite side of the vineyard, by the main entrance to the farm, was a line of small buildings, which I guessed were used for processing grapes for wine. We found M. Martin near this row of buildings.

Shortly after Alain introduced me to my new host, we hugged like longtime friends and he left to return to Pantin. M. Martin escorted me toward the big white house on the hill. We entered the house through a huge mahogany lacquer-covered door and found ourselves in a large hallway with a marble spiral staircase. M. Martin led me up the stairway to a room on the second floor. As we walked into the room, I faced a large group of men.

"My God," I said. "Americans!"

Some of them were still wearing their khaki army garments. A few wore leather flying jackets.

"Voilà [There]," M. Martin said. "Meet your American friends." They looked at me curiously, and I wondered what they were thinking, seeing me in my civilian clothes. I approached a guy with lieutenant's bars on his flying jacket.

"You must be in the air force," I said. He told me that he and the other men in the room were all B-17 and B-24 crew members.

"I am Lt. Steve Pisanos of the 4th Fighter Group," I said, and started to explain how I had come to meet them there. "How many of you are here?"

"With you," he said, "we are now thirty-two. A few of us have been here for some time, but others have been arriving here in the past few days. I'm Bill Smith."

The room was crowded. All these men were confined to this room and a few more down the hallway. That night and the nights that followed, I joined the majority of the pilots sleeping on the floor in the main room. It was not very peaceful; many of the men snored and some had nightmares that caused them to cry out. We couldn't see where we were going at night, and if we had to use the bathroom, we'd inevitably step on our neighbors along the way or run into furniture in the hallway.

A few days after my arrival at this safe house, M. Martin discovered that I could speak French fluently and asked me to walk with him around his vineyard estate, which extended from the main road to the top of a distant hill. He proudly showed me the upcoming harvest of grapes.

At the end of the tour we walked toward the edge of his property, which ran along the main road. We entered a small storage shed, and M. Martin pulled me toward the window that overlooked the paved road outside. I looked and saw hordes of Germans, both civilian and military, passing by in all sorts of vehicles. Well-secured to the roofs of these vehicles were bundles of furniture, boxes, and other goods.

"What on earth are those bundles and boxes they have on top of the automobiles?" I asked.

"Ah, my friend," said the Frenchman angrily, "that is French property. These thieves pass through here and on other main roads on their way east to Germany. They came to France in 1940, as conquerors, and are going away now with humiliation from the fear that the advancing Allied armies will soon be in Paris. Some are buying things they need, others are just taking anything they can put their hands on from houses they were renting and hotels they had taken over. You know, someday le Boche will pay for all the suffering France has endured."

When I returned to the lounge in the house, I told the pilots about what M. Martin had shown me. A few days later, I was able to take Lieutenant Smith to see the German thievery. From the window of the storage building, we could see both lanes of the two-way road, including the wide unpaved sidewalks on both sides of the road, being used as a one-way passage by the fleeing Germans in trucks, staff cars, and other military vehicles, many loaded with the stolen goods. We saw four-wheeled horse buggies being pulled not by horses but by able-bodied German soldiers and carrying not stolen goods in the back but wounded soldiers wrapped in white bandages. The scene confirmed that the German wounded were being taken out of hospitals to continue their recuperation in Germany.

After lunch that day, M. Martin invited me to take a ride with him to the city on his motorcycle, to see how things were there. When he pulled the bike out of a small barn, I saw that it looked as if it had been delivered from the factory the day before. M. Martin mounted the Harley, and after a few tries, the motor caught. I climbed on the back, and we were off toward the back gate of the property, away from the main road. As we reached the gate on top of the hill, we came out onto a dirt road parallel to the main road in front of M. Martin's property.

After driving slowly on the dirt road for two to three kilometers, M. Martin made a left turn onto a paved road that took us to the main road. This road looked like a boulevard, as it had a divider in the middle and trees on both sides. While the right side of the two-lane road was empty of traffic, the two lanes on the other side were fully occupied by German military vehicles, staff cars with occupants, and heavy and light trucks, all loaded with human cargo and stolen property headed for Germany.

We cruised along at a leisurely pace on the empty right side of the road toward central Paris. Then, suddenly, one of the German staff cars well ahead of us on the other side of the road stopped. An officer jumped out and walked across the divider to our side of the road and stopped in front of our motorcycle. He removed his Luger from its holster with his right hand and pointed it toward us. At the same time, he raised his left hand upward, signaling M. Martin to stop. I noticed the guy wore the uniform of a Luftwaffe officer. M. Martin had no choice but to obey the German and stopped in front of him.

"What's the matter?" he said to the German in a trembling voice.

"Get off the bike," the German said in broken French, pointing his pistol at M. Martin's head.

I was frightened and could feel the panic building up inside of me. I dismounted the bike and took refuge behind a nearby tree. M. Martin

258

dismounted his beloved bike and, at the same time, reached into his pocket and pulled out a big roll of French paper money, but the German didn't want any money. What he wanted was the motorcycle. He got onto the bike, and for a moment I thought M. Martin was going to resist. But, luckily, the Frenchman remained calm. The German holstered his Luger, started the Harley, and disappeared down the wrong side of the road.

As M. Martin stood frozen, watching the German thief vanish into the chaotic eastbound traffic, I walked over to express my sorrow for the loss of his beloved bike. When I approached him, I could see that he was crying. Tears were dripping down his cheeks from behind his thick spectacles. M. Martin looked at me as he started to wipe his eyes and said, "Let's go home, my friend."

We left the commotion of the German traffic and reached M. Martin's place through back roads. Although M. Martin had hardly opened his mouth on our way back to the house, I knew well that he was most furious at the loss of his treasured motorcycle. As we entered the vineyard grounds through the back gate, M. Martin said, "Stephan, the situation in Paris is very grave. Unless the Allied armies come soon, the Germans are planning to blow up the city."

When we entered the house on the hill, M. Martin went directly to his room on the ground floor and I ran upstairs to the lounge to tell the men what had happened. As we talked, we could hear P-47s, P-51s, and Spitfires flying overhead, hammering the fleeing Germans. That evening, after supper, we all gathered around the small radio M. Martin had given us. Surprisingly, the news that night was all good.

"The Germans are evacuating Paris by the thousands," the BBC commentator said, "and are taking with them everything they can put their hands on. Gen. Philippe Leclerc's French 2nd Armored Division is approaching Paris from the southwest and is ready to charge into the city. Also, the American 4th Infantry Division, under the command of Gen. Ray Barton, has left the village of Rambouillet on its way to Paris from the south, proceeding slowly behind General Leclerc's armored division."

When the news was over, Lieutenant Smith approached me and whispered, "Say, Steve, things look good out there. What do you say you and I make a run tomorrow and go south? The Germans are moving out of the city, and the French and American troops are ready to come in. We're bound to run into the 4th Infantry Division troops somewhere south of Paris. What do you say?"

"Funny," I said, "I had the same idea."

"OK, then, let's do it, and not a word to anyone," Smith said.

The following day, August 23, 1944, after a hefty breakfast, Lieutenant Smith and I left M. Martin's safe house without saying a word to anyone. We walked up the hill and snuck out through the back gate. We walked southward, avoiding the main boulevards, which were being used by the fleeing Germans. Luckily Smith had brought a small map of Paris and the surrounding areas. After quite some time, we found ourselves entering the heart of Paris from the area of Les Lilas. We walked down on Avenue Gambetta, all the way to the Cimetière du Père Lachaise.

Here we encountered, for the first time, automatic weapons firing. Fleeing Germans were evidently trying to sneak out, and resistance snipers were firing at them from rooftops and balconies. We stopped in a doorway to take cover until the firing had ceased. Then we started to move again—cautiously.

After walking for a while longer, we arrived at the Place de la Bastille, where we ran into a big fight between fleeing German soldiers and a group of resistance fighters. Smith and I had to take cover in doorways a couple of times more to avoid being hit. Just as we reached another door, we ran into a man about twenty years old who had taken shelter nearby.

We didn't greet him, thinking that he was a Frenchman, but when he heard Smith and me speak English, he exclaimed loudly, in English, "Are you fellows Americans?"

"Why, yes," replied Smith. "We're Army Air Force pilots who came down in France and have been evading the Germans. We were staying at a French house northeast of Paris and decided to leave the place and go south, hoping to meet up with the American army."

"And you?" I asked him. "You speak good English for a Frenchman."

"I'm not French. I am American too," said the man. "My name is Aaron Bluemski."

Sheltered from the sporadic firing in the area by the huge door, Smith and I listened to Bluemski's story of how he came to be in Paris. His family had moved there before the war so that his father could help his brother with the family business. Shortly after France was occupied by the Germans, Bluemski's mother and father, who were Jewish, were taken away by the Gestapo. Bluemski lived with his cousin and aunt for a while, but they too were taken away. He had been on the run for a while, and like us, after hearing the BBC report the previous night, he had decided to try to meet up with the U.S. Army unit on its way to Paris.

Smith and I felt sorry for Bluemski and invited him to join us. The three of us walked down Boulevard Bourdon, crossed the Seine at Pont d'Austerlitz, and through Boulevard de l'Hospital, arrived at Place d'Italie. Through Avenue d'Italie, we walked down to the Porte d'Italie. Bluemski guided us using Smith's map. We walked south, past the airport of Orly, and as we reached the small town of Barbizon, spotted a small, disorganized group of German soldiers walking in the opposite direction toward Paris.

We immediately took cover behind some bushes and stayed there until the Germans had passed. We started to move again until we reached what appeared to be a no-man's-land. By this time, twilight was upon us, and we were getting worried. We kept walking, dodging freshly made holes in the ground probably caused by aerial bombing or cannon shells. Finally, I spotted something up ahead.

"Hold on a moment," I said to my friends. I pointed ahead.

"Yes," Smith said, "I think they are soldiers."

"My God!" I shouted. "They are Americans. Look at their helmets."

"Well, I'll be damned," Smith exclaimed, and the three of us hugged each other as if we had won the lottery.

We started to run as fast as we could, but the soldiers didn't want to take any chances. When we neared them, they pointed their rifles at us, hollering for us to stop. We did, and Smith shouted, "Don't shoot! We are American pilots."

The soldiers dropped their rifles and waved at us to come closer to their line, but still they held their ground just in case. I gave my name and affiliation.

"First Lt. Spiro Pisanos, 334 Fighter Squadron, 4th Fighter Group, 8th Fighter Command."

Smith did likewise. The sergeant in charge asked Bluemski for his rank and name. I told him that Bluemski wasn't an airman but rather an American trapped in Paris since before the war. Bluemski gave his name to the sergeant and his address in the United States. A Jeep, driven by an army second lieutenant with a sergeant at his side, arrived.

The sergeant we had met told the lieutenant in the Jeep, "Lieutenant, here are two more aviators and an American civilian."

"Come on, gentlemen, hop in, and I'll drive you fellows to the rear," the young officer said.

We hopped on the back of the Jeep and soon arrived at a tent where officers had their meals. Inside the tent, the lieutenant presented us to a major who, in turn, took us over to a brigadier general on the other side of the tent. We introduced ourselves to the general, who chuckled and said, "You flyboys have had some vacation here in France. Ever since the invasion, we have been picking up your buddies everywhere, in basements, in the arms of women, hiding in trees. God knows what we may find in Paris."

A major general walked into the tent and the brigadier general introduced us to Major General Barton, the commander of the U.S. Army's 4th Infantry Division.

"Good to have you, boys," he said and told us to have a bite to eat. He went on to ask the major, who was standing by, to see that we were fed, to find us some army clothing, and to put us up for the night. He also told the major to contact the 6th U.S. Army and see what they wanted to do with Bluemski.

After we had dinner, the major took us to a tent farther down the row, where we spent the night on army folding cots. The major told us that he would pick us up in the morning for breakfast.

The following day, August 24, we had breakfast, and Smith and I were fitted with army khakis displaying our ranks. The major told Aaron that he'd take him to personnel to check with the 6th U.S. Army about his repatriation back to the United States. Smith and I bid Bluemski good-bye, and he thanked us.

While we were in the tent putting on our khakis and tossing our smelly civilian attire, a sergeant walked in and told the two soldiers in charge of clothing supplies to prepare to move again. When Smith asked one of the clerks where they were moving to, the soldier replied, "We are moving into Paris this time."

All day long, and into the night, everyone prepared for the move. With no assigned duties, Smith and I spent another night in the partially torn-down tent. The next day, we found that the division was moving toward Paris, behind General Leclerc's French 2nd Armored Division. Although we were happy to be with the American troops, both Smith and I wanted to return to England and not to Paris. When we told the army major as much, he told us that he couldn't change the plan at this point.

"Why don't you fellows come along with us to Paris," he said, "and we'll see from there what can be done for your passage to the United Kingdom."

Not having a choice, we tagged along in the major's Jeep while the division proceeded slowly behind the French 2nd Armored Division. The rumor was that General Eisenhower wanted General Leclerc's troops to be the first liberators to enter the French capital. The division slowed its forward movement as it was approaching the gates of Paris, and at one point, it came to a complete stop, waiting to receive the signal that General Leclerc's troops were well inside the city.

Finally, we heard word that the division was on the move again. The French troops were indeed in the heart of the city, and the French general had accepted an unconditional surrender from the German garrison in Paris. General Barton gave the orders to his troops to move full-speed ahead.

After driving some distance in a column of trucks, Jeeps, staff cars, and soldiers on foot, we entered the city of Paris from the suburbs in the south, first passing through where we had come a few days before: the Porte d'Italie. As we began to approach the center of the city, the division troops were met by a wild uproar of excitement from the people of liberated Paris. The streets and boulevards were strung with people of all ages, young and old. The women were wearing their best dresses for the celebration. Some carried flowers in their hands and threw them at the tired passing soldiers, as the motorcade wended its way through the streets.

Hundreds of thousands of jubilant and triumphant Parisians tried to get close to the passing troops, wanting to hug and kiss the Americans as an expression of their gratitude for the liberation of their beloved city. Major Jack's Jeep, in which Smith and I were riding, was full of flowers. I told the major, "The people think that we are part of your group. If they only knew that we were living in Paris all along, evading the Germans."

"Hey, Lieutenant," the major said, "you guys are part of us now, so enjoy this great welcome."

CHAPTER 24

HOMECOMING

Bill Smith and I spent another day celebrating with the 4th Infantry Division. Then, on August 27, we and several other liberated Allied airmen were driven to Evreux Aerodrome. There, we boarded an Army Air Force C-47 for our flight to London.

My first day back in England, August 28, was spent being interrogated by U.S. Army Intelligence in a secluded village in the outskirts of London. Late in the day I was given 200 pounds' advance pay, along with a special paper showing that I had returned from being missing in action and that I was on the way to join my unit.

BACK TO DEBDEN

When the guard at Debden's gate boarded the bus to check the IDs of those inside, I showed the special temporary document I had been issued at the Interrogation Center. After the military policeman checked it over a bit closer, he said, "Welcome back, Lieutenant." At about midmorning, I was at the officers' mess, where I secured a room and then headed for group operations. There, I found Blakeslee, who had been promoted to full colonel four days after I had gone down, still going strong.

Over coffee, I told Colonel Blakeslee what had happened on the March 5 mission to Bordeaux and how I had spent the last six months in occupied France. That evening, he and almost every other officer at Debden spent some time drinking with me at the bar, as they had in the old days. Aside from Colonel Blakeslee, Capt. Jerry Montgomery and Lts. Joe Lang and David Howe were the only ones left from the old group. Everyone wanted to know what had happened to me. They had heard only confusing reports from those who came back from that March 5 mission. Someone had reported that I had gone down in the English Channel north of Le Havre. Others thought that my aircraft had exploded south of Le Havre. I told them what had really happened.

I inquired about my friends from the old days. Deacon Hively had been promoted to major and was in command of the 334 Squadron but was on leave in the United States. Major Jerry Brown was acting CO. Several of my buddies had been killed in combat, including Maj. Mike Sobanski, Capt. Vic France, Lt. Ralph Hofer, Thomas Biel, and Edmond Whalen. Others, including Duane Beeson and Hank Mills, were being held as prisoners of war. Some of my friends from the other two squadrons had also been killed or became POWs: K. D. Peterson was a POW in some stalag, and Peter Lehman of 336 Squadron was killed in an accident near Duxford. Maj. Jim Clark, who had been my commanding officer when I went down, had been transferred to the U.S. embassy in London after spending a short time in group operations. My roommate and friend Captain Gentile had returned to the United States after he had destroyed twenty-eight enemy aircraft, twenty-two in the air and six on the ground. In all, I was told, the 4th Fighter Group had lost some forty-five pilots on various missions in the six months I was gone.

I walked down the flight line and had a small, but enthusiastic, reunion with my old crew chief, Sgt. Paul Fox and Sgt. Jerome Byrge, his assistant. Both of them had crewed my Spitfire XR-K, P-47 QP-D, and the P-51B QP-D. Sergeant Byrge was now crewing his own Mustang. Other crew chiefs dashed over to Fox's aircraft to welcome me back. The reunion with the men on the flight line was somewhat sentimental, and I had to tell them what had happened on that last mission.

I wanted to get back into combat again as soon as possible. At the mess the next evening, I ran into Maj. Fred Heene, from group personnel, and asked him about my flying status. Unfortunately, as a returned evader, I could not fly in combat and risk being shot down. If the Germans captured me on the ground, I could be forced to compromise those in the French Underground who had helped me. The good news was that Heene had found me an assignment under General Anderson, who was now commander of 67th Fighter Wing. When Anderson had learned of my return, he had asked for me to be assigned to his wing in operations. The post would allow me to fly over England but not over hostile territory.

I took the assignment, and on September 9, 1944, I was officially transferred from the 334 Fighter Squadron to the 67th Fighter Wing. I was assigned in combat operations under Lt. Col. Eugene D. Roberts, an ex-78th Fighter Group pilot with nine kills to his credit. We were responsible for the operational control of several fighter groups and the coordination of missions that involved both fighter and bomber groups. After I had settled into the job, I began flying out of Debden in staff aircraft.

In mid-September, I received a telegram from Captain Gentile:

Just learned that you have returned to England safe and well. I had the feeling that you weren't ready to go. I am getting married at the latter part of November and would like to have you as my best man. Come home and see if you can get an assignment to the Fighter Test Section at Wright Field in Dayton, Ohio. Regards, Your Pal, Don. Piqua, Ohio.

Don's telegram piqued my interest, and I began to think about returning to my adopted country. But I didn't have the courage to tell General Anderson that I wanted to leave his wing, until one day, when I caught him sitting alone at his table in the dining room. I approached him and asked for permission to talk to him about a personal matter.

"Sure, Steve. Sit down and have some coffee with me," he said. And before I had the chance to say anything, he added, "I'll bet you want to go home."

"But, Sir," I asked, "how did you know?"

"I can see it in your eyes," the general said. "You can't fly in combat—and with your buddies gone, you feel kind of lost in front of all the new pilots at Debden. I know about Gentile's marriage and I know you and he were close. In fact, when you went down on that mission to Bordeaux, Don flew over the channel alone to look for you. You'll be happy to know that as an evadee, you have your choice of assignments stateside. Where would you like to go?"

267

"Captain Gentile is assigned to Wright Field in Dayton, Ohio, at the Fighter Test Section, and I would love to go there," I said.

The general said he would help me get the assignment. I thanked General Andy, and when I left the dining room, my heart was singing. That evening, I went to Debden Aerodrome for dinner and learned that Colonel Blakeslee had gone back home on leave. As I walked into the lounge, I ran into Maj. Deacon Hively, who had just returned from his leave in the United States. We had dinner and a couple drinks together and retired to the lounge to talk about the old days. I asked him what had happened to the two ME-109s he went after when we split up during my last mission, and he told me that he had engaged in hair-raising combat with both of them and had scored hits on both. One of the planes burst into flames and blew up.

"The other guy saw what had happened to his buddy, came around, and tried to get on my tail," Hively said. "We started to go around and around as each of us was trying to get on the tail of the other. After I dropped some flaps down, I was able to outturn him and slowly found my way behind the guy. But the bastard started to try to shake me off his tail. He went into a dive from about 3,000 feet and headed eastward toward the cloud deck. I pushed the throttle forward to get closer and fired at him before he flew into the cloud deck. But I missed him, and he dropped down below the clouds. I followed him under the overcast and started to gain on him fast. I must have been some 200 to 300 yards out when I gave him a short burst but missed. I then gave him another long burst, as I was bouncing around behind his prop wash, and nailed him. The plane burst into flames and crashed.

"But as I was turning around at the spot where my second kill had crashed, I saw another crashed ME-109, smoking badly. I didn't pay much attention to the crashed 109 until I was about to climb through the low, soupy deck of clouds and head for home, when I saw a second crashed 109, also smoking."

"Those were probably the two 109s I had hit," I told him. "Both were smoking badly when they dropped into the low cloud deck and disappeared—but I never saw them crash."

"Well, Greek," Hively said, "they have to be yours. No one else has filed a claim of engagement in that area."

Hively promised to submit a revised report to Fighter Command and request that I be given credit for these two crashed 109s, which would give me a score of four destroyed on that mission, including the two that had already been confirmed by Captain Beeson and Lieutenant Peterson.

"Also," Hively said, "I'll put you in for the Silver Star—you've definitely earned it. I'm glad to see you back, Greek. What are your plans now?"

I told him that I was not allowed to fly in combat, that I had been assigned to General Andy's wing, and that I was hoping to be assigned to Wright Field in Dayton, Ohio, where Gentile was assigned. I spent almost all of my remaining evenings with Hively, Montgomery, Lang, Howe, and Colonel Blakeslee—after he had returned from leave in the States. Finally, on October 27, 1944, I received word from wing personnel that I had been assigned to the headquarters of the Air Technical Service Command (ATSC) Aircraft Test Division, at Wright Field, in Dayton, Ohio.

THE INCREDIBLE DON BLAKESLEE

On October 30, 1944, I was on duty at the wing's combat operations center, monitoring the several fighter groups as they were returning from escort missions over Germany.

It was then when we received the information from returning 479th Fighter Group pilots that Col. Hub Zemke, the ex-commander of 56th Fighter Group, who was leading the 479th P-51B Mustang Group, was shot down and had bailed out over Germany.

On the same day Col. Don Blakeslee was leading the 4th Fighter Group on a B-17 escort mission to Hamburg, Germany. This was Blakeslee's third combat mission since his return from leave in the United States on October 20, 1944.

Shortly after his return to Debden from that mission, he was personally grounded by Gen. Kepner, the chief of 8th Fighter Command. He didn't want to lose him as he had lost Col. Zemke, he told Brig. Gen. Anderson, our wing commander.

This was certainly a great blow to Don Blakeslee, who had led the 4th Group to greatness and who had always wanted to lead his pilots to the end, until the Luftwaffe was destroyed.

Who was this man Blakeslee, who had flown more combat missions and accumulated more combat hours flying against the Luftwaffe, who had commanded the 4th Group longer than any other pilot, and who believed that fighting the Luftwaffe was a grand sport?

Don Blakeslee was born in September 1917, in Fairport Harbor, Ohio. He joined the Royal Canadian Air Force in 1940, and after completing his training in Canada in May of 1941, was posted to the 401st RAF Fighter Squadron [FS] in England, flying Spitfires. Later on, he found himself in the newly formed 133 Eagle Squadron [ES], which he commanded briefly before the three RAF ESs were absorbed into the American Army Air Force.

I first met Don Blakeslee when the 133 ES moved into Debden Aerodome, just prior to our transfer into the 4th Fighter Group in the USAAF at the end of September 1942. He was without a doubt an impressive and striking individual with an athletic six-foot frame. He had a magnetic personality, a pair of piercing eyes and the bearing of a born aerial warrior. But above all, he loved to drink beer with his pilots after a mission.

After he was taken into the 4th Fighter Group, he was promoted to major and was given command of 335, FS in the group. Because of his exceptional skills and ability to lead in the air, Col. Chesley Peterson, deputy 4th Group commander, used Major Blakeslee most frequently to lead the group on fighter sweeps and bomber escort missions across the channel.

I was fortunate to have flown numerous times as a wingman to this great aviator in Spitfires and P-47s Thunderbolts, and I can attest that, in the air, Blakeslee was a genius aerial leader. In preparing to attack an enemy formation, he could judge precisely when and how to execute the maneuver for the attack. And, when a melee developed, he was in total command of the situation.

At the latter part of 1943, when Colonel Peterson took over command of the 4th Group from Col. Edward Anderson, he made Major Blakeslee his deputy for operations and continued to utilize him, now a Lieutenant Colonel, to lead the 4th group deep into Germany with a force of 75 P-47s.

When Colonel Blakeslee assumed command of the 4th Group from Colonel Peterson on January 1, 1944, the group's tally was less than 100 enemy aircraft destroyed. Ten months later, the group's score had surpassed the 700 mark. Don Blakeslee had fought the Germans longer than any other American pilot. He had flown more than 1,000 combat hours and had piled up close to 500 missions. On those missions, he had destroyed 15 enemy aircraft in the air, and two on the ground. He also had three probables and 11 damaged. He could easily have had more victories—even though he always claimed that he couldn't hit the broad side of a barn—but his aim was to lead his pilots into battle and protect the bombers at all cost during escort missions.

On an escort mission to Berlin, with P-51 Mustangs that involved a large number of bombers and escorting fighters, Blakeslee was chosen by fighter command to direct all the fighters involved on that mission.

It is also interesting to note that when the shuttle mission to Russia was planned and executed in June 1944, General Kepner selected Don Blakeslee to lead the augmented 4th Group on that one and only mission to Russia via Berlin.

Don Blakeslee's outstanding leadership in the air had also caught the attention of his superiors early. Debden Aerodrome was visited more than any other fighter station by Generals Spaatz, Doolittle, Eaker, Hunter, Kepner and others, just to observe the briefings given by Blakeslee before a mission, and to watch the group take off.

The same generals spoke extremely well of Blakeslee during and after the war in Europe. General Hunter, the first boss of 8th Fighter Command, described him as "a unique aerial commander who had set his objectives and direction at the beginning of nothing less than the obliteration of Goering's Luftwaffe." General Eaker portrayed Blakeslee as "a courageous leader in the air and on the ground." General Kepner had said once after the war that he had two great aerial commanders, "Don Blakeslee and Hub Zemke." Blakeslee's skills and abilities as fearful aerial opponent were also recognized and respected by the enemy he was fighting in the sky over Europe.

After the war, I was invited to attend the June 1987 Paris Air show at Le Bourget Airport by my friend, Dimitri Countouris, a retired Hellenic

Air Force Lieutenant General and a representative of Bell Helicopter Company in Greece. I was to meet my friend at the Bell Helicopter Chalet at Le Bourget. Upon my arrival at the Chalet, I was astounded when I spotted among my friend's guests no other than the Luftwaffe's wartime renowned aerial warrior, Gen. Adolf Galland. As we were taken to our table, after the usual introductions, I found myself sitting next to my ex-enemy, who I found most pleasant, and naturally, we began to converse.

272

At first the general thought that I was a Bell Helicopter pilot, but he was quite surprised to learn that I had flown Spitfires during WWII in England. "You flew Spitfires," he exclaimed.

"Oh, yes," I said, ''then Thunderbolts and lastly P-51s Mustangs. I was with the 4th Fighter Group that on the 3rd and 4th of March 1944 we escorted the B-17s to Berlin." By this time, everyone around our table was attentively listening to our conversation.

"Ah," he exclaimed, ''that was Blakeslee's organization."

I confirmed this, and asked him if he knew Colonel Don.

"Yes," he said, "we knew him well in the Luftwaffe," and added, "You know, my friend, when it was reported that Col. Hub Zemke had been shot down, I told Marshal Goering that if we could now get this fellow Blakeslee, our troubles with the Americans would be lessened. Zemke was a good catch, but Blakeslee was the one we really wanted." That's what the famed wartime Luftwaffe, 4th Fighter Group Aerial antagonist, Gen. Adolf Galland, had to say about Col. Don Blakeslee, when I met him at the Paris Air Show in 1987.

But it's interesting to note also that after Blakeslee had relinquished command of the 4th Group to Col. Everet Stewart, he and those who followed him and the pilots of the 4th Group continued to raise havoc against the Luftwaffe where, at the end of the war in Europe in May 1945, the 4th Group had destroyed 1,016 enemy aircraft in the air and on the ground, more than any other USAAF unit. Only Colonel Zemke's 56th Group came close behind the 4th Group with the destruction of 992 enemy aircraft in the air and on the ground.

I would be remiss though, if I failed to point out that the credit for the greatness the 4th Fighter Group achieved at the end of the war in Europe goes not only to those who commanded the group, the squadrons and the pilots who flew the Spitfires, the Thunderbolts, and the Mustangs but to all those on the ground—the crew chiefs, their assistants, the armorers, mechanics in the hangars, the refueling boys, supply clerks, cooks, military policemen, and all those who served in the 4th Group during WWII.

RETURN TO AMERICA

I left Debden on a Friday in early November 1944. The flight back to the United States was long but pleasant. When we arrived at LaGuardia Airport in New York, I was a bit surprised to find a pack of reporters waiting to meet the aircraft. I did my best to answer their questions about what aircraft I had flown in the war and what sort of air combat I had experienced.

When I finally broke away from the crowd, I took a cab to Hotel Astor by Times Square. I called Don in Piqua and told him that I would stop off in Plainfield before heading for Dayton. When I called Mr. Stender at the Park Hotel in Plainfield that evening, he was pleased to learn that I had arrived in New York.

Once I made it through the formalities at the army reception center in Atlantic City, I arrived in Plainfield on November 21 and took a cab to the Park Hotel. When my friends saw me enter the lobby in my uniform, they enveloped me. Word of my arrival spread through the halls, and soon Mr. Stender emerged from his office to greet me with open arms.

Two days later, Mr. Stender hosted a banquet in my honor. Many distinguished guests, including Senator Clifford Case, the mayors of Plainfield and nearby towns, newspaper publishers, and members of the American Hellenic Educational Progressive Association (AHEPA), attended. Several people gave speeches, and at the end of the meal, Mr. Stender briefly introduced me and asked me to say a few words. When I got up to speak, I discovered I was trembling, but I managed to say a bit about my experiences in Europe and to thank all the guests for coming. Finally I thanked America itself: "I am indebted to America for having given me the opportunity to fulfill my boyhood dream of becoming an aviator. To me, that was a great gift from Uncle Sam. I am proud to have served in the defense of America, and I am proud to wear the uniform I have on, but above all, I am proud to have been baptized as a citizen of this great republic and I am proud to call Plainfield my home."

Several days later, when my train pulled into Dayton, Gentile was waiting for me on the platform. He introduced me to his lovely fiancée, Ms. Isabel Masdea; his sister Edith; and Isabel's father, Mr. Masdea. At his home on Wayne Street in Piqua, I met Gentile's mother, Josephina, and his father, Patsy. Both had immigrated to America from Italy. The family welcomed me as though I was one of their own.

That night I was treated to a real Italian pasta dinner, and at Gentile's insistence, I spent the night in the family's small house. The following day, we woke up early, to get to Wright Field. Even though I was still on leave, I wanted to check in and get settled. On our way to the base, Don told me that as training for my new job I would be sent to test pilots' school, where I'd be taught the theory and practice of testing new and modified aircraft to determine their performance and capabilities. It was my responsibility as a test pilot to ensure that the performance characteristics of an airplane, as certified by the manufacturer, were verified.

"Test flying is completely different from the combat flying we did in Europe," Don told me.

Upon arriving at the field he took me to the Flight Test Division, where I met Col. Mark Bradley. I handed him the letter of introduction from General Anderson, which he read quickly. The good Colonel then told me to report to Maj. Fred Borsodi at the Fighter Test Section. When we arrived at the Fighter Test area, the parking apron in front of the hanger was full of fighter aircraft of all kinds. Major Borsodi welcomed me to his outfit and introduced me to Majs. Dick Johnson and Gus Landquist; Capts. Kenneth Chilstrom, Ira Jones, Jack Sullivan, and Bill Glasgow; Lts. Jim Little, Jim Fitzgerald, and Jim Martin; and, finally, Maj. Colman Kuhn, the chief of engineering and maintenance, responsible for the upkeep of all Fighter Test aircraft. Later on, I became an assistant to Major Kuhn, which allowed me to get more flying time than the other test pilots in the section.

Later that day, Don dropped me off at the bachelor officers' quarters (BOQ) at Patterson Field, where I had planned to stay. But I soon found out that I would get a better deal if I didn't stay in the "free" BOQ accommodations (for which I had to forfeit my officer's monthly quarters allowances). I moved my stuff instead to a comfortable room for one dollar per night at the Dayton YMCA, where other officers from Wright Field were staying.

On November 29, 1944, Don married Isabel in a full military ceremony at St. John the Baptist Church in Columbus, Ohio. Several other test pilots were in attendance, and I, of course, was the best man. After the ceremony, Don and Isabel went off on their honeymoon—and I reported for duty.

TESTING FIGHTER PLANES

In December 1944, I was selected to attend the test pilot school. The school wasn't easy; I had to work hard and make practice test runs with T-6, P-47, P-51, and P-63 aircraft. Determining the performance and characteristics of a new aircraft required not only specific technical knowledge but also certain skills. A test pilot needed always to be ready to abandon a crippled or unflyable aircraft. All of the test pilots I encountered in school and then at Wright Field were deeply aware of the ever-present danger of our work.

The real testing adventure began after I graduated from the test pilot school, when I began to test the numerous fighter aircraft we had at Wright Field. These included Japan's Zero fighter and Germany's ME-262, as well as the ME-109 and FW-190, the two German fighters I had met in combat over Europe. At the time I conducted test flights at Wright Field, few of the aircraft I worked with had automated data-collection systems mounted in their cockpits. (Today, of course, testing supersonic aircraft is accomplished with more sophisticated computerized equipment.)

My job required that I work closely with various engineers from the several laboratories on the base. The engineers assigned test runs for particular projects. They arranged the schedule so we were kept busy testing aircrafts' engines, systems, and equipment. The engineer who kept us the busiest was Capt. Nathan "Rosie" Rosegarten. His knowledge was vast, and his briefings before and after a test flight were, without a doubt, the best of all given by the engineers.

Shortly after I completed test pilot school, Gentile and I were assigned on temporary duty at the north base at Muroc, California, where we would take part in the accelerated service test of the YP-80 jet aircraft. The Army Air Force wanted the service tests of this plane expedited so that it could be used in Europe against Germany's ME-262, the new Luftwaffe jet fighter that was raising havoc with our bomber formations. The P-80, named the Shooting Star by its manufacturer Lockheed, was a single-seat, low-wing, cantilever monoplane with a knife-edge laminar-flow wing section. The jet engine was installed in the rear section of the fuselage with two air intakes, one on each side of the fuselage up front. The prototype XP-80 was powered by a 3,000-pound static thrust De Havilland H-I engine. The next two prototypes built were equipped with General Electric (GE) I-40 turbojet engines that produced some 4,000 pounds of static thrust at sea level. The aircraft had a maximum takeoff weight of 16,856 pounds, a service ceiling of over 40,000 feet, and a speed of about 580 miles per hour, or .80 mach.

In January 1945, the USAAF had twelve flyable P-80s. Three of those were XP models, and the other nine were YP models. From the YP-80 inventory, three had been shipped to England. One of these was lost when our colleague, Maj. Fred Borsodi, was killed in a crash while demonstrating the YP-80 to RAF officials in Bortonwood, England. Two other YPs were diverted to special projects in the United States (one of those two was delivered to Wright Field later). The remaining four were at the Lockheed plant in Burbank, being prepared for use in the accelerated service test program in which Gentile and I were to participate.

Col. George Price, the chief of the accelerated test program, and the five of us—Capt. Don Gentile, Capt. Jim Little, Capt. Jim Fitzgerald, and me, plus a pilot from the 412th Fighter Group (the unit that was scheduled to be equipped with the P-80 Shooting Star and then deploy to Europe)—waited at the North Base for the aircraft to arrive from Burbank. When the four, glossy P-80s arrived, Lockheed test pilot Tony Le Vier gave us a thorough cockpit indoctrination check and sent each of us aloft. After I took off with this magnificent flying machine on the dry bed of Muroc Lake, I climbed to 35,000 feet with almost full power.

I found the acceleration of the Shooting Star to be an amazing experience that has remained with me all my life—no torque and no vibration, except for the whining light noise from the jet engine.

We started the tests without difficulties, but there were times, of course, when we were left idle while our people and Lockheed technicians worked on all four aircraft at the same time. The deficiencies we encountered during the test were few. Minor ones were fixed locally; for major problems the aircraft had to be flown to the Lockheed facility in Burbank.

PANCHO'S PLACE

During our stay at Muroc, most of our nights were spent at a dude ranch not far away from our north base sanctuary. This ranch was owned by a woman named "Pancho" Barnes, and she was, without a doubt, one hell of a lady. Pancho's place was on a large plot of land in the middle of nowhere. It had several nice rooms for visitors, a restaurant that served good food, a bar and pool hall, and a stable with several horses for those who wanted to be cowboys. Naturally, she also had a landing strip for those who could afford to fly in.

As we learned during our frequent visits, Pancho Barnes was born Florence Leontine Lowe. She had learned to fly in the 1920s, and so was an aviatrix—the name women aviators used during those early days of aviation. Her surname came from the first of her five husbands, a clergyman. Although she never told us where she had gotten the name "Pancho," we learned from Tony Le Vier that she had acquired it from the Mexican revolutionaries while making gun runs for them.

She had become a stunt pilot, flying for Howard Hughes in the movie, *Hell's Angels*, and in various aerial exhibitions across the country. She befriended quite a few aviators, including Maj. Tooey Spaatz (the four-star general who commanded the USAAF in Europe during World War II), Paul Mantz, and Jimmy Doolittle. She had lost the family wealth while living in high society with the Hollywood crowd and had settled in the Mojave Desert. There, she opened her ranch, which became famous after the war.

Pancho was a colorful woman with a foul mouth, but she was shrewd and knew about almost everything. All of us from Wright Field, as well as the Lockheed and GE representatives, loved and admired her. She was a good sport and could tell incredible stories about her early flying days.

One night while we were having dinner, she sat with the five of us test pilots, plus Tony Le Vier and Col. George Price, our boss at Muroc.

During the conversation, she turned to me and said, "And you, Captain: where the hell did you get that goddamned accent?"

I told her that my mother had given it to me when she bore me.

"And where in the hell was that?" she responded tartly. After I had told her a bit about myself, she snorted into her beer.

"Oh, a Greek," she mumbled. "I have met a few Greeks in my life, including Spiro Skouras of 20th Century Fox in Hollywood. A good man."

She then excused herself from our table, as she was called from the kitchen. That was Pancho Barnes, the queen of her place in the Mojave Desert, and a lady with an unforgettable personality.

The testing of the YP-80, America's first jet fighter aircraft, was certainly a challenge to all of us involved in the program at Muroc. For me, being part of that unusual project was an experience where I was convinced that the Shooting Star, the aircraft Clarence "Kelly" Johnson of Lockheed had designed, was going to be a match for the German twin-axial flow powered, ME-262.

In early May 1945, as we were getting close to completing the service test on the YP-80, the war in Europe ended, and Washington decided that it was unnecessary to expedite the service test on the Lockheed aircraft. Colonel Price, was directed to stop the testing altogether and return with everyone to Wright Field. On our flight back to Dayton, I glanced at my log book and was surprised to see that during our stay at Muroc, I had accumulated more than one-hundred hours' jet time in the YP-80 and the Bell P-59 Airacomet, more than anyone else in our group.

Back in Dayton, we learned that the branch had a new chief, Maj. Russ Schleeh, and had also gained another pilot, Maj. Richard "Dick"

Bong, America's leading ace from the Pacific who had flown with the 9th Fighter Squadron, 49th Fighter Group. He had forty aerial kills to his credit and was a holder of the Congressional Medal of Honor. Dick was a rather modest fellow with sandy hair and a boyish looking face. He had a small frame, was quite handsome, and somewhat quiet, but gracious when he spoke. I got to know Dick and his wife Marge as they would occasionally join us (the bachelor group from the base who lived at the "Y") for dinner at the Eight Ball Restaurant on North Main Street. Although both Dick and Marge were from Wisconsin, Marge hated the Dayton weather. They didn't, however, stay long in Dayton, as Dick was able to get an assignment as an acceptance Air Force test pilot at the Lockheed plant in Burbank for the production model of the P-80 Shooting Star.

In July 1945 we gained another pilot, Capt. John Godfrey, Don Gentile's wingman in 336 Fighter Squadron, 4th Fighter Group with thirty kills to his credit, eighteen in the air and twelve on the ground. He was also assigned to the fighter branch. It was certainly a great surprise reunion for the three of us to be together again. Not long after Godfrey's arrival, our test branch had gained two more pilots: Capt. Chuck Yeager, an ace with eleven kills, and Lt. Bob Hoover. From Yeager I learned that he and I had gone down on the same mission to Bordeaux on March 5, 1944. Chuck had been with the 357th Fighter Group, the unit that was assigned to relieve the 4th Fighter Group on that mission. He had been lucky though to go down near the Franco–Spanish frontier, and in a few days later he was helped and walked over the Pyrenees to Spain and freedom. Because I had gone down in the northern part of France, the Underground up there had different ideas, and I was taken to Paris for safekeeping. I, of course, had to wait until Paris was liberated in the latter part of August 1944 before I could return to England.

Captain Yeager and Lietenant Hoover found temporary quarters at Patterson Field. But when they learned where a few others and I lived in town for a dollar a day, they too decided to move into the YMCA. That made the number of us test pilots living at the "Y" to eight. And I had now another fellow pilot to bum a ride to and from the field—Chuck

Yeager and his Chevy convertible. No sooner had Yeager and Hoover settled in on the job of testing, yet another pilot was assigned to the fighter branch, Lt. Col. Francis "Gabby" Gabreski, the leading European Ace with twenty-eight aerial kills to his credit. I had met Gabby in England during the war while he was flying with the 56th Fighter Group. He, too, moved into the YMCA.

With the assignment of Gabby to the fighter test branch, we now had six fighter aces in this unique organization. Dick Bong, Gabby Gabreski, John Godfrey, Don Gentile, Chuck Yeager, and me, with a combined score of 147 enemy aircraft destroyed, in the air and on the ground. This was certainly an amazing achievement by six aviators who included the leading aces from the Pacific and European Theaters of Operations.

There was another superb test pilot assigned to the branch, Capt. Kenneth Chilstrom, who had managed to survive ninety-three dive bombing missions, flying the P-51A Mustang in North Africa and the mainland of Italy. Ken wasn't an ace, but he was a sharp test pilot like the great Maj. Gus Landquist. Ken eventually took over as chief of the fighter branch and ended up as commandant of the Air Force's test pilot school before it was moved to Muroc in the Mojave Desert at the Air Force's Testing Facility, which was renamed Edwards Air Force Base.

AFTER THE WAR

On August 6, 1945, the United States dropped an atomic bomb on Hiroshima, and three days later a second bomb on Nagasaki. This action ended the war in the Pacific and World War II and, as expected, caused big changes in the U.S. Army Air Force. Military plans, programs, and projects on the drawing board were either canceled or postponed, and aircraft testing slowed down significantly at Wright Field. Thus, my colleagues and I were forced to hunt for new jobs. Those of us with flying experience had two options: the aircraft industry or the commercial airlines. The aircraft companies were about to transition from building war planes to building four-engine airliners, and the airlines, the *Dayton Daily* had reported, were planning to absorb the majority of the out of-work military pilots to accommodate anticipated domestic and international expansion of the industry.

Unfortunately on this date also, we were saddened to learn that Maj. Richard Bong was killed when he experienced engine failure on take off from Burbank Airport while on a production P-80 test flight. America's top ace of aces was dead.

In October 1945, I flew test runs with the YP-80, using kerosene, pure alcohol, and gasoline as fuels, in order to determine the best type of fuel for the jet engine. Because of high tailpipe temperatures, the Wright Field petroleum engineers realized that kerosene and alcohol were not satisfactory fuels. From these test runs, the engineers learned that a mix of kerosene and gasoline was most effective for jet engines, and this fuel came to be known as J-P fuel in the aviation industry.

The remaining months of the year we kept busy with limited testing and participating in air shows at home and away from Wright Field. In late 1945, Col. E. Leonard Harmon, our division chief, left Wright Field and was replaced by Col. Albert Boyd. Col. Williams Council remained as the deputy for operations. I had the good fortune to be able to show Colonel Boyd the P-80, who at once wanted to fly the Shooting Star. After I sent him off on his first flight, he, of course, pronounced it as a "splendid" plane upon landing.

Just before the end of December 1945, I was assigned to test an Allison-built engine equipped with a water injection system that was installed in one of our P-63 Kingcobras. The procedure was to climb and level off at 30,000 feet, set the RPM and manifold pressure at the required readings, and fly the aircraft for five minutes with the water injection system on, then reduce power to a setting for another five minutes with the water system on. On the third test, I was to open the throttle to full power and stay on this setting for another five minutes with the water system on. I was cruising along at 30,000 feet southeast of Cincinnati when I opened the throttle for the third part of the test. I started to jot down the instrument readings on my knee pad when the fire warning light suddenly came on. The light was followed immediately by a loud explosion from the engine behind me. Thinking that the plane was on fire, I cut the throttle off and released both cockpit doors. Before I committed myself to the empty sky, I banked the P-63 sharply left and right to see if I was actually on fire. I could see only smoke behind me but no fire. After a few moments, the smoke had diminished, but the fire warning light remained on.

"That's odd," I mumbled, "the light is on, but there's no fire."

There was, however, a continuous banging coming from the engine. Something evidently had become loose inside the engine housing. I declared an emergency, turned around, and started to descend toward Wright Field, thinking I'd make a dead stick landing, if possible. I called the tower and reported that my engine had failed and that I would attempt to put the aircraft down on Runway 27. Seconds later, the tower replied that the field was open and prepared for my arrival. I continued to descend and, at the same time, tried to relax and plan my approach. As I neared the field, I could see fire trucks, an ambulance, and several cars waiting on the side of the runway.

When I was over the field, I maneuvered the engineless P-63 into a sort of haphazard downwind leg, dropped the gear and flaps, and turned into final approach early, realizing that I was still a little high. Despite some side slipping, I didn't touch down until I had passed the halfway mark of the runway, and I quickly realized I was going to overrun the end of the runway; as I was going too fast to stop. I slammed on the brakes with all my strength, but only succeeded in locking them. Seconds later, the tower controller came on the radio and said in a rather screaming voice, "Aircraft on the runway, your wheels are on fire." Evidently, part of the rubber from the tires sheared off and sparks had begun to fly from the wheel rims that were scraping the surface of the runway. The remaining rubber on the wheels caught fire as the aircraft was skidding to a halt. Finally, I came to a complete stop well off the end of the runway.

I unstrapped myself, took my helmet off, and jumped down from the cockpit. In the meantime, firemen, who had already reached the spot where the P-63 had come to a stop, tried to extinguish the fire on the two wheels underneath the aircraft. As my feet hit the ground, I was covered from head to foot with the fire-retardant foam used by the firemen. Blinded, I lost my balance, and the next thing I knew, I was in the ambulance on the way to the hospital at Patterson Field. At the hospital, the doctors checked me over and cleaned my eyes, where I was able to see my friend Don and others who had driven over to see me.

Among them was Lt. Col. Jim Philpot, a TWA pilot on active duty in the bomber test branch, who was trying to recruit pilots for TWA. Just as the others were walking out of my room, Philpot leaned over my bed and said, "Hey, Buddy, I am flying to Kansas City on Monday in a B-26 to visit TWA headquarters and I need a co-pilot. What do you say?"

I told Philpot I would go with him. He had contacted me previously about joining TWA and the incident with the P-63 had convinced me to rethink my job as a test pilot. Two days later I was on my way to Kansas City in a B-26. Not an hour after we landed there I had submitted my application for employment with TWA and had been accepted, pending my release from the Air Force.

On January 6, 1946, I was separated from the U.S. Army Air Force and placed on reserve status. I said good-bye to all my friends at Wright Field, including my buddy, Don Gentile, who hated to see me go, but I promised to keep in touch with him. I reluctantly bid farewell also to the Zavakos family I had met when I first came to Dayton and told them how I had met their son, pilot officer Frank Zavakos in London while in the RAF, like me, well before I joined the 71st Eagle Squadron, where Frank was assigned at the time. Frank's father, George Zavakos, had come to America from Greece. Frank and I had much to talk about in addition to our Greek heritage. He told me a lot about Dayton, Ohio, where he was born. Frank's father owned a couple of restaurants and the famous Varsity Bowling Alley in Dayton, and Frank had promised that if I ever passed through Dayton, to stop by and he would treat me to a good steak.

Unfortunately, Frank was killed in June 1942 when he lost his engine over the English Channel and went straight in. I felt that it was my responsibility to call upon the Zavakos family as a tribute to Frank. I called Frank's father, George, one day, and he insisted that I join them for Sunday dinner. The first time I brought up Frank's name, Mrs. Zavakos started to cry. Nevertheless, they welcomed me into their home and I began to visit the Zavakos home regularly. Thus, it became common for me and two other Greek-American bachelors, Capt. Harry Lake and Capt. Peter Vlahakis, who both worked at one of the labs on the hill at Wright Field, to enjoy Mrs. Zavakos' Greek cuisine. As I was leaving the Zavakos residence, Pop Zavakos reminded me not to forget to look up his friend in Kansas City, Michael D. Konomos, an attorney, with whom George had come to America years ago from Greece on the same ship.

FLYING WITH TWA

In mid-January 1946, I reported to the TWA building at the Kansas City airport and checked in with Capt. Paul Frederikson, the chief pilot. Frederikson hired me on the spot as a TWA copilot with a salary of $220 a month and told me I would be attending a co-pilot school that was scheduled to start in two days.

At that time, Jack Frye, the president of TWA, was expanding the airline's routes overseas. These new routes would be served by four-engine, Lockheed-built Constellation airliners. I was one of many army- and navy-trained pilots hired by TWA who needed to learn to fly the airline way, which was distinctly not like military flying. As a friend of mine jokingly put it, "There are bold pilots, and there are old pilots, but there are few bold, old pilots. The airlines are not looking for bold pilots!"

My intensive training covered the basics of commercial aviation areas and everything there was to know about the DC-3, the main and only twin-engine airliner in the TWA fleet. Emphasis was placed on the importance of the aircraft's safe operation and the comfort of the human cargo we carried in the cabin. An airline pilot has to make takeoffs, turning, and maneuvering in preparation for landings as smooth as possible. In addition, we studied the company's operating manual and learned about the captain and copilot's responsibilities from preparation for a flight to arriving at another terminal. The copilot was expected to assist the captain and take over if he became disabled.

A month later, in mid-February 1946, after I had made two training flights in a DC-3 in the middle of the night, I was given a check ride by a captain named Walt Gunn. I passed the check and was declared qualified to fly as a copilot on a DC-3. On February 17, I went on my first flight as a third crew member on a DC-3 cargo flight from Kansas City to New York City and then back to Kansas City.

When I finished copilot school in mid-March, I started to fly as a regular first officer on the line. A variety of highly experienced captains trained me on the job. Since we weren't allowed by CAA to fly more than eighty hours a month, we had a lot of time off between flights. I took advantage of that free time one day and contacted Mr. Konomos, the prominent attorney recommended by George Zavakos in Dayton who had told me to look up his friend once I was settled in Kansas City. After dinner one Sunday at Mr. Konomos' residence where I met Mrs. Angela Konomos and their young daughter, Vickie, I was introduced to their Greek friends down the street, Mr. and Mrs. Nick and Virginia Smernes.

Virginia Smernes had two sisters, Lena and Sophie, the youngest, and three brothers, Gregg, Charles and Jimmie, all of whom I met that evening, except for Jimmie who was away serving in the U.S. Army. Virginia's brothers and sisters lived with her and Nick as they had lost their parents at an early age. It was at the Smernes' residence where I met my future wife, Miss Sophie Mary Pappas, Virginia's sister. At the very beginning I was impressed with Sophie's beauty and manners and I didn't lose any time to start dating this pleasant girl, almost every time I was back from a flight. I took her to dinner and went out on double dates with friends a few times. It was one day in March 1946, when upon my return from a flight, I took Sophie out to dinner and proposed to her. Surprisingly, she accepted joyfully.

We broke the news to Nick and Virginia and on April 7, we were engaged. On June 30, 1946, we were married at the Greek church in Kansas City, and I had my good buddy, Don Gentile, who flew in with Isabel, to be my best man. I continued to fly the line with TWA, east and west and occasionally I would be used locally as co-pilot on test flights on DC-3s and Boeing 400, a four-engine airliner. On January 4, 1947, I had my first co-pilot flight in a Constellation. Early that morning I caught a flight to Burbank with a flight engineer and Capt. Bush Voigts to bring back a new TWA "Connie" to Kansas City.

Once we had landed in California, I had a chance to walk around the parked Connie and admire the sleekness of the fuselage and the wings that held the four Wright R-3350-35 duplex cyclone radial engines of some 2,200 horsepower each. I climbed aboard the plane, walked up to the cockpit, and sat in the copilot's seat. I was immediately impressed with the instrument panel, flight controls, and the cockpit layout. As I read the preflight checklist to Captain Voigts, he explained the significance of each item so that I could become familiar with the aircraft. Captain Voigts let me fly the Constellation all the way back to Kansas City, then he took over for the landing.

When we returned to Kansas City that evening, I decided to check my box in the mailroom. There I found a letter from the company that read, "Dear Mr. Pisanos: Due to unexpected circumstances, you are being placed on furlough indefinitely, effective January 5, 1947. The company will notify you when to return to duty." The letter was signed by Mr. John Mullen, the director of personnel. I was shocked with the news and disappointed, and wondered whether leaving the Air Force had been the right decision. I was furloughed for almost four months before I was recalled to duty on April 25, 1947. Once I was back on the line, my career with TWA continued quite smoothly. I acquired the airline transport pilot's (ATP) license on my own, after a rigorous exam and a check flight. Then I graduated from DC-3s to Constellations and began flying in the right seat to La Guardia nonstop.

On February 26, 1948, Sophie and I were blessed with the birth of our first child, a boy of 8.3 pounds. We named him Jeffrey. Shortly after my son's birth, I began to worry about the lack of stability in my job with TWA. I was furloughed again in 1948, and soon after my recall, the pilots went on strike for a few days. The strike shook me up somewhat, as I now had to support a family and I had just put a down payment on a new house at Prairie Village.

In early October 1948, I received a call from Don Gentile, who was living in Washington, D.C. He told me that he had returned to active duty and was given a regular commission in the new U.S. Air Force. With little convincing from Don, I decided to return to active duty also. I was able to meet Don on a flight to La Guardia via Washington

National a few days after his call. Over coffee, I told him how unhappy I had become with TWA. A few days later, after I had returned to Kansas City, I received a letter from Gentile along with a USAF application form for an officer to return to active duty. I filled it out and mailed it to Headquarters USAF in Washington, D.C.

Two weeks later I received official orders from USAF headquarters, instructing me to return to active duty by October 30, 1948, and report to the Pentagon in Washington, D.C. Sophie and I began making preparations to move to Washington, and the following day, I quit my job as an airline pilot with TWA.

CHAPTER 25

JOINING THE NEW USAF

Sophie and I and our almost eight-month-old Jeffrey said good-bye to everyone in Kansas City on October 27, 1948, and headed for Washington in our two-door Chevy. When we arrived on the East Coast two days later, the Gentiles let us stay with them while we searched for a place of our own. Soon we found a two-bedroom apartment in Falls Church, which we furnished by canvassing every possible place in the area for good bargains.

I had been assigned to the Air Force Division (AFD) in the National Guard Bureau (NGB), the organization responsible for all Air National Guard (ANG) units. I was to help certain ANG units switch from P-51s to P-80s. When I checked in at the AFD, I met my new commanding officer, Maj. Gen. George Finch; Col. Peter Remington, the division chief; and Lt. Col. Buck Bilby, chief of Current Operations Branch, the office I was assigned to.

In addition to Lieutenant Colonel Bilby, four of us worked for the Current Operations Branch: Maj. Bob Walker, Capt. William McCall, Capt. Bob Terrill, and me. We were all pilots, and we were often called on to fly our bosses around the country to visit various ANG units in the United States and its territories. Since I was the only one in the branch with jet experience, I handled training matters for the conversion of ANG pilots to P-80s in Florida, Maine, Nebraska, and California. I also had the chance to fly the C-47, B-25, and B-26 aircraft from Bolling Air Force Base, as well as the T-33 from Andrews Air Force Base.

In the midst of all this, I managed to start on my college degree at the University of Maryland by attending classes at night and applied for a regular commission in the USAF. About a year later, in 1950, I was one of 200 selected for regular commission. It was at the Pentagon also where I got my promotion to major.

FAREWELL TO GENTILE

On Friday, January 26, 1951, Don Gentile called and asked me to join him on a flight in a T-33 from Andrews Air Force Base on Sunday. I turned him down, even though we had for a long time wanted to fly together in a T-33, because I had missed several classes and needed to study for two upcoming exams.

Late afternoon that Sunday, January 28, while I was sitting on our small porch with my books scattered around me, Sophie, who had been watching TV, ran outside and, in an alarmed tone, said, "You take hold of yourself now, dear, but come inside, quick."

I followed her inside just in time to hear the TV announcer say, "This program is interrupted again for the announcement of the crash of a jet aircraft some 4.5 miles northeast of Andrews Air Force Base. The pilot in the aircraft, who was killed, was Capt. Don Gentile, a highly decorated pilot and an ace from the European war."

When I heard my friend's name, I was stunned and saddened. Sophie turned the TV off, and I sat on the couch trembling from shock. I started to cry for the loss of my dear friend. Once I regained my strength, I decided I needed to visit Isabel and the three children he left behind. When I arrived at the house in College Park, I found Isabel in a state of shock, surrounded by friends and neighbors. We embraced and she started to cry.

Two days later, I escorted Gentile's remains to Columbus, Ohio. On February 2, 1951, Gentile was laid to rest at the St. Joseph Cemetery in Columbus with the full honors of a military funeral. It was hard to believe that the man who had knocked twenty-two enemy aircraft out of the sky and destroyed six on the ground during World War II, the fighter pilot whom General Eisenhower had called "a one-man air force," would be killed in a training accident. It took me a long time to get used to the fact that my closest friend and wartime buddy wasn't around anymore.

ON THE MOVE AGAIN

In mid-1952, I was reassigned overseas to the Office of the Director of Operations at the headquarters of the 12th Air Force (Advance) in Wiesbaden, Germany. My family and I had to say good-bye to the many friends we had made in Washington, D.C., the Pentagon, and Falls Church, and I took Sophie and Jeff to Kansas City, where they would stay with Sophie's sister, Virginia, until housing was available at my new station.

Before I arrived at my new duty station, however, I was informed that my assignment had been changed. I was now assigned to the headquarters of Allied Air Forces, Southern Europe (AIRSOUTH) in Florence, Italy, in the Office of the Director of Operations. Because I could speak Greek, the air force decided I would be of more service at the newly organized AIRSOUTH, which had operational control of the Greek air force.

Before I left for Italy, I headed for Berlin to locate my brother Jimmie, whom the Germans had kidnapped from Athens during World War II. I found Jimmie in the east sector of Berlin at an address my father had sent me, and the following day, the two of us drove to Florence through the Brenner Pass.

When I reported to the headquarters in Florence, I met Lt. Gen. David Schlatter, USAF, the commander of AIRSOUTH, and his deputy, an Italian air force major general. Officers from the air forces of Italy, Greece, and Turkey also worked at the command. Col. Nathan Abbott, USAF, was the director of operations and training, and he had two deputies: Col. Ulio Finali of the Italian air force and Col. Dimitrios "Theo" Theodossiades of the Greek air force. Two aircraft were assigned to AIRSOUTH: a C-54 from the USAF and a C-47 that belonged to the Greek air force. After being in Florence for only a few days, I discovered that working with the air forces of Italy, Greece, and Turkey at the same time was quite an interesting challenge.

Colonel Theo and I quickly became friends. Because he was not certified to fly the C-47, he would frequently ask me to let him be my copilot in the Greek aircraft when we started flying to visit NATO units in the field. Also, through Colonel Theo, who spoke Italian and English perfectly, my brother Jimmie was able to secure a job in the command's motor pool.

About a month after my arrival in Florence, Sophie and Jeff arrived in the Port of Livorno aboard a U.S. troopship. A few days later, we moved into an apartment in the "Picolo Skyscraper," as it was called, in the city of Florence.

Once Sophie and Jeff had settled in our apartment, Colonel Theo asked me if I'd like to fly him in the Greek C-47 to Athens. I accepted with pleasure. It would be my first visit to my birthplace in fourteen years. We took off from the Florence airport and headed for Athens in a glorious, cloudless sky. I let the colonel do most of the flying. When we arrived over Athens, I flew over Kolonos Hill just to see it from above.

When we landed at Ellenikon Airport, we were met by an air force staff car and taken to the Grand Bretagne Hotel in town. In the late afternoon I took a taxi to Kolonos, to the house where my parents still lived. When my mother answered the door, she screamed; I thought she was going to faint. The noise brought my father out from the back room. I hugged and kissed both of them, feeling as happy and excited as they were. My father examined my uniform closely and said, "Son, that dream of yours about airplanes did come true, and I am proud of you. Bravo!"

The news of my return to Kolonos spread rapidly, and soon relatives, friends, and neighbors surrounded me, admiring the uniform I was wearing. During my visit I spent most of my evenings at either the Karolos Taverna or the coffee shop on the hill of Kolonos, where I heard unbelievable stories of the cruelty inflicted on the Greeks during the German occupation. Also during this visit, I was able to spend some time at Tatoi Aerodrome, where, to my great surprise, the commandant of the Air Force Academy, thanks to Colonel Theo, had arranged to have the Academy Cadet Corps do a march on the parade grounds in my honor.

About a year after my trip to Athens, AIRSOUTH headquarters moved to Naples, Italy, closer to the other two commands, the army and COMSTRIKEFORCE SOUTH, a part of the U.S. 6th Fleet. In Naples, my family and I were lucky to find a small villa for rent in Ano Posilipo, a hilly area of the city that overlooked the Bay of Naples, the Island of Capri, Mount Vesuvius, and, in the far distance, the beautiful Sorrento.

The move was marked by the birth of our second child, Diane, on December 23, 1953.

During my assignment in Naples, I had my father and mother visit from Greece by ship. They, of course, were thrilled to see Jimmie and me and also to have the chance to meet Sophie and our children. When they were ready to return to Athens, Colonel Theo requested and got permission from the Hellenic Air Force for me to fly my parents home in the C-47. What a thrill both had to see me piloting the aircraft, especially when we flew over the Island of Kefalonia in the Ionian Sea, where my mother was born.

But good things always come to an end. In December 1954, I was reassigned from AIRSOUTH to the 27th Air Division (Defense) at Norton Air Force Base in California. Before reporting to my new job, however, I was diverted under USAF Operation "Bootstrap" to attend the University of Maryland full time in order to complete the remaining semester hours I needed for my degree. After six months of hard work, I graduated from the university with a bachelor's degree in military science. After my graduation, we packed up and headed for California

After my stint as chief of flight operations at the 27th Air Division, I was selected, in 1957, to attend the Air Command and Staff College at Maxwell Air Force Base in Montgomery, Alabama. When I graduated in the summer of 1958, I returned to the 27th Air Division at Norton Air Force Base. This time I was assigned to combat operations in the blockhouse. During the latter part of 1959, I was reassigned to Air Defense Command (ADC) headquarters in Colorado Springs in the Office of the Deputy for Materiel.

The Missile Division where I was reassigned was responsible for all airborne, conventional, and nuclear missiles used by ADC fighter aircraft, including the BOMARC ground-to-air missiles. While on this assignment, I was promoted to lieutenant colonel and also received my Air War College diploma, which I had completed through the Air University's Extension Institute Program. My diploma was presented to me by Gen. Von Shores during a small ceremony in his office.

In 1964, I was assigned overseas again, to U.S. Air Forces in Europe (USAFE) headquarters in Wiesbaden, Germany, in the Office of the Deputy for Materiel. In Wiesbaden, I was the chief of the Avionic and Missile Division, which made me responsible for the air-to-air missiles carried by the various fighters in Germany, France, and Holland and an F-102 squadron in Spain; MACE ground-to-ground missiles on a few bases in Germany; and all airborne and ground avionic equipment, including the few electronic calibration laboratories in USAFE.

Everyone in the family enjoyed the Wiesbaden assignment. The Germans we met were friendly, possibly because Wiesbaden was spared from heavy bombing during the war. I was able to fly on this job, mostly with the T-39. On weekends I flew into Athens, the Island of Crete, Tripoli, Spain, and cities throughout western Europe, including Naples, where my brother Jimmie still lived—now with an Italian wife.

In early August 1964, France planned a big celebration to commemorate the twentieth anniversary of the country's liberation from the German occupation. The main event of the celebration, in which Gen. Charles De Gaulle planned to take part, was at the naval base in Toulon. I was invited to attend, as one of six American aviators who had gone down in France, evaded the Germans during the occupation, and been housed by and fought along with the French Underground. Two other officers from the Wiesbaden area also were selected to participate: Col. Charles C. Williams and Lt. Col. Thomas J. McGrath.

On the last leg of our trip, after we were flown into Nice, we settled into a first-class compartment in a special train for the short journey to the naval base, where we were to meet and have lunch with General De Gaulle and other dignitaries. Shortly after we boarded the train, a tall, dashing U.S. Navy commander walked into our compartment and sat next to me.

"I know this man," I thought.

"Fairbanks, Douglas Jr., U.S. Navy Reserve," our companion said by way of introduction.

"My God!" I exclaimed. "You are the man who played in the movie *Dawn Patrol* with Richard Barthelmes."

I told him that I had fallen in love with airplanes in part through his movie. Commander Fairbanks sat with us for the entire journey to Toulon and joined us for the luncheon as well at a huge table with General De Gaulle at the head. I was elated to spend this time with him.

Later on, the Department of the Air Force informed me that I had been awarded the French Croix de Guerre with the Silver Star "for services rendered in the liberation of France during World War II." The letter that accompanied the award was signed by General De Gaulle.

In early 1966, USAFE received a message from the Pentagon with instructions to deactivate the 38th Missile Wing, remove all MACE missiles from alert, dismantle each missile in place, remove and secure all J-33-A-41 turbojet engines, warheads, and classified electronic equipment for shipment to the United States. All aluminum airframes were to be turned in to the German civilian market for sale.

This was a chance for me to save U.S. taxpayers some money. I suggested that the air force use the missiles as target drones in practice runs by interceptor pilots. After compiling a feasibility study, I was sent to Washington to brief the Air Staff. So, with charts and papers in hand, I caught a Pan Am flight out of Frankfurt for Washington. Once at the Pentagon, I briefed the Air Staff with my proposal, impressing upon them the need for quick action.

By the time I had returned to Wiesbaden, we had received amended orders. The missiles would be returned to the United States and put to good use. Months later, the Air Defense Command began to use some of the MACE missiles as targets for the F-101s, F-102s, and F-106s out of Tyndall Air Force Base in Florida, firing their air-to-air GAR missiles on real targets over the Gulf of Mexico.

In May 1967, I was alerted that my rotation back to the United States was forthcoming, but I wasn't in favor of a stateside assignment. The Vietnam War was in full swing, and I went to the USAFE personnel to inquire about the availability of spots in Vietnam. I was informed that I simply had to volunteer and fill out several forms—which I promptly did. Then I went home to break the news to Sophie.

At first, she felt somewhat concerned about my leaving her behind with the children, but eventually she was able to see my point of view. I was determined to go to Vietnam and defend my adopted country. By June 1967, I had received orders to report to Williams Air Force Base in Arizona for training and checkout in the F-4, before proceeding to Fairchild Air Force Base in Washington to attend survival and escape school.

While I was on leave in Kansas City, before departing for my assignment, I received a telegram telling me that my orders to report to Williams Air Force Base had been canceled. I had been reassigned to the 483rd Air Lift Wing, Cam Rahn Bay, Vietnam, and I was to proceed to Sewart Air Force Base in Tennessee for C-7 checkout. I was rather disappointed by this change in orders; as an old fighter jock, I had been looking forward to flying the F-4.

I was puzzled by my new assignment. I did not know what the C-7 was because we had no such aircraft in the USAF inventory. When I checked in at Sewart Air Force Base for my training, however, I quickly discovered that it was a pretty tough and resourceful bird. Named the Caribou, it was a high-wing machine, built by the De Havilland Aircraft Company of Canada for the U.S. Army. It had a fuselage some 72 feet long, a span of 96 feet, and a height of 32 feet. Its weight, empty, was about 17,630 pounds, and it was powered by two P&W R-2000 radial engines, each producing some 1,450 horsepower that could drive the Caribou to a maximum speed of 216 miles per hour. Its gross weight was about 28,500 pounds, and it could carry a combination of loads: thirty-two fully equipped troops, twenty-two stretchers and two Jeeps, or three tons of cargo. The U.S. Army had purchased some 210 C-7s from Canada, but the soldiers had experienced difficulties operating them, so the Department of Defense transferred the entire fleet to the USAF during the Vietnam War.

My training and checkout in the C-7 at Sewart Air Force Base was short and swift. Not only was I easily checked out on the unique machine, whose two throttles in the roomy cockpit were mounted overhead, but I also learned to air-drop supplies from 400-feet altitude via the low-altitude parachute extraction system (LAPES), which was designed for troop airdrops and quick extraction of cargo on the ground. The part of the training that was most fascinating was learning to reverse the props in order to stop short. We were taught this technique because we would have to operate into and out of many short and rough landing strips in Vietnam.

After I had completed the training course at Sewart Air Force Base, I headed west to Fairchild Air Force Base in Washington to attend the USAF survival and escape school, a mandatory treat for all combat air crews destined for Vietnam. The school was intended to teach us how to be POWs in a Vietnamese prison camp, and to give us the best chance of surviving the experience. Those in charge of the camp wore North Vietnamese Army uniforms and began to harass us, especially the high-ranking officers, upon arrival on base. We were told that anyone who violated the rules of the camp would be punished severely.

The officers of Fairchild Air Force Base excelled at realism. Shortly after I arrived, the guards placed a black hood over my head, and after a short walk assisted by one of the guards, the hood was removed and I was jammed, standing up and unable to turn around, into a wooden cage the size of my frame. A few holes had been cut in the cage so that its occupant could breath outside air. I spent my first night at the so-called survival school standing up in this cage, with no food and no water. It was hot inside the cage; my avocado green fatigues were wet from the sweat and I could feel the darned stuff dripping down my spine. My arms and legs became numb after hours of being unable to move.

At daybreak we were freed. We were taken to the camp compound and given some hot liquid soup that smelled of filthy feet for breakfast. Afterward, each of us was taken to a separate room for what turned out to be interrogation and harassment. I faced a North Vietnamese Army captain. The walls of the interrogation room were covered with large photographs of various demonstrations and riots that had taken place in American cities at different times, showing policemen hitting black people with clubs and fist fighting among people. At the outset, the captain asked me in broken English to tell him something about myself. I gave him my name, rank, and serial number, and immediately, he fired back and said, "Ah, Colonel, you speak with an accent. You are not an American. You must be a spy the Americans have sent over here to spy on us. What do you say to that, Colonel?"

I repeated my name, rank, and serial number and told him, "I am not a spy. I am an American airman."

"So, you want to play games with me," he snapped back.

He showered me with allegations and threats for hours. Eventually the line of questioning shifted to American democracy.

"So, you people in America think that your democracy is better than the communist society, hey?"

I wanted to give the guy the same old thing—name, rank, and serial number—but I thought for a moment and said, "The American democracy provides something to its people that your society and system of government does not."

"And what could that be?" he asked.

"Freedom and equality, not tyranny," I told him.

As we continued our discussion of democracy and the communist ideology, I stood my ground. When the interrogation was over, my interrogator said, "Colonel, you are handling your part very well. Just stick to your beliefs."

299

We finished school on August 18. I spent that afternoon under the shower, scrubbing the filthiness from the ordeal off of my skin. Then I headed to the bar to have a cold beer with some of the men who had survived the course with me. Who was behind the bar serving drinks? The North Vietnamese captain who had interrogated me, now wearing a USAF sergeant's uniform. I congratulated him for a job well done.

After a few days' leave, I was to report to Travis Air Force Base in California on September 5 to catch a flight for our long journey to Clark Air Force Base in the Philippines. There I would attend a jungle survival school before I set foot in Vietnam.

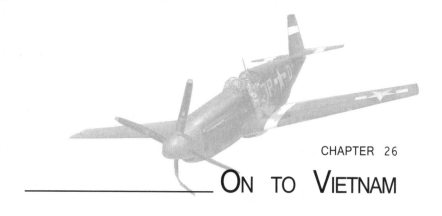

CHAPTER 26

ON TO VIETNAM

I spent some time in Kansas City with Sophie and the children before I caught a TWA flight to San Francisco and then a flight in a C-141 across the Pacific. After we landed in the Philippines, we were driven to the Pacific Air Forces (PACAF) Jungle Survival School grounds, away from the base activities. The following morning, we changed into army jungle fatigues and were rushed into a classroom.

We spent five days at this place. We learned to find edible vegetation and roots during field exercises in the nearby thick jungle. We learned what kinds of snakes to look for and how to catch them, skin them, and cook their tails in an open fire. We were also taught how to extract water from a banana tree. For our last lesson, we were sent in groups of seven into the distant jungle in covered trucks to spend the night in the wild. The following day, after spending a most miserable night in the thick jungle while it was raining, we made contact with searching helicopters. Everyone in my team was hoisted up and into one of the choppers through the thin foliage and brought back to the school grounds.

When our five days were over, we boarded a C-130 transport for Cam Rahn Bay Air Base in Vietnam. Cam Rahn was the home of several USAF units, including a small navy detachment. South of the base was a large U.S. Army Quartermaster's depot.

When we arrived at Cam Rahn, I checked in with the 483rd Air Lift Wing, where I met the commanding officer, Col. William H. Mason, and the deputy of operations, Col. Robert Kinney. After a welcome by Colonel Mason and a short briefing about the wing organization and its mission with the six assigned squadrons, Colonel Kinney took me over to the 457th Squadron and introduced me to Lt. Col. Milo Larson, the squadron commanding officer, and Lt. Col. Jim Townsend, the operations officer. I was assigned as Colonel Townsend's assistant.

My first flight over Vietnam was with Townsend. We flew a bunch of Vietnamese paratroopers to Pleiku, in the central highlands, for a practice jump south of Pleiku Air Base. After the jump, we landed at Pleiku and picked up a mixed load of ammo, beer, soft drinks, and other foodstuffs for Dak Seang, a Special Forces camp north of Pleiku and not too far from the Laotian border.

Townsend had me fly the leg from Pleiku to Dak Seang so that I could experience the "thrill" of landing on the most difficult jungle strip in Vietnam. While we were in the air, Townsend passed on a few hints for flying over Vietnam.

"The secret," he said, "is to stay around 6,000 to 7,000 feet above the jungle terrain. Then, when you arrive over the strip where you intend to land, chop your power and use a spiral maneuver to drop down to a lower altitude, but remain close to the landing strip. Then position your aircraft for a low approach and sneak into the strip. This way, you'll avoid being hit by those Viet Cong bastards who hang around the Special Forces camps waiting for a chance to pop off some small arms fire at low-flying aircraft or choppers. They'll fire at you if the foliage allows them to get a glimpse of your aircraft, so be aware."

When we arrived over Dak Seang, I asked him where exactly we were going to land.

"Down there," he said, as he pointed to a narrow strip of dirt road on the side of the camp.

"Down there?"

"You'll try first, and then you'll make it on your second pass," Townsend said. And that was my first landing in the jungle of Vietnam.

I flew almost every day and visited every Special Forces camp in our area of responsibility. We'd normally take off at 6:00 or 7:00 every morning, seven days a week. We'd head up to Pleiku, sometimes empty, to pick up cargo that was brought in by C-130s and C-141s. Loading crews on the ground would break down the cargo and place it on Caribou pallets so that we could carry it in our aircraft for delivery to Special

Forces camps. We also had loads out of Cam Rahn for camps that were located between Cam Rahn and Pleiku. We'd drop the load on the camp, then proceed up to Pleiku and operate from there. By the time we returned to Cam Rahn, the stars would be out. Every day each aircraft logged seven to eight hours in the air.

On January 15, 1968, Jim Townsend took over command of the squadron from Lieutenant Colonel Larson who was rotating back home. Townsend appointed me squadron operations officer. I chose, with Townsend's recommendation, Lt. Col. Donald A. Zeine as my assistant. As time went by, I discovered that Townsend was an exceptional leader and a personable and thoughtful commander who gave me freedom to act and operate on my own and who cared about the people we had in the squadron.

As the squadron operations officer, I spent my mornings on the flight line observing the entire spectrum of operations. In the days that followed my appointment, I began to feel that something was wrong with the way we launched our mission aircraft. Out of our sixteen aircraft, plus the two spares that were assigned to each squadron by the table of organization, we could commit only eight to ten aircraft to missions because at least six to eight of our aircraft were continually out for maintenance.

We assigned aircraft to missions a night in advance, and by the time we sat down to plan, we had an idea as to the number of serviceable aircraft each squadron would have for missions to be flown the next day. We would give this number to the 834th Air Division Air Logistics Control Center (ALCC) in Saigon, and the center would set up the missions as appropriate. The ALCC people in Saigon always expected and demanded that scheduled takeoff times be adhered to because deviations would create problems with subsequent missions.

I made it a point to get up well before sunrise each morning, have coffee, and wander around the flight line in my Jeep to observe the activities in progress. The more I observed the activities on the flight line each morning, the more I felt that tasks weren't moving along in an expeditious manner. For example, if during early morning run-ups an aircraft was discovered to have a radio problem or if an aircraft returned to the flight line after an aborted takeoff, unreasonable takeoff delays would ensue. I discovered that these delays were directly related to the leisurely manner in which the flight line mechanics went about fixing encountered problems.

We had a spare aircraft standing by on the flight line, but we couldn't use it unless we received permission from the wing chief of maintenance. It seemed that wing maintenance believed that the spare aircraft should be used only if an aircraft scheduled to fly a mission encountered a major problem; minor problems should be fixed on the flight line.

Because of this unwritten rule, however, the spare aircraft was hardly ever used and some of the squadron aircraft committed to ALCC didn't depart on the scheduled takeoff times. Almost daily, one, two, or sometimes three aircraft in my squadron were unable to meet their scheduled takeoff times. This situation wasn't peculiar to the 457th Squadron at Cam Rahn; the other five squadrons were suffering the same quandary, as initial takeoff delays were common throughout the wing. Yet no one was doing anything to fix the problem. This was the way it had always been, and changing procedure would be virtually impossible. In the meantime, our failure to launch our mission aircraft on time each morning continued, ALCC criticized the wing a number of times, and the army's Special Forces camps were unhappy because supplies were being delivered late.

Things then came to a head one day when I decided that I had reached the limits of my patience. One morning as I watched the aircraft taxiing out for takeoffs, the pilot of one of the Caribous that had pulled out earlier called me on the wing frequency to tell me that he was returning to the flight line because his VHF radio wasn't working. I told the pilot to hurry back, and to keep his engines running, when he parked on the flight line, while I had the radioman check his VHF radio. I immediately drove off and intercepted the squadron maintenance van roving on the flight line and told Lt. John Lutz that one of the Caribous was returning to the flight line because VHF radio was out.

The radioman, who was riding in the van, cut in and said, "Looks like a black box only replacement, Colonel."

"Do we have a black box in the van?" I asked.

"No, Sir. I have to go to Supply and draw one out."

"You better get going," I told him, "and hurry it up because I want that aircraft off on time."

After some waiting, the radioman returned with a replacement VHF black box, climbed onto the aircraft, and with engines still running, he installed the new black box. The pilot gave me the thumbs up and started to taxi away for take off. He made it just on time.

That day, I had lunch with my commanding officer, whom I briefed about the event on the flight line. I told him I had an idea that would improve our mode of operation. Townsend said, "You go right ahead, and I wish you good luck."

In the afternoon, I had a meeting with Lieutenant Lutz and some of his senior NCOs and suggested that they consider keeping one or two VHF black boxes and other essential parts in the maintenance van so that when we needed to replace a VHF black box in a hurry on a waiting aircraft, they wouldn't have to run to supply. Lieutenant Lutz assured me that he would work up a small list of items he could draw from supply and store in his van.

After the meeting, I made a change to my morning routine. Zeine and I began to wake up early in the morning and drive to the flight line in my Jeep. With coffee in one hand and a flashlight on the other, and with the assistance of the night maintenance shift, we would run up engines and check the radios on every Caribou scheduled to fly on a mission for ALCC that morning. If we ran into a radio problem, we fixed it immediately. We also changed spark plugs if necessary. If time didn't permit for a repair, I would take that Caribou off the schedule and use the spare aircraft in its place. The results were unbelievable. Once we started our morning inspections, we rarely had an aircraft return to the flight line for radio or mechanical problems.

The next problem I wanted to solve was the status of the spare aircraft. I didn't think we should have to get the wing chief of maintenance's permission to use the spare. Thus, I visited Lieutenant Col. Joel Geister in his office to discuss the status of the spare aircraft. I told him that the spare aircraft belonged to operations and that the commander or operations officer of a unit should be free to use the aircraft whenever he deemed it necessary.

I was most surprised when Geister replied, "Steve, you go right ahead and use the spare aircraft if you have to. You don't need to call my office."

Needless to say, after this conversation, with our new procedures in place, our squadron achieved an unprecedented record of launching mission aircraft on time every morning.

In mid-May, Colonel Mason called me into his office and, in the presence of Colonel Kinney, said, "Steve, as you know, Jim Townsend is rotating back to the United States, and I want you to take over the squadron."

Two days later, we had a wing ceremony with all personnel in formation, and the 457th Air Lift Squadron was officially turned over to me to command.

The 457th Squadron was now on its fifth month of launching aircraft without a single delay. Because of our continued success, the wing commander invited the other Caribou squadron commanders to observe our operations. The 483rd Airlift Wing, with its six squadrons, continued to achieve new records in the prompt delivery of supplies to the Special Forces in the jungles of Vietnam. Letters and messages began to arrive at wing headquarters, from not only the Special Forces Command but also the 834th Air Division, 7th Air Force, and the army chief in Vietnam, Gen. William Westmoreland, congratulating our wing for the unprecedented accomplishments in the support of airlift operations with the Caribou.

But our airlift operations into the jungles were not free of problems. We lost a number of aircraft to enemy ground fire as well as to accidents that were attributed to pilot error. My mind was always occupied with thoughts about how to minimize losses, and part of me was always out there, mentally accompanying our guys on each mission. Since I was commanding officer of the squadron, I was unable to do much flying. I flew only a mission here and there just to keep abreast of activities in the field.

As September gave way to October, my return to the United States neared. I had the chance to fly a few more missions during the Tet Offensive, at which my aircraft was riddled a couple of times with small arm bullets and shrapnel.

At the end of my tour, I learned that I had taken part in 375 sorties and had logged 325 combat hours. I had flown all sorts of missions throughout central Vietnam and Thailand in support of some hush-hush CIA operations there. I had done troop and cargo airdrops on temporarily besieged outposts in the jungle. I also learned that the 457th Squadron had launched more on-time combat missions and had carried more tonnage of cargo and passengers than any other Caribou squadron, an achievement that made me, as well as the squadron, proud and happy. I only hope that whoever takes over will carry the airlift missions with the same pride, spirit, and aggressiveness.

304

In the latter part of October, after I had received my new assignment to Vandenberg Air Force Base in California, I said farewell to the loyal people of 457th Squadron and to my two great bosses, Colonel Kinney and Colonel Mason, who both wished me well.

The night before my departure for the United States, my incredible and invaluable assistant, Lt. Col. Don Zeine, surprised me by having a whole roasted pig for dinner at our squadron's officers' small club, which we had built with scrounged material from different bases. The pig was compliments of the distinguished mayor of Cam Rahn Bay and his staff, for whom my squadron had occasionally provided airlift support to Saigon and back.

That night, a major from the Wing Staff handed me a sealed envelope and told me not to open it until I was on my way home over the Pacific. It was confidential, he said, and he'd deny he had even given it to me. The next morning I said good-bye to Zeine and caught the C-141 flight to Travis Air Force Base. When the C-141 was flying over the Pacific, I opened the envelope my wing friend had given me. To my surprise, it contained a copy of the efficiency report Colonel Kinney had submitted about me, which read as follows:

> Through outstanding managerial ability and supervision, this forceful leader has set an operational record second to none. His squadron has launched almost 1,500 consecutive missions without an initial launch delay. This impressive record was accomplished by an equally superb en route reliability rate of 98.7 percent on

time departure in slightly over 14,000 sorties. The result has been customer satisfaction and record tonnage movement. An aggressive and energetic individual, who is always on the job and knows no set working hours. His dynamic personality has infused this same spirit throughout the squadron, creating a positive can-do attitude. A professional pilot himself, Lieutenant Colonel Pisanos leads by example, exposing himself to the same hazards of enemy ground fire, primitive strips, and monsoon weather encountered by his aircrews. The broad leadership exercised by Lieutenant Colonel Pisanos has produced timely administration and quality maintenance. Forceful, aggressive commander who leaves no doubt who is in command. Energetic, perceptive and practical who stays ahead of the situation. Pinpoints problem areas and takes immediate corrective action. Truly dedicated to the mission and very strong on loyalty and straightforward with his people. Clearly a professional career officer with an optimum balance of the most desirable leadership qualities.

The glowing praise of this report completely surprised me and confirmed the sense of satisfaction I felt about my job in Vietnam. I felt a great sense of professional success.

RETURNING TO THE STATES

The most wonderful part of my return to the States was seeing Sophie open the door of our house upon my arrival in Kansas City. I dropped my gear, grabbed her, and held her in my arms for a long time. I was home at last, happy to be with my family—and I only now fully appreciated how much I had missed them.

After spending some time in Acapulco with Sophie, I returned home to find that I had been promoted to full colonel and had also been reassigned to the 308th Ballistic Missile Wing (BMW) at Little Rock AFB, in Arkansas.

When my leave was over, I checked in at the wing and met my new boss, Col. Don La Moine, the Wing Commander. He told me that before I take over as Deputy Wing Commander for maintenance, I had to attend a ten week mandatory course at Sheppard AFB in Texas to learn all about the Titan II Missile with which the wing was equipped.

With Sophie in Kansas City, I headed for Sheppard where I discovered that I was the only student in the class. The daily lecturing I received at that course I learned, not only about the Titan II Missile itself, but also the nuclear weapons the missile carried to its target.

Upon completion of that special course, I returned to Little Rock and assumed my duties as Deputy Commander for Maintenance in the wing.

As the days rolled by I discovered that the job was extremely high pressure, with periods of calmness and times of frustration. You had to be on your toes to stay ahead of the frequent problems encountered with the 18 missiles I had to maintain on alert in the silos throughout Arkansas.

The biggest problems I was confronted with were two, fuel leaks and corrosion. The small problems were taken care of easily, but the major ones, where we had to remove first the weapon, then the missile and move them both to the base, was a task that involved military police, the Highway Patrol, the FBI and the use of helicopters.

My stay with the 208th BMW, was almost a little over two years and I had mastered the job as missilcr very well. Then one day in March 1971, I received a telephone call from Col. Kenneth Tallman, Chief of Colonels/Generals assignment office at headquarters USAF.

The Col. offered me an assignment to Athens, Greece, as Chief of the Air Force section with the military mission for aid to Greece (JUSMAGG). Col. Tallman felt that I had all the qualifications for the job, especially my ability to speak Greek.

Naturally, I accepted the assignment and about a month later, I received orders to report to Athens, not later than May 24, 1971.

I traveled to Washington before leaving Little Rock to be briefed at headquarters USAF and other government agencies, about my new job. The group in Athens was comprised of officers and enlisted men from the U.S. Army, Navy, and Air Force who were assigned to Greece specifically to assist and advise the Hellenic Armed Forces and to supervise the distribution of military aid allocated to Greece by the U.S. government. JUSMAGG had been formed because of the U.S. commitment to

306

provide military assistance to Greece and Turkey to fight the extension of Soviet communism.

While in Washington, I picked up our diplomatic passports also for myself, Sophie and Diane, who was going to accompany us while Jeff was going to remain in Kansas City.

As we closed our house in Little Rock, Sophie and I felt that we were embarking on an assignment that would be some of the best years of our lives. On May 23, we said goodbye to our folks in Kansas City and boarded the plane for Athens.

CHAPTER 27

MISSION TO ATHENS

On May 24, 1971, Sophie, Diane, and I arrived in the place where my odyssey to America had begun. I came as a citizen of the United States of America and with a diplomatic passport in my hands. I had tears in my eyes and nostalgia in my heart as we checked in at the Congo Palace Hotel in Glyfada, which served as the officers' club and temporary living quarters for incoming and outgoing officers of JUSMAGG. Two weeks later, we moved into an embassy house in Psyhico, a suburb of Athens.

On our first evening in Athens, a JUSMAGG staff car picked us up and took us to Kifissia, a beautiful residential area north of Athens, where the chief of JUSMAGG, Maj. Gen. John Hightower, U.S. Army, was hosting a reception for us at the American Club. A number of officers from JUSMAGG and some civilians from the embassy were present, but I was most surprised to see among the guests my old friend Lt. Gen. Dimitrios Theodossiades, who had recently retired as chief of the Hellenic Air Force. I learned from General Theo that the present chief of the Hellenic Air Force was Lt. Gen. Dimitrios Kostakos—another friend I had made in Naples.

When I reported to JUSMAGG headquarters the following day, General Hightower briefed me on the JUSMAGG mission and also introduced me to my two counterparts, Col. Frank A. Athanason, chief of the U.S. Army Section, and Capt. Robert Ewing, chief of the U.S. Navy Section, and also to Lt. Col. Gage Mersereau, the acting chief of the Air Force Section. The officer whom I was replacing, Col. Philip Karas, had already departed Athens for the United States.

Later, I had the chance to meet those on my staff with whom I would be working: Lt. Col. George Jatras, Lt. Col. Roland A. McGuire, Maj. Chester Cavoli, Maj. Nicholas Karras, Maj. James G. Rothrock, Maj. Earl L.B. Hamilton, Maj. Nathan Blackwell and George Petrou, the office technical translator.

After a few days on the job, I paid a courtesy call to the U.S. ambassador, Henry J. Tasca. He welcomed me warmly and after a short discussion, said to me, "I am sure you are aware, Colonel, that the Greek government is in the market to buy a new fighter aircraft for their Air Force. The competitors, as far as we know, will be three: the French with their Mirage F1, the British with their Jaguar, and the United States with our McDonnell F-4 Phantom. We are going to depend on you to do your utmost in support of the F-4. And if I can be of any help, let me know." I assured Mr. Tasca that I'd do my best.

My next official visit was to the Greek Pentagon, where I had a brief reunion with my other friend from the period in 1953 when I was assigned to the Headquarters AIRSOUTH in Naples—the chief of the Hellenic Air Force, Lt. Gen. Dimitrios Kostakos. While in his office, I also had the chance to meet his deputy, Maj. Gen. Thomas Mitsanas, and Brig. Gen. Elias Tsamoussopoulos, the director of operations.

During those first few days in Athens, I also managed to visit the place of my birth, Kolonos. Since my parents had passed away, I had a quiet reunion with my brothers and sister, as well as my boyhood friends. Everyone was quite surprised when they first saw me being chauffeured in a staff car and wearing the uniform of a colonel in the American Air Force. They were all proud of me for what I had been able to achieve in America.

I also had to devote a considerable amount of time attending various social affairs at the embassy and elsewhere. It was part of the business of diplomacy; I was told I would occasionally have either a cocktail party or a sit-down catered dinner at my home for certain select people. It was the custom of the mission, my boss told me, and funds were allocated to cover the costs of official entertaining.

Eventually, I was able to turn over daily, routine activities to my staff so that I could be free to focus on the promotion of the F-4 Phantom.

Of all the projects my office was involved in, I had given the F-4 project in Greece number-one priority.

One day General Kostakos asked me to visit his office so that he could go over some aspects of the Phantom with me. I rushed to the Greek Pentagon, equipped with some charts my staff had prepared that compared the F-4 to the other two fighters. While in the chief's office, I answered a number of questions he had and reminded him of the three significant advantages the Phantom had over the other two aircraft. I placed one of my charts on his desk and pointed out that (1) the Phantom was tested extensively in combat during the war in Vietnam; (2) the Phantom could carry a combination of several loads of weapons in addition to electronic countermeasure equipment and it could carry and deliver nuclear weapons; and (3) the aircraft would be supported with spare parts for the next twenty years. General Kostakos was particularly impressed with the spare part support.

Of course, the French and the British aircraft companies' representatives were similarly promoting their own aircraft. I often spotted the cars of British and French military attachés parked inside the grounds of the Greek Pentagon when I was there on official business.

As part of my effort to promote the F-4, I made courtesy visits to almost every aerodrome of the Hellenic Air Force to highlight for them the F-4's capabilities. I was encouraged by the enthusiastic responses I received at every installation. But I still had to make one more visit, to Tatoi Aerodrome.

Early one glorious Athenian day, I got into my staff car and told George, my driver, to head for Tatoi. Part of me felt like a kid again as we made the drive to the place where my love for the airplane had begun. The visit was a decided success. I was warmly received by the station commander and the commandant of the Air Force Academy, Brig. Gen. Fokion Fotiades-Negrepontis.

My visit to Tatoi had inspired me. On my way back to Athens, I decided to look into acquiring some F-4s from a USAFE unit that I could use to demonstrate the aircraft for the Hellenic Air Force. I discussed the idea with my staff when I arrived back at the office, and all felt that the tactic could indeed be effective. Within minutes, we had dispatched a message to USAF headquarters in Washington with our request. A few days later, we received two F-4s from one of our bases in Germany. The pilots not only demonstrated the Phantom to the Hellenic Air Force but also gave rides to selected pilots, who were impressed with the way the aircraft maneuvered.

In late February 1972, General Kostakos called to tell me that the chief of the Hellenic Armed Forces, Gen. Odyseas Anghelis, wanted me to brief him on the Phantom. My presentation for General Anghelis went smoothly, and I was able to answer all the questions that were asked by both the chief and his deputy, Lt. Gen. Nicholas Broumas. The two army generals were clearly impressed not only with the Phantom's capabilities in comparison to the other two competing aircraft but also with the twenty-year guarantee of spare parts support.

When I returned to the office after the meeting, I briefed General Hightower, who listened carefully. He had only one comment: "Steve, you have done all you can and now we just have to wait."

Our efforts and our patience were rewarded when, in the following month, the decision was made. The Athens morning papers broke the story: the Greek government had decided to buy two squadrons of the McDonnell F-4E Phantom fighter for its air force. At JUSMAGG, relief accompanied jubilation, and none of us were happier than General Hightower. The afternoon newspapers broke the story also, and I received a congratulatory telephone call from the ambassador. He too had learned about the decision when he saw the morning papers.

The total sales price of the aircraft spare parts and training came to over $300 million. It took several days to finalize the sale and sign the legal documents, including a request for a U.S. loan in the millions of dollars. My office had prepared everything for the team that came over from Washington to handle the transaction, and I also took part in many meetings at the Greek Pentagon. Some of my staff and I chaperoned the members of the team during their free time at night. I also flew back and forth between Athens, Washington, and St. Louis, along with Hellenic Air Force officers, to discuss and coordinate the logistics and eventual delivery of the aircraft to Greece. When I returned to Athens from my second visit to the United States, I found a letter awaiting me in my office. It was from General George M. Seignious II, the officer to whom the head of the team from Washington reported. He wrote a glowing commendation, one that was later seconded and endorsed by General Hightower (see Appendix A).

As the commendations came in, I learned that the manufacturer of the French Mirage, the Dassault Aviation Company, was quite upset with us for having dashed their hopes of selling their aircraft to Greece. It was rumored that Dassault had spent big money to entertain high-ranking officers of the Greek air force, both in Athens and in Paris. The French had been certain that they would beat the British and the Americans out, but they had been foiled by our efforts and our aircraft's superiority.

In October 1972, after the hubbub surrounding the F-4 sale died down, we received word that Vice President Spiro Agnew was planning to visit Greece. To celebrate his arrival, Ambassador Tasca had arranged for a reception at the Athens Hilton Hotel for the vice president and several Greek and foreign dignitaries, including Prime Minister Georgios Papadopoulos. Only four officers from JUSMAGG, including myself, were invited to the reception.

Ambassador Tasca introduced me to Mr. Agnew and added, "Mr. Vice President, Colonel Pisanos was born here in Athens and look at what he has earned while serving in the American air force." The vice president congratulated me, while admiring the decorations on my dress white uniform.

Shortly after the introduction, the prime minister of Greece appeared at the reception. He approached the vice president, shook his hand, and conversed with him through an interpreter. After a while, the vice president turned around and signaled me to come forward.

"Come here, Colonel," he said. Then, he addressed Mr. Papadopoulos: "Mr. Prime Minister, this is Col. Steve Pisanos of the American air force. He was born here in Athens. You see what we do with Greeks you send to America?"

His words were translated as he gestured toward the medals on my uniform. The prime minister seemed impressed and congratulated me in Greek.

I replied in Greek, "I was born in Kolonos, Sir, and went to America when I was eighteen years old."

I told him that I had taken part in World War II and the Vietnam War and that I had been serving in the American air force for a number of years. He looked at me again, with amazement, and said, "But you speak Greek well, Colonel." He turned to his aide and said, "Why have I not met this man before?"

His aide, of course, was somewhat at a loss. The prime minister didn't realize that I wasn't on the list of those he was to be introduced to. The prime minister and I shook hands, and I returned to the group of JUSMAGG officers who stood on the side.

The next time I saw the prime minister was October 28, the No Day, a day when Greeks celebrate Gen. John Metaxas's refusal to let Benito Mussolini's troops invade Greece from Albania during World War II. Sophie and I were standing among high-ranking military and diplomatic corps dignitaries, many with their wives, by the monument of the unknown soldier in front of the House of Parliament. We were behind Prime Minister Papadopoulos while he was reviewing the procession of members of the Hellenic Armed Forces, including tanks and armored vehicles.

After the ceremony a reception was held inside the House of Parliament, Prime Minister Papadopoulos and I came face to face. He said, "Ah, my Colonel, so nice to see you again."

I introduced him to Sophie, and as he was shaking hands with her, I said, "Everyone was impressed with the parade, Mr. Prime Minister."

He thanked me and broke away, smiling as he turned around to shake hands with some of the guests who had surrounded him. Mr. Papadopoulos might have been a dictator, but he appeared to me to be a sincere, caring, and straightforward leader. He had done more for the country at that time than the elected politicians who, prior to the military takeover in April 1967, had converted the House of Parliament into a fighting arena. Still, I hoped Mr. Papadopoulos would turn over the reins of his military government to some capable civilian leaders, so that they could provide a true democratic government to the Greek people.

In June 1972, our distinguished chief in JUSMAGG General John H. Hightower left Athens for the U. S. to go into retirement. General Hightower was a fine gentleman who fully supported my efforts with the F-4 project in Greece. Major General Charles W. Ryder, Jr., U.S. Army, a Vietnam veteran replaced him. Just about that time, the chief of the Hellenic Air Force Lt. Gen. Dimitri Kostakos retired from active service and was replaced by his able deputy Maj. Gen. Thomas Mitsanas, who was promoted to Lieutenant General. Maj. Gen. Vassilios Papavasiliou became his deputy.

In mid-December 1972, I returned from a visit to West Germany, where I had met with Maj. Gen. Royal Baker, chief of MAAG Germany in Bonn, to learn about Germany's transition to the F-4. My office was planning to present this information to the Hellenic Air Force so that its pilots could be prepared for the days ahead. On walking into my office after being absent for a few days, I found a large sealed envelope, addressed to me from the chief JUSMAGG. Inside I found a letter from General Mitsanas, who by this time was the chief of the Hellenic Air Forces, addressed to Ambassador Tasca, commending me for my work on the F-4 project (see Appendix A). The letter was accompanied by written remarks from the ambassador, the USAF chief of staff, the deputy commander in chief of the U.S. European Command, and General Ryder, the new chief of JUSMAGG, all endorsing Mitsanas's praise. I was certainly pleased and thankful for the kind words, and I felt proud that I was able to contribute to U.S. efforts in the country of my birth.

INTO RETIREMENT

The year 1973 came and went fast as I kept busy with meetings and traveling to Washington and St. Louis, sometimes by myself, other times escorting Hellenic Air Force officers involved with the Phantom project. After the purchase of the aircraft was concluded, we became deeply involved in the logistics of providing spare parts for the airframe and engine. We were also involved in the arrangements for the training of pilots and maintenance personnel in the Untied States as well as in Germany at USAFE F-4 installations. As time passed, I accompanied Hellenic Air Force officers to the McDonnell Aircraft Company plant, where we actually observed the production line of F-4 aircraft destined for the Hellenic Air Force.

My tour in Athens was scheduled to end in November 1973. Sophie and I decided that, upon the completion of my tour with JUSMAGG, I would retire to enjoy life with our two grown-up children. At that time,

Diane was attending college in Columbia, Missouri, while Jeff was living in Overland Park, Kansas. I felt that after some thirty years in the service of my adopted country, plus almost a year with the RAF, it was time for me to move on and say a final good-bye to my beloved USAF.

In the latter part of October, we were swamped by invitations to farewell parties. We were entertained lavishly by the many friends we had made in Athens during my tour. I said good-bye to my brothers, my sister Chrisoula, and my boyhood friends in Kolonos, who I had visited frequently while in Athens. Then, on November 15, 1973, Sophie and I, with tears in our eyes, said farewell to the people from my office and their wives and boarded a TWA flight to New York.

As it happened, only two days after I left Athens, Brig. Gen. Dimitris Ioannidis successfully headed a countercoup that toppled the Papadopoulos regime. Although my friends in JUSMAGG and the American embassy were not harmed, I learned from the press that my friend, the chief of the Air Force Gen. Thomas Mitsanas, and many others in the Papadopoulos government were placed under house arrest. Others yet were put in jail.

At the end of November 1973, I began the process for retirement at Richards-Gebaur Air Force Base south of Kansas City. On my last visit to the base in December, I walked away from the installation for the last time as a retired air force warrior. When I returned home, I began to take off my uniform, and as I did so, I thought about the past, about the time I had spent in the RAF and the USAAF in England during World War II, about the friends I had made in the 4th Fighter Group; about my six months with the French Underground, about my experiences in Vietnam, and about my almost three decades spent in Uncle Sam's new USAF. I wish to express my heart's profound gratitude to this great country, the United States. I am indebted to America for the opportunity that was given by Uncle Sam to be who I am. The USAF educated me, promoted me, and let me live in many wonderful places. I thank the Army Air Force that ruled the sky over Europe in World War II and the USAF that gave me the most satisfying years of my life. And from the bottom of my heart, I can sincerely say that I am proud to be an American.

APPENDIX A:
LETTERS OF COMMENDATION

DEFENSE SECURITY ASSISTANCE AGENCY
WASHINGTON, D. C. 20301

17 APR 1972
In reply refer to:
IT-5410/72

MEMORANDUM FOR COLONEL S. N. PISANOS
                       CHIEF, AIR FORCE SECTION
                       JOINT U.S. MILITARY AID GROUP
                       ATHENS, GREECE

THROUGH   MAJOR GENERAL JOHN HIGHTOWER
                       CHIEF, JOINT U.S. MILITARY AID GROUP
                       ATHENS, GREECE.

SUBJECT: Commendation

I wish to commend you for the outstanding support you rendered to the
Department of Defense team that recently successfully concluded negotiations with the Government of Greece on introduction of F-4 aircraft
into the Greek Air Force inventory.

I am also aware that the excellent relationship and continuing dialogue
you have established and maintained with the Greek Air Force significantly
contributed toward F-4 acquisition by Greece.

Please accept my grateful appreciation and thanks for your valuable
contribution to this significant NATO force modernization.

George M. Seignious, II
Lieutenant General, USA
Director
Defense Security Assistance Agency

HEADQUARTERS
JOINT UNITED STATES MILITARY AID GROUP GREECE
APO NEW YORK 09253

317

JUSCH(17Apr72) 1st Ind
SUBJECT: Commendation

TO: Colonel Steve N. Pisanos, Chief, Air Force Section, Joint United States Military Aid Group, Greece.

1. I take pleasure in forwarding the attached letter from LTG George M. Seignious, II, Director, Defense Security Assistance Agency commending you for your wholehearted assistance and support rendered the Department of Defense team during their recent visit to JUSMAGG.

2. Your resourcefulness, professional competence and energetic application contributed to the success of this visit and reflects great credit upon yourself and the military service.

J. M. HIGHTOWER
Major General, USA
Chief

Cy furn:
1141 USAF Sp Acty Sq

CHIEF HELLENIC AIR FORCE
ATHENS - GREECE

His Excellency
Henry J. Tasca
Ambassador of the United States of America
Athens

318

Athens, September 18th, 1972

Dear Mr. Ambassador,

Now that the fiscal year 1973 Credit Agreement is complete and actions for acquisition of the F-4E by the Hellenic Air Force are well under way, I wish to bring to your attention the superlative support provided by Colonel Steve N. Pisanos, Chief of the Air Force Section, JUSMAGG, in bringing the whole procedure to bare a most appropriate handling.

Colonel Pisanos personally provided the Hellenic Air Force Command unparalleled advice during our early evaluations for the selection of a modern fighter aircraft for our Air Force. His guidance, knowledge, and background of the operational aspects and overall USAF logistical system of supportability enabled us to effectively finalize our decision for the selection of the American fighter. He personally and singularly made significant contributions that led to the final decision for selection of the United States F-4E rather than other types of fighter aircraft for the Hellenic Air Force.

As a professional military man, it has been a source of great satisfaction working with a USAF officer of the caliber and potential of Colonel Pisanos. I consider him capable of rising to the very highest military echelons and I want to express my personal appreciation to you and to the the United States Department of Defense for the services rendered by this officer which greately helped us reach a decision indeed sound.

Yours faithfully,

T. B. MITSANAS
Lieutenant General, HAF
Chief Hellenic Air Force

CF : Chief, JUSMAGG

EMBASSY OF THE
UNITED STATES OF AMERICA

Athens, Greece

October 3, 1972

General John D. Ryan
Chief of Staff
United States Air Force
Washington, D. C. 20330

Dear General Ryan:

I was very pleased to receive recently from the Chief of
the Hellenic Air Force the enclosed letter praising the
role of Colonel Steve Pisanos in effecting the sale to
Greece of F-4 Phantoms. This sale is an extremely
important step in keeping Greece's armed forces oriented
toward American equipment and methods, and throughout the
lengthy discussions and negotiations which culminated
in the Greek decision to "buy American" Colonel Pisanos
played a key role. It is equally worth noting that the
sale to Greece was an important determinant in the subsequent Turkish decision also to purchase F-4's, thus
considerably more than doubling the value of the work
channeled to America's aerospace industry by Greece's
decision to buy F-4's.

I commend to you Lt. General Mitsanas' letter as a reflection of the great effectiveness as "diplomats in
uniform" with which our JUSMAGG officers perform their
duties.

With personal best wishes,

Sincerely,

Henry J. Tasca
Ambassador

Enclosure:
As stated

cc: Commander in Chief U.S. European Command
     Chief JUSMAGG Athens

DEPARTMENT OF THE AIR FORCE
OFFICE OF THE CHIEF OF STAFF
UNITED STATES AIR FORCE
WASHINGTON, D.C. 20330

REPLY TO
ATTN OF: CC

1 Nov. 1972

SUBJECT: Appreciation

320

TO: USCINCEUR (Gen Burchinal)

1. The attached correspondence from Ambassador Tasca and Lt Gen Mitsanas, Hellenic Air Force, is noted and forwarded with great pleasure. Colonel Pisanos has performed a commendable service to the United States and has significantly enhanced the image of the USAF nationally as well as internationally.

2. Please convey my appreciation to Colonel Pisanos for his noteworthy achievements.

JOHN D. RYAN, General, USAF
Chief of Staff

1 Atch
Ltr fr Amb Tasca,
dtd 3 Oct 72, w/atch

PRIDE IN THE PAST   FAITH IN THE FUTURE

HEADQUARTERS
UNITED STATES EUROPEAN COMMAND
Office of the Deputy Commander-in-Chief
APO NEW YORK 09128

IN REPLY REFER TO

ECDC   21 November 1972

SUBJECT: Letter of Appreciation

321

THRU: Major General Charles W. Ryder, Jr.
           Chief, Joint United States Military
               Aid Group, Greece
           APO 09223

TO: Colonel Steve N. Pisanos
           Chief, Air Force Section
           Joint United States Military Aid
               Group, Greece
           APO 09223

1. It gives me great pleasure to add my congratulations
for a job well done to those expressed by Ambassador
Tasca, General Ryan and Lieutenant General Mitsanas.
Your contribution to the Greek choice of the F-4E is
deserving of great praise.

2. I appreciate your excellent performance as a member
of the JUSMAGG Team.

1 Incl   DAVID A. BURCHINAL
  Ltr fr Gen Ryan,   General   USAF
  dtd 1 Nov 72,   Deputy Commander in Chief
  w/atchs

HEADQUARTERS
JOINT UNITED STATES MILITARY AID GROUP GREECE
APO NEW YORK 09253

322

JUSCH(21Nov72) 1st Ind   14 December 1972
SUBJECT: Letter of Appreciation

TO: COL Steve N. Pisanos, Chief Air Force Section, Joint United
     States Military Aid Group, Greece, APO 09253

1. I take pleasure in forwarding you the attached letters of
appreciation for the support and advice that you provided the Hellenic
Air Force Command in the acquisition of the F-4E fighter.

2. I am pleased to be able to pass on expressions of appreciation for
your fine work in this most inportant purchase. Thank you for a job
well done.

CHARLES W. RYDER, Jr.
Major General, USA
Chief

CHUCK YEAGER'S LETTER ABOUT **THE FLYING GREEK**

I first met Steve Pisanos at Wright Field when we both served there as test pilots. He was a tireless and dedicated individual, and I have always admired his unswerving will and determination when, at a young age, he left his birthplace of Greece on a voyage to America as a crew member on a freighter with one goal in mind: to learn to fly.

In World War II, Steve served as a fighter pilot in the RAF and later the USAAF, where he became a double ace.

The Flying Greek is an incredible autobiography, a fast-moving adventure that will hold the reader's attention to the end as Steve describes the episodes of his life as they happened. He is certainly a rare immigrant and a proud American whose story exemplifies what the goodness of America is all about. He is a role model for youngsters of our world today."

—Brig. Gen. Chuck Yeager, USAF (Ret.),
chairman of the Gen. Chuck Yeager Foundation

APPENDIX B:
NOTES

Note 1. At the time the 71st RAF Eagle Squadron was transferred from the RAF into the USAAF 4th Fighter Group on 29 September 1942, its pilots had destroyed 45 enemy aircraft, probably destroyed 15 ½ more, and damaged 24 ¼. The squadron also produced four aces, as follows:

Pilot's Name and Rank	Aerial Kills
Squadron Leader Gus A. Daymond	8
Squadron Leader Chesley G. Peterson	6
Pilot Officer William R. Dunn	5
Pilot Officer Carroll McColpin	6

Note 2. At the end of the war in Europe, the 334th, 335th, and 336th Fighter Squadrons of the 4th Fighter Group (formerly the RAF 71st, 121st, and 133rd Eagle Squadrons) had tallied 1016 German planes destroyed in the air and on the ground. The following table shows the final score of each Fighter Squadron:

Squadron	Air	Ground	Total
334 Fighter Squadron	210.17	185.25	395.42
335 Fighter Squadron	165.17	97.33	262.50
336 Fighter Squadron	174.66	183.42	358.08

Note 3. In 1943, 8th Fighter Command allowed the destruction of enemy aircraft on the ground to be credited as a kill in the air. The following tables depict the total score of each of the 4th Fighter Group air and ground aces at the end of the war in Europe.

324

334th Fighter Squadron

Pilot's Name and Rank	Air	Ground	Total
Lt. Ralph K. Hofer	16.50	14	30.50
Major Duane W. Beeson	19.33	4.75	24.08
Major Gerald E. Montgomery	3	14.50	17.50
Major Louis H. Norley	11.33	5	16.33
Captain Nicholas Megura	11.84	3.75	15.59
Major Howard D. Hively	12	2.50	14.50
Captain Joseph L. Lang	7.84	4	11.84
Lt. Hipolitus T. Biel	5.33	6	11.33
Captain Donald M. Malmsten	3.50	7	10.50
Lt. Steve N. Pisanos	10	0	10
Captain Victor J. France	4.33	4.33	8.66
Captain David W. Howe	6	2.50	8.50
Lt. William E. Whalen	6	2	8
Lt. James W. Ayers	1	7	8
Lt. Grover C. Siems, Jr.	4.33	3.50	7.83
Captain William B. Smith	2.50	4.75	7.25
Major Gregory A. Daymond	7	0	7 (all with RAF)
Lt. William O. Antonides	0	7	7
Captain Vasseure H. Wynn	5	2	7 (2.5 with RAF)
Captain Raymond C. Care	6	.50	6.50
Major Henry L. Mills	6	0	6
Major Michael G.H. McPharlin	5	1	6 (including score with RAF and 339 F.G.)
Major Winslow M. Sobanski	5	1	6
Lt. Frank E. Speer	1	5	6
Lt. Arthur R. Bowers	0	6	6
Lt. Col. Oscar H. Coen	5.50	0	5.50 (1.5 with RAF)
Captain Archie W. Chatterley	4.50	1	5.50
Captain Carl G. Payne	2	3.50	5.50
Captain Thomas R. Bell	0	5.50	5.50
Major Gerald C. Brown	5	0	5 (all with 55th F.G.)
Lt. Alex Rafalovich	4	1	5
Lt. Gordon A. Denson	0	5	5
Lt. Kenneth G. Helfrecht	0	5	5
Lt. Jack D. McFaddan	0	5	5

325

335th Fighter Squadron

Pilot's Name and Rank	Air	Ground	Total
Major Pierce W. McKennon	12	9.68	21.68
Major George Carpenter	13.33	4	17.33
Captain Charles F. Anderson	10.50	5.50	16
Captain Albert L. Schlegel	10	5	15
Captain Frank C. Jones	5	5.50	10.50
Captain Ted E. Lines	10	0	10
Lt. Paul S. Riley	6.50	3	9.50
Major James R. Happel	4	4.68	8.68
Captain Bernard L. McGrattan	8.50	0	8.50
Major William J. Daley	8	0	8 (all with RAF)
Lt. Brack Diamond, Jr.	1	6	7
Lt. Col. Roy W. Evans	6	0	6
Lt. Loton D. Jennings	0	6	6
F.O. Charles E. Poage, Jr.	0	6	6
Lt. Clemens A. Fiedler	4.33	1	5.33
Captain Kenneth B. Smith	3	2	5
Lt. George W. Ceglarski	1	4	5 (including score with 355th F.G.)

336th Fighter Squadron

Pilot's Name and Rank	Air	Ground	Total
Major John T. Godfrey	18	12.60	30.60
Major James A. Goodson	15	15	30 (1 with RAF)
Major Don S. Gentile	21.80	6	27.80 (2 with RAF)
Major Frederick W. Glover	10.30	12.50	22.80
Captain Willard W. Millikan	13	2	15
Major Carroll W. McColpin	12	0	12 (including score with RAF & 9th AF)
Captain Kendall E. Carlson	6	4	10
Lt. Van E. Chandler	5	4	9
Captain Joseph H. Bennett	8.50	0	8.50 (including score with 356th F.G.)
Lt. Joe H. Joiner	4.50	4	8.50
Captain Carl R. Alfred	3	5	8
Lt. Vermont Garrison	7.33	.25	7.58
Captain Donald R. Emerson	4	3	7
Lt. Robert F. Nelson	1	5	6
Lt. Douglas P. Pederson	0	6	6
Captain Harry N. Hagan	2	3	5
Captain Robert D. Hobert	2	3	5
Captain William J. O'Donnell	2	3	5
F.O. Donald P. Baugh	0	5	5
Captain Nelson M. Dickey	0	5	5
Lt. Gilbert L. Kesler	0	5	5

Headquarters, 4th Fighter Group

Pilot's Name and Rank	Air	Ground	Total
Lt. Col. Claiborne H. Kinnard	8	17	25 (including score with 355th F.G.)
Col. Donald J.M. Blakeslee	15.50	2	17.50 (3 with RAF)
Lt. Col. James A. Clark	11.50	4.50	16
Col. Everett W. Stewart	7.83	1.50	9.33 (including score with 355th F.G.)
Lt. Col. Sidney S. Woods	8	1	9 (including score with 479th F.G.)
Lt. Col. Jack G. Oberhansly	5	4	9 (including score with 78th F.G.)
Captain Shelton W. Monroe	4.33	4.50	8.83
Col. Chesley G. Peterson	7	0	7 (6 with RAF)
Lt. Col. Selden R. Edner	5	0	5 (all with RAF)

Note 4. The table below depicts the final tally of German aircraft destroyed in the air and on the ground by each of the 15 Fighter Groups, as indicated by the VIII USAAF's historical records.

Group	Air	Ground	Total
4th	550.0	466.0	1016.0
56th	664.5	328.0	992.5
355th	339.0	502.3	841.3
352nd	504.5	287.0	791.5
353rd	328.0	413.8	741.8
357th	595.5	106.5	702.0
78th	326.0	358.8	684.8
339th	235.0	440.5	675.5
55th	303.5	268.5	572.0
364th	262.5	193.0	455.5
20th	211.5	237.0	448.5
479th	155.0	279.0	434.0
359th	255.5	98.0	353.5
361st	222.0	105.0	327.0
356th	200.0	75.5	275.5
	5152.5	4158.9	9311.4

SELECTED BIBLIOGRAPHY

Alexander, Richard L. *They Called Me Dixie*. Robinson Typographics, 1988

Barker, Ralph. *The Thousand Plane Raid*. Ballantine Books, 1965

Baumbach, Werner. *Broken Swastika*. Dorsey Press, 1992

Baumbach, Werner. *The Life and Death of the Luftwaffe*. Ballantine Books, 1960

Beck, L.O., Jr. *Fighter Pilot*. Wetzel Publishing Co., 1946

Brickhill, Paul. *Reach for the Sky*. Ballantine Books, 1967

Brown, Anthony Cave. *The Secret War Report of the OSS*. Berkeley Medallion Books, 1976

Caine, Philip D. *Eagles of the RAF*. Defense University Press, 1991

Caine, Philip D. *Spitfires*, Thunderbolts, and Warm Beer. Brassey's, 1995

Caidin, Martin. *Black Thursday*. Bantam Books, 1960

Caidin, Martin. *Flying Forts*. Ballantine Books, 1968

Caldwell, Donald L. *JG-26—Top Guns of the Luftwaffe*. Ivy Books, 1991

Causer, Philip H. *MIA—Missing in Action*. Phipps Publishing, 1997

Childers, James S. *War Eagles*. Heinemann, Ltd., 1943

Chilstrom, Ken and Penn Leary. *Test Flying at Old Wright Field*. Westchester House, 1993

Clostermann, Pierre. *The Big Show*. Bantam Books, 1979

Coleman, J.D. *Pleiku*. St. Martin's Press, 1988

Collier, Basil. *The Battle of Britain*. Berkeley Medallion Books, 1969

Collins, Larry and Dominique Lapierre. *Is Paris Burning?* Pocket Books, 1965

Dunn, William R. *Fighter Pilot*. University of Kentucky Press, 1982

Eight Air Force Tactical Development August 1942—May 1945. Eighth Air Force Document dated 9 July 1945

Everest, Frank K. *The Fastest Man Alive*. Berkeley Press, 1958

Freeman, Roger A. *Zemke's Wolfpack*. Pocket Books, 1991

Friedheim, Eric and Samuel W. Taylor. *Fighters Up*. MacRae-Smith Comp., 1945

Fry, Garry C. and Ethell, Jeffrey L. *Escort to Berlin*. Arco Publishing Inc., 1980

Galland, Adolf. *The First and the Last*. Ballantine Books, 1967

Gabreski, Francis "Gabby". *A Fighter Pilot's Life*. Bantam Doubleday Dell Publishing Group, 1992

Gentile, Don S. with Ira Wolfert. *One Man Air Force*. L.B. Fisher Publishing Group, 1944

Germain, Gregory St. *Resistance*. Signet Books, 1983

Glines, Carrol V. *The Compact History of the United States Air Force*. Hawthorne Books, 1963

Godfrey, John T. *The Look of Eagles*. Ballantine Books, 1958

Goodson, James. *Tumult in the Clouds*. St. Martin Press, 1983

Gunn, Walt. *From DC-3 to 747*. Wings Publications, 1998

Hall, Grover C. *Mr. Tettle's Tenants*. Sanders Philips and Comp, 1944

Hall, Grover C. *Death Squadron*. Zebra Books, 1946

Hall, Grover C. *1000 Destroyed*. Aero Publishers Inc., 1978

Harris, Sir A. *Bomber Offensive*. Collins, 1947

Harvey, Frank. *Air War – Vietnam*. Bantam Books, 1967

Hammerton, Sir John. *ABC of the RAF*. Amalgamated Press, 1942

Haugland, Vern. *The Eagle Squadrons*. Ziff-Davis Flying Books, 1979

Haugland, Vern. *The Eagle's War*. Aronson Jason, 1982

Haugland, Vern. *Caged Eagles*. Tab Aero, 1992

Hess, William N, and Ivie, Thomas G. *Fighters of the Mighty Eighth*. Motorbooks International, 1990

Hess, William N. *P-47 Thunderbolt*. Motorbooks, 1944

Hess, William N. *Fighting Mustang: the chronicle of the P-51*. Doubleday and Comp., 1970

Hirsch, Phil. *Through Enemy Lines*. Pyramid Books, 1967

Hoover, Bob R.A. *Forever Flying*. Pocket Books, 1996

Humble, R. *Battle of the Atlantic*. Military History, 1983

Hymoff, Edward. *The OSS in World War II*. Ballantine Books, 1972

329

Jablonski, Edward. *America in the Air War*. Time-Life Books, 1982

Johnson, Robert L. with Caidin, Martin. *Thunderbolt*. Rinehart and Company, Inc., 1958

Kaplan, Philip and Saunders, Andy. *Little Friends*. Random House, 1991

Kaplan, Philip. *Fighter Pilot*. Aurum Press, Ltd., 1991

Kelley, Terence. *Hurricane and Spitfire Pilots at War*. William Kimber, 1986

Levier, Tony. *Pilot*. Bantam Books, 1990

Liddell, Hart B. *History of the Second World War*.Cassell, 1965

Mahurin, Walker "Bud". *Honest John*. G.D. Putnam and Sons, 1962

Manvell, Roger. *SS and the Gestapo*. Ballantine Books, 1969

Marchetti, Victor and Marks, John D. *CIA*. Dell Publishing, 1974

Marshal, S.L.A. *Night Drop*. Jove Books, 1962

McCrary, Captain John R. and Scherman, David E. *First of the Many*. Simon and Schuster, 1944

Merrill, Sandra. *Donald's Story*. Tebidine, 1996

Michel, Henri. *The Second World War. Volume 2*. Praeger Publishers, 1975

Miller, Robert A. *August 1944*. Warner Books, 1998

Moszkiewiez, Helene. *Inside the Gestapo*. Dell Books, 1985

Moore, Robin. *The Green Berets*. Avon Books, 1965

Perret, Geoffrey. *Winged Victory – The Army Air Forces in World War II*. Random House, 1993

Porter, Bruce R. with Hammel, Eric M. *Ace*. Pacifica Press, 1985

Robinson, Donald. *The Day I Was Proudest to Be an American*. Doubleday and Comp., 1958

Rawnsley, C.F. and Wright, Robert. *Night Fighter*. Ballantine Books, 1957

Sevier, Elisabeth with Sevier, Robert W. *Resistance Fighter*. Sunflower University Press, 1998

Spangnuolo, Mark M. *Don S. Gentile: Soldier of God and Country*. College Press, 1986

Speer, Frank. *Wingman*. Hearth Stone Books, 1993

Speer, Frank. *The Debden Warbirds – the 4th Fighter Group in World War II*. Schiffer Publishing, Ltd., 1999

Spilken, Aaron. *Escape*. New American Library, 1984

Stevenson, William. *A Man Called Intrepid*. Harcourt Brace Jovanovich, 1976

Strategic Bombing Survey Team. *U.S. Strategic Bombing Survey Summaries*. Air University Press, 1987

Terraine, John A. *A Time for Courage*. MacMillan Publishing, 1985

Toliver, Raymond F. and Constable, Trevor J. *The Blond Knight of Germany*. Ballantine Books, 1970

Toliver, Raymond F. and Constable, Trevor J. *Fighter Aces*. MacMillan Publishing, 1965

Toliver, Raymond F. *The Interrogator*. Aero Publishers, 1978

Toliver, Raymond F. and Constable, Trevor J. *Fighter General – the life of Adolf Galland*. Ampress Publishing Co., 1990

Turner, Richard E. *Big Friend Little Friend*. Doubleday, 1969

Townsend, Peter. *The Odds Against Us*. Zebra Books, 1947

USAF Test Pilot School 1944-1979. Book published by the school.

USAF Test Pilot School 1944-1979, 45th Anniversary Ed. Book published by the school.

USAF Historical Studies #156. *Development of the Long Range Escort Fighter*. Ma/Ah Publishing.

Vader, John. *Spitfire*. Ballantine Books, 1969

Yeager, Chuck and Janos, Leo. *Yeager*. Bantam Books, 1985.

Wineland, Lynn. *In the Shadow of the Devil*. Squiggle Press, 1991

Wykeham, Peter. *Fighter Command*. Putnam, 1960

331

INDEX

339

340

About the Author

Col. Steve N. Pisanos, USAF (Ret.) retired from the U.S. Air Force in 1973, after thirty years and service in three wars. He is the recipient of numerous U.S., British, French, and Republic of Vietnam awards and decorations, including three Legions of Merit and five U.S. Distinguished Flying Crosses and the Purple Heart. He lives in San Diego, California.